Tables

CW01499648

Identifying with Nationality

Columbia Studies in International and Global History

Columbia Studies in International and Global History

The idea of "globalization" has become a commonplace, but we lack good histories that can explain the transnational and global processes that have shaped the contemporary world. Columbia Studies in International and Global History encourages serious scholarship on international and global history with an eye to explaining the origins of the contemporary era. Grounded in empirical research, the titles in the series transcend the usual area boundaries and address questions of how history can help us understand contemporary problems, including poverty, inequality, power, political violence, and accountability beyond the nation-state.

Cemil Aydin, *The Politics of Anti-Westernism in Asia: Visions of World Order in Pan-Islamic and Pan-Asian Thought*

Adam M. McKeown, *Melancholy Order: Asian Migration and the Globalization of Borders*

Patrick Manning, *The African Diaspora: A History Through Culture*

James Rodger Fleming, *Fixing the Sky: The Checkered History of Weather and Climate Control*

Steven Bryan, *The Gold Standard at the Turn of the Twentieth Century: Rising Powers, Global Money, and the Age of Empire*

Heonik Kwon, *The Other Cold War*

Samuel Moyn and Andrew Sartori, eds., *Global Intellectual History*

Alison Bashford, *Global Population: History, Geopolitics, and Life on Earth*

Adam Clulow, *The Company and the Shogun: The Dutch Encounter with Tokugawa Japan*

Richard W. Bulliet, *The Wheel: Inventions and Reinventions*

Simone M. Müller, *Wiring the World: The Social and Cultural Creation of Global Telegraph Networks*

Identifying with Nationality

Europeans, Ottomans,
and Egyptians in Alexandria

WILL HANLEY

Columbia

University

Press

New York

Columbia University Press
Publishers Since 1893
New York   Chichester, West Sussex
cup.columbia.edu
Copyright © 2017 Columbia University Press
Paperback edition, 2022

Library of Congress Cataloging-in-Publication Data
Names: Hanley, Will, 1974– author.
Title: Identifying with nationality : Europeans, Ottomans,
and Egyptians in Alexandria / Will Hanley.
Description: New York : Columbia University Press, [2017] |
  Series: Columbia studies in international and global history |
  Includes bibliographical references and index.
Identifiers: LCCN 2016042344 (print) | LCCN 2017000063 (ebook) |
  ISBN 9780231177627 (cloth) | ISBN 9780231177634 (pbk.) |
  ISBN 9780231542524 (e-book)
Subjects: LCSH: Alexandria (Egypt)—Ethnic relations—History. |
  Nationalism—Egypt—Alexandria—History. | Citizenship—Egypt—
  Alexandria—History. | Group identity—Egypt—Alexandria—History.
Classification: LCC DT154.A4 H375 2017 (print) | LCC DT154.A4 (ebook) |
  DDC 962/.1—dc23
LC record available at https://lccn.loc.gov/2016042344

Cover design: Rebecca Lown
Printed and bound by CPI Group (UK) Ltd, Croydon, CR0 4YY

To the memory of Yaguine Koita and Fodé Tounkara.

Contents

Part III Other Nationalities

Illustrations

Acknowledgments

Thanks to Adam McKeown for his generous engagement with my manuscript, to my anonymous reviewers for their suggestions, and to Matthew Connelly, Anne Routon, and Rob Fellman for bringing this book to light at Columbia University Press. Numerous people inspired and encouraged me in the years I've worked on this book; I can name only a few here. Hussein Omar, Elena Chiti, Matt Ellis, Beth Holt, Cécile Shaalan, and Khaled Fahmy referred me to source material, and Khaled taught me to read these documents in the first place. Workers at all of the archives I consulted helped me find materials; special thanks to Anne-Sophie Gras in Nantes. Aaron Jakes, Jeff Culang, Shane Minkin, John-Paul Ghobrial, Mary Dewhurst Lewis, Sarah Abrevaya Stein, Valeska Huber, and Lale Can commented on portions of the book. Robert Tignor, Molly Greene, Dirk Hartog, and Roger Owen continued to support my work long after they were relieved of duty. Elizabeth Dale, Mitra Sharafi, and Barbara Welke were patrons of my reorientation toward legal history.

I am grateful to the funders, organizers, and fellow participants of five extended seminars where I was able to develop this book: an NEH Summer Seminar at George Washington University (Dina Khoury), a Rechtskulturen fellowship at Berlin's Forum Transregionale Studien (Alexandra Kemmerer), the Hurst Summer Institute in Legal History in Madison, the ZMO Berlin summer academy in Istanbul, and the Harvard-Koç Ottoman Summer

School in Cunda. I also benefited from invitations to present some of the contents in Montreal (Laila Parsons), Berlin (Christian Sassmannshausen), Washington (Shira Robinson), Philadelphia (Eve Troutt Powell), Toronto (Willem Maas), Jerusalem (Liat Kozma), Durham (Edward Balleisen), Göttingen (Irene Schneider), Aix (Angelos Dalachanis), Brussels (Pieter Lagrou), and New York (Lale Can and Jeff Culang). I have incorporated portions of two articles into this text: "Grieving Cosmopolitanism in Middle East Studies," *History Compass* 6, no. 5 (2008): 1346–1367; and "When Did Egyptians Stop Being Ottomans? An Imperial Citizenship Case Study," in *Multilevel Citizenship*, edited by Willem Maas (Philadelphia: University of Pennsylvania Press, 2013), 89–109.

The research and writing of this book were supported by funds from Princeton University and its history department, the Social Sciences and Humanities Research Council of Canada, the Tomlinson Postdoctoral Fellowships (McGill University), and Florida State University. At FSU, my chairs Neil Jumonville, Elna Green, Jonathan Grant, and Ed Gray offered support, funding, and patience. I am grateful for the research assistance of Alex Shelby, Erica Johnson, and Jonathan Moury. Special thanks to my mentors Peter Garretson and Fritz Davis and my friend Adam Gaiser.

My sister-in-law Dominique Leman and my neighbors Sion Doman and Angelica Baeza offered me space to write. I am grateful to my parents for their examples as writers—I wish I could write as quickly as my dad or as carefully as my mom—and to my brother Bede for his presence in my life. Loving thanks to Marie-Claire Leman for her abiding respect for this book, and to our children, Emma, Sabri, and Ingrid, for their long-suffering and unreasonable accommodation of it.

Abbreviations

AJ	Fonds Alexandrie: Jugements
AOM	Archives d'outre mer, Aix-en-Provence
ASMAE	Archivio Storico del Ministero degli Affari Esteri, Rome
BLJE	*Bulletin de législation et du jurisprudence égyptiennes* (Alexandria, 1889–)
BOA	Başbakanlık Osmanlı Arşivi, Istanbul
CAA	Cour d'Appel d'Aix archives, Archives Départementales des Bouches-du-Rhône, Centre d'Aix-en-Provence
CADN	Ministère des Affaires Étrangères, Centre des Archives Diplomatiques de Nantes
DI	Dabtiya Iskandariya
DWQ	Dar al-Watha'iq al-Qawmiya, Cairo
FA	Fonds Alexandrie
FO	Foreign Office records, National Archives, London
MQDQ	Maljis Qawmi lil-Dirasat al-Qada'iya, Cairo
MRMA	*Al-Majmuʿa al-Rasmiya lil-Mahakim al-Ahliya* (Cairo, 1900–)
RA	Fonds Alexandrie: Recensement—Algériens
RT	Fonds Alexandrie: Recensement—Tunisiens
USNA	National Archives of the United States, College Park, Maryland
WM	*Al-Waqa'i al-Misriya* (Cairo, 1828–)

Identifying with Nationality

Introduction: Nationality Grasped

When I was arrested by the police, I had to submit to interrogation. But I don't know Arabic, how to speak it, or even how to write it. I don't know any language but Greek. . . . The police told me that they were sure to kill me, saying that because I was a local subject, I was certain to be killed. Had I been of another nationality, I might have had some hope, but because I was a local subject, there was no hope for me.

—*Niyaba* case #256 of 1914,
Maljis Qawmi lil-Dirasat al-Qada'iya (Cairo) 14004/7

Nationality was a matter of life and death, as far as Theodore Sava Joannides could tell. It was 1914. In a suburban police station of Alexandria, his interrogators shouted at him for hours. Only when they stripped him of his clothing in preparation for torture did he agree to sign an Arabic-language document accusing a coworker of murder. Much later, after he was sentenced to death, he recanted this accusation and made the statement quoted above. Theodore's words describe two kinds of fear. The first, that of an outsider fearing for his life, was an old terror. The second fear, spun from subjecthood and nationality, was something new. This new element surprised Theodore, and he insisted on it in his statement.

This book is about the many moments of surprise when nationality, an abstract tool in the burgeoning domain of international law, became vivid in the lives of ordinary people. Theodore was the sort of person who could be labeled hybrid, liminal, or cosmopolitan. This book avoids such indefinite constructs, employing a more rigorous set of categories of sociolegal description to determine precisely what we can and cannot know about such individuals. We can say that Theodore was Greek by language, Cypriot by birthplace, Christian by sect, a grocer by profession, and an Egyptian national for the purposes of the law. However, none of these labels, alone or in combination, gives us access to his identity. What is clear is that he was a human being in trouble, and in this moment these labels washed over him, some offering him dead ends and others paths forward.

Theodore felt himself a stranger in the hands of the Egyptian police. He could not understand their words, and even his dragoman (translator) seemed in cahoots against him. He was not one of these men, but a new and special kind of status—nationality—meant that he belonged to them and, more remotely, to the state they represented. This belonging was neither cultural—he could not understand the words they spoke— nor political, and it had nothing to do with the nationalist and anti-imperialist debates playing out in the streets and newspapers of the city. Nationality was instead a legal form of affiliation, a technical parameter to be specified on new administrative forms and documents. No one knew Theodore's nationality at the moment of the crime, but during the investigation the police determined it using remote laws of birth, residence, migration, and naturalization. Cyprus, his birthplace, was Ottoman territory under British occupation; so, too, was Egypt. Despite social differences with most Egyptians, legally he was a member of the same category. For decades, his nationality had been latent, unnamed, and without meaning, but suddenly it meant everything.

Few people came to law or to the nation spontaneously. Although from the first half of the nineteenth century a handful of elites used nationality as an auxiliary tool of privilege, it emerged in the lived experience of ordinary people only later. Over many decades, they discovered it one by one in their own moments of need or trouble. If nationality came to Theodore as a terrifying thing, others discovered in it protection, liberation, burden, or wealth. Newly minted nationals, from Theodore to the wealthy European traveling on a diplomatic passport, found ways to take up this legal identity and use it to shape their lives. The international sphere of nation-states became a meaningful reality when nationality laws engaged a critical mass of individuals. This book offers a pointillist account of nationality (and, consequently, of the nation) as an aggregate phenomenon that came into being case by case by case.

Even though he was in extraordinary trouble, Theodore was an ordinary person.[1] Stories that privilege remarkable individuals (the pioneer, the liminal, the elite, the exception) can reveal many things, but they are the wrong tool to explain the general phenomenon of membership in collectivities such as nations and empires.[2] Histories of the rise of the nation also give pride of place to its life as an idea, without attending much to the diffusion of that idea beyond the small circles of the literate.[3] A global social history of the nation requires a different approach, one that privileges large numbers of relatively ordinary individuals.

By attending to the experiences of these individuals, we can reduce the phenomenon of the nation to the sum of its parts: governments and bureaucracies, borders, flags, anthems, textbooks, passports, visas, and, critically, nationals. We are not obliged to grant the nation the epic imaginary proportions that certain proponents claim for it—those who ask "sons" to die for the nation, those who would write triumphalist histories of the fatherland, and indeed those who would wrestle to defeat such histories. The nation can be cast as less than all that. Instead of dismissing the nation as fiction, it is more constructive to probe the banal work of nationality and thus to assign the nation to its proper curtailed realm.

Nationality was imposed on Theodore, but once he was free of his captors, he accepted its terms. Most creative appropriation of nationality took place far from the two interpretive extremes—crushing state power and endlessly creative agency—that trouble the literature on the state.[4] The formal and discursive structures of modern state power—the law, for instance—matter a great deal, but they do not determine everything.[5] Agency, whether of the individual or of the state, also has its limits. Individual adoption of discourses of nationality or other forms of communitarian identity, for which the eastern Mediterranean is a key laboratory, happened in private moments, not in public spectacles.

By disaggregating complex societies into their constituent membership regimes, we more accurately depict many of the policies that governing bodies adopted during the modern period. From criminal law in eighteenth-century Istanbul to sectarianism in Tanzimat Lebanon to municipal development in mid-nineteenth-century Izmir, it is clear that top-down reform projects suggested communitarian frames for populations, and individuals and groups responded in the same idiom by adopting those frames.[6] By the late nineteenth century, communitarian frames were an accepted rubric for political organization and social identification. These newly reified communities reproduced the hierarchies of the society as a whole, however. Emancipation of sectarian communities, for example, appeared to answer demands for inclusion but only did so for elites. The generality of the population persisted in a subject position.

The mechanisms by which individual subalterns became members of these newly constituted communities have not been clearly explained for the pivotal decades before the First World War. The nature of late nineteenth-century documentation allows a closer look at the process of ascension to subaltern membership in newly emerged communities and redefined collectivities.[7] By looking carefully at the contingencies through which membership was taken up by individuals and attributed to them, this study suggests that the problem of scale should be considered in other communitarian moments. Individuated processes of subject and community formation deserve attention alongside the more typical narratives of collective, national, and transnational movements.

The history of international law, too, has been told as a top-down story. A number of recent studies reveal the non-European roots of international law.[8] These studies describe the emergence of the diverse, interlocking global regime of law that characterizes the modern world, but they do so above all in terms of public international law. States and entities that look like states are the main players in these studies, which work to retrieve distinctions among forgotten and occluded judicial categories.[9] This book examines the same process in terms of private international law, in which persons are the main subjects. States and persons differ markedly as sites of legal change. While states offer a certain variety of historical examples, persons are vastly more numerous and their range of experiences more complex.[10] As this book makes clear, histories of nationality law that depend on statute and doctrine describe the exception and not the rule. The lived experience of international law is an obscure subject, but its pursuit is a meaningful objective.[11]

Nationality is a critical (and overlooked) category for the historical analysis of the nation-state, community identities, and international law. This book works to specify nationality's meaning, using turn-of-the-century Alexandria as a proof text. Only a close study can denaturalize the phenomenon of nationality by demonstrating its novelty and diversity. In the present day, the legal concept is familiar and ubiquitous because almost everyone has come to nationality. But it was new to Theodore in 1914 and new to thousands of others in Alexandria in the decades straddling the turn of the twentieth century. And nationality had the power to supplant previous statuses while maintaining their functions. Nationality was modular and unified in appearance, but it played many roles. As a general phenomenon, nationality emerged fitfully in law codes and treatises. A social history of the rise of the nation through its diffusion to hundreds of individuals can describe the phenomenon without reliance on a killer anecdote or impersonal generalization. This approach changes the way the phenomenon looks—we find we know less, which is good.

Grasping Nationality

Nationality is a familiar word, but its use is typically imprecise. In the academic literature, it appears as an anodyne synonym for two more densely theorized concepts: nationalism and citizenship. Benedict Anderson's seminal text on the nation, for example, incorrectly equates nationality with "nation-ness."[12] To specify nationality's particular meaning, it may be simplest, first, to define its difference from these more familiar terms. Nationalism, citizenship, and nationality each describe relations among individuals, communities, and states. But nationalism's concern with ideas and sentiments in the political register differs from nationality, which concerns practices in the legal and civil registers.[13] The distinction might be reduced to thought versus action; there was no nationalism—no concern for voice or community—in Theodore's encounter with nationality. The difference between nationality and citizenship, meanwhile, begins with the distinction between international and municipal settings. Citizenship concerns political participation, standing, and voice within the state of membership. Nationality, on the other hand, concerns legal standing outside this domestic sphere.[14] As Paul Weis puts it, "Conceptually and linguistically, the terms 'nationality' and 'citizenship' emphasize two different aspects of the same notion: State membership. 'Nationality' stresses the international, 'citizenship' the national, municipal, aspect."[15]

For those familiar with the concepts of nationality and citizenship, this negative definition (of what nationality is not) may already form an outline of the subject of this book. But nationality's relationship with nationalism and citizenship is not as clear as this negative definition pretends. Nationality begins in law, but it becomes a malleable social fact with political and cultural functions. Some scholars minimize the importance of the distinction between legal and social meanings of nationality.[16] Eliding these meanings is a dangerous act of forgetting, however, with powerful political consequences. Treating nationality as an organic human characteristic conceals its fundamental work, which is to discriminate among human beings according to the accidental circumstances of their birth. This book's account of legal status as lived in a specific time and place is thus a call to be sure that we mean what we say when we invoke nationality in any context. Chapter 2, which defines a number of keywords in legal identity, further clarifies nationality's semantic field. Here I wish to enumerate five characteristics of nationality as a category of historical analysis.

First, nationality is legal.[17] A legal study from the middle of the twentieth century gives the term its barest definition: it is "the status of belonging to a state for certain purposes of international law."[18] It is often misidentified as a "sociocultural concept," but this characteristic is secondary and derivative.[19] In the first instance, nationality is a category of legal affiliation used by state and administrative bureaucracies and law courts. Individuals who self-identify by nationality typically do so to make a legal claim. When that legal claim is not explicit, for instance, in the case of administrative requests, it is usually implied. Without reference to law, nationality is an empty signifier.[20] Nationality was once a key issue in private international law. In the present day, most questions of private international law relating to the nationality of real persons are settled as a matter of routine (though corporations are a different matter); in fact, nationality is sometimes considered a part of immigration law. A century ago, this was not the case, as the categories of the field were in flux. The first Arabic textbook on private international law, which appeared in 1924, is dominated by questions of nationality.[21] If those questions appear largely settled today, *Identifying with Nationality* argues that they have simply been submerged in the contemporary international order and subsumed in doctrines of universal rights. The law of nationality is not settled now, and it was not settled then.

Second, nationality is personal and practical. As we saw in the case of Theodore, it is a latent quality that only becomes real when individuals are tested by concrete circumstances. This practical character is one reason that nationality is less obvious than nationalism. It does not and cannot emerge in collective, revolutionary moments. It cannot be led. Instead, it emerges person by person, family by family, case by case, over years and decades. As a result of its personal, practical nature, nationality appears contingent and strategic. Most Alexandrians self-identified (whether as Egyptian, Ottoman, or European subjects) circumstantially and non-exclusively, and they did so in order to access legal and civil (as opposed to political) rights. This individual, nonpolitical genealogy of national membership is an important supplement to existing conceptions of the rise of the nation. In fluid circumstances, people learned to address legal and state bureaucracies in terms that would win a response; hence, they learned to make claims in communitarian terms, notably sect and nationality. That communitarian self-identification had its origin in individual impetus, and the general phenomenon can usefully be analyzed through its individual parts.

Third, nationality is novel. Modernity gave a number of specific forms (what Novak calls "common law[s] of membership") to generic associationalism, including sect, ethnicity, and nationality.[22] If the nation tradition was invented no earlier than the eighteenth century, its nationality component has an especially weak claim to be immemorial: European jurists first referred to the concept of nationality near the middle of the nineteenth century.[23] The diffusion and individuation of nationality reached its peak in the years after the First World War. This modern phenomenon is also secular. Parolin's study of citizenship in the Arab world distinguishes among three types of belonging: kin, religion, and the nation-state. In the modern period, he suggests, nation-state membership trumps kin and religion.[24] If certain nationality laws enshrine religion and kinship in a primal position, these principles are articulated in secular language.[25] Secularism offers nationality special force in the modern world, which kin and religious associationalisms recruit by adopting secular terms. The concept has been naturalized in such a way as to conceal its novelty and erase its contingency.

Fourth, nationality is colonial. It is a "rule of difference" that bears the hallmark of colonial governmentality.[26] In the period considered by this book, nationality was prominently deployed in explicitly colonial and imperial contexts. But even outside of these contexts, the influence of colonialism is critical to the work that nationality does. Colonialism's will to categorize populations, its pervasive expression of power through small mechanisms and technologies, and its modernity are recognizable in nationality. This colonial character is an important distinction from citizenship, which was a key aim and claim of decolonization movements.[27] Nationality is also colonial in the sense that it is about difference rather than equality. Although the term is used for internalist accounts of a single "nationality," it finds its true sense in settings that require distinction between differing nationalities.[28] As we have seen, nationality's legal setting is necessarily international; indeed, as this study will argue, in the modern period there is no position that is not international. This lesson is repeated in various fields of study, from American history (where the transnational has overturned the exceptional) to the colonial (where metropole and colony can no longer be considered in isolation).[29] The internationalist critique of the political philosopher John Rawls shows that history is not the only field that has moved beyond the isolated national analytical forms of the twentieth century.[30] Furthermore, as recent studies of international law make clear, the colonial is the essence of the international.[31] If this case is clear in public international law, it is also rather abstract; the concrete work of nationality in private international law reveals a more vivid colonial face.

Fifth, nationality is modular but not universal. As a legal status, it derives legitimacy from its universal claim, for instance in article 15 of the Universal Declaration of Human Rights.[32] Universal state nationality is a necessary component of the nation-state's claim to be the legitimate constituent unit of the modern world order. We know quite a lot about the international system of commensurate citizenships that was consolidated in the decades after the First World War, which the sociologist John Torpey describes as "a system that presupposed mutually exclusive citizenries all of whom were distributed uniquely to one state or another."[33] This logic is supported by conflict-of-laws jurisprudence, which insists that every person (whether natural or legal) has a nationality that jurists can discover. But there is little space in this scheme for the exceptions that are the necessary companion of any legal order.[34] In practice, nationality is not universal. From the interwar problem of statelessness to refugee law to dual nationality to present-day "illegals" and "*biduns*," it is clear that not everyone has a nationality and that not all nationalities are equally efficacious.[35] Instead, nationality is a modular phenomenon, a status that is transportable and can be compared across legal contexts but has a particular character in each.[36] Nationality's particularities are historical products, and the story of its incomplete standardization needs telling. Modern nationality operates via a limited set of forms whose apparent uniformity conceals a diversity of functions. *Identifying with Nationality* shows the particular circumstances of nationality's ascent in Alexandria, which offers views of an especially revealing version of this global process.

Global Historical Context

Nationality succeeded widely varied systems of affiliation and membership. In the last decades of the eighteenth century, old ideas of membership started to crack as a result of political revolutions, tensions of empire, liberal ideology, industrialization, and increased mobility. Recent scholarship has revealed the foundational place of exclusion in the regimes of rights and citizenship that emerged, particularly in France and America.[37] Even within these signal nations, political membership was limited by gender, slavery, and religion. Meanwhile, economic and labor membership became ever more widely distributed as previously remote populations were drawn into unmediated state membership as soldiers, taxpayers, or laborers. The preponderant influence of private and corporate institutions such as guilds, churches, towns, firms, tribes, castes, and estates gradually unraveled under the pressure of centralizing states. A host of scattered conflicts over land ownership, military service, protection, and extradition during the post-Napoleonic expansion of state power built a large volume of new membership forms and procedures. The key move during this period was the widespread disaggregation of populations into standardized individuals visible to responsible authorities. While political episodes such as the 1848 wave of European protests, Italian and German unification, and the American Civil War have attracted the most attention, historians are now revealing the steady accumulation of a host of new mechanisms of civil membership and exclusion during this period.

Outside of Europe, laissez-faire migration policies during the third quarter of the nineteenth century combined with new transportation technologies to produce unprecedented global population flows.[38] It was in this context that new mixed port cities such as Alexandria became prominent. At the same time, a new idea of borders was beginning to gather momentum. Until the mid–nineteenth century, border controls were meant to capture and retain populations, to keep them in. Now the idea emerged that borders were meant to keep out migrants who might threaten the individual freedoms (as "free" laborers, for instance) of the inhabitants of a territory. This engine of membership and exclusion became all the more important after the abolition of slavery because it produced new markers of difference to replace those that had been lost.

Struggles over status increased in number and variety during the 1880s as centralizing states fought to overcome a vast variety of forms of local corporate organization. The concepts and categories produced through these struggles formed a gossamer fabric of remnants and novelties. Each setting was its own bellwether, and this widespread pattern of unique variations on the same theme justifies many local studies. In France and the United States, the battles were over access to the citizenship that constituted the republic under law. Struggles both internal and external revealed the limits of the citizenship model.[39] In Britain, there were no border controls and no explicit citizenship until much later; instead, access was open, and membership was defined in terms of a flat form of subjecthood that spread from the metropole to the farthest colonies of the empire. These practices created innumerable headaches as the state worked to control its population for its own needs and in response to its neighbors and colonies. The leading European state presided over one of the most muddled membership polities in the world.

The issue of which powers have the responsibility to identify and protect individuals and where individuals could be placed in space was a consistent thread running through these various forms. From the late nineteenth century, the international system grew to address these issues in increasingly uniform ways. Nationality laws spread as part of this process, alongside other measures of international standardization. High imperialism brought with it the decline of free-trade ideologies and the rise of "universal" extraterritorial norms and shared mixed courts in a number of parts of the world.[40] Under this new regime of international law, the civilization of states and of individuals belonging to those states were tightly associated and organized into three broad tiers: civilized, barbarian, and savage. In the decades before the First World War, homogeneous state forms and individual forms cogenerated.[41] The standardized membership norms and procedures that emerged during the 1910s and after the First World War were entrenched by the Second World War. These general trends in the history of persons and groups are clear in the historiography, but their relationship to the modern international system is still being articulated. Detailed local studies of these global processes are a critical step in this discovery.

Egypt's Institutional Context

In its more immediate context, two moments of broad institutional change define the chronology of this study: the Egyptian legal settlement of 1876–1883 and the extinguishing of Ottoman sovereignty over Egypt at the start of the First World War. While this book is not a general account of Egypt's legal history, I discuss the particular legal conditions of nationality's rise in Alexandria throughout the study. Here, as a general orientation I provide a thumbnail account of the legal landscape that structured the events described in this book.

Two earlier periods are essential to the story: the half-century of state centralization and change that preceded 1876 and a longer, more stylized period of Ottoman "tradition" that preceded it. This earlier period, in which Alexandria's law more closely resembled that of the rest of the Ottoman Empire, was by no means fixed in character.[42] From the perspective of the late nineteenth century, however, it inevitably assumes the role of a relatively uniform "tradition." From this retrospect, the salient feature of the system was its decentralization. Despite a measure of central supervision over judges' appointments, localities and various minority communities (sectarian communities [Coptic, Armenian, Greek, and Jewish], guilds, and clans) controlled their own legal situations. Alexandria's distance from the imperial capital compounded this decentralization.[43]

Within this system, subjects of certain European powers were governed by a regime of derogations called the capitulations. The Ottoman capitulations emerged in the sixteenth century as a set of privileges that the Ottomans granted to agents of Poland, France, and England. Over time, capitulations were extended to other European countries; eventually subjects of some nineteen foreign states enjoyed these special rights. Notably, they were exempt from Ottoman taxation, conscription, prosecution, and search. Historians tend to describe early modern capitulations as a kind of diplomatic immunity from arbitrary Oriental despotism.[44] It is more accurate simply to consider them part of the logic of the so-called *millet* system: foreigners, like Jews, Christians, and guild members, were a minority given substantial responsibilities of self-regulation in the Ottoman world.[45] Until the middle of the nineteenth century, protection was the ubiquitous medium of legal standing in the eastern Mediterranean. The protection that local notables and patrons offered to their clients (typically in the form of guarantees [*damana*]), the protection that the Ottoman sultan offered to his subjects (*ri'aya*), and the protection that foreign states offered their protégés (*himaya*) were drawn from the same well. Protection came in various forms: mutual protection within communities of residence, sect, family, and occupation; the protection of thugs ("protection rackets"); the protection of documents and guarantees; guild protections; and the protection of the state against invasion and public disorder. The Ottoman state never delegated the personal jurisdiction that came with such protections, nor did it ever really claim it. As far as the individual was concerned, there was no paramount authority or system of affiliation in the eastern Mediterranean to resemble the uniform nationalities of the twentieth century.

Between the sixteenth century and the early nineteenth century, capitulatory consulates were bit players serving tiny constituencies in an Ottoman cultural idiom. But during the eighteenth century, as the Mediterranean balance of power shifted in favor of the European powers, the capitulations became irrevocable and their application increasingly one-sided.[46] By the nineteenth century, they had become the legal basis for extensive extraterritorial rights for Europeans and their protégés. The change in rights was not restricted to foreigners, however. The ancien régime of Ottoman subjecthood was overturned by the complex social, economic, and jurisdictional transformations of the first half of the nineteenth century, which accompanied the global changes in membership outlined in the previous section.

In the half-century before 1876, Ottoman "tradition" was displaced by new systems of justice that emerged out of imperial and economic reconfigurations. In the second quarter of the nineteenth century, the Tanzimat invoked the notion of uniform and equal subjecthood. Although this uniformity was not realized in any practical, widespread manner for the better part of a century, it triggered new kinds of political rhetoric and institutional rearrangements.[47] For the most part, however, its early influence was corrosive of previous forms without constructing new forms in their place. Egypt became the principal site where new forms of power were practiced. And the centralization and rationalization of state control under Mehmet Ali Pasha had a clear judicial face.[48] The court and police reforms of the 1820s, 1830s, and 1840s were swamped by Egypt's incorporation into the world economy, however.[49] During the middle years of the century, a marked influx of European subjects into the Ottoman Empire (the result of European imperial expansion, changing transportation technologies, and new labor conditions) put a strain on the existing justice system.

Under Mehmet Ali, the Ottoman province of Egypt became independent of Istanbul in all but name. Western powers were able to press their claims for capitulatory privileges even further in Egypt than they did in the rest of the dwindling Ottoman Empire. From the middle of the nineteenth century, the massive expansion of Western-subject populations in the port cities of the Ottoman Empire changed the function and weight of the consulates. The network of consulates became far more extensive, placing agents in all significant towns of Egypt. In the 1830s and 1840s, Britain and France first codified the laws and procedures to be used at their consulates.[50] They did so because ad hoc adjudication, which had worked so well under the ancien régime, had become unmanageable. The first problem was subaltern foreigners, who now overwhelmed the foreign elite. Consular justice has been described in the secondary literature as an instrument of "self-control," allowing upper-class foreigners to keep their unruly lower-class compatriots in check. The capitulation system was designed to let people off scot-free, and foreign elites were concerned not to extend this liberty too far down the social scale.[51] A second and more pressing problem concerned resolution of the commercial and civil disputes of the wealthy. Most such cases of any significance had become the subject of simultaneous litigation at multiple tribunals, typically one for each nationality involved. Settlement of the increasing volume of legal disputes involving two or more capitulatory powers had become too complex, unpredictable, and interminable for comfort, so in the second half of the century, foreign and local authorities sought to standardize the chaotic judicial system.[52]

This study begins in 1880, two years before Britain invaded Egypt and became the real power behind the Turkish dynasty that had ruled Egypt, independent of Istanbul, since the early decades of the nineteenth century.

This book's story involves a set of new legal institutions and instruments, what I will call a "settlement," that emerged in Egypt between 1875 and 1885.[53] These years witnessed the establishment of the Mixed Tribunals (1876); the deposition of Isma'il, the last powerful khedive (1879); the 'Urabi revolt (1881–1882), the British invasion and occupation (1882); and the establishment of the Native Courts (1883). This pivotal period integrates great domestic and foreign legal reforms into one moment.

Under the terms of this settlement, the population of Egypt was divided into jurisdictional spheres corresponding to four major judicial institutions. The Mixed Tribunals had jurisdiction in commercial and civil cases between parties of mixed nationality. The Native Courts dealt with local subjects (such as Theodore), and consular courts managed foreign subjects.[54] A parallel system of sectarian courts—Islamic, Christian, and Jewish—handled many cases of personal and civil status. In the theory that typifies conflict of laws, everyone in the city could answer a series of either/or questions in order to define or discover her or his place in the kaleidoscope of statuses.

This settlement was implemented over the decades that followed. The key outcome of the settlement was to relieve consular and Egyptian courts of any jurisdiction over commercial and civil cases involving more than one nationality, which had constituted the bulk of their work. These cases were transferred to the Mixed Tribunals, which do not figure prominently in this study. Although they were the prestige venue, with the best lawyers and the strongest jurisprudence, nationality questions figure less prominently there than elsewhere because simply establishing the fact of mixed nationality was sufficient for the Mixed Tribunals to win jurisdiction.

This study draws instead on the consular courts, which were the site of most intensive nationality work. These courts handled all criminal cases with foreign defendants and civil and commercial cases in which all parties were nationals of the consulate. Only a tiny number of commercial cases fit this category, but rather more civil disputes fell under consular purview. Marriage, divorce, and inheritance cases were questions of personal status, and as such they were typically referred to private, sectarian authorities. However, consular and state courts received the responsibility to certify judgments, respond to appeals, and enforce money issues that arose from these personal-status cases. It was some time before this settlement, this new judicial order, found its legs. This 1870s and 1880s period

TABLE 0.1 Jurisdiction after 1883

Case type and defendant		Plaintiff or petitioner		
		Local subject	French subject	British subject
Civil or commercial	Local	Native Courts	Mixed Tribunals	Mixed Tribunals
	French	Mixed Tribunals	French consular courts	Mixed Tribunals
	British	Mixed Tribunals	Mixed Tribunals	British consular courts
Criminal	Local	Native Courts	Native Courts	Native Courts
	French	French consular courts	French consular courts	French consular courts
	British	British consular courts	British consular courts	British consular courts

Note: "French" and "British" appear merely as examples, for which any foreign nationality can be substituted.

of institutional and status transformation was not unique to Egypt, but Egypt, compact and controlled, was a focused legal space where even the exceptions depended on permission rather than neglect. Its various institutions interacted intensively, despite their different sources of law. The archives of the consular courts, small institutions dependent on the Egyptian police for enforcement, preserve a mass of correspondence with the other institutions.

A history of Alexandria starting in 1880 faces archival opportunities and lacunae. Before the 1882 British bombardment of Alexandria, which triggered an inferno that gutted the consular quarter of the city, the British consulate's chancellor grabbed a few bundles of recent records and rowed out into the bay. Because everything else was lost in the fires, the earliest of the thousands of judicial dossiers held in the British archives date from 1880. The French archives lack such dossiers but contain two dozen registers summarizing every judicial hearing before its consular court in Alexandria between 1880 and 1914, as well as personal dossiers for all French subjects and protégés registered in the city. While Egyptian police and judicial records for the period before 1883 are abundant, those for the period following the British invasion are currently beyond the reach of any researcher—probably hidden in the Dar al-Mahfuzat—but a small separate collection of capital cases as well as correspondence in other archives has allowed me access to this history. The full archives of the Mixed Courts are also inaccessible at the moment. Italian, American, and Turkish state archives offer valuable (if less complete) sets of information.[55] In total, this study draws on more than four thousand cases, in five languages, from archives in six countries, concerning more than ten thousand individuals. The documents on which it draws are very diverse in type: interrogation transcripts, identification documents, wills and receipts, log books, judge's notes, and letters.

This evidence reveals the ways in which residents of Alexandria identified themselves in the three and a half decades before the First World War. *Identifying with Nationality* tells the story of nationality's triumph over rival categories of affiliation. Archival records show that in the 1880s, self-identification depended on a wide range of categories, including name, profession, family, quarter, sect, guarantor, and many others; nationality was almost never invoked. By 1914, when Theodore faced the police, nationality was a ubiquitous and primary element of all identification. The First World War brought structural changes to the justice system in Egypt. If the wartime termination of Ottoman sovereignty was of largely theoretical importance at the level of the state, as Britain had wielded military and administrative control over Egypt since 1882, for Ottoman nationals it meant a significant change in status. Martial law disrupted the normal routines of all courts and police (as well as their archives). German nationals in Egypt saw their protection shift to American hands, and Russians lost their capitulations after 1917. The 1919 revolution in Egypt, meanwhile, marked the beginning of widespread Egyptian nationalism beyond the educated elite. Beyond these circumstantial factors, the First World War was a moment of global change in nationality practices. Universal nationality became a normative presumption of postwar international law. As the epilogue shows, Egypt was one of many states scrambling to accommodate this new expectation.

Why Alexandria?

The emergence of nationality was a global phenomenon, and it rewards study in any of the global cities—Bombay, Calcutta, Shanghai, San Francisco, São Paolo, New York, London, Marseille—which became laboratories of

jurisdiction in the late nineteenth century. Alexandria's diverse population, its proximity to Europe's many nationalities, and the exceptional
situation of Egypt under public international law give the city a distinc-
tive place on this list.[56] Critically, and unlike its Mediterranean cousins
Izmir, Istanbul, Salonica, and Tunis, it was a city with many authorities
but no hegemon.[57] In Alexandria, dozens of formal legal institutions drew
on international law to ask and answer questions about the categories of
affiliation of individuals like Theodore. Alexandrians' practical articulation
of identity before these myriad institutions illustrates arguments about the
banality of nationality and the circumscribed nature of citizenship. Drawing on this setting, this book departs from existing narratives of colonial
legal history in three ways. First, it sets legal doctrine and practice in a single frame, treating law as a socially constituted product. Second, it considers people as subjects of international law, along with states, and it sets the
experiences of ordinary people on equal footing with those of the wealthy
and intellectual. Third, it seeks to counterbalance the preponderance of
Euro-American stories in legal history by privileging the law of the rest of
the world in a transimperial (not merely comparative) context. Together,
these interrelated agendas aim to depict not the origin of nationality but
(something like) its median, when it became a truly global legal practice.

Histories of law in practice have only recently begun to look beyond
Western settings.[58] There are good reasons for this—the sources and structures of many non-Western legal institutions await systematic description,
and their sources are difficult to access both linguistically and practi-
cally. The rich body of anthropological work on non-Western legal practices, meanwhile, has offered many insights into legal pluralism, but its
application to formal legal institutions is less obvious. In addition, this
work typically focuses on the present rather than the past.[59] Alexandria's
jurisdictional complexity, in which some two dozen national, sectarian,
policing, and judicial institutions maintained often separate, sometimes
overlapping spheres of responsibility, depended on strict application of
legal categories to individuals. This sociolegal structure, clear enough in
theory (see table 0.1), was not so straightforward in practice. As a result,
social historians mining the rich pool of turn-of-the-century Mediterranean legal sources often skirt its legal content and rarely situate the
sources as essentially legal products. Of course, clear, consistent social
segmentation by nationality was a legal fiction. Alexandria was rife with

category distinctions and colonial ironies: European-born foreigners were distinguished from those born within empire (such as the Maltese, Algerians, and Tunisians), rich from poor, and foreigners from locals. The historical record contains numerous examples of double nationality, uncertain nationality, absence of nationality, misread nationality, and so on. But the gap between legal plan and sociolegal practice resulted not because complex jurisdiction was an inherently "intractable problem" but because of the incidental nature of nationality.[60] Before the First World War, a small and wealthy Alexandrian coterie defined itself consistently according to nationality. But many more residents of the city declared national affiliation only on the rare occasions when it was advantageous for protection or identification, and most did not identify themselves by nationality under any circumstances. This book describes numerous experiences of many such individuals and the ways that these individuals lived in exception to the official vision of clear nationality. Their instrumental practice of nationality was a force in the subsequent constitution of the doctrine.

Much sociolegal history aims to show how law is "constitutive of consciousness," how legal ideas shape and are shaped by social life.[61] This worthy aim lies somewhat beyond the reach of this book for several reasons. The historical literature on global nationality law and practice is too sparse to support such a lofty goal at present, and the source material is terse and dispersed. Second, and contrary to the prevailing sense in the Euro-American historical literature of law as a pervasive force, in Alexandria nationality law's constitutive force presented itself punctually, not permanently. Though this book narrates nationality's increasing prominence in social life, it remained one constitutive ingredient among many; global histories of legal pluralism show that few legal modes were all-pervasive all the time. Third, as Robert Gordon reminds us, the notion "that law is partly constitutive of social life, because law distributes powers and immunities, and because all social actors internalize and enact legal identities and roles, tends to get mixed up with another issue entirely, that of the relation between elite/official and everyday/lay legal actions."[62] This book's evidence describes the latter relationship better than the former; while it is clear that legal concepts and social practices are mutually constituting, any overall theory of that relationship in the context of nationality is premature.

Whether describing constitutive theory or everyday action, the history of practice demands a focus on ordinary people.[63] This study distinguishes between nationalism and nationality in order to deemphasize questions of elite intellectual culture and formal politics. This methodological premise is also a reaction to the deafening preponderance of elite culture and politics in the historiography of the nation-state in general and Egypt in particular. These factors were important, but I wish to see the themes that emerge when they are held in check. I am encouraged by my sources, which reveal power without formal politics, feature plans and schemes but few abstract ideas, and show nationality without the nation, citizenship without politics. The story that emerges is meant to complement existing narratives, not replace them. The adjective "national" ought to refer as much to nationality as it does to nationalism.[64]

The conventional focus on political citizenship impoverishes analysis of Middle Eastern citizenship in at least two ways. First, it condemns analysis of Middle East citizenship to the role of pathology of a body that is either immature or broken, situating conventional definitions of citizenship as prescriptions that will heal it. Second, it sets Middle Eastern historians seeking to restore honor to the region's past on an impossible quest for a Holy Grail of indigenous political citizenship that was destroyed by outside forces.[65] That citizenship which is (in Linda Bosniak's words) "portrayed as the most desired of conditions, as the highest fulfillment of democratic and egalitarian aspiration" haunts attempts to describe the global history of imperialism.[66] In their efforts to situate Middle Eastern experiences vis-à-vis this ideal historians must keep in mind the differentiated nature of Western citizenship.[67]

The existing literature on citizenship focuses overwhelmingly on political rights, especially issues of democratic and electoral politics, taking 1789 as its point of departure. While this focus largely corresponds to the major problematics of Western citizenship, it deadens analysis of other forms of citizenship (legal, social, civil, and so on). My account of nationality in Alexandria brackets the political—there was no democratic citizenship in Egypt—and excludes it from analysis. This move is not an idle, contrarian thought experiment. It is a corrective effort to get at citizenship as a global (and not merely Western) phenomenon. *Identifying with Nationality* argues that turn-of-the-century Alexandria offers a privileged view of citizenship's emergence in a world not merely confined to its

European province. This was a time when people of all classes, races, and genders—not merely white bourgeois men—began to engage with the law of the expanded state in their everyday lives. To win access to protection and identification under the law, they had to self-identify by nationality. Unlike the archetypal North American and European settings of citizenship, Alexandria was a place where legal nationalities of many regions and types were on offer, and the conversation between them is at the core of this book.

The bourgeoisie has dominated the urban history of the modern Arab Mediterranean, primarily through the sources they produced—their books and newspapers and their chambers of commerce and municipal organizations provide the basis of most of the historiography.[68] Literacy is one of the foundations of bourgeois hegemony (in this case in cultural history). Wealth is a foundation of bourgeois domination of economic history, and nationality is the basis of their prominence in legal and political histories. The wealthy are also prominent in recent studies that break new methodological ground in describing networks and migration in the Mediterranean, the Indian Ocean, and beyond.[69] In large part, this literature describes networks in which the vulnerability of diasporic communities— Armenian, Jewish, Hadrami, radical—was in some ways balanced by strong internal connections and considerable economic power. Many of the individuals I describe experienced no such advantages. Poor and poorly connected, they searched hard for protection; nationality proved a network of last resort.

Global legal histories that focus on the practice of ordinary people must deemphasize questions of public law. Public law is the concern of the most important studies of global legal history.[70] But beyond a handful of leading cases that occasioned diplomatic intervention—Don Pacifico (Athens, 1850), Koszta (Izmir, 1853), Joris (Constantinople, 1905)—public law appeared in the lives of ordinary people only indirectly, if at all.[71] If (as I suggest) nationality is personal and practical, its private-law character deserves special attention, for instance, to practices of protection and identification that states and individuals share. Widespread, varied private implementation of nationality's forms illustrates the modular character of the phenomenon.

Perhaps the chief virtue of Alexandria as an object of study is its situation between European imperial nation-states.[72] It requires a transimperial approach to law that goes beyond mere comparison and does not endorse the national frame.[73] In Alexandria (and perhaps only in Alexandria), twenty-odd states were obliged to work together, each in a way that was legally justifiable in the terms of the home state. In other words, here more than anywhere it was necessary to develop universal, complementary international law practice. A full study of Alexandria's history demands work in the archives of more than one empire—more, indeed, than I have used. British archives alone are insufficient: add French, Ottoman, and Italian archives for a start, as well as the Egyptian national archives. The virtue of this burdensome requirement is liberation from the blunders of the narrowing tradition that has grown up around the history of each imperial nation-state. The most critical and engaged studies can suffer from national blinders, failing to transcend the universal pretenses of French republicanism, the "conventional oppositions . . . between the national and the transnational"[74] (and even this Gary Wilder book is all and only about France and its world). And the whole body of imperial historiography flows through these national channels. Edited collections sometimes bind the channels in parallel proximity, to useful effect, but they do not blend. Egypt demands otherwise and points the way toward an imperial historiography while still attending to the constraints of the nation-state.

A novel phenomenon such as nationality can be studied at its point of origin—this is a certain type of genealogy. In Jacques Berque's classic survey of modern Egyptian history, he states (with characteristic exaggeration) that Egypt is the world's oldest nationality.[75] Less eccentric accounts point to France as the birthplace of modern nationality.[76] France's strong normative discourse of nationality was confronted with its children in the late nineteenth century when, as Patrick Weil argues in his history of French nationality, France became Europe's first "country of immigration."[77] But a global-historical approach must privilege instead the moment of widespread adoption. It is common use, rather than original use, that best describes the reality of the phenomenon. Alexandria was an even more indeterminate setting because there was no strong norm. The nationality of Egypt's "local subjects" was as weak in Egypt as the nationality of French citizens was strong in France. Alexandria was thus a bellwether for nationality changes that would spread worldwide in the twentieth century, and its experience more closely conforms to the norm than that of France's early adopters.

Outline and Narrative

The book is divided into three parts, and its chapters come in pairs. Part 1, "Settings," offers microhistories of the place (Alexandria) and of the field of law (private international law) that this book employs in its work to recast global genealogies of citizenship. Chapter 1, "Vulgar Cosmopolitanism," shows how the city's inhabitants elaborated systems of identification outside of state institutions. It gives a vivid taste of life in the city's streets. Chapter 2, "Keywords," is a survey of the meanings of a dozen terms used in legal and historical discussions of nationality and citizenship. It draws on international legal sources as well as the writings of Ottoman and Egyptian lawyers. In form, it is inspired by Raymond Williams's indispensable work of the same name.

Part 2, "Means," offers a close examination of four practices that inculcated nationality in the everyday lives of the general population. Identification papers (chapter 3) and the census (chapter 4) were key sites of modern state labeling practices, which trained the population to self-identify using a new (and efficacious) vocabulary in order to claim rights. Papers and censuses show the convergence of identification protocols from two directions: the individual and the institutional. Both chapters treat the categories that these protocols produced, the former in the details of particular instances and the latter in the effects of aggregation. Money (chapter 5) and marriage (chapter 6) were two leading reasons that people came to define themselves according to nationality. Both were engines of discrimination between different kinds of people: rich and poor, male and female. These sites of class and gender practice triggered especially anxious nationality debates that tested the capacities of novel means of status definition. Microhistories of these four phenomena (which were operative elsewhere in the world at the same time) illustrate nationality's grasp at fine resolution in a manner that is scalable to world history.

Part 3, "Other Nationalities," tells of statuses that lost out to nationality after the turn of the twentieth century. Europeans (chapter 7) occupied the dominant rank of sociolegal status in Egypt as elsewhere in the world. What was unusual in Alexandria was the presence in their midst of non-European foreigners (chapter 8), notably imperial subjects such as Maltese, Algerians, and Tunisians, who were able to exercise privileges in Egypt unavailable to them at home or elsewhere within their own empires.

These foreigners outnumbered the Europeans in Alexandria, and the legal institutions of the capitulations, intended to guarantee European privilege, were encumbered by this non-European majority. Protégé status (chapter 9) was a formalized system of protection for deserving compradors that was particular to the Ottoman Mediterranean. The status of bad subjects (chapter 10) was also morally defined, but these undesirables were local representatives of a global category of undesirables. The final pair of chapters concerns two statuses that were tightly bound together. Ottomans (chapter 11) were that minority of residents of the eastern Mediterranean that could deploy the Ottoman nationality invented in 1869 and gradually elaborated in the decades that followed. Locals (chapter 12), meanwhile, describes the overwhelming majority in Egypt who had no form of nationality and no use for it—until, after 1900, a few of them did.

To modern eyes, these six statuses might appear nebulous, inconsistent, and ill defined. This reaction is largely the result of the normative position that nationality occupies in the present day. These chapters, which engage literatures on legal history and especially private international law, show that nationality was once an equally contingent and contested category. How and why did standardization of affiliation status occur, and why did nationality survive while other categories faded away? Each of the six "other nationalities" that this book examines followed its own trajectory. European status was permanent; there was no trajectory toward the top for those already there. The same was true of bad subjects, the perennial bottom status. Protégés, on the other hand, knew already in 1880 that their days were numbered, and indeed the status vanished in the first years of the twentieth century. Foreigners—non-European subjects of empire—did not see the fate of their status until well into the twentieth century, when anticolonial thinking began to encourage them to disaffiliate with their imperial protectors. Along with the last two "other nationalities" I study— Ottomans and locals—they engaged in "choice of nationality" during this period. These political communities learned that the path of least resistance was to follow the international legal playbook, and that playbook offered nationality as its plan. Already in the 1860s the Ottomans were beginning down this path, and they refined their approach as the decades passed. Egyptians were bound in imperial relationships that limited their sovereignty, and their nationality agenda only began to clarify at the turn of the century (and was enshrined in law a quarter-century later).

The epilogue of the book, "Egyptians in a World of Universal Nationality," explains the mechanisms by which Egyptian nationality was established in the years after the First World War, when national citizenship became ubiquitous. Public international law and private international law are far more tightly integrated than we have been led to believe. After the turn of the century, both fields standardized in a single process. The First World War and its settlement created a clear rupture in public international law, and it had the same effect in private international law. The shock that swept away empires also swept away nonconforming categories of personal status. The First World War was a violent consolidation of questions and answers. In the interwar years, nationality became so prominent as to be ubiquitous, and it disappeared as it was folded into citizenship after the Second World War. Nevertheless, its discriminations remain with us today. There is no better indicator of the endurance of nationality than the persistence of statelessness, a mirror that reveals nationality's essence, which is to protect the strong from the weak.

PART I

Settings

1

Vulgar Cosmopolitanism

In the high heat of July 1886, two young British navy men set out to enjoy a free afternoon in Alexandria. They followed the usual path of sailors on leave, walking from their boat to the nearest busy spot, a street called al-Sabᶜ Banat (the Seven Girls) in Arabic, Rue des Soeurs in French, and Sisters' Street in English. Even under occupation, Alexandria was one of the most lively ports in the world. Like counterpart streets the world over, al-Sabᶜ Banat was set up to deal with the rising human tide arriving on steamships, offering them supplies, beds, and work, as well as grog shops and brothels—and special detention rooms in its police stations.[1] Ground-floor shops lined the sidewalks of al-Sabᶜ Banat, selling food, alcohol, and everyday goods and services. The sidewalks were crowded, and the roadway's ceiling was a thicket of tram cables. Most of the two- to four-story brick buildings along the street were built during a cotton boom twenty-five years earlier. The debt crisis and revolution that followed that boom led to a British occupation, which brought these two sailors to the city.

During brief stays in this port of call, sailors would often indulge in alcohol and violence. As they appear in the court records, these visits usually followed a set pattern: disembarkment, a walk to al-Sabᶜ Banat, drinking, drunkenness, return to ship. Sometimes: fighting with police, falling off the quays, falling asleep on railroad tracks. On this afternoon, the men stopped first at the German Bar, where "there was a lot of skylarking going on amongst merchant seamen and girls." They crossed the road, looking for somewhere quieter, and paused to chat in front of another bar. A man sitting nearby overheard their conversation and believed himself to have been insulted. He said something to the sailors, who in turn became angry. A brief fight followed, chairs flew, and men ran from the bar into the street. Both sailors were stabbed.[2]

The dossier of evidence for the criminal prosecution that ensued is a cosmopolitan dream. It contains transcripts in four languages, with the testimony of almost every witness recorded in a language not his or her own. Evidence given by Maltese men was written down in Italian; the accused, Guglielmo Farrugia, signed his deposition with the name "William." The testimony of four Englishmen was taken in French, even though their interrogator bore the distinctly un-Gallic name of Percy Bagwell (Lieutenant in 2nd Essex Regiment).[3] The testimony of an illiterate twenty-four-year-old Austrian barmaid was recorded in Arabic. The police scribe took down her oath in two Islamic formulas: "I testify by God (Praised and Exalted be He) that what I witnessed was . . . " opens her account, and it closes with "This is what I witnessed, and God (Exalted be He) is the Best of Witnesses."[4] The charm of this evidence derives from its incongruities: a man named Percy Bagwell should not speak French, Austrian barmaids should not speak Islamic oaths. But our sense of surprise (and indeed pleasure) at such incongruities is based on a series of assumptions about identifiers, the implications of which go beyond historical inaccuracy.

The golden image of late nineteenth- and early twentieth-century cosmopolitan Alexandria depends on reflexive reference to a vocabulary of categories—cosmopolitan, foreign, native, European, citizen, subject, national, Levantine, protégé, local, and others—that act as distorting abstractions because their significance is implied rather than explained. The cardinal sin of histories of fin-de-siècle cosmopolitanism is pleasure in the anachronistic use of present-day categories, especially those of modular and indelible nationality.[5] This book offers a different pleasure: corrective precision concerning the legal force, historical circumstances, and global context in which individuals and groups came to be labeled by nationality and its rival categories. Unlike twenty-first-century readers, residents of late nineteenth-century Alexandria were not fluent in the vocabulary of nationality. For them (like us), social categories were a shorthand of convenience. Naturally, their use was contingent, temporary, and subject to error. Those most prone to err were outsiders (like us) clinging too closely to overdetermined categories of their (our) own choosing. Vocabularies of description legible in one context do not necessarily carry over into other contexts, and they can fail—as the British navy men attacked at the bar discovered—when they organize description and action unsuccessfully.

The police were slow to make arrests, in part because the details reported by the stabbed sailors were so unclear. One victim said his assailant "looked like a Frenchman [*avait l'air d'un français*], with a little mustache and a Napoleon-style beard." The other victim testified that the attackers had spoken in French to each other. These descriptions were of little use to the police, who knew that the clientele of the bars in question were not French speakers. A patrol of British soldiers was sent from bar to bar to determine where the attacks had taken place. Here too ethnic and national coding were misleading. The "German" grog shop, part of a notorious cluster of three trouble spots, was frequented by British soldiers. The "Union Jack," in the same knot, was run by an Italian woman. If taken as identification categories, these labels were poor guides, crutches for outsiders.

Mistaking Maltese for French was only one aspect of a confrontation that turned on misunderstanding and misidentification. The sailors (bold enough to curse in a police report) claimed that before the attack, they had been complaining to each other about the "bloody noise" at the first bar. Somehow, they said, their French-looking, French-speaking interlocutors had misunderstood their English words. They reported that one of the men said to them "*sacré bleu*" or "*sacré bousse* [*buse*?]" or "*sacré boof*." One of the sailors, confident of his comprehension, told his companion that this phrase meant "bloody bugger." On this basis, the fight was on.[6]

Instead of a contest between British, Greek, French, and Maltese nationals, the fight and the charges that followed it can be read as a contest between those possessing local knowledge and those who lacked it. Alexandria's population grew rapidly during the second half of the nineteenth century. Long-term residents shared the city with newcomers and sojourners, and the social distinctions between them constitute a major social boundary that does not map onto received legal or ethnic schemas. The seamen did not know who was who or where they were. They walked along a few key avenues, leaving the rest of the city alone. They did not know the name of the bar where they were attacked, or if it had a name, or what language was spoken there. These sailors were true outsiders, in the sense that their stays in Alexandria were very brief, and their conduct in the city was often obnoxious to its society. But even peaceable newcomers experienced the geography of the city in a different way from residents. They worked, slept at hostels, and cobbled together a social life based on language, acquaintances from their homeplace, religion, and money. They operated despite a lack of knowledge about the places where they were living, the company they were keeping, or even the name of the street in which they stood.

Long-term residents were very different kinds of social actors. The Maltese assailants, when pursued after the attack, escaped by ducking around corners and out back doors in a neighborhood that they knew well. And their neighbors certainly made better witnesses in court; some of those who appeared seemed to know every actor in a crime or crowd personally. Certainly they recognized outsiders, such as sailors and soldiers, immediately. In the end, the police were able to identify Maltese suspects thanks to the help of "native" witnesses.

Length and nature of residence were critical categories of identification in turn-of-the-century Alexandria. Every police interrogation record began with the same protocol of identification: name, occupation (sina'a), residence (sakan), the name of the neighborhood headman (shiyakha), and place of origin (balad).[7] For anyone whose place of origin was other than Alexandria, their length of residence in the city was noted.[8] In a relatively rootless society filled with newcomers, protection became a major social distinction. As we will see in chapter 3, the purpose of identification was to determine which authority could protect or control an individual. Traditional forms of protection—family, friends, neighbors, wealth—served this purpose, but so too did newer kinds: employment (in the army, for example), officialdom, and nationality.

The most powerful protectors were able to impose a reordering of hierarchies of knowledge and power. Although they were outsiders, the British victims possessed an important advantage over their assailants: they belonged to a military occupying force that offered them maximal protection. The power of their patrons compensated for their lack of local knowledge, and colonial officialdom intervened to settle the two sailors' case and impose its own legal categories, which did not "privilege local knowledge over outside knowledge."[9] When he learned of the attack, the captain of their ship immediately wrote to the three centers of official power: the governor, the general commanding the British garrison, and the British consul. The governor arrested the perpetrators, and the Maltese men (who were British subjects because of the British military occupation of Malta) were charged before the British consular court. Legal proceedings were hurried, as the captain was anxious to set sail. The navy paid the wages of a prosecuting lawyer, who won a conviction.[10]

The same vocabularies of identification that hindered the investigation were essential to prosecute the case in Alexandria's patchwork of complementary jurisdictions, which depended on nationality to assign litigants to the proper tribunal. Modular nationality made the incident "legible," in James Scott's convincing sense.[11] Legible nationality is equally essential to a particular vision of cosmopolitanism operating in many retrospective accounts of turn-of-the-century port cities: it is elitist, grieving, nostalgic, and privileges label over content.[12] This vision varies from site to site, but it is particularly prominent in the memory of Alexandria. The conventional image of cosmopolitan Alexandria ignores locals, just as it fails to tell an accurate story of Alexandria's foreign community. Instead, this field of writing amplifies the experience of a tiny group of elites and broadcasts it across the whole of a heterogeneous social past. Informed above all by the modern-day context of the secular nation-state, this cosmopolitan fable serves certain presentist political agendas but fails history.[13]

In this study, I wish to move beyond that critique to propose a revised view of the social history of cosmopolitan Alexandria. One might call this picture "vulgar cosmopolitanism," in contradistinction to the conventional image of gilded, cosmopolitan Alexandria. By "vulgar cosmopolitanism" I intend not obscene but low, unrefined, plain, common, ordinary cosmopolitanism.[14] "Ordinary cosmopolitanism" is something of an oxymoron, but that is part of my point: the conventional image of cosmopolitanism depends on (usually unacknowledged) conditions of wealth and the vocabulary of difference authorized by privilege. The sources on which most historians of Alexandria depend—books, newspapers, letters, and memoirs—announce and record social interactions of the wealthy and privileged and reproduce and normalize their category vocabulary. Parallel processes in the much larger plebeian population, which go largely unrecognized in these sources, were in fact the mainstream of Alexandria's social history.[15]

At its heart, cosmopolitanism is an attitude toward categories of social identification, notably those of nationality, religion, and ethnicity. As far as social history is concerned, the problem with conventional cosmopolitan accounts lies in their unconsidered use of these categories. When categories are employed more consciously, the best of the cosmopolitan attitude—transgressive, open-minded, even utopian—becomes a sound basis of critical inquiry.[16] Ordinary people employed a broad range of social categories and boundaries in their cosmopolitan interactions. Recognition of these categories and interactions is an essential part of this story. What the philosopher Charles Taylor calls "the politics of recognition" plays a generative role in identities (including national identities) and also in claims for minority rights. Such claims suggest that

> our identity is partly shaped by recognition or its absence, often by the *mis*recognition of others, and so a person or group of people can suffer real damage, real distortion, if the people or society around them mirror back to them a confining or demeaning or contemptible picture of themselves. Nonrecognition or misrecognition can inflict harm, can be a form of oppression, imprisoning someone in a false, distorted, and reduced mode of being.[17]

Legal rights—such as those enjoyed by the seamen—were a form of recognition, and the absence of a counterpart legal personality for locals was a form of misrecognition. But philosophers of cosmopolitanism have not given serious attention to the problem of divergent vocabularies of identification.[18] Instead, they assume that a single vocabulary can be developed in which to accomplish the hard work of recognition. The evidence of Alexandria's vulgar cosmopolitanism shows that its inhabitants employed multiple vocabularies of social identification. The forms of misrecognition that characterized the society—including misunderstanding, mistranslation, and miscategorization—were often a product of incommensurate vocabularies.

In arguing for a reassessment of Alexandria's cosmopolitan places and societies, I suggest that common vocabularies of Mediterranean social description—sect, class, language, nationality—were neither constant

nor universal. Certain vocabularies were sometimes of the first importance, and at other times they faded into the background to be misrecog-
nized, forgotten, or replaced by other vocabularies; the rise of nationality
to prominence is the prime example. When they fought in front of the bar,
the navy men were more outsider than Briton, and the bar's clients were
more insider than Maltese or French. Before the court, however, vocabularies of nationality were most important. This chapter offers other social
categories of vulgar cosmopolitanism, including walker and driver, public
official, newcomer and native. The chapters that follow probe one vocabulary of identification—nationality—but other vocabularies—class, gender, race, and religion, but also ability, emotion, and others—are equally
deserving of historians' attentions.

The first section of this chapter examines how geographic and social
maps of cosmopolitan Alexandria reveal sharp distinctions between newcomers and long-term inhabitants. Clear but idiosyncratic native geographies map uneasily onto the grid of outsiders' expectations and priorities.
While local systems of social and spatial description were eventually overwhelmed by standard top-down categories, scholars who take dominant
schemes at face value misrecognize the city's centers and margins.

The second section of the chapter plunges into the experience of
mobility in Alexandria's streets, where walkers met crowds both faceless
and friendly, drivers elaborated codes of circulation, and tram and train
employees enforced rules of conduct. The practice of social mixing shows
distinctions improvised around contextual understandings of authority, class, and order. Who made the rules, and where were they practiced?
Nationality and the other sociolegal identifiers examined in this book
played no small role in those understandings, but they cannot tell us
everything about the stubbornly inaccessible codes of the vulgar cosmopolitan streets in which this story is set.

Mapping Cosmopolitan Alexandria: Rue de Rosette Versus Shariᶜ al-Sabᶜ Banat

Those who celebrate the memory of cosmopolitan Alexandria put its center at Rue de Rosette (later Shariᶜ Fuʾad, now Hurriya). Rue de Rosette runs
perpendicular to al-Sabᶜ Banat, in space and in significance. It is lined

with grand buildings of stone—villas, hotels, okellas, courts. The durable spectacle of such substantial buildings bolsters Rosette's status as a site of memory. In *Alexandria: City of Memory*, a book that typifies the traditional discourse on cosmopolitanism, Michael Haag asserts that Egyptians were a marginal presence on this latter street, a long, straight line of urban grandeur:

> From the Place Mohammed Ali and along the Rue Chérif Pasha at the centre of town, and eastwards along the Rue Rosette past the elegant enclave of the Quartier Grec and on out through the suburban villas of Ramleh there might be the occasional Egyptian laundry but hardly one Egyptian shop.[19]

In this nostalgic account, an unsupportable assertion ("hardly one Egyptian shop") is shaded with the mourning of change and of invasion by Arab Egyptians.

The buildings of al-Sabʿ Banat were wooden; like Rosette, it is a long, straight street, but while length is a virtue of the former, it is a fault of the latter ("interminable," Haag calls it).[20] But al-Sabʿ Banat also intersects Muhammad Ali Square; the seat of the Mixed Tribunals dominates this intersection. At its south end, the street meets the Mahmudiya Canal in the warehouse district of Minaʾ al-Bassal. In the conventional literature, the street appears under its French name (Rue des Soeurs) as a vulgar place of prostitution, violence, and poverty. Al-Sabʿ Banat was more densely populated than Rue de Rosette. It was the main street of Labban, a quarter of the city built up after the 1860s. Skirting the old port of Minaʾ al-Bassal, the new port, and Anfushi (the heart of Ottoman Alexandria), Labban was settled by newcomers without the social capital to inhabit a traditional neighborhood and by subalterns without the financial capital to move to a more affluent area.

Two caracols (a Turkish word for police station) anchored the northern and southern ends of the street (the caracol of the Square/Manshiya and the caracol of Minaʾ al-Bassal). The middle of al-Sabʿ Banat was dominated from the 1880s until the end of the twentieth century by a third, Caracol Labban. This two-story building governed the T-intersection of al-Sabʿ Banat and Bab al-Karasta Street, which led directly to the port. Even the stabbed seamen, ignorant of almost every place in the city, knew

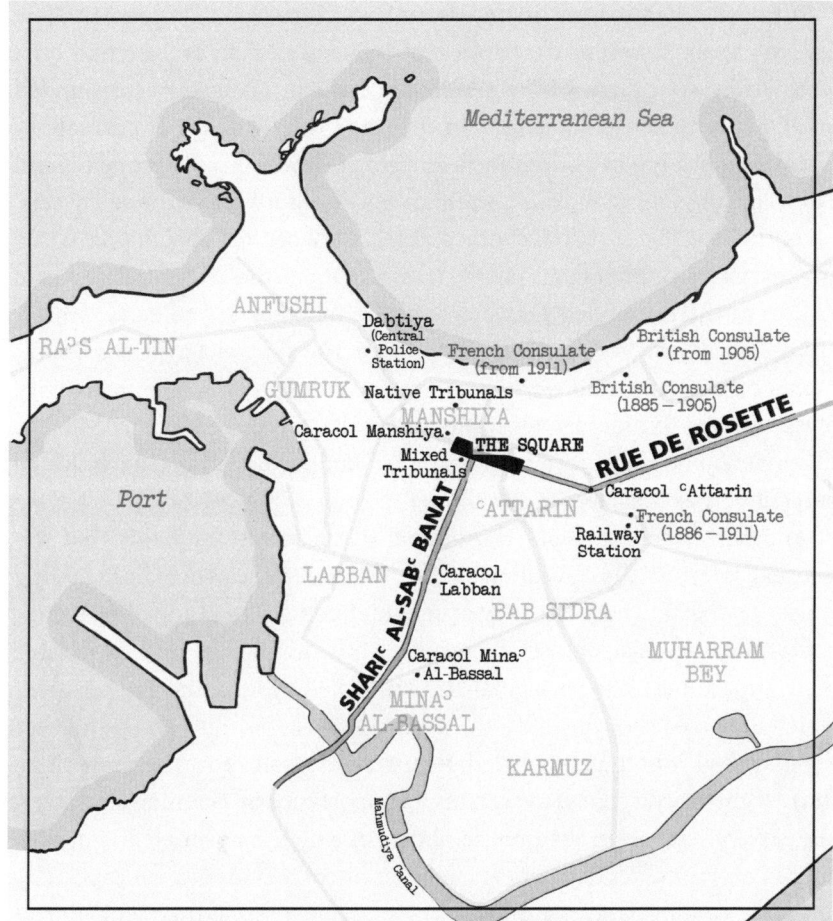

FIGURE 1.1 Alexandria's cosmopolitan axes (Mike Swallow, cartographer).

to stumble to this caracol for help. Whereas Muhammad Ali Square is the landmark of Alexandria's golden cosmopolitanism, Caracol Labban is the pole of its vulgar cosmopolitan geographies.

In both spatial and social terms, the historiography of Alexandria relies on the notion of a center bolstered by the presence of a margin. The bounded space of maps, featuring a key index, a center, margins, and exclusions, embodies the vocabulary frames used to describe diverse cities. Maps make explicit frames that often remain implicit in historical narration:

a certain kind of margin is necessary to a certain kind of center. How else to explain a recent description of Pompey's Pillar as "perched on a weedy ridge south of town," when in fact it sits in a cemetery surrounded on all sides by dense housing?[21] In the same way, acolytes of cosmopolitan Alexandria typically describe a margin of "lower-class" Europeans and Egyptians in order to make a certain category of foreigners the social center of the city. The essential characteristic of the center is belonging, while the margin is unimportant, alien, foreign: "As in the ancient Hellenistic city, so in the refounded Alexandria of the nineteenth and early twentieth centuries, the 'foreign' population were the simpler Egyptians, immigrants off the land who were drawn to the city by the economic activity of its overseas founders whose culture they hardly shared."[22] According to this inversion, Haag's foreign margin of "simpler Egyptians" includes 80 percent of Alexandria's population.

Another discourse about the liminal in social history holds that the unusual is especially revealing of the nature of the whole.[23] Assigning stories to the category of the marginal (defined as "the individual's nonconformity to legal or social norms") both diminishes and overstates their importance. The "marginal" is diminished by its name and position, which endorses the centrality of "legal and social norms" and of all that the marginal is not: male, settled, secular, and wealthy. At the same time, the marginality discourse overstates its importance by claiming a mysterious explicative power, the precise nature of which is never clearly articulated. This hermeneutic claim encourages historians to seek out especially unusual, striking, and marginal stories. Meanwhile, it fragments social history by preventing historians from examining (or even acknowledging) the ordinariness that dwells in their stories. In writing history, we sometimes describe the margins because we are unable to distinguish the center. The theoretical justification for this focus on the liminal draws heavily on Foucault, who (correctly) considers power at its point of implementation.[24] But the fascinating detail of a single capillary is less important than an encompassing view of a system extensive enough to develop capillaries; the liminal ought to be a means to this end. Historians should aim to proceed from reading at the bottom or the top or the edge to writing about societies at their thickest midpoint.

Insofar as al-Sabʿ Banat appears in the conventional historiography of Alexandria, it is also lurid and violent, the street of prostitutes and "services to sailors."[25] It is also the street of the violence of June 1882 that offered the pretext for Britain's invasion. This study depends on court records, especially those of criminal cases, which contain much that is engrossingly lurid and violent alongside much more that is ordinary and everyday. These sources are valuable because they contain all manner of noncriminal material, which describes the plain cosmopolitanism of Alexandria that is the center of this study. It is a major contention of this study that the so-called margin is misidentified; its basic character is in fact both ordinary and central. As Jennifer Robinson argues, those who isolate extraordinary "global" cities do so to their analytical peril.[26] To that end, this book makes al-Sab‵ Banat its center and focuses on its ordinary places and ordinary activities.

E. M. Forster's *Alexandria: A History and a Guide* (1922), a proof text of conventional Alexandrian cosmopolitanism, directs visitors to blind themselves to the present while moving through the city's streets, fixing their gaze on the shadowy remnants of pre-Islamic antiquity.[27] In 1922, the municipality of Alexandria sponsored the reprinting of *Alexandrea ad Aegyptum* (1914), which offers a cartographic articulation of the exclusive, elitist cosmopolitan vision. The map that accompanies the book (figure 1.2) emplots the image of the past (in red) over just enough of the present (in dull gray) to make navigation possible. The main avenue of that vision is the Rue de Rosette, which follows the path of the ancient "Canopic Way"; its antique echoes are essential to the cosmopolitan image of the city.

Caracol Labban is gone now, but many of the grand buildings of Rue de Rosette are being preserved.[28] Despite important efforts by Egyptians to protect, restore, and improve Alexandria's built heritage, narrators of the loss of cosmopolitan Alexandria continue to lament contemporary Egyptians' disinterest in a history that *should* matter to them. Haag describes his attempt to visit the room in the Majestic Hotel (on Muhammad Ali Square) where E. M. Forster stayed for several months in 1915 as follows:

The hotel, no longer majestic in name or appearance, has been converted to commercial offices, its unlit rubbish-strewn entranceway the resort of idle characters in galabiyyas. . . . It is pointless explaining your curiosity to the shrouded young secretaries wearing the hejab, that veil covering their heads, necks and shoulders, and revealing only their faces, who despite the evidence around them deny that the building could ever

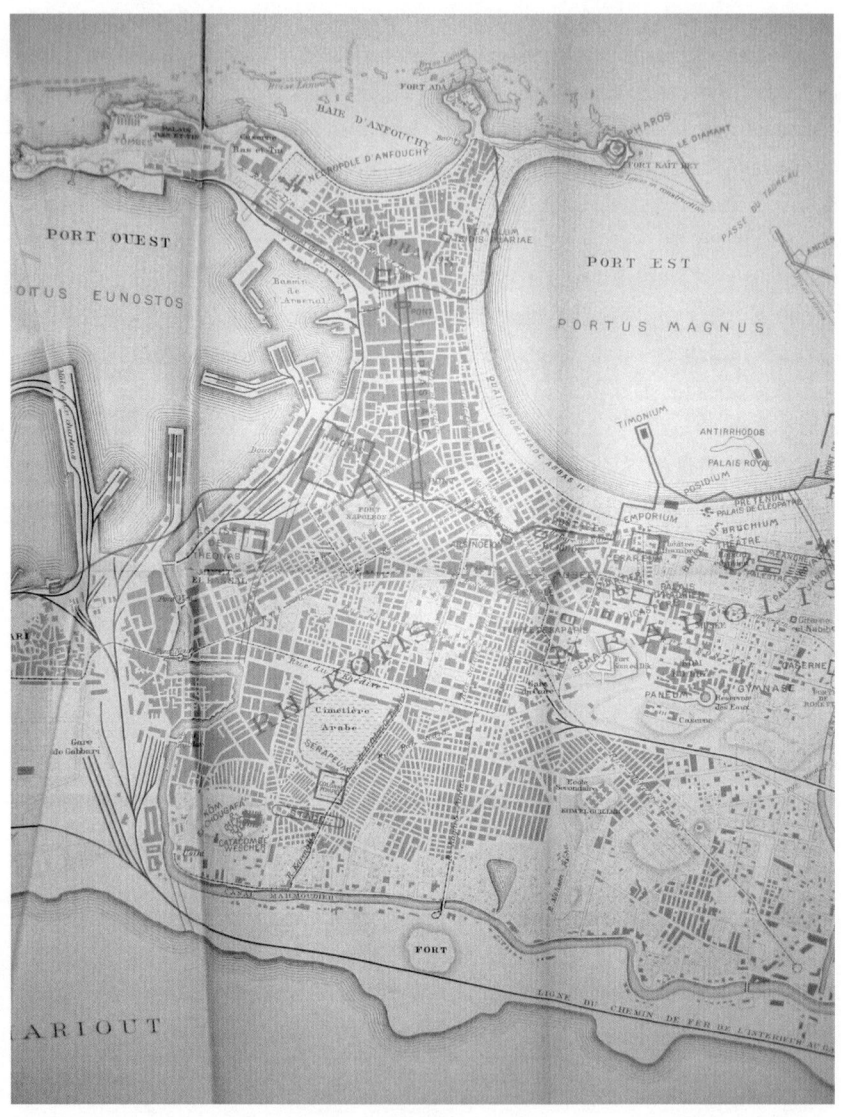

FIGURE 1.2 Ancient and modern Alexandria.

Source: Evaristo Breccia, *Alexandrea Ad Ægyptum* (1922).

have been a hotel at all. Nor can they comprehend your wish to step onto a balcony for the view. A great sea change has washed over Alexandria and its populace inhabits a history disconnected from the city's past.[29]

Even if Forster mattered to most Alexandrians, it is unfair to expect a randomly chosen local resident to share a historian's interest in or knowledge of Forster's peregrinations.[30]

Alexandria has a history that matters to its inhabitants, and it has nothing to do with E. M. Forster or Lawrence Durrell. While visiting the site of Caracol Labban, I too asked "idle characters in galabiyyas" about the area. I was immediately taken to a site of great historical significance: the building dozens of meters from the caracol where Raya and Sakina, a legendary pair of sisters from Upper Egypt, ran a brothel. Between 1919 and 1920, they were involved in their husbands' murders of seventeen women, killed for their jewelry. This story of migration, social dislocation, encounter, scandal, and sex resonates throughout Egyptian society. It has been the subject of numerous books, films, and television miniseries.[31] I frequently heard Labban referred to as "the neighborhood of Raya and Sakina," vivid testimony to Egyptians' tight connection to a history that is central to them.

If figure 1.2 is a map for visitors from another time and place, the hand-drawn map in figure 1.3 offers a translation of native spatial vocabulary for an outsider. The constable of the British consular court produced this map of the neighborhood surrounding al-Sabᶜ Banat in order to situate significant events in an 1897 assault trial. Alfredo Vassallo, a Maltese painter, and his friend Franceso Zammit (nicknamed Macchina) had spent a Saturday evening with other friends, strolling from café to wine shop along the route traced on the map. At the end of the evening, they returned to their own street. They had hoped to fight a certain rival that evening, the husband of one of their mistresses, but were unable to find him. Instead, the friends fought each other, and Francesco stabbed Alfredo seven times. Alfredo spent eight weeks in hospital. Francesco was sentenced to one year of penal servitude in Malta.[32]

This case file abounds with marks of intimate connection between these Maltese men and the places on the map. Unlike the British seamen, who were strangers on al-Sabᶜ Banat, Alfredo and Francesco knew people everywhere they went. The map records, at a close scale, the key sites of the evening. The men spent an hour drinking at the shop of the victim's

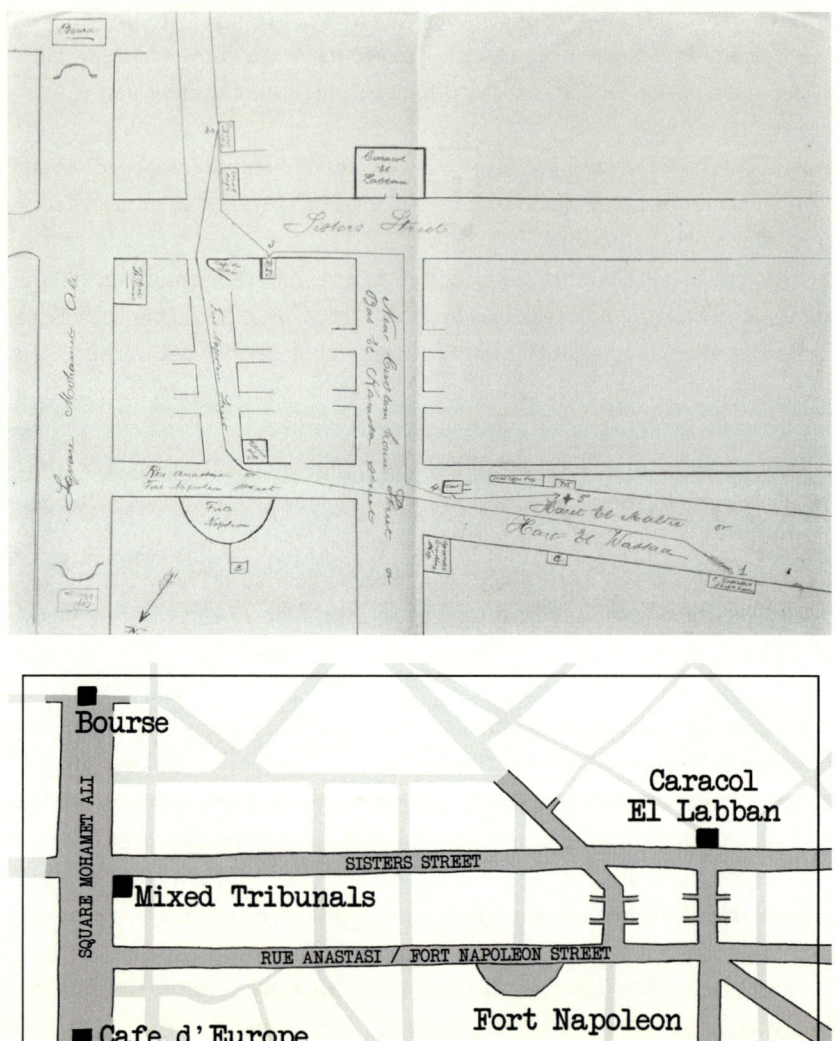

FIGURE 1.3 Hand-drawn 1897 map of al-Sabᶜ Banat with transposition.

Source: FO 847/27/2, with permission of the National Archives of the UK; Mike Swallow, cartographer.

brother (labeled 1 on the map) below the victim's home. They then headed east, drank coffee at a tobacco shop on their way to another Maltese drinking shop (Antonio Bajada's, 2), then another (Peppo Fayar's, 3) on al-Sabᶜ Banat. One of the group stopped to talk to an Arab vegetable seller, "his friend," who parked his cart at a corner (4). Other men drank at a Greek drinking shop opposite the cart (Apostoli Paolo's, A); an Arab coffee house behind it (where some of the men were habitués) is also indicated. Francesco and Alfredo then returned to the diagonal street at the bottom right of the map (5), where they both lived. Neighbors in the two- and three-story buildings along the blocks where the stabbing took place recognized their voices.

The judge who came from Istanbul to try Francesco Zammit knew nothing of the streets where the men walked. For his orientation (and only his), the map also presented key sites in an elite outsider's mental geography of Alexandria: Muhammad Ali Square, the Bourse, the Mixed Court, Fort Napoleon, and Caracol Labban. In this way, the map translated witnesses' experience of local place into the foreign context of the court. The insider and outsider geographies are represented at different scales. The lower figure is a transposition of the constable's lines onto a proportional plan of Alexandria's streets. It shows that the constable gave the tiny alleys of the neighborhood of Labban (which surrounds al-Sabᶜ Banat) as much space as Muhammad Ali Square itself. Indeed, it is not clear which is the city's center and which is its margin.

Labban's new straight streets were the product of limited but powerful central planning.[33] These streets appear in a series of twenty-nine Goad fire-insurance maps, covering the economic center of the city in 1898–1905 (including both Rosette and al-Sabᶜ Banat) in building-by-building detail.[34] The systematized depiction of the plan did not transfer to residents' descriptions of place, however. Apostoli Paolo, the Greek drinking-shop keeper, testified in court that his shop (A) was located on Jamiᶜ al-Nazir street. When this street's name rang no bells (and failed to correspond to the map), he claimed at first that it had no other name, then allowed that he did not know what other name it may have, being a newcomer: "I am only there since six months." He then appealed to authority rather than local knowledge: "The municipality has put a plate with the name Haret Jami El Nazir in the street." An Arabic-speaking policeman sought to clarify the issue:

> Some call the street Sharia el Kerasta & some call it Sharia Anastasi but its real name is Sharia Nazir as it leads to the mosque of that name. It is a little way from the Caracol Lebbane. . . . Nearly half the street is inhabited by Maltese. The Haret El Maltia is near the old caracol Lebbane. It is another street.

The hand-drawn map, an outsider's touchstone like the municipal street sign, seemed to disagree. On the map the street in question was doubly labeled: Haret El Maltie (Maltese Lane) and Hart El Wassaa (*harat al-wasiʿa*, Broad Lane). The rationalizing document bears other marks of contingency and indeterminacy: Bab El-Karasta Street is also New Custom House Street, and Rue Anastasi is also Fort Napoleon Street.

This book is about standardization of identification, about how insiders and outsiders learned to describe places and persons according to a common vocabulary. The hand-drawn map and the court's discussion of it embody the flexible and subjective forms of recognition that were reclassified during this period. There is a distinct lack of consensus regarding toponymy (to say nothing of centers and margins) in the dozens of maps of Alexandria that were produced between 1880 and 1914.[35] The identities of straight streets shift. On these maps and elsewhere, Maltese Lane is given yet other names, including Haret al-Warsha (Warehouse Lane). As the policeman suggested, some of this indeterminacy is simply error. Several witnesses did confuse one street with another, and translation caused further misunderstanding. (An Arabic-speaking watchman's reference to al-Sabʿ Banat (Seven Girls or Sisters), for instance, was transcribed as "Seven Cisterns.") But why would both the north-south and east-west streets opposite Fort Napoleon be labeled Fort Napoleon Street? Perhaps the mapmaker simply conveyed relational descriptions used by Labban's inhabitants: Fort Napoleon Street was the street (or streets) leading to Fort Napoleon; the Maltese lived on Maltese Lane. In the same sense, the rambling scale of the hand-drawn map is of little consequence when its linear itinerary and place markers are clear. The geography that mattered to residents of Labban was relational. The seamen were stabbed in the bar *across from* the German Bar. Witnesses did a great deal of walking up and down, going away and coming back, with reference to fixed landmarks rather than street names. The clearest picture that emerges from court records identifying places and people is one of relationality.

The 1886 seamen's case that opened this chapter showed the interaction of different systems of identification: the accurate ambiguity of natives, the legible errors of the outsiders, and the authoritative categories of the occupiers' justice system. In this 1897 map, we see a similar range of registers. It is a practical document reflecting the intimate relationships of the witnesses. It represents "objective" knowledge by reference to outsiders' landmarks. It came into being at the behest and hand of a justice system that demanded legible space for a legible society, just as it straightened streets and named nationalities.

In modern, cosmopolitan visions, the street is the archetypal site of the politics of difference that makes up robust citizenship.[36] As the evidence of Alexandria shows, streets were also sites of miscomprehension and misrecognition, where the classification schemes of foreign elites and local subalterns coexisted but did not meet. It was the standardized vision of the modern state, both in space and society, that organized diversity according to a common vocabulary. If that vocabulary, of which nationality was one part, eventually offered insiders and outsiders a common idiom, as the next section will show that idiom did nothing to eliminate difference or inequality.

Popular and Official Rules of the Road

The evening described above, which ended with one friend stabbing another in Maltese Lane, began with the words, "Today is Saturday, let us go and have a walk."[37] Pedestrians were undoubtedly the most important segment of traffic: turn-of-the-century Alexandrians could walk from one edge of the (center) city to the other in an hour; walking was accessible, affordable, efficient, and democratic. Vulgar cosmopolitan streets were the site of social hierarchies with little to do with ethnicity, religion, or nationality; for example, a boundary of social practice existed between those who always walked and those who sometimes traveled in other ways. Furthermore, three kinds of people—natives, newcomers, and officials—described streets differently, and they moved through them differently. In fact, the distinctions between walkers and nonwalkers, between officials and nonofficials, and between locals and newcomers show the challenge of discernment in this vulgar cosmopolitan setting.

Al-Sabᶜ Banat was filled not just with walkers but with other forms of privately owned or hired personal transport: carriages, above all, but also horses, bicycles, and, from the start of the twentieth century, automobiles. Commercial and industrial transportation was also a significant presence on the streets: loaded donkeys, freight carts, and so on. Transport was noisy: consular court records describe people chasing carts and policemen running with whistles to clear the way for ambulance carriages.[38] Carts were a source of wildness, of unintended collateral violence. Court records are filled with accounts of death and injury caused by carts and horses. The lowliness of the cart and carriage drivers' professional position gave poor local subjects a virtual monopoly on the work—and also on the violent force that cart accidents deployed. Cart drivers were licensed, taxed, and issued with numbers (duly recorded in police reports), but this was the extent of government regulation of the industry. Victims rich and poor, foreign and local, proved no match for the force and weight of the carts. Legally, too, victims had little redress. The death and injuries caused by carts were almost never deliberate, but carelessness or recklessness (a socially produced notion) was often a contributing factor.

As Alexandria's streets became more crowded, the rules of the road emerged as a field of concern. When a Tunisian carter named Ahmad ᶜAbd al-Hamid Halluwag drove his heavily loaded cart over the legs of a seven-year-old girl named Shafika (who died two days later), the claim of her father for two thousand francs in damages was rejected by the French consular court. The court agreed with the defense lawyers that Ahmad had shown no "clumsiness, imprudence, inattention, negligence, or failure to observe regulations" (criteria set out by articles 319 and 320 of the Code Pénal, the law for accidental homicide). But the case seemed to balance on a more commonsense explanation of the rules of the road. It was repeated several times that Ahmad had kept a straight line and watched his horses' heads. The girl fell under the rear wheels of the cart, but he could not have noticed this and watched in front of him at the same time. The expert operator knew his business.[39]

Traffic conflicts intensified after 1903, when the first automobile appears in consular court records.[40] Automobiles were at once more dangerous and more elite than the horses and horse carriages of the nineteenth century. Automobiles, like horse carriages, were driven by experts ("mechanics") rather than the owners themselves.[41] In May 1904, Alphonse

Gagnon, a French-born "*mécanicien-ajusteur*" was driving Prince ʿAziz along cosmopolitan Alexandria's grand avenue, Rue de Rosette. Prince ʿAziz did not own this car but had hired it (and, presumably, its driver) from another man, a Mr. Gylmenopoulo. Caught behind two horse carts, Gagnon did not see Salih ʿAwad Muhammad until he hit him. The invisibility of this local subject fits the received image of cosmopolitan Rue de Rosette, but the presence of slow-moving, animal-drawn transport does not. Gagnon stopped quickly, while Salih was still under the car. The victim did not answer his summons to Gagnon's dangerous-driving trial at the French consular court, nor did any of the witnesses, so the case was dropped.[42] It is unlikely that Gagnon would have been convicted in any event: the court record showed considerable deference to his expertise.

Conflict between diverse users of roads is a universal feature of city streets; in this sense Alexandria is unremarkable. The city's streets were politicized in the violence of 1882, certainly, and again during the protests of 1919. But self-conscious political struggle in the streets, of the sort Elizabeth Thompson describes in 1930s Damascus, where walking itself (particularly by women) could be a public statement, belonged to another time and place.[43] The ordinariness of street conflicts gets to the heart of this revision of Alexandria's cosmopolitanism. Most encounters between local and foreign took place in public places; above all, this meant streets. Passing, ignoring, jostling, speaking, fighting, coexisting: these were the modalities of interaction. Encounter was conditioned (in theory and in legal reaction to conflict) by expertise and rules of conduct. Drivers and walkers were expected to conduct themselves in certain ways, and division was made between those who followed rules and those who did not. The same was true of trams and trains, to which we now turn.

Trams ran down the center of al-Sabʿ Banat (but, significantly, not on Rue de Rosette). Egypt had one of the earliest and best-developed systems of train and tram transportation outside of Europe and North America.[44] Alexandria's first trams came into service in 1860, and the system developed rapidly. Steam and electric power replaced horse-drawn trams during the early decades of the British occupation. Trams were inexpensive, convenient, and widely used. Open to all (who held tickets) yet enclosed, these public spaces were a fertile setting for encounter and conflict, where the problem of social mixing of classes, genders, and foreigners and locals was thrown into sharp relief. Unlike the streets, public conveyances were constantly regulated spaces: passengers were subject to the authority of conductors and other agents.

The sanctity of rules and notions of propriety were paramount in court reflection on disorder on trams and trains. In the spring of 1912, a French wine merchant beat Ramadan Ahmad, a tram employee who had asked to see his pass. This caning was severe: Ahmad could not work for ten days. The accused claimed that he had shown his card, but every witness (including the witnesses for the defense) contradicted him. Even if the wine merchant had received blows in his turn, the court ruled, this was his own fault: he was the aggressor because he had broken the rules by not displaying his card. He was sentenced to six days in prison and fined six Egyptian pounds.[45] He had broken the rule of access (by not showing a ticket) and also rules of conduct. The penalty was severe, and the outcome shows that although many foreigners were accustomed to privilege vis-à-vis locals, the justice system did not always uphold their social advantage.

In a society in which foreigners were free from most forms of local jurisdiction, workers on trams and trains were among the very few native subjects who could claim authority over foreigners. This authority was simple: the right to see tickets, to seat passengers, and to regulate outrageous conduct. Just as the violent power of carts was controlled by poor locals, however, tramway class distinctions were policed by conductors and ticket takers of inferior social status to the passengers themselves. This irony was a source of tension. Foreign subjects who contravened class and gender divisions on the tram asserted social distinctions when disciplined by the conductors, and order was reestablished only by reference to those of superior hierarchical status.

Tram workers' authority had its limits and peculiarities, however. In 1913, a Swiss citizen was acquitted of assault in a conflict with two local conductors. His complaint that too many people wanted to sit on his bench in the second-class carriage drew insults from the conductors, and a fight ensued. The court ruled that while its protégé should have shown more calm, the conductors must show particular care in the execution of their public service, as their job is to "avoid conflict."[46] This definition of their role is striking. The maintenance or enforcement of social order was not a positive task to be pursued; instead, disorder was to be avoided. It is difficult to imagine how employees could adopt this approach in practice.

A reactive vision of social management was, however, essential to the logic of the consulates.

This notion of order meant that most cases were decided not on the basis of tramway rules concerning tickets, seating, and so on but by measures of social offense. Passengers of high social rank were allowed special latitude in their treatment of local employees. In October 1903, a notable French protégé was rebuked by a railroad agent at the Tanta station for crossing tracks to catch a train to Alexandria. As the incident escalated, the stationmaster and the Tanta consular guard became involved; finally, the governor (*mudir*) of Gharbiya province complained to the French consul in Alexandria. In the end, however, the protégé was acquitted of assault; the court ruled that the stationmaster should have accorded him more respect because of his reputation.[47] In similar circumstances, individuals of lower status were typically found guilty: a French citizen of unsavory reputation who could not produce a ticket and insulted a stationmaster, for example, was jailed for two weeks.[48] A Tunisian French subject who engaged in a similar dispute in 1909 was found to have brought trouble on himself by resisting the ticket taker and stationmaster and was fined sixteen francs.[49]

Although there was no hard and fast line of local guilt and foreign innocence in tram and train conflicts, certain foreigners seemed to enjoy greater leeway. In June 1900, a French citizen and tramway inspector named Ferdinand Lacoste head-butted a local subject (an off-duty soldier of the Egyptian army) who objected when Lacoste refused him a military discount. In July, Lacoste hit a man who intervened in an argument he was having with a third party on the train. In August, he struck a man who tried to stop him from beating another railway employee. In September, he kicked a municipal guard. In October, he was tried by the French consular court on these four charges of assault. Each incident had taken place while Lacoste was on duty, and in every case his violence was directed toward a local subject.

It is clear that Lacoste was a hothead and a bully, and the court in its judgment noted his "regrettable attitude." But he was acquitted on all four charges, on various pretexts: lack of evidence, self-defense, or accidental injury. While these verdicts show a pattern of permissive treatment of this foreigner, the judgment itself is explicit about authority structures on the tramway itself. While it is regrettable that Lacoste lacks calm ("*un défaut de sang-froid*"), the judge and his two assessors wrote, his attitude can be explained in part by the difficult relations between the native public and the (foreign) tramway personnel.[50] Here the typical social inversion of the tramway (locals policing foreigners) assumed more familiar dimensions. The colonial relationship was reproduced on the micro level in this version of foreign-built, foreign-operated technology offered to local users. But the associated picture of orderly foreigners and difficult natives was not so easily framed. Despite the court's excuses for Lacoste, he failed to play his assigned, civilized role.[51]

There were many measures of standing in Alexandria, and an individual could change position rapidly. The court records contain many episodes of "passing," of mistaken identities. Nationality could be a hidden attribute only revealed under the light of prosecution. Official standing could also be concealed and revealed. Lacoste's assaults were permitted initially because of his office and eventually because of his nationality. Other tram employees warranted respect so long as they were on duty. When they were not working, however, they lost their standing. In February 1907, Selim Effendi Abadir was thrown out of a compartment of the Alexandria–Cairo train by a French civil engineer named Paul Talbot. The dispute arose when Selim tried to take a place that Talbot was saving for his wife. In the aftermath of the conflict, when authorities became involved, Selim made it known that he was a railroad inspector. Because Selim did not make his official position known to Talbot, however, Talbot rebuked his request—justifiably, in the court's opinion.[52] Locals needed to announce and display any authority they possessed in order to impose it on foreigners; without it, their standing as mere humans was insufficient protection.[53] In cases of conflict, individuals invoked their role as representatives of institutions, such as the Railroad Administration, the Egyptian state, or foreign consulates. Rules for the maintenance of calm and order across these lines faltered, however, as the hierarchy of positions was neither established nor stable.

These dramas of social and official power were performed in public. In November 1884, a large crowd, including many of the city's notables, was awaiting the departure of an express train from Alexandria's station. This crowd witnessed a French subject's assault on the stationmaster. The foreign passenger, displeased with the compartment he was assigned, called the stationmaster a "pig looking for money," then pushed and kneed him. More seriously, he called the Railroad Administration the "*administration de merde*" and its stationmaster a "servant" (*domestique*). These latter insults, as well as their publicness, drew the condemnation of the French court, which fined its subject. Agents who are constantly dealing with members of the public cannot be allowed to be insulted and brutalized by travelers, the court ruled, placing special emphasis on the "authority and dignity" of the agents.[54]

Officials depended on this authority in the public setting of the streets, where mixing aggregated individuals into groups. While the solitary, contemplative walker rarely figures in Alexandria's court records, the crowd was far more prominent. Juan Cole's important study of the roots of the 1882 ʿUrabi revolt presents the image of crowds of Euro-Egyptian conflict in politically charged, identity-coded streets.[55] Cole broke new ground by demonstrating that not all crowds were Egyptian and by bringing poor and working-class Europeans into the picture of late nineteenth-century Egyptian social history. His description of national crowd violence makes teleological sense in an account of the roots of the 1882 battles between the British and Egyptian armies.[56] Certain crowds described in consular court records also conform to Cole's interpretation: they divide along European/Egyptian lines and threaten violence. Ibrahim Salama, a soldier at the Caracol Labban, released a Maltese suspect from custody in 1880 so as "not to gather many Europeans before the Caracol as this case was after midnight."[57] A French purse snatcher born in Bône, Algeria, who ran off when his victim screamed, used fear of an Arab crowd to explain his flight: "if he started running when [the victim] Madame Vais began to shout, it was out of [his] fear of the Arabs who (it was said) gathered at the sound of the commotion."[58]

The image of potentially violent, nationally coded crowds is far from universal. The court gave the purse snatcher's claim only slight credence, for example. Judges knew, and most consular court evidence shows, that in fact most crowds were rarely dangerous or violent. People were thrown together by the busyness of the streets, and the crowds they formed typically showed little coherent character beyond everyday proximity. Crowds such as the one that pursued the purse snatcher were animated by curiosity more often than animosity. Following a 1905 shooting on the street (for which an Italian police officer was accused), curious crowds swarmed the police station where he was held: "there was a great crowd and much pushing and confusion." Members of this crowd pushed their way into the station in an effort to satisfy their curiosity, and others identified the shooter when he was (illegally) released from the station.[59] Police witnesses treated this crowd as a nuisance rather than a threat. Elsewhere, there are reports of screams from within private houses that rapidly gathered crowds on the sidewalks outside, crowds that sought to render assistance.[60] In these urban crowds, the social divide in everyday practice between the curious and the cautious was at least as important as the divide between Europeans and Egyptians.

Furthermore, these mixed, curious crowds tended to assist investigation rather than create victims. In an 1883 murder, unidentified voices from a crowd gathered in the street shouted out that the killer was "Giovanni, the butcher with the curly hair." This accusation was accurate, phrased in terms legible to an audience of insiders, and sufficient to warrant an arrest.[61] The crowd was no faceless, anonymous mass. Some years later, a secret policeman testified that while chasing a shooter, he was held up by a thick crowd that was also chasing the same man and thus was unable to reach him. Again, however, the crowd did nothing to preserve the anonymity of the suspect; the secret policeman simply arrested him later at his home.[62]

Despite his attention to the class diversity of Egypt's population, Cole reproduces his elite witnesses' categorical distinction between European and Egyptian. He invokes "larger networks and loyalties" of "unthinking allegiance" that joined, for example, Maltese and Italians with Greeks, or Egyptians with Nubians.[63] Were foreigners (Europeans) and locals (Egyptians) really divided so categorically and naturally? What was the basis of this division? Language? Maltese spoke Arabic, not Greek. Religion? Many Egyptians were Christian and Jewish, and many Maltese, Italians, and Greeks were Jews. Ottoman subjects from the Levant, many also Christian and Jewish, have no place in Cole's crowds. Nationality? Europeans shared no nation, and there was a sharp social distinction between Egyptians and "Nubians."[64]

It is a reflexive practice in urban histories of the nineteenth century to classify groups of people by national or sectarian categories. This manner of classification is convenient, but it constrains social history. It certainly fails to differentiate between the foreigners and locals who appear in consular court records. Coding people by practice rather than birth category is one way out of this cul-de-sac. Everyday social practices are particularly useful markers of social boundaries in port cities. Consider the consumption of alcohol, for example, which is forbidden in Islam. Sectarian affiliation is an inflexible measure of identity for those Muslims in Alexandria who frequented wine shops because it entails questions of essence rather than practice. Classifying these people by sect entails defining them as "bad" Muslims before considering anything about the way that they lived. In the same way, to define a fight between an Egyptian-born tram conductor and a Maltese-born passenger as a Euro-Egyptian conflict invokes international politics rather than the everyday practices of petty pride, economy, and physical comfort that often lay at the heart of such disputes. Curiosity, speech, dishonesty, obedience, familiarity, residency, foreignness, and citizenship practice: these are *candidates* to join nationality, religion, class, and other traditional measures of social boundaries.

"I know the Rue des Soeurs well—at 8:30 pm the street is much frequented," a British soldier testified concerning the evening of a shooting. "There were people of all nationalities round about."[65] The soldier invokes nationality here not as a category of social description but as a signal of mixity in general. Streets were often sites of violence: the human violence of fights, thefts, and insults but also the impersonal violence of transportation accidents. Histories of late nineteenth-century global port cities often purvey a narrow, bourgeois concept of encounter, packaged as cosmopolitanism. Encounters that took place in streets like al-Sabʿ Banat, beyond the tourist hotels and elite salons, provide an antidote to this convention. This vulgar cosmopolitanism, lubricated by liquor and misunderstanding, was neither sublime nor rare, and it reveals the mainstream content of global history. Posed in a global context, Samuel Moyn's provocative question— "What if cosmopolitanism was easy to achieve historically?"—helps dissolve notions of ultimate diversity past and present.[66] Although al-Sabʿ Banat was the scene of the notorious rioting crowd of 1882, most life on the street was utterly pedestrian: people going somewhere, gathering out of curiosity, some familiar to those they met, others indistinct and uncategorized. Asserting the easiness—the ordinariness—of cosmopolitanism is a critical foundation for the exploration of everyday practices of social life in the mixed cities of the turn of the twentieth century.

Humble streets should be put at the center of global urban history, and rosy scenes of elite urban social mixing and segmented communitarianism

placed on the margins. Witnesses who speak in a vocabulary already familiar to us are often poor witnesses, ones lacking the local knowledge and
descriptive vocabulary to see into the crowd in the center of the city. To
make this crowd legible, we must attend to ordinary witnesses' categories
and vocabularies of identification, which are often unfamiliar to us. This
chapter has traced vocabularies of identification moving through Alexandria's streets. The chapters that follow trace the descriptive schema
that formed around nationality in official settings. Many other vocabularies operated in parallel to nationality; some are better studied (class
and religion), while others remain little understood (ability and emotion).
No single vocabulary is a key index of identification. If the systems of the
state or the occupying power imposed their standards in some contexts,
reordering existing categories through their regimes of protection, they
did not hold a monopoly on meaning. As the next chapter shows, even the
most universal vocabulary—the vocabulary of private international law
triumphant—was shifting and multivocal.

2

Keywords

In order to map this book's conceptual territory, this chapter glosses key terms used to describe the affiliation of persons to states in the modern world. Its five sections establish a baseline of definitions clustered around nationality, citizenship, residence, foreignness, and subjecthood. These glosses, while necessarily schematic and incomplete, provide a sense of the range of meanings that each term encompasses. Special attention is paid to the turn of the twentieth century, the specific conditions of Egypt, and the languages of Alexandria. This chapter is concerned with these words as technical terms of "mandarin law," particularly as they appear in private international law treatises.[1] The rest of the book describes their use in practice.

The most salient reason to insist on more precise use of "citizenship" and "nationality" is the need for world-historical comparison. The challenge of comparison is well illustrated by the case of nationality in Russian history. Nationality had a peculiar sense in Russian imperial and Soviet use: it was a domestic category referring to ethnolinguistic and sectarian status, its effects more cultural than political.[2] Nationality was considered an immutable attribute.[3] As a result of this particular path, scholars who study naturalization and alienage in the Russian context quite naturally eschew the concept of nationality. In a comparative context, however, this language choice makes less sense. A scholar who recently framed a book on "citizenship" defined as "a status denoting membership in a country, usually documented with a passport" was compelled explicitly to exclude rights-based concepts of citizenship from his analysis.[4] His context-specific use of nationality and reactive definition of citizenship appears eccentric in the broader frame of his avowedly comparative study. Comparison and translation lie at the heart of the challenge of global histories of legal concepts.

Translation is a particularly useful indicator in the context of turn-of-the-century Alexandria. Translation freezes a snapshot of the sense of concepts produced in a particular legal and linguistic system at a particular moment. In the present day, for example, we equate nationality with citizenship because international conflict of laws concerning real persons who are subjects of strong states has largely faded from view. The differing equations and translations of the past reveal the character of legal practice in those earlier periods. The late nineteenth century was a period of rapid vocabulary development in Arabic.[5] While much of this development took place in literature and the popular press, the legal field was also a key site of vocabulary innovation. The terms glossed in this chapter show conceptual uncertainty as regimes of membership changed at the turn of the century.

In the decades before the First World War, international law was a very different field from its mid–twentieth century counterpart. Critically, it was not yet monopolized by questions of public international law and the state actors with which it is concerned. The topic that became known as "conflict of laws" was a driving question in the field as a whole, and leading jurists devoted sustained attention to the effects of international law on real persons. Leading jurists such as Joseph Story (1779–1845), Henry Wheaton (1785–1848), Friedrich Carl von Savigny (1779–1861), John Westlake (1828–1913), A. V. Dicey (1835–1922), and Carl Ludwig von Bar (1836–1913) gave prominent place to choice of law, conflict of laws, and other questions of private international law.[6] In the middle of the nineteenth century, a prominent scholar such as Pasquale Mancini (1817–1888) could make the argument (unimaginable today) that the fundamental subject of international law *in general* was the nationality of individuals rather than the relations of states.[7] Even a general treatise such as the first volume of Lassa Oppenheim's *International Law* (1905), which firmly situates individuals as objects rather than subjects of international law, devotes many pages to these questions.[8] The contents of these classic references in international law surprise those expecting public questions to dominate the field. Private questions—nationality, marriage, inheritance, real property—were given priority.

The conceptual flux of the late nineteenth century finds a counterpart in the twenty-first. As I argued in the introduction, nationality is often used imprecisely in historical scholarship. Meanwhile, as citizenship has become a malleable vessel for all manner of reflection on political activity and identity, present-day theory about citizenship is not a reliable guide to counterpart phenomena in the past. Citizenship studies takes as its object the practices of political subjectivities. Historians speaking to this question have often been eager to read its preoccupations and definitions back onto their historical sources. This tendency has been exaggerated by the nature of many non-Western sources' references to citizenship, which occur in relative isolation from their broader context. Historians seeking to engage the vital debate in citizenship studies quite naturally seize on historical data that appear to offer the glimmer of recognition or correspondence. Unfortunately, making connections between the "citizens" of the past and the present can erase historical particularity. Citizenship, nationality, and other kinds of status were diverse legal technologies that migrated from one setting to another and adapted to local conditions in diverse ways. As Frederick Cooper has shown for the concepts of identity, globalization, and modernity, overlapping contemporary analytic concepts and historical indigenous categories "need to be understood in the often conflicting ways in which they are deployed."[9] Nationality is unquestionably an indigenous category, but it is used in the historical literature as thesaurus filler rather than as an analytical category. Using "nationality" as an unrigorous synonym enables weaknesses in other categories, allowing nationalism, citizenship, and ethnicity to extend into territory where these concepts do not belong. Global legal history is sufficiently complex on its own empirical terms without inputs from latter-day synthetic definitions. These definitions also conceal the contested nature of international law itself. As a result of such blurry synthesis, institutions far removed from the sites of international law's thickest practice have been able to capture its terms, much to the detriment of global visions both realist and utopian.[10]

National

"Nation" is a concept with a long and complex history, well treated in a host of studies.[11] In English, nation was used from the thirteenth century with a racial or ethnic sense, and its political sense is clear from the seventeenth century.[12] The ethnic and political branches of meaning are also relevant to the two derivatives on which this book focuses: "national" and "nationality." While the semantic relationship of these words to "nation" is obvious, they have a distinct set of meanings.

"National" was an adjective before it was a noun.[13] In English, the earliest citation of "national" in the nominal sense in the OED is 1887; the adjectival sense from which it springs ("Of or relating to a particular nation or country, as opposed to another or others") is of earlier vintage. But the designation of individual members of the nation as nationals is quite recent. In addition to its novelty, the term's scope is narrow: the concept is operative largely within the confines of international law. Legally, it is most clearly organized by means of a test: if an individual is offered protection by a state's diplomatic or consular services abroad, he or she is a national of that state.[14] In this sense (and perhaps only in this sense) were colonial subjects on par with citizens. Thus slaves were afforded consular protection by the antebellum United States, as were Filipinos and Native Americans under the Nationality Act of 1940.

"Nationality" does not seem to have derived from the status of nationals (which emerged later) but rather from the idea of the nation itself. Nationality, according to Raymond Williams, "acquired its modern political sense" in the late eighteenth and early nineteenth centuries.[15] The French nationalité appeared in 1835 in the Dictionnaire de l'Académie Française.[16] But by the turn of the century, this direct link with the nation had been superseded by nationality as the status of nationals. The leading twentieth-century scholars of international law (Oppenheim and Lauterprecht) state simply that nationality is "the link between individuals and the benefits of the Law of Nations."[17]

The simplicity of this definition did little to influence the diverse uses given to "nationality" in various contexts, of which I will give only a few examples here. As noted above, nationality is an important concept in the historiography of late imperial Russia and the Soviet Union. In that context, the term came to mean belonging to an ethnolinguistic community.[18]

In his general definition of nationality, Boll defines this "other use" thus: "Legal subclass used to group persons in the municipal law of certain states, usually according to ethnic background."[19] Referring to the English context, meanwhile, Williams insists on the "political" sense of "national" and all its derivatives, which mingles with a sense of "racial" grouping. This capacious use of "political" is unilluminating as regards the members of the nation-state. He argues that this word is "clearly political," in a moment of uncharacteristic imprecision: in fact, the national—the individual member of the nation—is among the least political derivations of "nation."[20]

Political rights were generally reserved for citizens rather than nationals.[21] French allows certain circumlocutions of national: *"Qualité de français," "qualité d'Ottoman,"* and the like suggest that an individual possesses, rather than is possessed by, her or his nationality.[22] The term *ressortisant* offers another shade of meaning. In treaties of the early twentieth century, it appears as the translation of the English "national," or, rather, the English is the translation of the French. Jurisprudence has shown its meaning to be slightly more extensive than "national," covering some non-nationals who "come from" the state in question; in the 1920s, for example, certain Egyptians were considered British *ressortisants* and certain Tunisians as French *ressortisants*, given their subjection to these empires.[23]

In the Egyptian context, *watan* came to mean "nation" by the end of the nineteenth century, and *watani* was the first iteration of "national."[24] But the resonances of the terms are diffuse. In 1892, a British judge in Egypt named Donald Cameron (who would later be consul-general in Alexandria) published an *Arabic-English Vocabulary for the Use of English Students of Modern Egyptian Arabic*. This book offers a revealing glimpse of the changing legal vocabulary around nationality during the period. Cameron defined *watani* as "native, national, *indigène.*"[25] The term had not stabilized, and neither had other Arabic terms corresponding to nation: *umma, qawm,* and *milla.*[26] The single translation he offered for "nationality" (and "allegiance") was *tabaʿiya*, from *tabiʿ* ("follower, servant, dependent, subject, annexe.")[27] While this term (and the related *tabiʿiya*) might appear more stable and unified, it would be superseded by the current Arabic term for nationality, *jinsiya* (a term derived from *jins* ["type"]), which settled only in the twentieth century.[28]

The use of *tabaʿiya* for nationality was made official as early as 1869, when the Ottoman Nationality Law (in Turkish, *tabiiyet-i osmaniye kanunnamesi*) was promulgated.[29] In legislative terms, nationality law is a recent development, and the Ottomans were among its early adopters.[30] While many modern European states made membership regimes a part of their fundamental laws, it was only in the last years of the nineteenth century that membership began to be defined in terms of nationality. Metropolitan France had its first nationality law in 1889.[31] In Britain, explicit nationality laws came especially late. The wartime British Nationality and Status of Aliens Act (1914) was the first, and it was a stopgap.[32] Only in 1948 (after much of the Commonwealth had their own nationality laws) did Parliament pass a thorough British Nationality Act.[33] Each of these laws was primarily concerned to describe the conditions of acquisition and loss of nationality, rather than the rights associated with it, which are more typically questions of citizenship. Confusion about the function of these laws is compounded by latter-day glosses, from Brubaker to Heater to Fahrmeir, which inaccurately treat them as "citizenship laws."[34] Although the citizen is a far older figure than the national, as the next section will show, statutes referring to citizenship are even more recent than those referring to nationality.

Citizen

Conceptually, "citizen" is much more straightforward than "national": it is the fullest form of state membership. Fullness of membership can be measured in possession of rights such as civil standing, political enfranchisement, and access to social welfare.[35] "Citizen" is also a much older term than "national"; the citizenship established in France and the United States at the end of the eighteenth century drew on classical referents.[36] This heritage bolsters the claim of citizenship to be conceptually self-sufficient. The other four poles treated in this chapter (nationality, residence, foreignness, and subjecthood) are driven by inequalities and latent others (the alien, the nonresident, the native, and the sovereign, respectively). Citizenship, meanwhile, claims not to require negative definitions.[37] In practice, however, citizenship depends on a set of rights *superior* to other classes of membership. The hierarchical standing of the citizen is especially clear in the context of French empire, where the *nationalité française* enjoyed by imperial subjects in no way implied citizenship (see chapters 7 and 8).[38]

Historians of American citizenship, even while arguing for ascension to full equality, reveal the discrimination inimical to citizenship practice before and after the Fourteenth Amendment, female franchise, the civil rights movement, and so on.[39]

Citizens enjoy their top-tier rights in the domestic or municipal sphere.[40] In the international sphere, on the other hand, the citizen/national/subject distinction is typically less important.[41] Outside the home state, citizenship is subsumed by nationality: "Every citizen is a national, but not every national is necessarily a citizen of the State concerned; whether this is the case depends on municipal law; the question is not relevant for international law."[42] As early as the second half of the nineteenth century jurists lamented the confusion of nationality with citizenship.[43] Then as now, the statuses belong to different contexts, but this distinction has not been scrupulously applied in the current wave of literature on citizenship.[44] In arguing against the common and stereotypical contrast between civic, jus soli France and ethnic, jus sanguinis Germany, Patrick Weil correctly notes that "nationality law has its own trajectory and its own characteristic features, independent from the history of citizenship."[45] In so doing, however, he reproduces and reinforces the nationality/citizenship dyad. This dyad was far from universal—each status has many other tempting counterparts. In the British context, for instance, subjecthood was the highest form of membership until (and even after) citizenship emerged as an active legal category with the British Nationality Act of 1948. Crucially, however, nationality also exists *without* citizenship—not in modern France, perhaps, but certainly in many other places and times.

In the Egyptian context, the early nineteenth-century Egyptian historian Jabarti used the loanword *sitwayan* for *citoyen*, suggesting that the idea did not have an obvious Arabic counterpart.[46] Over the course of the century, Arabic political vocabulary developed and diversified, but the figure of the citizen still had no agreed-upon equivalent: in 1898, the path-breaking writer Jurji Zaydan relied on the commonplace term *raʿaya* (subjects) to refer to the American citizenry, even in a discussion of their political rights.[47] The slippage between these terms persists: in his 1974 translation of Muhammad al-Muwaylihi, Roger Allen uses "Egyptian citizen under the jurisdiction of the government" for *"rajul min raʿaya al-hukuma."*[48] More than anything, the translations of Zaydan and Allen show the preconceived categories of their target readership. Just as later twentieth-century Anglophones have an anachronistic expectation of citizenship as local membership, late nineteenth-century Arabophones considered subjecthood the norm.

The distinction between individual citizens and individual subjects was slow to emerge; it was clearer in collective description. Political voice was accorded to "the people" (*al-ahali*) in the 1876 Ottoman constituent assembly, and this term was soon succeeded by the more populist, rights-bearing concepts of *al-sha*ʿ*b* and *al-umma*.[49] Neither of these latter terms had much legal significance, however—local and native rights were almost exclusively described in terms of *al-ahali*. Only in the twentieth century did the term *muwatin* emerge to describe the individual citizen. As Gianluca Parolin observes, however, this term referred to republican and not liberal citizenship.[50] It is revealing that this term is semantically linked with *watan* ("nation"); the figure of the citizen and *muwatin* "signified relation to a place, rather than subordination to a ruler," and it generated rights on the basis of territory of residence, to which we now turn.[51]

Resident

"Residence" is a status derived from practice and animated in time and space. Specifically, it binds a person to the place where she or he habitually makes a home or conducts business. Within the broad category of resident, we can distinguish two streams. One is the resident by birth: the native or local. The second is the resident by election: the denizen or naturalized resident.

"Native," linked etymologically with birth, identifies individuals with their place of birth.[52] As status marker, it is primarily social and political rather than legal in nature, conveying a strong sense of belonging. It is a permanent status, and one can remain a native of a place even when no longer resident there. A 1906 dictionary makes a rare allusion to the legal status of a native, in which territory is less significant: "Legally, a person is a native of the place or country where the parents have their domicile, which may or may not be the place of natural birth."[53] This unusual definition hints at a distinction essential to the term: the native is "a member of the indigenous ethnic group of a country or region, as distinguished from foreigners, esp. [in the view of the *Oxford English Dictionary*] European colonists." From the sixteenth century, "native" carried the negative sense of "inferior inhabitants of a place subjected to alien political power or conquest."[54] An obsolete mid–nineteenth century usage well illustrates the term's detachment from its "birth" etymology and attachment to racial hierarchy: "in Britain and the United States during the period of colonialism and slavery: a black person of African origin or descent."[55]

In his well-known study of colonial and postcolonial Africa, Mahmood Mamdani extends this thinking, equating the "division between the citizen and the subject" with the division between "the nonnative and the native."[56] But in turn-of-the-century Egypt, outside of formal colonial control and without clear citizenship or subjecthood, the division was never so stark. "Native" residents were indeed non-European, but the term was not always perceived as pejorative. The French *indigène* was widely and generally used in Egypt.[57] The central equivalent for "native" in Arabic was *ahli*.[58] Thus the *mahakim ahliya* established in 1883 were the *tribunaux indigènes*, or Native Courts. Although this translation shifted to "National Courts" in the late 1930s, the difference between "native" and "national" was apparent earlier.[59] Already in Cameron's 1892 vocabulary, translations of *ahli* bear a slightly different—and inferior—shade of meaning from *watani*: "domestic, native, *indigène*."[60] If domestic rights were often inferior rights, the most neutral of all renderings of this concept of *ahli* was "local." Yet even though birth was not at issue in the term "local," it was reserved for non-Europeans all the same. In the Egyptian context, "local" was a fundamentally spatial Arabic word: *mahalli*, derived from *mahall* (place). This legally anodyne (and therefore politically useful) term was frequently used for individuals, and it will be treated in detail in chapter 12 of this book.

Turning from birth to residence by election, "naturalized" refers to "a foreigner or immigrant: admitted to the rights or privileges of a native citizen or subject; taken to be a native by virtue of (long) residence."[61] Whereas nationality and citizenship present as permanent and unalloyed statuses, naturalization implies change over time and a plural history. Nor does naturalization necessarily grant equal rights with all other citizens. In the nineteenth century, France distinguished between *grand naturalisation*, which conveyed political rights, and *petit naturalisation*, which did not.[62] The English legal term denizen, dating from the fifteenth century, bears a similar meaning: a foreigner with the right to residence and certain other domestic rights, but without a full set of rights.[63] "Denizen" was superseded by "naturalized" in the twentieth century but was a vital legal concept until then.[64] In this sense, all naturalized persons and denizens were once aliens or foreigners. At its heart, "naturalized" is a term of contrast: a dweller in a territory who is *not* native born.

Until local residence in Egypt or the Ottoman domains offered positive rights or advantages under the law, there was little need for a precise Arabic equivalent for "residence." *Mahalli*—"of the local place"—sufficed. In 1892, Cameron offered *muwattan* for "domiciled, naturalised"; clearly this sense did not stick.[65] The Arabic *tajnis* ("naturalization") is a twentieth-century neologism. Until that time, all residents, native born or otherwise, were more or less equal subjects (*ri'aya*). But in the eyes of European law, a resident alien owed temporary allegiance, not the permanent allegiance of a subject. Of course, residence is supposed to be permanent, but it can also be established by habit or custom. In any case, the contrast with nationality and citizenship, with their concern for origin and descent, should be clear. Residence, like citizenship, was normally a category of municipal law without international effect. Only in the twentieth century did it become possible to conceive of illegal residents (or, slightly earlier, resident aliens). During the nineteenth century, the leading concept in this field was domicile. In questions of status, whereas nationality was the predominant test in Anglo-Saxon countries, domicile was predominant in Continental countries.[66] Thus the leading Egyptian jurist 'Abd al-Hamid Abu Haif, writing in the 1920s, could describe nationality as the natural successor of domicile.[67]

Residence—an apparently banal determination—showed the world's human and spatial divisions. Residents of Christian countries (i.e., Europeans) could never become residents of non-Christian countries.[68] Nineteenth-century jurists distinguished between "civilized" (*mutamaddin*) or even "Christian" countries and the rest of the world.[69] The rhetoric of residency and the legal claims attached to it differed markedly between these two solitudes. In practice, the greatest difference between "native" residence and "naturalized" residence is colonial. "Local" and "native" were not categories applied to Europeans; they were reserved for the majority in the rest of the world. Meanwhile, "resident" was reserved for Europeans.

Foreigner

Foreignness, like citizenship, is ostensibly a straightforward determination: whereas citizenship is the highest level of membership or belonging, foreignness is nonmembership as a "domestic or native . . . a citizen . . . [or] a member of the guild."[70] It is an essentially negative definition, animated by difference, that implies and shores up the positive statuses on which it depends. But just as the positive statuses have different qualities, so too do their negations. At least three shades of foreignness can be discerned in legal treatments: the stranger, the alien, and the expatriate.

The stranger is an outsider or barbarian—someone outside of the bounds of acknowledged or reciprocal status.[71] Foreigners from uncivilized countries could not simply regularize their legal status in lands governed by the rule of law. A more measured and bounded version of foreignness, which implies the possibility of recognition of the foreigner as counterpart, is alien status. The alien is not (like the savage) someone without allegiance—instead, her or his allegiance is to a foreign state. To alienate property is to surrender ownership to another; the allegiance of subjects of sovereigns functions in the same way.[72] When foreign status is articulated in terms of acknowledged counterpart territories and systems of law, foreigners living away from their home places sometimes receive legal accommodation as expatriates. Legitimate outsiders such as diplomats were the beneficiaries of hospitality, the cardinal virtue of the cosmopolitan international order envisaged by Kant. In some cases, and certainly in Egypt under the Ottoman capitulations, these expatriates are governed by the laws of their home country; international law uses "extraterritoriality" and "extrality" to describe the projection of a state's jurisdiction over its own nationals when abroad.[73] Law obtains in this place, but it is a rule of exception. For other expatriates, foreign residence resulted in loss of native status at home (to expatriate was, "in the Law of Nations, to renounce one's citizenship or allegiance") without necessarily becoming naturalized in the new place of residence.[74]

Ajnabi is the relatively neutral Arabic rendering of "foreign." In his 1938 Cairo University dissertation on conflict of laws, Ramzi Sayf shows that the precise meaning of the term was the subject of a half-century of debate. *Ajnabi* was woven into the fabric of the Mixed Tribunals, which used the term in its founding document and confirmed it in a ruling of March 1, 1877: *ajnabi* meant anyone not local (*"non originaire du pays,"* *"laisa min asl watani"*).[75] Egypt's 1890 patent law, applicable "to anybody in Egypt, whether *watani* or *ajnabi*," shows that this distinction had become a standard part of jurisdiction description.[76] The 1907 text of Muhammad al-Muwaylihi's classic *Hadith ʿIsa bin Hisham* also juxtaposes *ajnabi* and *watani*, though in the original 1899 newspaper version he used *ahl al-bilad* for native.[77] During the nineteenth century, the capitulations came to be called *al-imtiyazat al-ajnabiya* (foreign privileges) in preference to the older *ahidname* (pledge). Another group of outsiders enjoyed another system of privileges: *imtiyazat al-ʿurban* (the bedouin privileges).[78] In the populist political rhetoric of the late nineteenth century, *gharib* (stranger) and *dakhil* (intruder) were pejorative terms for foreigners applied especially to Ottomans of Syrian origin.[79]

Subject

Just as foreignness is animated by difference, subjecthood is animated by inequality: the term "stresses the quality of the individual as being subject to the Sovereign."[80] But if the difference of the foreigner is less than straightforward, the various versions of the unequal relationship between sovereign and subject are even more complex. An old and continuous meaning, dating in English from the fourteenth century, places the subject under the dominion and protection of a personal sovereign (a lord or monarch).[81] Later, under the influence of political reconfigurations, that sovereignty was invested in a government or state or other ruling power; in the nineteenth century, notions of British imperial subjecthood emerged.[82] In a world-historical context, two particular senses are prominent: subjects of a monarch and subjects of an empire.

In recent years, the distinction between subject (a subaltern position) and citizen (a rights-bearing position) has become prominent, but it was not always so.[83] There is no better evidence that this distinction is of recent vintage than the discovery that Thomas Jefferson's original draft of the Declaration of Independence used the word "subjects" instead of "citizens."[84] As we have seen already, the same situation applied in late nineteenth-century Egypt. The term ra*aya* was the most generic term for "members," and its more specific meaning of "subjects" drew on Ottoman and Islamic tradition. Cameron defined the singular ra*iya* as "sheep; Ottoman subject; Indian *ryot*"; he gave "*ra*iya* [*sic*] *wa himaya*" as "Ottoman subjects and foreigners under (Consular) protection."[85] Indeed, ri*aya* ("subjecthood") was not exclusive to Ottomans but was used for all manner of foreign subjects. In 1890, for example, a twenty-five-year-old domestic servant named Antonio Mascidri, when deposed at the Caracol Labban, was described as *min ra*aya dawlat al-nimsa* (one of the Austrian subjects).[86] The Arabic *tabi*ᶜ (follower, dependent) was also frequently used for subjecthood. As we have seen, however, the associated noun *taba*ᶜiya* was used for nationality from 1869 as well as in the 1876 Ottoman constitution. It had a far thinner sense of subjecthood because it implied mere affiliation, rather than protection and allegiance. Mere affiliation was a form of subjecthood that also found explicit expression, for instance in a bilingual 1892 letter in which the phrase "[they] claim to be Turkish subjects" is translated as "*yadda*ᶜuna bi-intima'ihim lil-dawlat al-*ᶜuthmaniya*" (they allege their affiliation with the Ottoman state).[87] As *taba*ᶜiya* or *intima'*, subjecthood was a banal sorting of humans into slots.

Cameron's translated phrase *ra*iya wa himaya* suggests that subjecthood could also be tightly connected to the idea of protection (*himaya*), which Cameron specified meant "consular protection, hence a foreign protected subject, not an Ottoman."[88] Chapter 8 is an extended discussion of the associated term protégé (*mahmi* in the Egyptian context). Scholars sometimes incorrectly substitute diplomatic protection, which has a narrow meaning, for protection itself, which has a much more general meaning.[89] What the protected owed their protector was allegiance. Boll argues that allegiance is a part of identity.[90] Shortly after the Second World War, the lawyer Maximilian Koessler argued that the idea of allegiance should be abandoned, as nationality had lost its contractual sense: rights and duties were no longer reciprocal. Instead, the national's duties to the nation are obligatory, not contingent on the nation doing something in return.[91]

Jurists aim to refine the meanings of these concepts and categories. The evidence of practice serves to broaden and diversify them. Referring to the end of the nineteenth century, Ayalon argues that "*ra'iyya* was now a flexible term, which inevitably blurred rather than clarified its subject, especially when the subject was a modern political concept in a foreign context."[92] This is indisputably true, but the problem can also be framed in another way. What if the signified ideal was the falsehood and the flexibility of the signifier the reality? Citizenship studies suggests this to be so and also suggests that the term's flexibility can be illuminating. The aim of this book is to explore that flexibility.

PART II
Means

3
Papers

A city of migrants, nineteenth-century Alexandria was full of
strangers. In familiar societies, a person's standing and conduct were controlled by reputation in his or her immediate
circle. Strangers lacked those circles, and their status was irregular as a
consequence. As we noted in chapter 1, newcomers were a distinct type in
Alexandria's social mix, marked by their lack of fluency and local knowledge and by their social disconnection. During the later nineteenth century, the state came gradually to assume the guarantor role previously
played by the social circle and to identify its subjects in ways that were
durable, portable, individual, and impersonal. Nationality and its paper
tokens—the passport, the identification document, the letter of recommendation—were a means of managing mobility and diversity.

Even as these practices developed, the city's strangers, unknown and
dislocated, remained a problem in life and death. In March 1880, police
discovered a skeleton on a salt flat at the western edge of Alexandria. Its
flesh had been consumed by dogs. Local authorities could not identify
these remains and proceeded to bury the body according to Muslim rites.
Near the body, a passerby found papers belonging to Henry Hampson, an
English customs house worker. Hampson had disappeared a month earlier when, after a day spent in a state of derangement, he walked off from
his rooming house into open land, carrying photographs of family and

business papers. The British consul, Charles Cookson, had been searching for Hampson. When he made the connection between the papers and the body, he demanded its immediate retrieval, then set out to "*reidentify* someone as the same person he once was known to be."[1] Government regulations prohibited exhumation of the body, so Cookson sent the British consular physician, who was obliged to perform a postmortem in the grave itself. He could not conclude definitively that the body was that of Hampson. Despite this inconclusive finding, Cookson claimed the body, rescued it from its Muslim burial shroud, and transferred it to British custody.[2]

The consul's urge to identify Hampson's remains was symptomatic of the logic of nationality. Because the civil rights that foreign subjects enjoyed in the Ottoman Empire—exemption from local tax, search, conscription, and prosecution—were exceptional and tenuous, their protectors made especially aggressive assertions of clear legal identity. Foreigners' status gave them systematic advantages over anonymous locals who could not access counterpart civil rights. Anonymity may have been acceptable for locals both dead and alive, but by 1880 every British subject had the right to a name.[3] An objective identifier of this sort, which evoked a comprehensive index of protection, was necessary to maintaining legal status outside of a home community, and any foreigner who could not be clearly identified diminished the status of the rest of the community. The same was not true for local residents of Egypt. Although an internal passport regime developed earlier in the nineteenth century to capture peasants fleeing conscription and corvée labor, until the closing years of the century everyday identification and monitoring of most locals was a personal rather than a paper process, delegated to neighborhood *shaykhs*.[4] Outside of a local subject's own neighborhood (where his reputation was known), locals announced identity with a personal guarantee (*daman*) from a notable individual, by which the guarantor agreed to be held responsible for the conduct of the guaranteed individual.[5] Those who could not find a guarantor lived in official anonymity, which meant that they, like Hampson, could be buried in an unnamed grave.[6]

The papers and photographs that enabled Hampson's circumstantial identification acted as external labels that transformed the meaning of the object they described (his body). In this function, they resembled the identification documents that were becoming the universal currency of nationality status in Alexandria. At the time of Hampson's death, passports were used only by a small and elite minority of people embarking and disembarking at Alexandria's port, giving them access to the city's institutions as they passed through. Certificates of consular registration, which allowed residents of the city to exercise the advantages of foreignness, were in more common use. Registration enabled consulates to count, list, and monitor subjects who had settled in Alexandria. But the definite status expressed by identification documents—foreign and not local, known and not anonymous, clear and not blurred—papered over the contested nature of nationality. In practice, it was those whose status claims were tenuous who employed documentary means most assiduously. Before the twentieth century, the wealthy, those with established reputations in local communities, and those living beyond the reach of the state had little need for papers. Local subjects, too, had no systematic need for identification papers. Like nationality itself, documents were most necessary for those whose standing was uncertain.

In the decades that followed the British invasion, however, documentation of status became increasingly widespread as more and more individuals had occasion to certify their identity in bureaucratic form. Local status gradually became a counterpart to foreign nationality, rather than its absence. The imperatives of rationalized administration combined with the rhetoric of benevolent, noncolonial protection, leaving a space for positive identification of individual subalterns, both local and foreign. Identification of these individuals, a task previously delegated to neighborhood *shaykhs* and community notables, became increasingly centralized in government hands. As was the case with the corvée and conscription passports of Mehmet Ali, the administrators were interested in collective demographic resources rather than individual identity. But by the last quarter of the century, demographic science held that the registration of births and deaths and the generation of population and public health statistics required centralized accounting of every inhabitant of the territory.[7] Consistent with this biological accounting, censuses and nationality laws became the key tools in an initiative to make identification a universal possibility for Egypt's inhabitants. Forensic methods based in biology and bureaucratic methods based in law both promoted identification. Although this endeavor would never be complete, by 1914 localness was no longer merely the default category for anonymous skeletons with no positive identity. Anonymous bodies, living and dead, became identified as Egyptian nationals or foreign subjects, and legal consensus emerged around the boundaries of those communities.

The chapter is made up of three sections. The first draws on a set of more than four dozen distinct documents to present a typology of the identification papers in common use in turn-of-the-century Alexandria and show how documents communicated the legal regimes they embodied by their physical aspect. The second section offers an aggregate analysis of the details recorded in these documents, showing the protocols of identification at play as nationality emerged in Alexandria. The third section describes the economies through which legal and social power were traded for documents and documents were exchanged for institutional access. Document bearers used them in all sorts of ways, which can be reconstructed from consular records and from marks on the documents themselves. Those who possessed the power of nationality can be distinguished from those who did not by their use of papers, which materialized their knowledge of the law and fluency in its procedures.

Forms of Identification

Seven types of identification documents were in common use in Alexandria during the late nineteenth and early twentieth century. The consular archives of Alexandria contain more than fifty different formats and thousands of copies of these seven types, which differ in content, form, function, and issuing institution. The typology presented here is a basis for the discussion of documents and nationality that follows and serves as a point of comparison with studies of documents in other contexts.[8] This typology emphasizes the relationship of the document holder with the issuing authority and treats the documents as symbols of that transaction.

The first type, the most plentiful in the archives I have explored, is certificates of protection: documents confirming an individual's identity, protection, nationality, residence, and so on, primarily framed for use within the holder's territory of residence.[9] They were aides-memoires for institutions that had direct contact with their small constituencies and would protect and control their subjects within the municipal setting. The documents were keys that allowed other authorities to check back with the issuing authority; in this sense, they were not impersonal documents issued by some distant third party.

In this they differed from the second prominent type: travel documents, passports, and other travel passes, both internal and external, formulated for use outside the territorial jurisdiction of the issuing authority.[10] At the most basic level (and *contra* the frequent and erroneous association of passports with citizenship), we can distinguish between mobility documents and residence documents.[11] Mobility documents were impersonal documents, functioning like letters of recommendation to counterpart institutions abroad. These documents rarely led to direct exchanges between issuing and receiving institutions.

The third type is population-registration documents. This category includes certificates of birth, death, and marriage, as well as extracts from official registers.[12] The primary purpose of such documents was to gather demographic data for the state; personal identification was secondary. While certain subjects (such as Algerian French subjects) could use birth records to substantiate identification claims, for the most part these population documents were treated as discrete and rather general descriptions of individuals. For example, documentation of a marriage at a British church did not mean that the parties were British or Christian. Population-registration records first appeared in the closing decades of the nineteenth century, decades after protection certificates and travel documents were in common circulation, and their use increased markedly in the twentieth century.

A fourth type of document was produced by institutions of public order: warrants, forms consigning individuals to prisons or asylums, death notices, and the like.[13] These documents, which resemble shipping dockets for human beings, were exchanged among authorities with existing relationships. The documents describe individuals in bare terms and were most concerned with the question of their custody and transfer.

A fifth type of document concerns employment: military and state employment, government-certified manumission papers, and sailors' benefits forms.[14] The British Shipping Board of Trade's return of births and deaths, completed by the ship's officers but endorsed by the consul, for example, was a critical tool for seamen and their widows seeking benefits.[15] Institutionalized labor benefits were still quite rare during this period, and the consular and judicial archives of Alexandria contain relatively few of these documents.

State authorities issued the five types of documents already described. To this list we can add two further types, produced by nonstate actors. At the end of the nineteenth century, nonstate documents were the subject of particular official anxiety as states moved to monopolize jurisdiction, and so the papers nonstate authorities issued were becoming less authoritative.[16] Nevertheless, state institutions and individuals alike continued to rely on nonstate communities to certify identities. Thus papers issued by sectarian authorities—certificates of birth, death, marriage, poverty, and notoriety—constitute a sixth type of document.[17] In this case, the sectarian and communitarian nature of issuing institutions—rabbis, churches, *qadis*— was the defining characteristic. As we will see, sectarian institutions continued to exercise authority delegated to them under the Ottoman system well into the twentieth century. The seventh type were private declarations of notoriety, letters of introduction, and other "personal" recommendations. Although these were private rather than institutional documents, here too the issuer was the defining feature.

All seven types of documents should be considered utilitarian tools in the first instance. Identification documents were auxiliaries for direct, personal knowledge and were meaningful insofar as they were useful to the institutions that issued or received them. For this reason, most of the documents were plain forms to be filled out, sometimes on official paper or bearing a revenue stamp, and occasionally bearing decoration as a security feature. But documents also had proper power as material objects that in many cases superseded their function as records of information. In the present day, documents substitute for direct knowledge by the state of the individual citizen, leading some scholars of citizenship to misconstrue documents as the location of citizenship itself. But already in the late nineteenth century, documents' mere physical aspect could protect and embolden their bearers and intimidate those who could not or did not read their texts. In this way, they replaced personal protection, which was a social expedient out of reach of migrants and strangers.

Did people in turn-of-the-century Alexandria carry identification documents? How did they use them? The evidence that might answer these simple but crucial questions is less than conclusive. Most documents in the archives are pristine, which might suggest that their users kept them in a safe place or that they were used on only one occasion. It was not necessary to repeat identification for official purposes so long as individuals remained in the same community of residence. Once they made their status known, they might have no further need for papers. This is confirmed by the fact that many "potential documents" were never retrieved or issued in the first place. Bureaucratic records show that most individuals did not collect the identification documents available to them, despite repeated exhortations to do so. Typically, a single document, used once, was enough to bring a person to nationality.

Consular archives contain contrary evidence of the preciousness of certain papers. Many are deeply creased from folding and refolding, and some have torn along a fold and been taped back together.[18] The quarter or eighth left exposed when the document was folded and carried in a pocket is often discolored or dirty. Because they were carried for use, they were also burnt, lost, torn, stolen, or otherwise damaged. Damaged documents meant trouble. The embarkation certificate that Joseph Deleuze presented at the French consulate in Alexandria in 1911, for example, was endorsed with a "visibly counterfeited" signature from the vice-consulate in Port Said. Deleuze, who was arrested on the spot, insisted that the certificate was authentic, but he admitted to forging the signature.[19] He had done so only to replace writing that had washed off when the document fell into the sea, however.[20]

Fraudulent use is a mark of the value of papers. Prosecutions for forgery and falsification of official papers make this material power clear. In March 1911, Pierre Merillan, a French citizen, was arrested in possession of a set of crudely forged passports and other documents. He had falsified these travel permits with invented signatures ("*signatures fantaisistes*") and affixed them with two forged stamps. One bore the mark of the Tunis Regency, and the other bore an effigy and inscription of the French Republic, which had been transferred from a French Indochinese piaster. The court observed that the documents were so poorly made that they would never have fooled officials in such a way as to win access to any positive rights of French subjecthood, either in Egypt or abroad. Instead, they were meant to dupe "Arab" buyers who would believe that the documents would win the favor of officials ("*de nature à attirer sur lui la bienveillance des agents du gouvernement.*")[21] We can speculate about the precise meaning of this favor: presumably the prospective buyers were local subjects who sought tax or conscription exemptions in Egypt.

The accuracy of the forgery, or the coherence of the fraud, was less important than the symbolic power of the document as a whole. This was true of nonfraudulent use as well. As in other contexts, "what was most important . . . was the general impression made by the passport."[22] The torn and reconstituted French residence certificate in figure 3.1, for example, remained useful despite the fact that several pieces were misplaced in reassembly and that the bottom left-hand segment was taken from another document altogether. The whole material object was more valuable that the sum of its parts; errors in its content were of secondary importance.[23]

Because passports were particularly useful to those foreigners who did not look the part, it was difficult to verify identity and protect against misuse. Although physiognomic information was often recorded, passports did not display photographs before the First World War.[24] Inevitably, forgery and trafficking became concerns, but opportunities to prosecute were rare.[25] In 1912, investigators discovered an altered passport in the possession of an Algerian arrested for morality crimes. Before proceeding with his trial, the consulate sought information from the Jedda consulate, which had issued this passport. Their formal investigation (*commission rogatoire*) discovered that all writing on the passport except the consul's signature and seal had been wiped away by scratching or chemicals. Curiously, however, the new information entered corresponded to the records in Jedda. In all likelihood, the consulate decided, the Algerian had sold (or rented) his passport to another, who used it with false information. The original owner then retrieved it and restored the former details. The accuracy of the entries was immaterial, the court ruled, because the Algerian was guilty if the passport was altered in any way at all. The court took the case very seriously and gave the Algerian the harsh penalty of eighteen months in prison and a five-year ban from civil rights.[26] Clearly, a passport verified by seal and signature was valuable enough to sell and useful enough to want back.[27]

Passports were subject to strict controls because they had value for individuals making claims on states. The states guarded their rights jealously and indeed used them as a primary means to distinguish subjects from nonsubjects. The result was often strange. The relationship of persons to the modern state was (meant to be) unmediated, but because it was also impersonal, subjects required paper keys to unlock access.

FIGURE 3.1 French residence certificate of ʿAli Muhammad bin ʿAli, 1894.

Source: CADN-RA 48/1167, with permission of the Ministère des Affaires Étrangères.

This was clearly a weak point in regimes of nationality. But this private function also paralleled a public function for documents: they were a modular tool representing the state as one of the community of nations.

The passport in figure 3.2 illustrates a number of gaps between the image of sound sovereignty and the reality of documentary practices. It is a French passport, valid for one year and a single journey to Algiers, issued by the French consulate at the Red Sea port of Jedda.[28] The Jedda consulate issued a good number of passports—the Alexandria consular archives hold many of them—and had a form printed expressly for the purpose. This particular form lagged some way behind political changes in France, however. The document was issued in 1877, half a dozen years after the fall of the Second Empire of Napoleon III and the establishment of the Third Republic. Yet this epochal shift from monarchy to republic, which was the site of considerable symbolic contestation in France, was a simple affair for the passport-issuing consulate in Jedda: "Empire" was crossed out and replaced with "République," and an "e" was added to the end of "Français."[29] This improvised document was issued to Muhammad bin Salih, born and residing in Mecca. In the box for "*signature du porteur*," Muhammad affixed his Arabic seal. Muhammad was a traveling man. Visas on the back face of the passport show that a month after he received the passport in January 1877, he was in Algiers. He proceeded quickly to Oran, then to Tangiers. In July, he received a visa from the Ottoman consul in Gibraltar (a man named Richard Edmund Cowell) to proceed to Alexandria. Muhammad's undated Alexandria file was probably produced in 1878, when he was given a fresh passport (in exchange for the passport retained in the file) in order to return to Mecca. The passport was the key that unlocked consular protection in Alexandria for a man passing through who showed no sign of connection with the French language and only an instrumentalist connection with the French territory of Algeria. We can infer from its terse contents, however, that he was a man of a certain standing. Whereas an uncertain claim typically foregrounded positive evidence of its validity, Muhammad's states that the passport was given to him "on the recognition of his identity and on his request." Furthermore, no physical description is given—a common mark of elite status. As we will see, passports and other identification documents were pressed into service above all to validate less-than-self-evident claims to nationality.

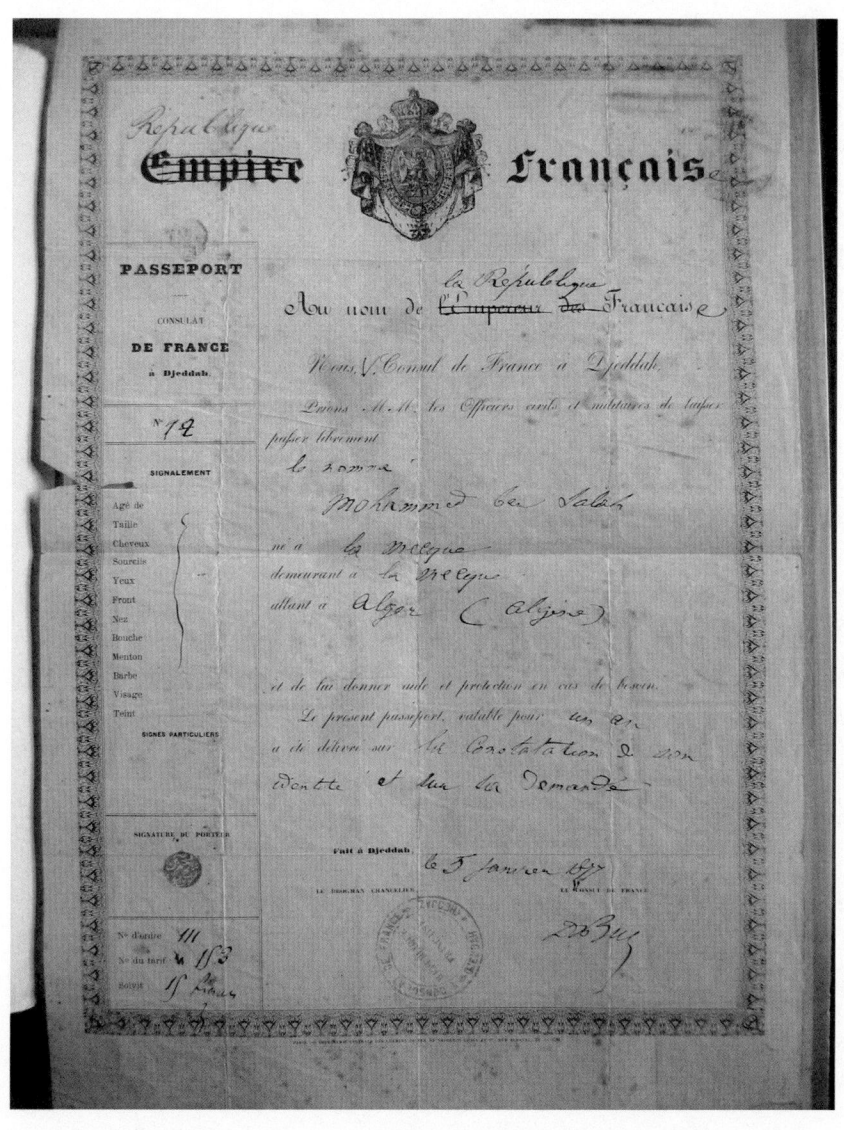

FIGURE 3.2 French passport of Muhammad bin Salih, 1877.

Source: CADN-RA 46/1008, with permission of the Ministère des Affaires Étrangères.

While nationality law would eventually develop in such a way that states became the sole authoritative dispensers of affiliation documents and nationals became the sole legitimate bearers of such documents, until the interwar period it was clear, in local practice at least, that states and subjects constituted each other. The authority of state institutions in Alexandria derived from the lists of individuals whom they protected and controlled. The various types of documents describing these relationships of affiliation formed a common field.

In the closing decades of the nineteenth century, certain Ottoman subjects—including elite Egyptians—used a passport (*mürur tezkeresi*) such as that in figure 3.3 that was a formal hybrid of older Ottoman internal passes and newer European passports. It was a product of the census bureau rather than the foreign ministry; ironically, its language and terms made it illegible to the non-Ottoman authorities it was (sometimes) used to address. But in the first decade of the twentieth century, a generation of nationalists carried the Egyptian passport in figure 3.4, which replaced the Ottoman passport around 1899. Two decades after the Jedda passport, we see similar symbolic dissonance in Egyptian passports. The new Egyptian passport offered the possibility of translation, but only two language choices: French and Ottoman Turkish.

The dissonant symbols of state in these passports, like the pieced-together shreds and the second-rate forgers of residence documents described earlier, suggest that documents were not always the site of pedantic bureaucracy. The piles of documents in the archives contain numerous empty spaces. Their "incompleteness" and their "errors" were normal, and they warn the historian not to insist on close readings of single documents.[30] Documents (like the nationality they represented) were meant to make an impression, not to make sense.

Protocols of Identification

Personal identification documents had value as material symbols of protection, but they were also information containers. Document makers elicited this information from the document holders according to specific protocols of identification.[31] Institutions developed protocols of identification according to their particular needs. Notaries in early modern Spanish

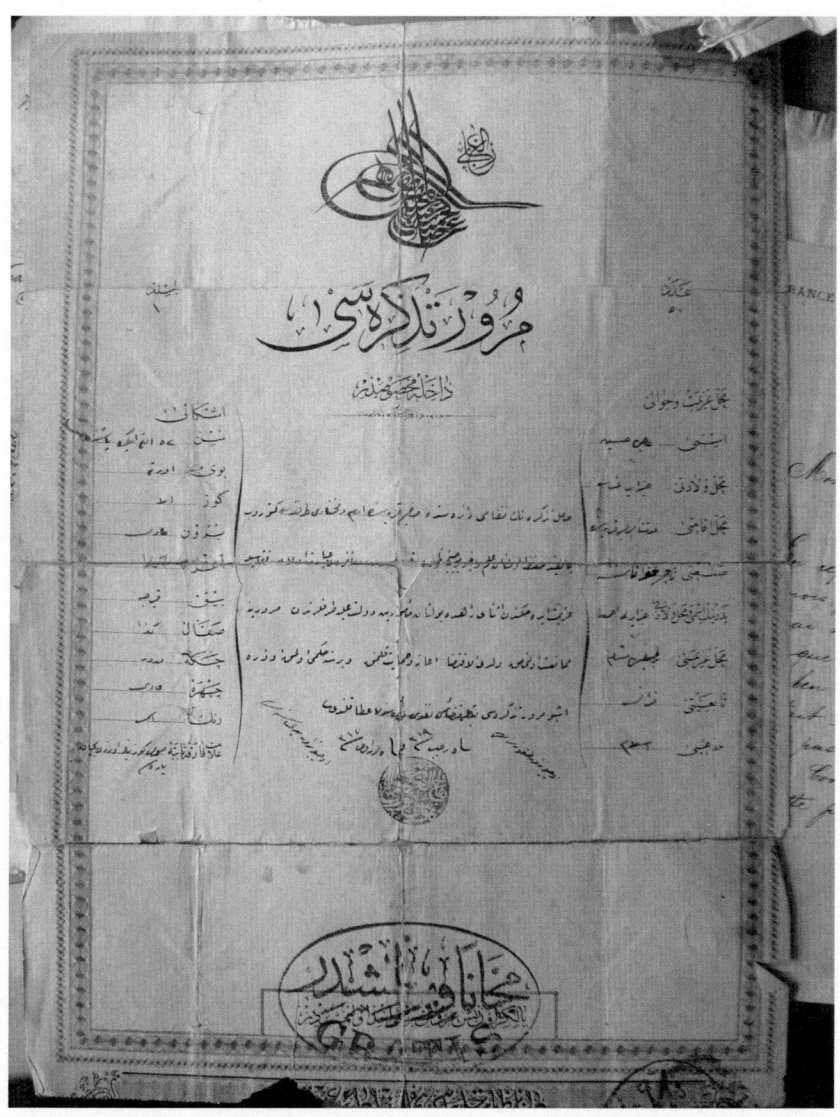

FIGURE 3.3 Ottoman passport of Haj Hussain bin Ahmad, 1901.

Source: CADN-RA 54/1531, with permission of the Ministère des Affaires Étrangères.

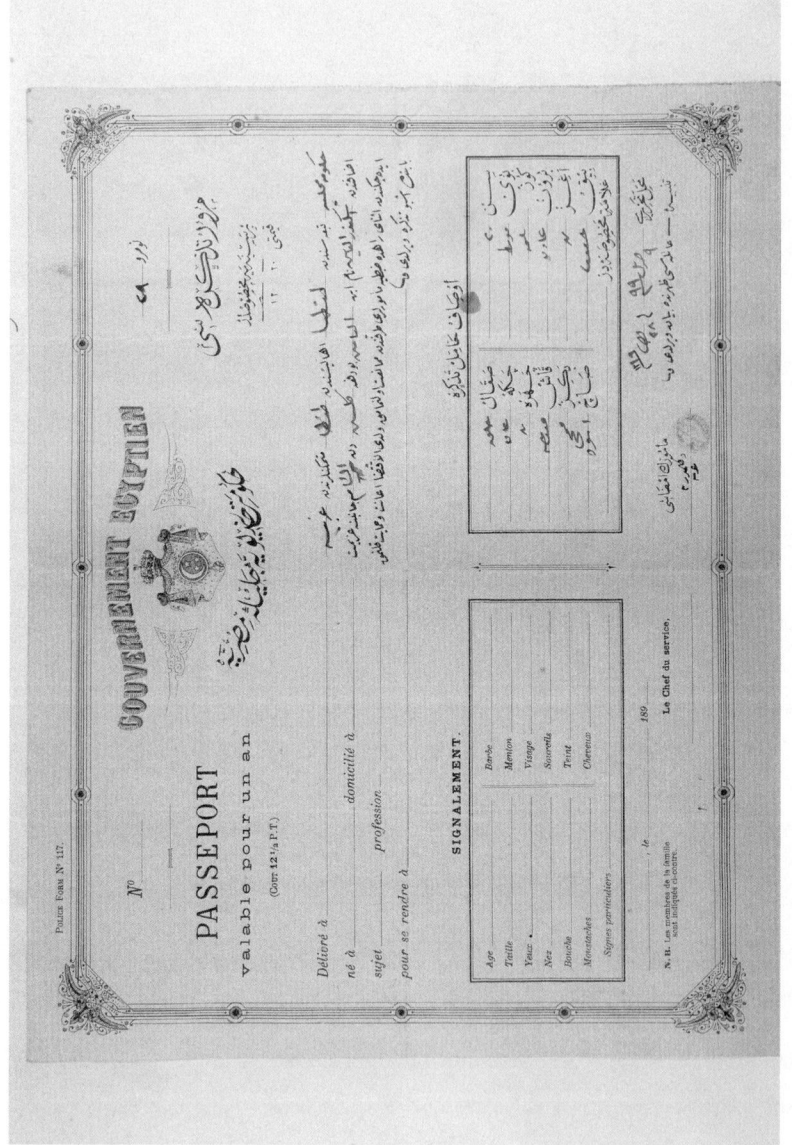

FIGURE 3.4 Egyptian passport of Iskander Ilyas, 1899.

Source: DH.TMIK.M 62/65, with permission of the Başbakanlık Osmanlı Arşivi.

America, for example, identified witnesses according to a formula: age, relation to parties, whether friend or enemy.[32] Medieval Islamic notaries also developed elaborate guides to best documentation practices.[33] The internal passports used to control Egyptian peasants in the first half of the nineteenth century listed name, father's name, physical description, and village.[34] In late nineteenth-century Alexandria, both state institutions and the people using them learned to imitate and adapt these protocols in their own best interests.

Table 3.1 summarizes the kinds of data recorded on almost four dozen different kinds of personal identification forms collected from the many archives of turn-of-the-century Alexandria and described in the typology above. The percentage figures indicate the share of all documents that contains the given category of identification. Under each category I have listed the particular terms used to designate it.

Naming was the ubiquitous identifier: every identification document surveyed had a field or fields for name. For James Scott, the "invention of permanent, inherited patronyms was . . . the last step in establishing the necessary preconditions of modern statecraft."[35] This was not so obviously the case in late nineteenth-century Alexandria. During this period, the state did not rush to reformat traditional names that defined identity in locally significant terms. Arabic naming practices endure: European and Egyptian records alike typically contain a given name (*ism*), followed by a father's name (preceded by *ibn*, *ben*, or *bint*, or not) and often some additional descriptive name (*nisba*) indicating origin, profession, or other attributes. These names were not standardized in orthography or format and were transliterated in multiple ways.[36]

Although they were key descriptors, names as common as Muhammad bin Salih, ʿAli Muhammad bin ʿAli, Haj Hussain bin Ahmad, and Iskander Ilyas could hardly serve as unique identifiers in bureaucratic indexes. A good deal of supplemental information was necessary. What is clear, however, is that the recording of a name or names—irrespective of invented formats—was itself a significant act of representation. In featuring a personal name consistently, identification documents differ markedly from the censuses discussed in the next chapter, which usually did not name names. Yet this was the major distinction between these two means of identification. The many other fields that feature in protocols of personal identification also feature in many censuses; the next chapter will show

TABLE 3.1 Protocols in Alexandria identification documents, 1861–1914

Name	100%
name, surname; le nommé, le sieur, nom et prénoms; ism wa laqab; isim ve şöhret	
Residence	**61%**
domicile, place of abode; demeure, addresse; mahall al-iqama, mahalli ikamet, al-maskan, balad, sakan; al-muqim, min al-musafirin hadiran min	
Origin	**52%**
place of birth, native of; balad, mahall al-wilada	
Occupation	**52%**
profession, rank, occupation; sana'a; sanaat ve sıfat ve maişet	
Age	**48%**
date of birth, né en; tarikh al-wilada, 'umr; sin	
Nationality	**39%**
condizione; inscrit comme; jins, jinsiya; tabiiyet	
Family	**35%**
father and mother's names, ages, origins, professions, residences; marital status; wife and children's names, ages, birthplaces, residence; "accompagnée de . . ."	
Physical Description	**30%**
Signature	**20%**
Religion	**17%**
diyana, madhhab, mezheb, mille; culte	
Sex	**17%**
sinif, nu'	

Note: n = 46. These documents were issued by French, British, Egyptian, Ottoman, American, Algerian, and Tunisian authorities.

how the identification logics of censuses and papers were cogenerated. Individuals who learned to answer identification questions for census takers would know how to answer document issuers, and vice versa.

After name, the next most prominent protocol of identification involved place. Current residence was clearly an important factor in identifying individuals, but it was not quite ubiquitous. Almost as important as where the individual *currently* lived was the separate question of where they or their ancestors had *once* lived. Origin, nationality, and family—ways of telling what kind of a person the bearer was—were used in (only) half of cases (though origin was sometimes implied by the context of the document itself). While birthplace might be considered a straightforward determination, like so many aspects of expanding identification protocols, its meaning was not self-evident. Often a city's name was given, but it had to be located in a larger geographic unit—a province or state.[37] In fact, it seems that birthplace elicited many general rather than precise responses. This information served to affiliate individuals to general communities of origin rather than specific sites of birth. Generalizations mapped well onto a category such as *ahali* ("of the people of"), used on Tunisian identification documents to show that an individual was of the people of a certain area. Intriguingly, these documents also specified birthplace. For those born in Djerba, Sousse, and Sfax, birthplace and *ahali* coincided in almost every case. For those born in Tunis, Alexandria, or elsewhere in Egypt, *ahali* pointed elsewhere in Tunisia, indicating a different sense of origin.[38] In legal identification documents (though not in population documents), this kind of belonging was more important and more revealing than place of birth.

Occupation was an important indicator of an individual's status. Guilds had only recently lost their position as guarantors of their members' status, and occupations were often indexed to class.[39] As we will see in chapter 10, certain occupations (musician, for example) or the lack of an occupation could carry a weighty stigma. Occupation was not a fixed characteristic and was inconsistently and multiply recorded. Certain occupations, too, were ambiguous by nature—*employé*, for example.

Age was not always a straightforward determination. It was often recorded approximately, typically in five-year intervals. Year of birth was sometimes recorded instead of age, but here too information could be ambiguous. In 1910, the Ottoman high commission in Egypt wrote to the

Ottoman census directory about a young man named Oseb, who was facing charges in Egypt. Oseb carried an Ottoman identification document (*tez-kere*) that stated that he was born in Constantinople in 1313 but did not specify the calendar. If 1313 was reckoned according to the *hijri* calendar, he was fourteen or fifteen years old and could be prosecuted as an adult. If the date was reckoned in the *rumi* calendar, however, Oseb was two years younger, hence a child.[40] It is striking (but characteristic) that the massive bureaucratic regime erected during the nineteenth century stumbled over such simple details—and indeed the commission also had questions about the orthography of Oseb's name. On the other hand, it is clear that the machinery of interdepartmental reference functioned quite efficiently, and the census bureau provided the information necessary to sentence the youth. Even more significant is the privileging of the determination by paper of a physical characteristic such as age, which would previously have been determined by medical examination.

More intimate identifiers, such as physical description and signature, were less prominent, at least until the advent of photography. One-fifth of the documents contained a field for the bearer's signature. Sometimes this space was signed; often it bore the print of a signet seal, which was a key tool to certify documents in the Arabic scribal tradition. Often too this field was marked "illiterate" or left blank. Literacy was itself a useful mark of class standing and bureaucratic fluency. For the highly literate, as for the wealthy, identification documents were often a less effective tool than other forms of social prestige that they possessed. For the illiterate, who often engaged bureaucracy through the intermediacy of a scribe, these documents were typically more critical. The issuing of documents without fee was another intimate indication about the bearer. According to official rhetoric, poverty was no barrier to documentation because the poor received documents gratis. Of course, this principle was incompletely diffused in practice. Jews received gratis documents at a greater rate than non-Jews, apparently thanks to better information rather than greater poverty: the Jewish community issued certificates of indigence quite routinely, while other communities did not. "Gratis" mattered because few documents were so labeled; physical description was left blank for those of elite class and for most women. For most of these rarely used forms of information, the asking of the question is as important a clue as the answer itself.

Those whose physical descriptions were taken down became participants in fledgling efforts at definitive unique identification that would
culminate in the use of photographs in the first decade of the twentieth
century. By this time, quixotic, local, contextual forms of identification
were disappearing from official use. In 1912, shortly before the identification watershed, the French consulate introduced an entirely new card format. Like the British certificates, the new French card was a generic form
for use throughout the Ottoman Empire. It was more permanent: each *certificat d'inscription* had spaces for ten annual endorsements (so was used
for a decade). In addition, it included a photograph of the bearer, employing identification technology that had been available for decades.[41] These
shifts in format demanded a shift in practice. The paper trail of endorsements was contained in the document itself, and the bearer had to present
him- or herself at the consulate regularly.

The various protocols operative in Alexandria omit categories prominent in contemporary settings elsewhere in the world, notably race, estate,
and caste. While these categories have their own particular characteristics
proper to the settings in which they were prominent, there are important
structural similarities between the work these categories did and those
operative in Alexandria. In turn-of-the-century Russia, for example, individuals were identified according to categories of religion, geographic
locality, nationality, and estate.[42] On the face of things, this protocol is very
different from its Alexandrian counterparts. It is especially notable that
religion, despite the prominence of sectarianism in the scholarly literature
on the period, was rarely an explicit part of paper identification in Alexandria. Of course, identification by religion was often tacit, either obvious because of choice of venue or bureaucratically irrelevant. Sometimes,
too, religious labels were added even where it was not part of the protocol. While late imperial Russia worked to concentrate sovereignty through
the benevolent grant of distributed justice, requiring compartmentalized and explicit jurisdiction, the shared sovereignties in Egypt favored
implicit designation of jurisdiction. Therefore religion could be left unin-
dicated, in order to defer conflict between authorities. The same is true
of the Egyptian equivalent of estate—the foreigner/city dweller/peasant/
nomad distinction. Legal practice shows that the justice system knew who
they were dealing with, even if it was not explicitly documented. Religion
and "estate" were locally relevant forms of identification, gratuitous in

documents meant to communicate over longer distances. Different identification and protection transactions required different paper currencies,
recording information according to different protocols. As the next section
argues, these documents were tools to mediate sociolegal interactions.

Paper Economies

We have seen the ways that the form and content of identification documents communicated power and defined people, but how and why did
individuals take out identification papers in the first place? They did so in
a manner that illustrates the pointillist manner through which the nation
became embodied through the affiliation of its subjects. Individually, in
family groups, or in communities, people exchanged guarantees of their
notability or reputation for paper tokens of status. These tokens could
then be traded for others, in the newly impersonal bureaucracy of subjecthood; eventually, nation-states established a monopoly over identity certification, and all tokens issued by previous regimes were exchanged for the
new currency of identification.

Papers incarnated elaborate and varied bureaucratic procedures that
defined an economy in which they were traded for other papers, or for
services, or for status. Whether forged or genuine, they were commodities.
Consulates and their courts treated foreign protection as a value communicated from a territory (such as Britain, France, Malta, Algeria, or Tunisia)
via reputable institutions and the documents they issued. Nationality was
precious and exclusive, and the consular officials who were its custodians
worked hard to limit its spread. The conventional image of loosely controlled distribution of protection, even in the early and mid–nineteenth
century, is exaggerated.[43] Based in large part on metropolitan formulas, consulates devised positive criteria with which they evaluated individual claims to protection. They applied these criteria to manage the
exchange of documents.

Nationality created a paper trail. Consular archives reveal the background investigation encapsulated in a single piece of paper. Consular
registration dossiers were the core of a system of individual recognition
and documentation; they were the reserve to the paper currency. This
function is most clear in the French consular archives: every Algerian

and Tunisian claimant on French protection had a numbered file, and these files recorded hundreds of different paths toward protected status. While those passing through used passports, residents wishing to access the services of the consulate needed to produce their annual registration certificate or at least a registration number. This number corresponded to a subject census (*recensement*) dossier in the office of the dragoman (translator). These dossiers were the central tool of the consulate's judicial and civil administration of its subjects.[44] Until the First World War, the *recensement* was divided into two series: Algerian (beginning in 1873) and Tunisian (beginning in 1881).[45] When French citizens (who were typically white skinned, Francophone, and Christian) registered births, deaths, and successions, requested notarization of documents, received passports, and performed other administrative tasks at the consulate's chancellery, they typically won access not with a document but with appearance, language, and reputation (*notoriété*). Regardless of class, the access of French subjects (typically brown skinned, Arabic speaking, and Jewish or Muslim) to the same services depended on the paper currency of identification documents, which they won, maintained, and lost through the *drogmanat*'s elaborate registration system.

Registration certificates were symbols of recognition issued to those whose claims to French protection succeeded. The French consulates' dragomans were personally responsible for registration dossiers and their system of identification, regulation, and surveillance. The *drogmanat* received one to three dozen requests for registration in each year, and the dragoman noted his verdict on the cover of each dossier: "approved" (*vu, bon à déliver*) or "refused" (*non admis*). Proving nationality was a key element of the developing procedures of private international law. As Patrick Weil has shown in the French context, those born abroad faced steep costs in order to procure documents that were readily available and conclusive evidence for those born in the metropole.[46] Protection depended on the documents that the subject could produce and had little to do with the subject him- or herself or the skin, language, and dress that marked European foreignness. The *drogmanat* systematically recorded the document that warranted production of each subsequent document. Certain requests were doomed to fail by any measure. When Tanco Abramovitz (a "poor roving musician" [*pauvre musicien ambulant*]) wrote to the consulate in 1881 without proof of his claim to have been born in Constantine, the dragoman dismissed his request in two words: "not recognized" (*non reconnu*).[47] Presumably, many less detailed or serious claims to protection were dismissed at an even earlier stage, before a dossier was opened. More than one-third of Algerian dossiers opened at the *drogmanat* between 1880 and 1894 did not win a registration number.[48] Although dragomans often refused certificates and even maintained a special series of dossiers for those persons removed (*renvoyé*) from protection, certain individuals were given the benefit of the doubt, particularly at the beginning of this period under study.[49] In 1880, for example, provisional registration cards were issued in the absence of conclusive evidence.[50] Certainly, consular staff knew that a certain number of the documents they received and issued contained errors.[51]

In 1887, Isaac Chakhowa attempted to register with the French consulate in Alexandria. In support, he offered a passport for travel to Haifa that the consulate had issued in his name in August 1882. The consulate considered this passport, produced in the immediate aftermath of the troubles of 1882, insufficient proof of nationality. On the cover of the registration dossier, the dragoman wrote:

> He has never registered with this consulate as an Algerian. He claims that he lived for several years in Syria, but holds no consular registration certificate from Syrian consular authorities. The passport he produced is insufficient to establish Algerian origin. He must provide a judgment from the civil tribunal of Oran, where he was born, demonstrating his Algerian origin.[52]

This note was not an expression of doubt (there was no implication that Chakhowa was concealing some other nationality) but a bureaucratic evaluation, judgment, and prescription. It told him exactly what evidence of nationality he had to present in order to register. The *drogmanat* measured documentary evidence of nationality against a scale of strength and weakness; identification papers were valuable and could only be traded for certificates of equal or greater value. Nationality decisions issued by French courts (in Algeria in most instances) were considered the strongest evidence and never questioned by the dragomans. The case of a money-lender (*changeur*) named Haïde (Eïd) Skinazi appeared hopeless: he claimed to have been a German subject, but this protection was revoked, and he became a local. His profession and personal history raised red flags, but an

1883 judgment drawn from the civil registers of Oran (the city in Algeria where he was born) answered all questions.[53] Skinazi's work presumably entailed frequent legal challenges, and he was one of few subjects to renew his certificate without fail every year thereafter.

Evidence of previous registration with a consulate was the next most persuasive proof of nationality. Registration certificates issued by French offices elsewhere in Egypt and the Mediterranean (Algiers, Beirut, and a dozen other cities) were often employed. More than half of all successful applications referred to a relative (father, brother, husband, son, or mother) already holding status with the consulate. *Drogmanat* interpretation of relationships was not always predictable, however, and family connections cut both ways. Just as a foreign brother could transmit his status, the discovery of a local sibling might trigger loss of foreign protection.[54]

Prominent representatives of Alexandria's Algerian and Tunisian communities also possessed some power to confer status on those they recommended. The *drogmanat* accepted certain letters of recognition (*certificats de notoriété*), in which notable foreigners attested to and guaranteed an individual's identity. The consulate was even more willing to defer to the judgment of the subject community when exempting poor subjects from registration and passport fees. Five percent of Algerians and almost 15 percent of Tunisians registered with the consulate presented poverty certificates (*certificats d'indigence*), which were produced on a sectarian basis.[55] As mentioned earlier, Jewish authorities issued poverty certificates frequently enough to warrant the use of specially printed forms. Muslims offered letters certified with three or more seals from a small group of men that the consulate trusted. Subjects were an administrative burden, and the French consulate was glad to pass on the responsibility to investigate their material circumstances.[56]

Sometimes, nationality conversion was wholesale and formulaic. In 1881, when France occupied Tunisia, the agent in Egypt of the bey of Tunis prepared lists of Tunisians, to whom he issued some 247 certificates (*tezkereler/tadhakir*, sing. *tezkere*, a generic Ottoman term for "permit" or "license") permitting them to register with the French consulate.[57] These documents listed the name, age, birthplace (more than 30 percent were born in Egypt), spouse and children, and occupation of each Tunisian.[58] Each certificate was the seed of a new dossier in the *drogmanat*, from which registration certificates were reproduced annually. By 1884, the bey's agent no longer possessed the authority of protection, and community notables took on the task of *tezkere* certification.[59]

Registration was meant to be an annual ritual in which a minor economic transaction accompanied the paper transaction. After a rush at the beginning of January, renewals slowed considerably by springtime. French registration records show that families—four brothers, for example—sometimes came to the office and registered as a group.[60] Subjects surrendered the previous year's certificate in order to receive a new one, and the expired document was added to the individual's file. As we have seen, however, many subjects found it unnecessary to take out new registration certificates every year, if at all. National authorities sought to encourage more regular registration. British certificates cost five shillings until the turn of the century, when the fee was halved in order to encourage participation. French certificates were more expensive, at ten francs (eight shillings), but both consulates offered free registration to the poor. Out-of-date certificates retained by the majority who did not renew represented an exposure for those issuing identification papers: outside the registration offices, the paper tokens were more powerful than the details they contained, and they could be falsified and traded for status. Thus new measures emerged in an effort to flag expired certificates: a 1909 certificate belonging to a Maltese man was stamped with the warning (in English and Italian) that it "must be Renewed in January."[61] As mentioned earlier, the French introduced ten-year, photographic, annually recertified certificates of registration in 1912.

The paper chain of transmission through which documents produced nationality could be revisited when necessary. Dossiers were reexamined in at least two circumstances. First, the consulate often had to vouch for its subjects' nationality in response to enquiries from local authorities, courts, and counterpart consulates in Cairo and elsewhere in the Mediterranean. The second occasion for reevaluation of dossiers was the periodic pruning of lists of protected subjects, a process discussed in the following chapters.

While the qualifications for recognition as foreign were relatively clear, there were fewer positive markers of local status. In the eyes of consular officials, localness was the condition of those who failed to show signs of foreignness—the less than foreign, the falsely foreign, and the unforeign—and who therefore descended or reverted to local status.[62] In 1889, the dragoman Alexandre Haggar dismissed the claim of Ahmad ʿAbdullah, who was brought to the consulate by the local authorities: "This individual, who was sent [to us] by the police, is not recognized (*reconnu*) [as a French subject]." The Cairo consulate had given him a travel permit (*permit de passage*) on February 5, 1883, in order that he might return to Algeria. This permit states "that the bearer cannot use it to claim protection. . . . He has been sent back to the [local] government."[63] Another foreigner failed by the paper exchange was Violet Peradon, a worker at the International Bar on Stagni Street who was given an 1897 British registration certificate "by mistake." The consulate refused to renew her certificate the next year. When she died, her nationality was undetermined, and the consulate referred all enquiries to authorities of sect (the grand rabbi of Alexandria) and nationality (the local authorities).[64] Even in French-occupied Tunisia, persons of Algerian origin were considered local (i.e., Tunisian) unless they held a valid certificate of French nationality (passports and other identification documents did not make the grade), and officials were on the lookout for individuals who "passed themselves off as Algerian, when in fact they originate from Tunisia."[65]

In the eyes of the great powers, the international exchange of identification was devalued by authorities that issued identification too cheaply. Greece came in for special criticism in this regard. In 1897, Ottoman provincial authorities in Beirut wrote to their foreign ministry in Constantinople, trying to figure out what to do with Greek nationals with Egyptian and Cypriot passports who were coming to Beirut and claiming protection from the French consulate.[66] In Egypt, too, Greek nationality documents caused anxiety. Because they were issued by mayors, rather than a national bureau, Greek passports were considered especially liable to fraud or influence.

Egyptian documentation—or no documentation at all—created similar anxieties. In December 1892, Anna Spanion passed through Alexandria on her way from Istanbul to Bombay. Acting on advice from colleagues in Istanbul that she was a "procuress," the Alexandria consulate investigated whether the six girls traveling with her (her nieces and their mother, Anna's sister) were being taken to India for "immoral purposes." The case dossier sheds little light on this lurid accusation—the consul found no cause to detain the party—but its details reveal rather more about how easily passports were accessed and how lightly they were carried.[67]

Spanion came to the British consulate in Istanbul with an English passport issued in Bombay but was unable to convince them to give her a new one. When she arrived in Egypt, "although in possession of no document to prove the truth of her assertion," she declared herself a British subject and was mostly treated as such. Spanion's sister and nieces spoke Italian and German and traveled on an Ottoman passport in which each girl's name was entered separately. (The consular constable visited them on their ship and "questioned the girls one by one and asked them what was their nationality and they all said Turkish.") When the group proceeded to Port Said, the Alexandria consul-general informed the consul there that he thought she might take an Egyptian passport, "unless you are satisfied that she is a British subject in which case she could take a British passport." What is striking here is the matter-of-fact treatment given these identification documents. Sir Charles Cookson, the Alexandria consul-general, was not a man to defer to others; that he delegated to his inferior the decision to grant a document he himself had declined to issue shows how little weight the passport was assigned. No one seemed particularly bothered that Spanion's claim to be British was undocumented or falsely documented; so long as the British authorities did not concede more than they had to, any Egyptian or even British passport she won was no great cause for concern.

Conflicting paper evidence in the dossier of a certain Mahri Hamawi shows the uncertainty of nationality exchange between foreign and local subjecthood. Over the first decades of the British occupation in Egypt, local authorities began to define local status as more than just the absence of foreign protection. In 1881, they claimed authority over Hamawi—ostensibly a French subject—whose father had "made a claim to local protection (*fait acte de raya*), by paying certain taxes, such as the [Mirka] fees [and] by accepting passports of the local authority (*l'autorité territoriale*) guaranteed by the shaykh of the Syrian community (*corporation syrienne*) of Alexandria."[68] Hamawi resisted the local claim on him and asked the French tribunal to verify his right to French nationality. He had been refused in an earlier attempt to register with the consulate, apparently because several of his brothers were local subjects.[69] It seems that he continued to represent himself as a French subject, however. The local authorities probably chose to press the case in order to curtail his de facto exemption from their jurisdiction.[70] But the French consular court quickly dismissed the arguments of the local authorities, ruling that "these acts, if proved, are not sufficient, according to the principles of the Civil Code, to make one lose one's French affiliation (*la qualité de Français*) and by extension, one's quality of French protégé." In the eyes of French authorities, the tokens of local status cited by the local authorities were of an inferior order and not to be compared with proofs of French nationality.

Hamawi was not out of the woods, however. It was one thing not to have quit French protection but quite another to prove possession of it. Hamawi's evidence of French nationality was an 1871 passport issued at Nice in his father's name, which attested that his father was born in Algeria before the French occupation. But the *drogmanat* files contained another passport, issued to Hamawi in 1878, which showed an impossible eleven-year difference in age between father and son. Based on this evidence, the consulate was not able to establish Hamawi's claim one way or the other. A major essay on statelessness takes as its framing anecdote the (ficti-tious) child of Puccini's character Madame Butterfly, who (in 1905) would not have carried a passport. But the passport was not always a trustworthy indication of state affiliation.[71] In fact, possession of a passport was never really the measure of anything but possession of a passport. Although Hamawi's son also produced personal references (*actes de notoriété*) for his father, issued in Algeria, the court decided it needed more powerful certification: a "confirmatory judgment" from judicial authorities in Alge-ria. The court gave Hamawi four months to produce this evidence. Until a definitive judgment was possible, the consulate gave him the benefit of the doubt and agreed to consider him an "*algérien français*."[72] No final judgment was recorded in the court records, and here the archival trail goes cold. It is possible that he demonstrated his foreignness to consular satisfaction and that the local authorities were forced to abandon their claim over him. It is also possible that the question was dropped and that Hamawi contin-ued to live his life without definite nationality.

In a certain sense, individuals who came to the consulate to collect a certificate of registration cannot be considered anything but foreign. I have suggested, however, that a single certificate went a long way for many subjects settled in Alexandria. Once their protection had been docu-mented, most foreigners had little need to maintain standing at the con-sulate or worry if their name was struck from the list of foreigners. So long as they avoided the police and the courts, a background check was unlikely, and thus they would not encounter the official question "who are you?"

In the meantime, they lived their lives without positive tokens of national status. But foreignness was not merely the product of documents. Many of the advantages of foreign status accrued to those who could project it without recourse to paper proof. Although social and legal status often coincided, they functioned somewhat independently. Certain foreigners exercised legal foreignness but made no similar social claim.[73] Others made social and legal claims to foreignness who did not in fact possess that status. Complexion and dress were key markers of foreignness. To return to the anecdote that opened this chapter: when Cookson overstepped the bounds of local regulations by rescuing Hampson's remains, he was driven to redeem Hampson's *social* foreignness. His flesh could not speak for him—if it had, it would have done so with more eloquence than any identification document.

Fahrmeir's "most precise" definition of "formal citizenship" is "the legal definition of a close relationship between individuals and one state, usually documented in passports or other citizenship certificates."[74] The prominence of identification papers in this definition suggests the presence of a fallacy in which a symbol substitutes for the relationship signified. As this chapter has shown, before the First World War, identification documents were quite simple tools. Sometimes they did identification work, often they did not; for their users in the past and for historians in the present, they are useful but indecisive pieces of evidence. Document holders and document issuers alike were learning how and why to use these tools, and they did not rely on them—as we might today—as a substitute for direct, personal knowledge.

Documents met banal needs. A woman wrote to the British consulate in 1897 trying to get a death certificate for her husband, who died in San Remo, so that she could collect a pension from the Egyptian government, for which he worked.[75] The Ottoman Interior Ministry wrote to the Khedivial office in 1899, wondering whether a Bulgarian Muslim who died while passing through Egypt on his way home from the Hejaz had left any papers or passports that would help settle his estate.[76] Each time a document of this sort was procured, an individual had occasion to be drawn into the regime of nationality. It was not only the documents but also the verification of identity that expanded the purview of the state. Although it did not monopolize identification, the state assumed the right to adjudicate and sanction identity fraud. Vincenzo Lombardi was charged with fraud in 1886, when he presented a false certificate of character, claiming it was produced by his employer, the Eastern Telegraph Company.[77] It was the state that sanctioned this private offense: objective identification had become a question of public order. But when James Scott argues that "categories used by state agents" of the sort cataloged in this chapter "are an authoritative tune to which most of the population must dance," he is listening to the music that the state played from its own bandstand.[78] Listening to the same tune from the midst the crowd, one might notice that only some people are craning their necks to catch snatches of its rhythms and melodies. Out here, no choreographer was disciplining the dancers. Those who managed to hear the song might try a few steps of their own accord; it cost them nothing, and if they danced well, perhaps they might be called up onto the stage.

Personal identification was specified in tens of thousands of documents, in hundreds of thousands of individual interactions. Some of these transactions proved fruitful for claims makers or order-seeking bureaucrats; most were rote recordings of newly defined characteristics. This individual practice took place alongside the expansion of the census, which is the topic of the next chapter. The two administrative undertakings were tightly connected. The census combined millions of minor determinations into a forceful policy instrument, just as millions of minor (and mostly inconclusive) dots on identification documents gradually resolved, like a pointillist painting, into the image of a populace universally identifiable according to the logic of a standardized category regime.

4

Census

Questions and answers conjured nationality into being. As we saw in the previous chapter, nationality was described and certified on a case-by-case basis, in response to individual petitions. Administrators' decisions to grant papers (and the bureaucratic recognition that they embodied) to an individual was a subjective process. The various nationalities and statuses they certified were modular in form, but they were incommensurate rather than counterpart categories. The apparently incomplete evidence and inconsistent principles on which their grants were based were part and parcel of the individualized process. The questioner and the answerer learned from each other, and the statuses they produced were mutually constituted.

Individuals and institutions do not share motives, however. Identification documents were delivered on petition from individuals, whereas censuses produced nationality for clerks insisting on answers from an often recalcitrant population. The questions and answers used to produce identification documents differed so widely from those used to produce censuses that the nationalities they revealed were also substantially different. The census was a tool for administration. It is thus a curious place to look for markers of identity—the questions that clerks asked were not meant to understand sentiment. These questions were, rather, a clear index of bureaucratic attention. As Stoler has argued, bureaucratic mentalities are the first and best fruits of the serial records they produced.[1]

Documentation was instantiation, the general category made manifest in an individual. On an individual scale, nationality was a partial and intermittent quality, as varied as the individuals who used it. But the personal name, which as we have seen was the indispensable attribute in personal identification and documentation, was categorically excluded from the census.[2] The census made a corporate body through what Anderson calls "anonymous seriality."[3] It did not make nationality a presence in the lives of the population, and the category retained its abstraction despite its ascription to the whole population in comprehensive nationality tables. If the few who had been called to prove their nationality individually might consider their answers to be of some significance, for most the label was of little consequence. The scope of each project determined the type of nationality it evoked. Documents were singular and necessary, while the census was universal and largely ignored.

But most social histories rely on a different scale, aggregating individuals into economic, sectarian, ethnic, racial, and national collectivities and describing the dynamics of their societies in these terms. This is especially true of histories of turn-of-the-century port cities and the cosmopolitan diversity they represent.[4] Aggregation was also a favorite tool of the rationalizing bureaucracies that emerged in the later nineteenth century. At the same time that these institutions individuated their subjects using the protocols of identification described in the previous chapter, they were also constructing panoptic views of their populations that abstracted and serialized the characteristics of those individual subjects. The pull of these census figures is difficult to resist because they stock the social-historical imaginary with the appearance of substance and assign souls to its empty signifiers. But the comparison of multiple aggregate counts reveals that census takers were no more certain than consular clerks or police officers about the meaning of social categories.

How many foreigners lived in Alexandria? This question encapsulates much that nineteenth-century administrators and twenty-first-century historians want to know about that city. They have answered it many times, in many ways. For the period 1836 to 1917, the answers range from one-tenth to one-third.[5] The heterogeneity of these answers suggests that the question itself is poorly formulated. But national census returns have

formed the basis of Alexandria's social history, in which demographic statistics are quickly translated into identity abstractions. Inconsistencies
observed in the attribution of nationality to individuals were not eliminated when foreigners and locals were clustered and counted. In fact, category failings were amplified, as the figures in table 4.1 show. While the
overall population of the city increased steadily from census to census to
census, the share assigned to each subgroup fell and rose and rose and fell.
This inconsistency was the effect of changing counting categories, not
changes in the people counted.

This chapter begins with an analysis of registers and partial surveys
maintained by British, French, American, Italian, and Egyptian offices. I
then turn to the Egyptian national censuses of 1882, 1897, 1907, and 1917,
which have established the baseline of Egyptian demographic and social

TABLE 4.1 Egyptian census returns for Alexandria, 1882–1917

	1882	%	1897	%	1907	%	1917	%
Population of Alexandria	**231,396**	**100**	**319,766**	**100**	**332,246**	**100**	**444,617**	**100**
Greeks	18,688	8.1	15,182	4.7	24,602	7.4	25,393	5.7
Italians	11,579	5.0	11,743	3.7	15,916	4.8	17,860	4.0
French	8,215	3.6	5,221	1.6	4,304	1.3	8,556	1.9
British	3,552	1.5	8,301	2.6	8,190	2.5	10,656	2.4
Other nationalities	7,659	3.3	5,671	1.8	6,356	1.9	22,257	5.0
Total Foreigners	**49,693**	**21.5**	**46,118**	**14.4**	**59,368**	**17.9**	**84,722**	**19.1**
Sedentary Egyptians	171,854	74.3	254,358	79.5	245,136	73.8	321,367	72.3
Bedouins	503	0.2	4,984	1.6	714	0.2	2,503	0.6
Ottoman[1]	5,169	2.2	14,306	4.5	21,827	6.6	28,912	6.5
Sudanese[2]	4,367	1.9	—	—	5,201	1.6	7,130	1.6
Total Locals[3]	**181,893**	**78.6**	**273,648**	**85.6**	**245,850**	**74**	**359,912**	**80.9**

Notes: Not all of these categories appear in the censuses themselves. Foreign and local totals are, for the most
part, my own aggregates. Note that in the 1917 census figures, the sum of foreign and local exceeds the city
population by 17.
[1] 1917 figure is an aggregate of all "local" categories except Egyptian, bedouin, Sudanese, and Berberi.
[2] 1917 figure includes Berberi.
[3] In 1907, this figure excludes Ottomans and Sudanese. Ottoman and Sudanese figures are not added to the
foreign total, either.

history. I examine the general circumstances of their production and presentation, then focus on their use and development of the category of nationality. The priority in this vision is the interest of the administrators. As identification became universal and its certification centralized, the number of partial surveys (which were signs of delegated responsibility) decreased. At the same time, the universal census also changed, adding more and more subcategories in an effort to describe the diversity formerly managed by decentralized authorities whose powers the state was now assuming. One of the major contentions of this study is that the meaning of the category "nationality" is transformed when it becomes a universal attribute. Universal coverage produced modular categories. While this argument is largely chronological—that is, that nationality was partial until the First World War, after which it became universal in aspiration— the census offered a mirage of universal nationality long before the status and its documents and advantages were the desire of every individual.

Registers and Partial Surveys

Local and sectoral surveys have been neglected in the rush to find aggregate answers in historical description. Surveys on this scale use idiosyncratic classification schemes and articulate alternate visions of identification that do not map easily onto modular modern categories. Partial surveys preceded the national censuses that became symbols of sovereignty in the late nineteenth century and continued afterward.[6] The endurance of these partial censuses suggests the limits to the reach of central government practices and principles.

Unlike universal censuses, partial surveys were not meant to depict the population as a whole. They do not contain aggregate statistics or abstract individuals. Because these lists of names represent those who were visible to their competent authorities, they offer the most accurate composite image of particular communities. While the collection of nine partial surveys in table 4.2 is far from exhaustive, it represents nationality at the scale on which it appeared to legal rather than census authorities.

An official log book, which aggregates but does not anonymize description, is a type of census. The categorization practices of these registers typically duplicate those of identification documents; the individual carries

TABLE 4.2 Partial national censuses preserved in archives

State	Type	Place	Year	Number
France[1]	Algerian subjects	Alexandria	1868–1914	3,519
Tunisia	Subjects	Alexandria	1881	c. 250
France[2]	Tunisian subjects	Alexandria	1881–1917	c. 1,700
Italy[3]	Protégés	Cairo	1883	77
United States[4]	Citizens	Alexandria	1883–1907	c. 300
France/Egypt[5]	Tunisian subjects	Alexandria	1884	293
Egypt[6]	Prisoners	Torah prison	1887	c. 500
United Kingdom[7]	Subjects	Alexandria	1888	3,165
Ottoman[8]	Subjects	England	1893	19
Italy[9]	Loss of protection	Egypt	1897–1903	53

[1] CADN-RA 35–54; Suppl. 197–201.
[2] CADN-RT 69–92; Suppl. 234–9.
[3] ASMAE Cairo 113/5.
[4] USNA 84/350/11/19/3 vols. 24–26.
[5] Filib Jallad, *Qamus al-idarah wa-al-qada᾿*, 3rd ed. (Cairo: Matba῾at Dar al-Kutub wa-al-Watha᾿iq, 2003), vol. 2, 296–300.
[6] I date this series from the period between the date that ῾Abdallah al-Sudani was imprisoned (30 Rabi῾ al-Akhr 1304) and the date that ῾Uthman ῾Abd al-Rahim was scheduled for release (3 Rabi῾ al-Awwal 1305).
[7] FO 881/5968.
[8] BOA Y.PRK.ESA 17/3.
[9] ASMAE Cairo 113/5.

the copy while the institution retains the source. This source then becomes an index of the registered population. Registration of births and deaths was made compulsory for Egyptians in 1891 and for foreigners in 1912.[7] The British consul sent an annual list to London of all British subjects born, died, or married in Alexandria during each year.[8] Birth, death, and vaccination registers generated vital statistics just as they produced identification documents. The Ottoman census bureau combined the survey function and the identification-certification function even more closely.[9] Ottoman bureaucrats referred numerous identification queries to the central census bureau, which was a clearinghouse for identification as well as a source of statistics.[10]

Discrete lists maintained by the French consulate in Alexandria of its Algerian, Tunisian, Moroccan, and Lebanese subjects offer perhaps the clearest example of the partial survey as a mechanism for control.

The consulate called these records a "census" (*recensement*).[11] When a clerk wished to access information about one of the consulate's registered subjects, he consulted one of four large boxes of index cards.[12] These cards reveal the very individualized focus of this census, which was anything but anonymized, but they also show the challenges inherent in using names as a comprehensive index of identification. They were grouped by first letter of "given name," so Salomons, Salvatores, and Sions were clustered together, Hameds went with Hassans, Ahmeds with ʿAlis, and Muhammeds with Moussas. Cards were marked A for Algerian or T for Tunisian, and they listed names in a variety of transliterated spellings, dossier number, birth date and place, residence, and the numbers of parents' and spouses' dossiers.[13] Whereas names tended to function as unique or all-but-unique identifying labels for Europeans (French citizens, Britons, and even Maltese), they did not serve the same function for French subjects from the Maghrib.[14] Arabic names and agnomens (*alqab*) varied by context and did not necessarily show family groupings in the same way that European names did. Many North African subjects were known by their first name and their place of origin; consular files contain references to countless men named ʿAli al-Maghribi (ʿAli from the Maghrib).[15] Without a common system of transliteration of Arabic into Roman characters, a single name might be rendered many different ways (for example, Abraham, Brahem, and Ibrahim).[16] The name-card index, which clustered various spellings of a single name or agnomen, was an indispensable tool for the surveillance and ordering of the French consulate's large non-Francophone subject population. As we have seen, surveillance and control—protection—was a key function of nationality in territory of mixed jurisdiction.

While partial surveys are not universally representative, they do a good job of capturing those who were actually engaged with the state. Registration records tended to underestimate populations because they counted only those who took the trouble (and derived some advantage) from registering. Short-term sojourners, those unwilling to pay the small registration fee, and those with no reason to or experience of using the consulate went unregistered. But in some ways, registration is a better measure of *active* nationality than Egypt's universal censuses. Counting those who actually used the consulate is at least as reliable as counting everyone who self-identified as foreign when asked on census day. Statistics of this type suggest, for example, that there was no immediate influx of British residents to Alexandria in the half-decade after the occupation. For the years between 1872 and 1887, paid registration at the British consulate rose to a peak of 956 in 1876, sank to a low of 720 in 1879, then hovered around 800 until 1887, when 916 British subjects registered.[17]

A careful partial survey of British subjects in Alexandria conducted the following year (1888) counted 1,084 heads of household. This remarkable document, produced in 1889, lists every registered British subject by name.[18] Not surprisingly, the numbers produced by the consulate's restricted criteria of nationality do not fit seamlessly with the Egyptian census results, either in proportional and absolute numbers. The community census summarized in table 4.3 used a protocol of personal details about every individual: name, age, profession, marital status and family size, birthplace, religion. Names and family relationships were important

TABLE 4.3 British subjects in Alexandria, 1882–1917

	1882	1888	%	1897	%	1907	%	1917	%
Total British Subjects	3,552	3,165		8,301		8,190		10,656	
Britons[1]		817	26	3,005	36	5,006	61	3,115	29
Army of Occupation				1,119	13				
Army families, women, children				163	2				
Maltese[2]		1.960	62	3,989	48	3,184	39	4,190	39
Indians		182	6	25	0			319	3
Gibraltar		148	5						
Widows		37	1						
Other[3]		21	1					1,223	11
Greeks								1,189	11
Egyptians								405	4
Jews								149	1
Australians, Canadians, South Africans								66	1

[1] The 1897 figure is not expressed in the census as such. It is the difference between "total British subjects" and the other categories specified. In the 1907 census, this group is labeled "English."
[2] In 1907, the category included colonial subjects.
[3] In 1917, "Other races."

tools used to ascertain foreignness, and place of birth was a demographic detail of particular importance in consular recording.

These accessory details were recorded for the purposes of administrators, not demographers. They provided the means to limit the spread of nationality. Careful measurement of origins and circumstances of arrival in Alexandria was important, for example, because welfare and repatriation costs incurred by Maltese British subjects born in Egypt were the responsibility of the Foreign Office, while it was the Colonial Office that paid for those born in Malta. At the French consulate, place and year of birth (or father's birth) was a critical determinant of eligibility for protection. Careful attention to the competing principles of jus sanguinis and jus soli became even more important in purges of protégé lists after the First World War. In this work, officials relied on the data of their partial surveys.

If diplomatic negotiations over nationality often employed the language of law and the form of treaties, decisions were enacted in many cases using censuses and lists. Periodically, consular authorities submitted lists of their acknowledged subjects and protégés to the Egyptian foreign ministry. These lists became references in future disputes over nationality.[19] These lists were semipublic and differ from internal subject counts because they were meant to assist relations between authorities. They were a primary tool in establishing agreement about jurisdiction sharing and were a frequent topic of correspondence between judicial and consular authorities. As mentioned above, when France assumed control of Tunisia in 1881, protection of certain Tunisian subjects (ba'da ashkhas min fi'a khususa) in Egypt shifted from the Ottoman sultan to the French consuls. The representative in Alexandria of Tunisia's "ex-bey" produced lists of individuals to be transferred to French protection in 1881 and 1884. The 1884 order from the Egyptian interior ministry shows how minutely this transition was managed: it lists the names of every individual who would change protection (himaya).[20] It was perhaps not merely coincidental that both Italy and the United States also produced subject lists in 1883. The Egyptian foreign ministry regularly requested information from consulates in reference to these lists, seeking to ensure that all details were in order.

What can historians do with this evidence? It was collected for use on a case-by-case rather than an aggregate basis and must be used cautiously indeed in describing contours of foreign communities. It is clear that data collection was episodic and sampling far from random. Rich description of consular documents and highly stratified internal censuses show the danger in aggregating the data they contain without supplying additional context. In large part, this context comes from study of the issuing institutions rather than of the individuals soliciting the documents. It was for institutional use that auxiliary information was recorded. When institutions did not need to know much, it showed—the 1897–1903 list of former Italian subjects who had lost protection, for example, contained names and nothing else. The protocols of identification used in internal censuses corresponded to clerks' administrative needs. The Tunisian *tezkeres* that were used to win French protection specifically labeled every Jew (*al-yahudi*). Muslims, on the other hand, were identifiable by name and title (*haji*). The same *tezkeres* rounded age into five-year segments; greater specificity was unnecessary. The same is true of professions: merchant (*commerçant*) was so commonly reported that it must have referred to many different functions. Salim bin Muhammad of Tanta was described variously as a porter (*portefaix*), cook (*restaurateur*), and cobbler (*cordonnier*).[21] This evidence is hardly suitable for a history of these occupations.

Institutions recorded just enough information to perform their surveillance work. Registers were meant to restrict the supply of status, which was (as argued in the previous chapter) a controlled commodity reserved for the deserving. At the same time, they were meant to facilitate the monitoring of certain individuals. A series of photographic cards indexing convicts incarcerated in Toura prison in the 1880s is a clear example of this manner of identification work.[22] The cards listed some identifiers: the individuals' names and nationalities (*jins*) are given—most were Egyptian (*misri*)—but fields for sect (*milla*), profession, and residence were usually left blank. The indexing function of the cards was more fastidiously observed: clerks carefully recorded the crime, the sentence, the date of imprisonment and projected date of release, and any adjustments to the sentence.[23] Partial surveys listed visible individuals, indexing them in a series for purposes of bureaucratic reference. The Ottoman archives contain a brief index of twelve Ottoman and seven Egyptian subjects resident in England in 1893.[24] This handful of individuals, abroad in semiofficial capacities, was monitored because they were part of a state anxious for its reputation. Comprehensive vision was not the aim.

Universal counting was the purpose of the national census. In the universal census, nationality was a secondary field, like occupation or evidence were in the partial surveys. Partial surveys filtered for the category of nationality—typically, the nationality of every member was clear by virtue of her or his inclusion on the list. But these partial counts do not match up with the nationality counts of the universal census. This noncorrespondence is a clue about the distance between active or visible nationality possessed by the minority who had proven their status and the latent nationality ascribed by census takers to the general population on the basis of a simple question or an evaluative glance.

The Universal Census

The primary aim of partial surveys was bureaucratic responsibility; in the universal census, it was the legitimation of the state and the management of its resources. National censuses carried out in 1882, 1897, 1907, and 1917 are the core of Egypt's population history during the British occupation. Certain historians reproduce these census figures without a gloss.[25] Others weigh the statistics more carefully, attempting to measure their accuracy. Critical examination of Egypt's censuses has typically focused on their statistical accuracy, rather than on the categories they employ and the mentalities that they reveal.[26] As a result, the explanatory power of relatively sound censuses has been exaggerated, and more questionable counts have been neglected. Most critics point out that the 1882 results lie well below the standard curve of nineteenth-century population growth. Given the disturbed condition of the country as well as other factors, it is estimated that as many as three-quarters of a million people in Egypt went uncounted.[27] The next three counts are better received.[28] Certainly the 1882 numbers do not add up, sometimes literally so.[29] But even the well-regarded 1917 census contains errors of addition that, though relatively unimportant in their own right, offer a hint that these censuses may be untrustworthy even according to their own logic.[30] Coherent (and even incoherent) population statistics tend to lull historians into complacent acceptance of census categories that are arbitrary and problematic.[31] Even before considering the statistics that the four censuses produced, it is clear that the measurement of nationality from census to census was inconsistent.[32] In attempting to recover the history of nationality, it is best to accentuate rather than to smooth these inconsistencies. To dismiss the results of the 1882 census outright on the grounds of statistical inaccuracy is to throw the analytical baby out with the bathwater. Instead, we should ask what mentalities its categories betray.

Population counting was only one aim of the census and not always the most important. The census, like legal reform, continued despite changes in authority, and the project as a whole presents a powerful argument for continuity during the 1880s. On the third day of December 1881, Khedive Muhammad Tawfiq ordered that a census be carried out on May 3, 1882; the results of this census were published at the end of 1884. Between order and publication, control of Egypt moved from khedival to ʿUrabist to British hands. None of the parties who fought for control of the state impaired the progress of the census; the rationalization of Egypt's population and territory was an indispensable tool for any government. The census was a state-building project that transcended the details of its population count. It was a lavish publication: two volumes in French and Arabic versions (a promised third volume never appeared), printed on heavy stock at the government's Bulaq press. Its text was repetitive, and many of its tables were redundant, but the census had bulk. The fashioning of an impressive physical object (bolstered by many blank pages) was part of the effort to substantiate the Egyptian state.[33] This paper incarnation resembles the symbolic function of passports discussed in the previous chapter.

The 1882 census was more concerned with space than it was with people. The authors themselves admitted shortcomings in their population count. They insisted, however, that this project was but a first step, the creation of an "administrative division of the country, which integrates in its many subdivisions each and every site inhabited by one or more individuals, on any single spot of the territory (*sur un point quelconque du sol*)."[34] The focus on geography, even at the expense of population, is evident in the division of the published work itself. The bulk of its (projected) three volumes was devoted to painstaking lists of a total of 3,615 localities, many of which were home to twenty, or twelve, or just three inhabitants. Meanwhile, the census dispensed with the populations of Cairo and Alexandria in about a dozen pages. When this ungranular count is compared to the street-by-street accounting of these cities in subsequent censuses, the 1882 census might be considered a partial survey of rural Egypt. The emphasis on rural centers had implications for the count of foreigners: only 10 percent of the total population lived in cities (*gouvernorats*), but 88 percent of the foreign population was urban, and 55 percent of all foreigners lived in Alexandria. Government interest in the centralization of authority (including the authority to identify individuals) demanded this complete map of Egyptian territory. Formerly, authority was delegated to neighborhood *shaykhs* and guarantors, who took the responsibility to know the small areas they controlled.[35] If the government was to assume universal direct authority, it also had to acquire comprehensive local knowledge. For this reason, the 1882 census focused on geography first.

A third concern of the 1882 census was Egypt's labor force. The census conceived of population as a human machine for economic growth, as shown by its privileged treatment of Egypt's sex ratio. In addition to population and settlement, the census collected information about six demographic characteristics: sex, nationality, age, religion, education, and profession. The two published volumes treat sex and nationality only; age, religion, education, and profession were supposed to form the bulk of volume 3, which never appeared. The census showed that Egypt had more men than women, and this question was discussed at greater length than any other. In one of several comparisons with censuses of India and Algeria, the authors found that Egypt is more like Europe than its fellow colonies in regard to its male-to-female ratio.[36] The French were centrally concerned about population growth and the male-to-female ratio during this period, which may help explain this preoccupation of Boinet, the French director of the census. Again, this demographic preoccupation helped signal Egypt's membership in the community of states. But it is clear that this male population, like the land of the state, was a critical economic input to be measured. These three qualities of the 1882 census demonstrate its rhetorical purpose.

Subsequent censuses also did modular representation work for the Egyptian territory, but they show the more elaborate statistical-management techniques of the British administration. The 1897 census offered a far more detailed picture of urban geography. It divided Alexandria into 108 districts, most containing between two hundred and seven hundred residences. This detailed study revealed the capitulations' sensitivities. For the 1897 census, it was agreed that census takers would not enter foreigners' homes unless invited; if the foreigner refused to reply, the census taker would merely note the refusal and report it to the consulate (which could presumably fulfill its traditional delegated administrative role by supplying replacement information based on its own partial surveys). The information collected was "merely information, and had no weight in determining civil status or nationality."[37] Yet "mere information" delivered an aggregating logic that rendered national and religious categories into a modular format.

The 1897 census shows certain national and religious clusters. A quarter of the population in the 292 residences in the seventeen streets around Qahwat al-Gezaz in Labban were Catholic British subjects, hence Maltese. Two-thirds of the three thousand inhabitants of al-Ginaina al-Kubra, surrounding St. Catherine's Church, were Christian. All of the 3,416 residents of Kafr ʿAshri in Minet al-Bassal, except eighteen French subjects and forty-six Copts, were Egyptian Muslims. Ninety-three individuals in the city were neither Muslim nor Christian nor Jewish. A quarter of the residents in both Suq al-Samak al-Qadim and Haret al-Magharba were Jews. If we exclude the 450 British soldiers stationed at Raʾs al-Tin, 99 percent of the 37,000 residents of the peninsula were local subjects.

In preparing for the 1907 census, legal authorities reconsidered the question of unforthcoming foreigners. Egypt had passed a census law stating that the whole of the information must be collected in a single pass, without refusals. The local government asked the Mixed Courts to impose penalties on those who avoided the census and arranged for census agents to collect information without entering foreign domiciles.[38] In the 1907 census, the district-by-district counts of foreigners were dropped; only literacy and religion were recorded on that fine scale. (Alexandria was divided into seventy-one districts this time around.) Perhaps for reasons of privacy, nationality was only reported in greater aggregations. The same is true of the 1917 census, which counted ninety-five districts in Alexandria. In this census, however, occupation information is broken down by nationality. Among Egypt's 13,849 beggars and prostitutes, for instance, census takers managed to find a Belgian man and a Belgian woman as well as a Spanish man and a Spanish woman; there were no Swiss beggars or prostitutes. The same census contains extremely detailed breakdowns by nationality of age cohorts, literacy, religion, language, birthplace, civil status, and the like, but always for the whole of the Egyptian territory rather than particular districts.

What questions did census takers ask? Little is known of the details of their data collection.[39] How would Mahri Hamawi, whose claim to protection is discussed in chapter 2, have answered the question "who are you?" Would he have self-identified by his nationality? What about Theodore Sava Joannides, who as we saw in the first pages of this book was denied the nationality he believed he possessed? It is impossible that all those identified as French or British held registration certificates; presumably some had already been refused consular protection. Did census takers ask for evidence? These unanswered questions are in many ways beside the point. The statistical accuracy of the census is less important than the rhetoric of the bureaucracies that produced it. The question of nationality categories warrants special attention in this regard, and it is the subject of the next section of this chapter.

National Taxonomies

The 1882 census was hardly the first to categorize Egypt's population by national type. The 1800 *Description de l'Egypte* distinguished between eight kinds of people: Egyptians, Turks, Arabs, Moors (i.e., Maghribis), Greeks, Syrians, Jews, and Europeans.[40] The 1848 census divided the population between those under local authority (*dakhil al-hukuma*) and those beyond government authority (*kharij al-hukuma*).[41] A contemporary study of the 1855 cholera epidemic differentiated between eleven categories: Europeans, Greeks, Armenians, Syrians, Copts, Israelites, Natives, Turks, Maghribis, Barbaris, and Blacks.[42] Whereas the eighteenth-century capitulations treated foreigners as communities of exception rather than individuals, in the 1882 Egyptian census it is the locals who are the crowd, while the foreigners are individuated by nationality.[43]

As we have seen, the 1882 census was characterized by uneven granularity. The largest cities were given cursory treatment, whereas the tiniest villages were enumerated in detail. The census makers adopted a parallel approach with respect to nationality. The greatest part of the population was blended into a homogeneous mass, which census takers rendered into an undifferentiated majority labeled "real Egyptians" (*misriyun asliyun* or "*Égyptiens proprement dit*"). Meanwhile, ten tiny minorities were carefully counted. In this way, the 1882 census grappled with tensions that characterized population description in the censuses to follow: Egypt's nomadic and transient population (primarily bedouin) could not be made to fit in the demographic scheme, and the place of Ottoman subjects and Sudanese—local but not Egyptian—was also obscure. Later censuses would struggle to account for local subjects of European origin (such as Greeks). These questions were not resolved until the 1917 census, and even then the resolution was not neat.[44]

The privileging of nationality, like that of sex, is purposeful: the census was an administrative tool guiding the state's understanding of its own jurisdiction. In some ways, the census was an index of the various authorities from whom individuals should request protection and of the partial surveys in which each individual should be identified. The pinnacle of the imbalance in granularity is the census breakdown of Egyptian population by nationality reproduced in table 4.4. Eleven different "nationality/settlement" categories are listed, of which "real" Egyptians form the vast majority and the rest mere fragments. In the words of the census makers,

TABLE 4.4 Nationality categories, 1882 census

Category		Proportion of the total population of Egypt
Settled Natives (*Muqimun*)		
"Real" Egyptians	*Misriyun asliyun / Égyptiens proprement dits*	92.70%
Residents of Ottoman origin	*Qatinun wa usuluhum ʿuthmaniyun*	0.42%
Sudanese	*Sudaniyun*	1.88%
Bedouins (ʿ*Urban*)		
Semisedentary	*Mukhalitun*	0.32%
Nomads	*Ruhhal*	3.29%
Foreigners (*Ajanib*)		
Greeks		0.55%
Italians		0.27%
French		0.23%
English		0.09%
Austro-Hungarians		0.12%
Other nationalities		0.08%

Note: Egypt, *Recensement général 1882*, sec. 2, 14.

"nomads and foreigners form a very small minority as against the dense mass of settled natives (*la masse compacte des Indigènes fixes*), who are the true people (*véritable population*) of Egypt."[45]

This distinction was the product of the census makers' prioritization of place over population. *Settlement* was the hallmark of a national population; bedouins and foreigners were anomalous because they were mobile. Egyptians were suitable for counting because they were tied to the land and isolated from other nations. Turkish and Syrian immigration having slowed, Europeans were now the principal immigrant group. Their "distinct social and political behavior (*al-mukhtalifiyin mashraban / situation sociale et politique à part*) prevent[ed] them being confused with the native population (*zumrat al-wataniyin*)," which was agrarian and sedentary.[46] The census makers claimed that this distinction was "social and political"; in reality, it was legal. Bedouins and foreigners were considered separately because they were exempt from the laws that ruled other subjects.[47]

The distinction between real Egyptians and all others made operative sense in terms of 1880s internal policy, according to which dangerous bedouins were to be taken under government control, foreigners were to be protected by their own authorities, and settled natives were to be taxed. Under the occupation, however, the divide between foreign and local became the decisive cleavage. This divide was most marked in the decennial censuses of 1907 and 1917, in which the social diversity of local nationals is more clearly designated. Local subjects were subdivided in the four censuses in question according to the schemes in table 4.5.

The 1897 census divided the local population much as it had been in 1882, but it dropped the Sudanese subcategory and set aside the categorical distinction between nomads and settled Egyptians. Sedentary, bedouin, and Ottoman were all clearly labeled as "real" Egyptians. Sudanese were reincorporated as a subcategory in 1907, while Ottoman nationals appeared for the first time as foreigners. This sea change was the result of changes in Ottoman nationality laws that will be detailed in chapter 11. As a result, four new non-native Egyptian types were introduced for persons with Ottoman roots but without Ottoman nationality: Turkish, Syrian, Arabian, and Armenian "locals." Even more subdivisions were employed ten years later, when the 1917 census distinguished Egyptians according to sect and added four further categories of origin (Berberi, Greeks, Jews, and "Other Races"). In 1882, 1897, and 1907, census makers offered

TABLE 4.5 Census taxonomy of locals, 1882–1917

1882	1897	1907	1917
"Real" Egyptians	Egyptians: settled natives	Egyptian sedentary	Egyptian Muslim non-Muslim
Bedouins Semisedentary Nomadic	Egyptians: Bedouins	Egyptian Bedawi	Bedouin
Those from other parts of the Ottoman Empire	Egyptians from other parts of the Ottoman empire	Turkish	Turkish
		Syrian	Syrian
		Arabian	Arabian
		Armenian	Armenian
Sudanese		Sudanese	Sudanese
			Berberi
			Greeks
			Jews
			Other races

an aggregate total of foreigners but no sum count of local subjects. Only in 1917, once it was divided a dozen ways, did "local" nationality emerge as a distinct, subdivided category given a cumulative population figure of its own.

Foreign taxonomy also expanded steadily over these decades. Five of the seventeen foreign nationalities counted in the 1882 census were classified as the "major communities" (*grandes colonies*): Greeks, Italians, French, Austro-Hungarians, and "English and British subjects." Joined by the newly foreign Ottomans after 1907, the nationalities listed in table 4.6 comprised the majority of Egypt's foreign population.

Although it was the first census to count Ottomans as foreign, the nationality typology of 1907 was otherwise restrained. It counted only twelve types of foreigners, as opposed to twenty-three in 1897 and

TABLE 4.6 Census taxonomy of major foreign nationalities, 1882–1917

1882	1897	1907	1917
Greeks	Greece	Greek	Greek
Italians	Italy	Italian	Italian Italians Egyptians Erythreans Greeks Jews Tripolitans Other races

English and
  British subjects
	Great Britain
	  Maltese
	  Indians
	  Army of Occupation Officers,
	  Non-Commissioned Officers,
	  Soldiers
	  Army of Occupation families,
	  women, children
		English
		  Maltese/colonial
			British
			  British
			  Egyptians
			  Australians
			  Canadians
			  Greeks
			  Indians
			  Jews
			  Maltese
			  South Africans
			  Other races

French	France
	  Algerians and Tunisians
		French
		  Algerian/Tunisian
			French
			  French
			  Egyptians
			  Algerians
			  Jews
			  Moorish
			  Syrians
			  Tunisians
			  Other races

Austro-Hungarians	Austria-Hungary	Austro-Hungary	Austro-Hungary

		Ottoman	Ottoman
			  Turks
			  Arabs
			  Armenians
			  Greeks
			  Jews
			  Syrians
			  Other races

fifty-three in 1917. These turbulent taxonomies show that nationality, both foreign and local, was a determination in flux in British-occupied Egypt. Census takers were uncertain about whether to define foreigners according to the narrower test of nationality law, which would unify each community under a single flag, or to define foreigners according to their social characteristics, which entailed counting the diversity within each nationality. The taxonomies of "minor" foreign nationalities display a different pattern, however.

The list in table 4.7 corresponds in large measure to the community of nations recognized under international law between the Congress of Berlin and the Treaty of Versailles. The small number of subjects of each of these states made further subdivision of little use. Instead, the presence of these minor nationalities in the census communicated an image of universality that served to normalize and substantiate the less coherent lists of major nationalities. Modularity depends in part on volume: the logic of nationality derives force from its repetition, even—perhaps especially—when the states making the claim are a negligible presence in empirical terms.

The danger of reproducing these incommensurate yet apparently modular national categories is illustrated in the demographic portrait that Michael Haag offers in his 2004 book on Alexandria. He writes that Alexandria

> was home to nearly half of all foreigners living in Egypt. About thirty thousand of these were Greek and twenty thousand Italian. . . . But citizenship and ethnic origin did not always coincide. About twenty-five per cent of all those who considered themselves ethnically Greek, for example, were not Greek citizens. With the outbreak of war, numbers of inhabitants who had been Ottoman subjects, including ethnic Greeks, Armenians, Syro-Lebanese and Jews, now found themselves stateless or were counted as Russians, Bulgarians, Persians, North Africans or Egyptians. Some foreign powers, the French especially in an effort to increase their influence in Egypt, sold or otherwise granted citizenship papers, while many British citizens were Maltese, Gibraltarians and Cypriots. Certainly in Alexandria the number of those who were not ethnically Egyptian was greater than the official citizenship figures indicated and amounted to something like a quarter to a third of the population.[48]

TABLE 4.7 Census taxonomy of minor foreign nationalities, 1882–1917

1882	1897	1907	1917
German	Germany	German	German
Russian	Russia Boukhariens, Khiviens, etc.	Russian	Russian
Belgian	Belgium		Belgians
Spanish	Spain		Spaniards
Portuguese	Portugal		Portuguese
Dutch	Holland		Dutch
Danish	Denmark		Danes
Swedish	Sweden and Norway		Swedes
			Norwegians
American	USA		US of America
Swiss	Switzerland		Swiss
Serbs, etc.			Servians
			Bulgarians
			Montenegrins
			Roumanians
		Other European nationalities	
Persians, etc.	Persia	Other nationalities	Persians
			Arabs of Arabia
			Abyssinians
	Other countries		All other and not stated nationalities

In this gloss of the 1917 census, Haag performs prose gymnastics to turn incoherent numbers into something resembling fluent description. Constant equivocation is necessary to this task ("nearly . . . about . . . not always . . . numbers of . . . some . . . something like"). Even more important is the insertion of two alien categories: citizenship and ethnicity. British subjects from Malta, Gibraltar, and Cyprus were not citizens, and "Egyptian ethnicity" is a truly elusive concept (is it about language, skin color, class, dwelling place, or what?). I have described nationality as pointillist, and this paragraph is also an exercise in pointillism. Here each dot of data ("half . . . thirty . . . Greek . . . ethnic . . . foreign . . . Egyptian . . . third") is untrustworthy when examined on its own, yet when the reader draws back, he or she has a sense of the paragraph's meaning. Thinking in terms of national (or citizenship or ethnic) categories is a habit of mind that fills ambiguities and empty spaces of the past with the patterns of the present. Haag recruits familiar national labels and a quantitative veneer ("something like a quarter to a third") to transform the implausible census into plausible prose. This remarkable passage manifests the allure of dividing a population into nationality categories that seem to possess some inherent validity. One effect of listing a large number of these categories as Haag does is to discourage critical probing of the substance of any one of these signals. As the changing schemes of the censuses show, modular nationality categories were arbitrary and experimental. Lending them the solidity of social description is unwarranted.

Social histories crave demographic baselines, and this book is no exception. If many historians express a healthy reserve about the numbers that they draw from the census, in most cases they adopt its categories wholesale. This chapter has argued that those categories are more interesting (and perhaps less reliable) than the numbers that censuses produce. Identification papers and the census—the means treated in the last two chapters—described two different kinds of nationality (and provide two different opportunities to misread identity labels). Census takers certainly elicited a genre of performance on polling day, but it was not the sort of calculated, nuanced performance that (as we saw in chapter 3) lay behind most individual claims to nationality. Of course, these two iterations of nationality were mutually constituting. But the judicial advantage that is the hallmark of foreignness under the Ottoman capitulations was not part of the lives of most of the foreigners of the census. These "foreigners" exercised another kind of foreignness, which was probably not restricted to their self-identification on census day.

The universal national censuses of the late nineteenth and early twentieth century propose the fledgling figure of the universally convertible human. But the censuses did not really treat individuals according to such terms; at least at first, some were counted much more carefully than others. Census takers employed a changing stock of categories, and the statistics that they produced were inconsistent. We see this, for example, in distinctions among types of Europeans and the lack of a similar distinction within the native population, presented as a faceless crowd. What was special about the national census was its pretense of comprehensivity; in this it was a key site of nationality's universal claim, which was made of precisely the same holey cloth. The census was a product of the state's appetite to centralize the certification of identity. As it assumed the role previously delegated to subsidiary authorities (producers of their own registers and partial surveys), its authorities began to elicit responses to questions about nationality that were both more specific and more modular.

Nationality—the status, not the sentiment—emerged as the result of two administrative vectors: universalization and the proliferation of specification (or even speciation) over time. The structures of data collection and reporting reveal much about administrators' thinking concerning nationality. Nationality was an administrative mode, a song pleasing to administrators' ears; the census form was one of nationality's cue sheets, a songbook from which the inhabitants of Egyptian territory learned to sing in the key of nationality. The philosopher Ian Hacking describes this process as an almost mystical transformation:

> National and provincial censuses amazingly show that the categories into which people fall change every ten years. Social change creates new categories of people, but the counting is no mere report of developments. It elaborately, often philanthropically, creates new ways for people to be. . . . People spontaneously come to fit their categories.[49]

In Egypt, the process was more mechanistic than this description suggests (and, critically, less complete). But censuses are sirens for social historians; their songs seduce us with numbers before smashing us against the rocks of their too-solid categories. So we should haul aboard what we can from this—description of two administrative trends, speciation and universalization—and sail on to safer waters, where we can continue our inquiry into how people identified themselves. The next two chapters discuss means that made the stakes of nationality utterly plain: money and marriage.

5
Money

In 1881, police arrested a fifteen-year-old native named Hassan ʿAli as he was running down Nabi Daniel Street, pursued by a Greek boy shouting "thief!"[1] The boy, who worked in a grocery store, accused Hassan of stealing cheese. When the police arrested Hassan, they found that he was carrying a mix of monies: a forged Spanish dollar (*riyal bi-midfaʿ*, marked by a cannon), a forged five-piaster coin, twenty-four single piasters, one standard ten-para piece, two pintos, a twenty-centime piece, and sixty single para pieces. (He was also carrying three pieces of hashish.) During his interrogation at the police station, Hassan was asked the origin of the counterfeit currency. He reported that the riyal was given him by a Greek near the port, as payment for his labor in the mill where he worked as a grain roaster. Hassan discovered that the coin was a fake only the next day. When he confronted the man who had given it to him, the Greek said it wasn't his, and Hassan left the matter to God because he could not prove it. The five-piaster piece, meanwhile, he had also taken as a fee, and it was only from the police that he learned it was counterfeit.

Hassan was charged for theft of the cheese but not for possession of counterfeit currency. "Coining" (the production of false money) and "uttering" (putting it into circulation) were crimes, but it appears that simple possession was not. Possession was a black mark, however: it proved that the possessor had been in contact with bad people. This sympathetic magic of possession was taken into account, as were prior convictions for theft, in framing new charges against Hassan: police recommended that he receive a harsh sentence to correct him and warn others.[2]

The diversity of coins in Hassan's possession is one issue of note in this case. He held a mixture of nationally coded and certified objects of value, manipulating them for his own purposes, uninfluenced by their nominal designation. This was a sort of vulgar cosmopolitanism: he was managing apparent diversity without interest or comment. But Hassan was not an expert on currency, and he lost out to those with superior knowledge because he could not identify the counterfeit. Even if he kept bad company, Hassan was no coiner himself. It took him some time to discover that the Spanish dollar was forged (presumably he found out when he tried to change it), and he never realized on his own that the five-piaster piece was a fake. As was the case with identification papers (and the deliberations that produced them), the detection of currency forgeries was the work of experts: experienced cashiers from the customs house and the tax administration were called as court witnesses to certify the counterfeit nature of coins.[3] One can assume that Hassan may have harbored some doubts about the coins; certainly he should have. In less monetized contexts, such as 1880s Sudan, we see generalized suspicion of newly introduced coins, and even inexpert users of coins in Alexandria did well to be alert.[4]

Anxiety about counterfeit and currency offers a hint about the ways that institutions perceived nationality. To official eyes, regimes of currency and nationality were kaleidoscopes: shifting mosaics made up of unalloyed essences. The day-to-day dance of different coins and nationals bewildered and confused, and officials were concerned to fix values and legal personalities in place. Furthermore, they were threatened by attempts to undermine the purity of these essences. Currency and official documents were symbols of official order, substitutes for economic value and administrative standing respectively. Both systems endowed an object—coins and identification documents, respectively—with powerful, abstract worth. In order for economic and nationality regimes to function, individuals had to honor these tokens. Both presented a complex spectrum of national types, plainly understood by those who used them but liable to confuse the present-day observer who focuses on type, rather than meaning or use. Both depended on popular cooperation and were subject to deceit. Those who challenged them challenged the roots of official order.

In this chapter, I develop this analogy between money and nationality. First, I describe the system of money that existed in Egypt, arguing that its similarities to the nationality system are not simply coincidences. I then look at coining and other kinds of currency tricks, which resemble identification fraud in numerous respects. I then discuss the legalized swindle of foreign moneylenders, who were the great villains in popular complaints about the capitulations, and show how the possibility to "forum shop" in inheritance and probate law created incentives for individuals to enroll in nationality.

Monetization in Egypt

Coins circulated in the Mediterranean and the Islamic world for millennia before the nineteenth century, but their use in Egypt was organized, standardized, and expanded as a result of the state reforms initiated by Mehmet Ali at the start of the nineteenth century. Different denominations assumed their place in the coin hierarchy organically. Until the middle of the eighteenth century, a gold coin (the *zer-i mahbub*) and a silver *fidda* (or *para*) were minted in Egypt. Because the difference in the value of these coins was vast, it became common practice to use a foreign currency, the *talari* or *riyal* (from the Austrian thalari and Spanish riyal), as

TABLE 5.1 Nineteenth-century currency denominations

Mid-nineteenth century				
talari		= 20 *qirsh*	gold	foreign minted
qirsh	piaster	= 40 *fidda*	silver	minted in Egypt
fidda	para		bronze	minted in Egypt
Late nineteenth century (after 1885)				
gunaih	pound	= 100 *qirsh*	gold	
talari or riyal	dollar	= 20 *qirsh*	silver	
qirsh	piaster tarif	= 40 *fidda*	silver [*sagh* and *darija*]	
fidda farda	para		bronze	

an intermediate denomination. In 1835, Mehmet Ali introduced a fourth denomination, the *qirsh* (piaster tarif), between the *talari* and the *fidda*.[5] As the *zer-i mahbub* fell out of use, the hierarchy of denominations changed.

When the value of silver declined after 1860, Egypt was unable to maintain the exchange rate between its domestically produced silver *qirsh* and the foreign gold *talari*. In 1885 Egypt abandoned silver and the bimetallic standard; henceforth it would produce its own gold *gunaih* (pound), which would be its denomination of account. It introduced a silver twenty-*qirsh* coin to replace the *talari*, maintained the silver *qirsh*, and renamed the *fidda* the 1/40 *qirsh*. The British pound was almost equal in value to the Egyptian gold pound and in far greater supply. Everyday currency after 1885, then, followed a new hierarchy. Values between *qirsh* and *fidda* were expressed as fractions of the *qirsh* (for example, *nisf qirsh*) or, less frequently, as multiples of the *fidda*. Ostensibly a rationalization and localization of the monetary system, the Egyptian currency reform of 1885 bears more than a passing resemblance to the Egyptian legal reform of 1876–1883. Despite the theory of a fresh start, in practice there was no great rupture. New currencies joined but did not supplant the old, and the fundamental dynamics of the previous system endured. Currency diversity was a practical response to a lingering money problem in Egypt: the lack of small currency. For much of the century, even the smallest denomination of coins on offer was too valuable for minor transactions, and residents of the city sought all means of instruments to make their exchanges.

The currency reform did not end currency diversity in Egypt, as various European currencies remained in circulation. European currencies were also being organized and standardized during this period. The basic unit of European currency was the franc, which was the standard currency of the Latin Monetary Union, which comprised France, Belgium, Italy, and Switzerland (from 1865), Spain and Greece (from 1868), and Romania, Austria, and several other states (from 1889). The largest European gold coin was the napoleon, or pinto, worth twenty francs. Five-franc silver coins were also in common use; these were often referred to as dollars (equivalent to the *riyal* and *talari*). Francs were divided into centimes, which were copper coins. Britain, Egypt's colonizing power, did not participate in the Latin Monetary Union, and its own currencies also circulated, the gold pound leading the way, and shillings and pence besides.

So: we have piasters, pounds, pintos, napoleons, francs, dollars, shillings, and thalers, all in a variety of denominations. Before we get caught up in the familiar fantasy of Alexandria's cosmopolitan mosaic, it is important to mention that currency diversity was a global phenomenon in the nineteenth century. The United States was the scene of strenuous administrative efforts to produce a "standardized national money" out of more than five thousand kinds of state- and private-issue banknotes in circulation.[6] The Latin Monetary Union was another such standardizing initiative. Indeed, the currency system displays the same modular character as the nationality system. Generic units, such as the Latin Monetary Union francs, were minted according to a standard weight, size, and value. Each member country minted its own variety, using its own language and iconography, according to the template. Thus we have the Spanish cannon, the German "Peter," and so on. Modularity can be understood through its exceptions, however. Here the critical exception is the Maria Theresa dollar, which was a prominent international currency. It was minted everywhere, using the iconography of late eighteenth-century Austria, but the coin was no longer used in Austria itself.

By the 1880s, monetized exchange was the major medium of exchange in Alexandria. The use of money was normal, banal, especially once large quantities of copper coins were in circulation. But it is clear that some used money more fluently and accurately than others. The variety of coins in circulation could create difficulties for newcomers, and counterfeiters and other tricksters used expert knowledge to prey on the innocent and the inexperienced. It must be said, however, that historians are in this case part of that group of innocents. A leading economic historian of the Middle East describes a confusing currency landscape in the nineteenth century: "A bewildering variety of coins were in use in the Middle East throughout the period, and in most cases their relative values were constantly changing."[7] While the present-day historian may struggle to make sense of currencies and transactions, the historical record offers a different view. Most actors appearing in court records, while bewildered by many procedures, were not bewildered by the diverse moneys in their purses. On the contrary, even the illiterate used and converted between various currencies with a fluency embarrassing to those, like us, who struggle to understand the system.

Again and again, the records reveal individuals who showed no "bewilderment." A Maltese man whose purse was emptied by the police was carrying

TABLE 5.2 Turn-of-the-century exchange rates of five common currencies

	Egyptian Pound	Piaster Tarif	British Pound	Franc	Talari (Dollar)
Egyptian Pound	1	100	1.025	25.92	5
Piaster Tarif	0.01	1	0.01	0.26	0.05
British Pound	0.975	97.5	1	25	5
Franc	0.04	3.86	0.04	1	0.20
Talari (Dollar)	0.20	20	0.20	5	1

five pounds and four shillings total, made up of four European currencies: one pound sterling, three and a half napoleons, two French five-franc pieces and five Maria Theresa dollars.[8] Another Maltese was arrested carrying two-franc pieces as well as dollars (*riyal*) classified as Spanish (*riyal bi-midfaʿ*, marked with a cannon), German (*riyal batira*), Ottoman (*riyal majidi*), and French (five franc: *riyal cinqo*).[9] When Aly al-Khuli, a local, was attacked by his Algerian creditor, he was carrying pounds, francs, dollars, and piasters in his galabiya.[10] This diversity gives an idea of what was taken as valuable and worth carrying. And complex purses were not the only area in which parties to the court showed striking financial fluency: frequent litigation between petty lenders and debtors reveals another dimension of the economic acumen of ordinary people in late nineteenth-century Alexandria.

Currency diversity shows how vulgar cosmopolitanism worked. Diverse coins coexisted in a single pocket without any sense of blurred or alloyed identities. Each of the coins was a *known* type. Their users were not confused, and when they mixed coins in transactions, they were not blurring boundaries or living dual monetary lives. There was nothing romantic about their exchanges. They simply held many different kinds of coins and knew how to use them. The connection that I am drawing between coins and nationality is not only metaphorical. The relationship is in fact one of analogy. Monetary and nationality reforms benefited elites and institutions in much the same ways by clarifying terms of impersonal exchange. And those who sought to subvert coins and identification documents, the symbols of value on which these reforms depended, made authorities anxious in precisely the same ways.

Counterfeit Anxiety and Nationality

Counterfeiters were treated severely in turn-of-the-century Alexandria. At a time when thefts and assaults were punished with a few months or weeks of detention, counterfeiters received one, two, three, or even ten years of hard labor. Although counterfeit and forgery accounted for only a handful of the thousands of cases I examined, it is clear that these practices were the occasion for special anxiety for legal authorities. This anxiety forms a part of the larger story of the rise of nationality as a means of legal and social identification. In 1880, a Maltese man named Antonio Magri (a recidivist and informant), when arrested for using counterfeit two-franc coins to purchase four dozen quails, claimed that he had received the coins as change for a napoleon from a liquor shop in Hamamil, where Rue des Soeurs meets Muhammad Ali Square.[11] Police already suspected Magri of bad character, but they also suspected that the shop, owned by a Greek, was a source of false coins. The bedouin quail seller, as well as the porter who carried the quails for the buyer, were key to the investigations. Although these men were illiterate and not even in possession of a seal (an essential tool for any paper transactions), they understood the game immediately. The quail seller discovered that the two-franc coins were counterfeit when he took them to a changer (*sarraf*) in order to get piasters (a more widely accepted coin in his circles, presumably, though he himself accepted the francs). He called on the authorities and won the prosecution of a foreign subject (showing once again that the conventional wisdom about foreign immunity in Egypt is false).

Magri was an ongoing source of trouble. The following year, he was arrested again, this time for buying shoes with false coins. He led police to his source, Sebastiano Scaffili, an Italian carpenter who had produced the counterfeit. The police urged the British consulate to prosecute their Maltese subject, arguing that he had conspired with the Italian (*nazir itti-hadahu*) in the "production and circulation of false coin" (*istina' wa tasrif al-'umla al-barrani*).[12] Magri was prosecuted rapidly and sentenced to three years of penal servitude and deportation from Egypt. This was his fourth conviction in three years for "uttering false coin"; the three previous convictions were six months each. Magri, who was eventually stripped of British protection, continued to cause trouble for the consulate until the end of the century.

Whereas genuine coins are stamped using industrial machines, counterfeit coins were made by pouring molten metal into a mold. In many
cases, this metal was then given a silver or golden veneer. The production
of convincing false coins was an elaborate process, requiring time, skill,
space, and tools. In February 1882, police searched the home of a Maltese
man accused of theft. In addition to the stolen property they sought, they
found materials for coining: yellow and black powder for the forms, bel-
lows, pieces of zinc, one false piaster (*qirsh sagh barrani*), and something
called "kicke Acqua forte" (*juz² ma² nar*). The puncheon was set for coining
Egyptian silver piasters. The fact that these items were found at his residence (*mahall niyamihi*), along with his bad reputation and antecedents,
were enough for the court to sentence him to three years in prison.[13]

Because counterfeiting was skilled work, recidivism was common. In
January 1883, Pietro Gameo was arrested for counterfeiting for (at least)
the third time.[14] He was homeless at the time, and an acquaintance gave
him a place to work only after much pleading. The police burst in twenty
minutes after he started work, as he was leaning over a crucible in the
kitchen. Investigation was held up when police discovered Gameo was
Maltese—they had mistakenly brought a janissary from the Italian consulate and were forced to wait for a British representative to arrive before
searching the premises. When they did, they found a considerable store of
coins: large quantities of Italian half-francs dated 1867, Greek half-francs
dated 1874, shillings dated 1878, and Turkish piasters tarif dated 1277 (i.e.,
from the reign of Sultan Abdul Aziz) and 1293 (Abdulhamid II). They also
found stamps with changeable chalk (gypsum) molds used to make the
coins. Gameo was sentenced to ten years of hard labor, and his unfortunate
host received a sentence of eight years (later reduced to two).

Five years later, another Maltese recidivist was caught in the act. Seven
officers burst into his home, running upstairs past his wife to find him trying to escape through a window. In his pipkin they found half-baked Egyptian five-piaster coins. He also had counterfeit Italian half-francs dated
1866 in his purse. Constanti Ferrari, the Italian policeman who arrested
him, knew of five previous arrests, for false dollars, "colomata," two-franc
pieces, and shillings. His sentence, one year of hard labor, was light considering his recidivism, but it is clear that his was a small-scale operation.[15]

The small scale of counterfeiting in Alexandria—coining for private use, by individuals rather than gangs—contrasts sharply with the

situation described in Eric Tagliacozzo's study of counterfeit currency in English/Dutch colonial Southeast Asia. He shows evidence of village coin factories producing tens of thousands of pieces of counterfeit money that circulated through Asia in the 1880s and 1890s.[16] Coining was not a big business in Alexandria. In 1887, police convinced a local subject whom they arrested carrying false coins to lead them to the source: Vincenzo Buhagiar, a Maltese tobacconist on Ibrahim Street.[17] Buhagiar, a recidivist known to police, gave the local subject thirteen of the newly introduced ten-piaster pieces in return for thirteen francs. Like most of the counterfeiters who appeared in court, Buhagiar was a small-time operator. He told the man buying coins that these thirteen were all he had but offered to sell him more eventually. In Alexandria, small-time coiners poured out a few coins at a time. In this instance, thirteen ten-piaster pieces for thirteen francs was not a huge return on investment: 130 false piasters for the equivalent of fifty-two genuine piasters. The return of roughly seventy-five piasters, less expenses, was the equivalent of a day's wages for a skilled laborer.[18]

Coining was subversive trickery, not big business. In 1888, Buhagiar was up to more mischief. A "native peasant" (*fallah*) named Muhammad Abu Shara of Damanhur reported to police that a bedouin (*ibn ʿarab*) stranger had engaged him in conversation in the street. While they talked, Buhagiar passed by and dropped his purse. When the bedouin picked up the purse, Buhagiar accused both men of suspicious activity and insisted on searching the peasant. The peasant agreed, and Buhagiar took a variety of coins from him—a pound, a gold napoleon (*bintu dhahab*), and silver coins worth one pound—saying that he would examine them to see if they were his. He then returned the coins, wrapped in paper, and sent Muhammad on his way. When the unfortunate man opened the paper, he found that it contained only three and a half copper piasters. He immediately alerted police, who captured the fleeing Buhagiar but failed to find his bedouin accomplice. In this case, we see Buhagiar playing another money game, preying on the uncertainties of a man from out of the city—the sort of stranger described in chapter 1. The peasant, though naïve enough to allow himself to be searched, knew exactly the value of the varied currencies he carried, rapidly realized the nature of the trick, and responded effectively. This confidence game was often repeated. Theft of purses was one of the most frequent types of petty cases treated in the limited available records of the Alexandria police from the early 1880s.[19] As we will see in chapter 10, other swindlers used false promises of alchemy and magic.[20]

Counterfeit was a shared concern—when a British subject (a previous informant) was charged with counterfeiting in 1880, the governor of Alexandria wrote to the consulate requesting that they drag the names of other counterfeiters out of him.[21] In correspondence, local authorities put a special emphasis on the crime: it was among the worst crimes. Consulates responded with draconian sentences. But the men just described can only be considered petty criminals, especially compared to the tyrants and murderers around them in the courts and prisons. Why were the states so concerned about a few false coins?

Their concern had two aspects. First, coining was a principal mark of "bad subjecthood," an administrative and moral category discussed at length in chapter 10 that emerged at a time when authorities were working to identify the whole population. The technical Arabic term for counterfeit, *muzayyafa* and its variants, was used infrequently in legal records. The commonly used adjective for false coins was *barrani*, meaning "outside, outer, exterior, external; foreign, alien."[22] Once again, the money/nationality simile is not merely metaphor: the same term was used for foreigners. Coiners lost their national protection, their legal personality, because they refused to abide by the rules. They were condemned to the purgatory of bad subjecthood. A second source of state anxiety was the fiction of the state's monopoly on power, in this case the power to circulate symbols of value. The state felt the same anxiety over its classification of land, mobility, and the state affiliation of persons through the census, the cadastral survey, and identification documents.

The counterfeit fear peaked in the 1880s, and prosecutions dwindle in the court records after that point. It may be that counterfeit cases were transferred to another administrative division, the records of which I have not discovered. It may be that the currency reform of 1885 was effective in standardizing money. The variety of currencies in use may have diminished to the point that producing counterfeits was far more difficult because users were more familiar with the narrower range. Unification of currency certainly shifted the tables against small-time coiners, who exploited diversity and thrived in an environment in which only experts could tell cheats. Even decades later, however, the anxiety had not entirely disappeared, and it retained its cosmopolitan character. In 1910, the Japanese embassy raised concerns that its bank's notes were being counterfeited in Egypt.[23]

But if authorities show marked anxiety about the act of counterfeiting, they show a remarkable *lack* of anxiety about certain other dimensions of currency use in Egypt. For instance, authorities were not particularly bothered by alchemy cases and those who subverted the metallic value of money. But more significantly, there is no sign of currency chauvinism: although coins bear clear national identification marks, these marks were insignificant to honest users, counterfeiters, and states alike. The literature on nationalism argues for the importance of specificity in national symbolism—Hobsbawm called money the "most universal form of public imagery," in the invention of tradition—but this does not seem to have been true in the case of Alexandrian counterfeit currency.[24] Viviana Zelizer has shown that money is not generic or standardized by nature.[25] As we have seen, coins (like persons) were not always modular or fungible. Often, those with local knowledge could trace coins to the last hands that held them, objects to the person who made them, and persons to their home place or to those who held authority over them. The knowledge to recognize an individual by his or her own character and personality was not accessible to outsiders, who had to depend on official marks.

Foreign Moneylending and Inheritance

Foreign moneylenders were the great villains of the capitulations. The Ottoman nationality policy that emerged during and after the 1860s was largely a response to fears and panics about men such as the Damascus moneylender protégés who in the 1870s ruined whole villages under the protection of their consulate.[26] But those men were tricksters and outlaws and were dealt with like counterfeiters and alchemists. Nationality law also created a legitimate space for private investors of foreign nationality to exploit legal personality to win advantage over those with less knowledge and power. Here we turn from illegal to legal activity, and the relationship between money and nationality moves from the metaphorical to the concrete. Everyday uses of money in the streets of Alexandria were key sites of state intervention. Money brought nationality into the lives of ordinary people by confronting them with judicial institutions that supported the wealthier population, which put money at the heart of its interactions with nationality. Their use of money to make money through the alchemy of interest was legal, and those with nationality used their legal powers to gain advantages over those without.

The Mixed Tribunals, founded in 1876, were the major site of foreign privilege in the domain of money. In economic terms, they were by far the most important site of legal work in Egypt, and foreign access to the institution was an acquired and (until the 1930s) largely uncontested right. These courts handled all commercial and most civil litigation involving people or capital of more than one nationality. In this jurisdictional definition, nationality operates as a generic rather than a specific characteristic: any two nationalities would do, and all mixed nationality had the same quality. In many ways, once litigants had access to the Mixed Tribunals, it became a legal space free of nationality. Of course, the price of admission was possession of a nationality.

The Mixed Tribunals await their historian, but the consular court records reveal something of the character of Egypt as a land of opportunity for investors and exploiters who used nationality as a business tool. Many property or inheritance dossiers that passed through the consular courts show parallel processes of litigation before the Mixed Tribunals. While inheritance was typically a national prerogative, the consular courts were only a weak auxiliary in property disputes, which were almost always settled before the Mixed Tribunals.

From time to time, however, probate cases offer glimpses of the ways that foreigners enjoyed the privileges of profit making under the rule of law in Egypt. When John Keill died in 1912, his petty lending estate was laid bare in probate proceedings before the British consular court.[27] From an office in the village of Shubra Khit, near Disuq and Damanhur, Keill lent small sums to hundreds of Egyptians living nearby. He had houses in Alexandria and Liverpool. His estate (shared by his wife and eight sons) amounted to almost eight thousand pounds, making it one of the largest probate settlements the court saw during that decade. Keill's debtors were more than four hundred in number. All but a handful came from five villages near Shubra Khit: Cheberece, Mahallat Farnowah, Kafr Mustanad, Mahalassa, and Mehallat Sase. As table 5.3 shows, the median loan was about five hundred piasters tarif, or about five pounds.

TABLE 5.3 Debts to John Keill estate, 1912, in piasters tarif

Status	Number	Mean	Median	Low	High	Total	Discounted
Good	357	1,784	463	23	52,500	644,424	644,424
Doubtful	131	2,125	902	11	36,349	287,483	143,741
Bad	13	1,417	685	125	6,513	18,724	0
Apostolides	1					£7,843	£400

Note: There are some discrepancies between my calculations and those of the probate file.

Keill's small loans are particularly remarkable: three dozen loans of under one hundred piasters, most of them classified "good" (though it was "doubtful" whether the estate would recover the eleven piasters owed by "Sud Ahd el Munawke" of Mahalassa). At the other end of the scale was the fortune of almost eight thousand pounds—equal to his total worth at death—that Keill lost to the firm of Messrs. Apostolides Frères in the investment bubble that burst in the half decade before his death. In probate, this investment was discounted 95 percent to only four hundred pounds. It seems that his petty loans were more secure, and his estate would have been wealthier had he not engaged in other forms of lending.[28]

Keill "got away" with his moneylending advantage. Like the rest of the users of the Mixed Tribunals, he enjoyed clear privilege through his access to capital and to legal personality. Not every foreigner made money in Egypt, of course. Especially during the period of the financial crisis in 1907, the courts saw many cases of bankruptcy, financial chicanery, and even of bankruptcy-induced suicide.[29] This question of access was not so clear in the case of inheritance. Inheritance was generative of nationality, as potential heirs sought to find paths to claim wealth large and small.

When Antun Yussuf ʿAbd al-Massih died in Cairo in February 1885, his will assigned his immense fortune of half a million pounds to his wife, Ellen. A Chaldean Catholic, Antun was born in Baghdad. He was thus an Ottoman subject by birth. For the last decades of his life, however, he lived in Egypt. There, he registered as a British protégé, and his widow took his probate to the British consular court, his usual tribunal, in October 1885. Five years of high-powered and high-priced litigation ensued, as Antun's sisters Angela and Cecilia challenged their brother's will and the jurisdiction of the probate court.

At the core of this litigation was a debate over jurisdiction. The widow argued that Antun was a British subject and that his estate should be disposed according to the formulation of his will, namely accorded to his wife. The sisters argued that Antun was an Ottoman subject and that probate jurisdiction belonged to the Ottoman state, which applied Islamic law of the Hanafi school to personal-status cases. This law stipulated that the testator could not leave more than a third of his or her estate to "strangers" (such as a widow) without the consent of blood heirs (such as the sisters).

The case proceeded from the Cairo and Alexandria British consular courts (February 24, 1886) to Britain's Supreme Consular Court in Constantinople (May 28, 1886) and eventually to the Privy Council in London (March 17, 1888).[30] This series of hearings considered the question of jurisdiction; finally, the Privy Council decided that in Antun's case, "the law of Turkey governing the succession of a member of the Chaldean Catholic Community domiciled in Turkey [should] be followed." But which law was that, precisely? A new round of litigation began treating this question. Now the widow's lawyers argued that although Antun was an Ottoman subject, jurisdiction in his case followed his personal status and belonged to the Chaldean Church. In this case, the will would also be considered valid. This interpretation led to competing claims between the Egyptian branch of the church, which automatically received 5 percent of any estate under its jurisdiction, and the Baghdad church, which received "what the family could afford to give." In the end, the case was settled, by binding arbitration, largely in favor of the sisters.[31] By this time, lawyers' fees had absorbed some 25,000 pounds sterling.[32]

Ironically, all of these arguments were again heard by the British consular courts, despite the sole conclusion of the first round—that the British courts did *not* have jurisdiction over Antun's estate. In the context of empire, European justice systems often moved to endorse and canonicize non-European law. The French justice system made such efforts in the Mediterranean context. But the Ottoman law that the British courts engaged in Antun's case had apparently already been codified in a Europeanized form during the third quarter of the nineteenth century.[33] Why did such vast ambiguity remain? And why was the British consular court the venue at which such questions should be decided?

The answer to these questions is outside the scope of this chapter, and the case of Antun Yussuf ʿAbd al-Massih certainly deserves a careful, detailed study of its own.[34] A number of observations serve our purposes, however. First, it is clear that despite the vast nineteenth-century expansion of codified law in the Ottoman Mediterranean, the principle that a single state held authority over a single individual had not been established. When large sums of money were at stake, as in Antun's case, lawyers had no trouble questioning exclusive national affiliation. The arguments deployed in the case show that the lawyers found many ways to argue the question. The new formulations of nationality were a puzzle, not a settlement, and this case revealed many of the inconsistencies of the emerging system.

Second, this case shows that courts of European imperial states (notably Britain and France) were preferred venues for jurisdictional litigation. This preference was the result of the authority and enforcement power of these strong states, rather than the regularity of their laws. Antun's case, settled in arbitration by the British justice system, had nothing to do with British law. Despite the venue in which it was delivered, however, the conclusion of this case was that an Ottoman subject could not become a member of the British community in Alexandria purely "so as to attract to himself English law."[35] But the principle asserted by the court—that nationality and protection meant more than mere legal convenience—had long been a fiction for many bourgeois protégés in Alexandria.

Nationality games began with the dead. If the nationality of Keill was always clear, often death was a moment for reclassifying bodies (such as those of Antun and of Hampson, in chapter 3) that had already been objectified through a legal process. There are numerous (but less lucrative) similar examples from various other courts. In the decades that followed, arguments over national classification of individuals moved on to the living, however, and came to involve those who could not be fixed in national space as easily or permanently as could an interred corpse. The agency of the living created problems, certainly, but the settlement marched ever forward in its effort to answer two interrelated questions: who gets which nationality, and what is that nationality worth?

Money—as wealth and as currency—was a medium for the spread of nationality in Alexandria. The wealthy were the earliest adopters of nationality practices such as the use of passports for travel and the acquisition of foreign protection. Poor foreigners, meanwhile, were a burden on foreign communities and consular authorities. This chapter examined official concern over forged currency, which was connected both figuratively and literally to institutional certification of personality through identification documents.

Money provided the content for many of the legal struggles through which nationality spread in late nineteenth-century Alexandria. It was not merely an occasion for grasping nationality, however. Money created occasions for individuals to discover and begin to practice nationality. This was not only a metaphorical relationship. The same administrators and the same subjects were working with money and with nationality at the same time. The legal system defended money and the systems that used it. Monetization advanced through the lenders we met. By the same gesture, the lenders advanced the logic of nationality. Money was a means to display the material advantages attached to affiliation with states. The regimes that defended lenders, in turn, showed that nationality was a critical means of access to adjudication. Those working with money had every reason to inscribe themselves into nationality.

6
Marriage

Nationality was a gendered practice. Women changed nationality more often than men. Conversion of nationality occurred most often through marriage: the principle that women followed the status of their husbands was endorsed by all authorities. Because some nationalities were more useful than others, marriage litigation became a leading means to test the theory of commensurate nationalities. Women who preferred the nationality of their fathers to that of their husbands (or vice versa) attempted to exercise choice of nationality at critical junctures: widowhood, remarriage, parenthood, separation, divorce. Was coverage permanent, or did the husband's power to determine his wife's status last only as long as their marriage?

As means through which nationality grasped and was grasped, money and marriage share several similarities. Nationality and money and women were controlled substances, subject to special attention and anxiety, especially in colonial contexts. Money and marriage were the leading themes in private international legal scholarship, in litigation, and in the individual practice of nationality.[1] Inheritance and marriage were occasions for sectarian law to confront state law, especially in places like Alexandria, where lawyers were well versed in jurisdiction conflict. But the moral shading of marriage revealed nationality problems that money did not. Paternalist work to protect "vulnerable" women, to control bigamy and miscegenation, at times occasioned episodes of rough justice that showed how gender control could be a stronger imperative than nationality jurisdiction.

The rule of colonial difference was meant to protect the strong, not the weak, and the perceived vulnerability of women and minors was a problem for the emerging system of nationality, which grudgingly granted them certain civil and social rights. Universalizing legal personality was a nationality project, and it was also a gender project. As we have seen, women and children figured as anonymous and subsidiary figures in most censuses. Covered by the male head of household, they were present as numbers but not as names, and their legal personality was latent. Women's nationality became active only in the absence of a male protector. In colonial societies, imperial governments, and nationalist movements alike, women were likewise empty signifiers.[2] At the same time, they were centers of administrative anxiety.[3] This pattern applied to nationality's development in British Egypt, in which marriage was the driving wheel of nationality litigation and legislation.

This chapter examines the cascading problems that marriage created for the theory of sound, commensurate, discoverable nationality. The first section shows how litigation over betrothal, separation, divorce, and maintenance offered an occasion for individuals to discover the usefulness of choice of law and thus to integrate nationality into their self-identification. The second section shows how the acquisition of nationality through marriage, typically a straightforward and relatively objective procedure, could be complicated on some occasions. The third section pursues this theme, considering cases of what I will call "nationality miscegenation." The fourth section, on bigamy, concerns doubts about the legitimacy of nationality produced by marriages of dubious legal legitimacy. The closing section returns to questions of secular and religious law, showing how under the sign of marriage, Protestant, Catholic, Islamic, and Jewish laws could conflict and cooperate with the state laws of various authorities in Alexandria.

Choice of Law and Nationality

Esther Gandour and Jacob Malca were fluent litigants. During interminable separation, divorce, and alimony proceedings between 1889 and

1912, they invoked status as French citizens, Algerians, Tunisians, protégés, and imperial subjects. They conducted parallel litigation at the French consular courts (including an appeal to Aix), the Mixed Tribunals (where Jacob was an *employé*), and the Jewish courts. Although their saga is exuberant, it represents much of the normal business of the courts. Esther and Jacob were not looking to duck or to change or to embrace their nation; they were merely grasping the tools that nationality offered them.

Jacob Malca was born in Tunis in 1853. He acquired French nationality through his father, Haim, who was Algerian. Haim registered with the Alexandria consulate in 1869, having lived in Tunis for at least a decade beforehand.[4] Esther was born in 1866 in Alexandria to parents of two prominent Jewish families.[5] She became a French national when she married Jacob in April 1888.[6] The marriage was not a success. She first took her estranged husband to court in May 1889, winning a "pension" of one hundred francs per month.[7] He failed to attend a second session later that year and suffered an adverse judgment as a result.[8] When he appeared in January 1890 (this time with a lawyer), he was identified as a Tunisian protégé.[9]

Three hearings in the year that followed settled the terms of their separation.[10] Esther had brought a dowry (*dot*) of twenty thousand francs to the marriage. She wanted it returned and wanted to maintain the hundred-franc monthly pension. Jacob argued that Esther had abandoned him and committed infidelity. He refused to accept her back in his home. According to Judaic law, he argued, he did not owe her anything. He was, however, willing to pay her six thousand francs. Esther argued that it was he who had forced her out and that Judaic law did not apply.

The couple finally divorced in June 1896.[11] At this point, his monthly payment to her was reduced to fifty francs per month. The payments were adjusted several times in the years that followed. In 1905, with the pension now at seventy-five francs per month, Jacob sought a reduction. He reported that he was earning 325 francs monthly, of which 16f went to retirement, 66f to pay debts, and 75f to his ex-wife. This left only 168 francs for his current wife and their child. Payments were halved.[12] In 1909, he returned to request another reduction. His salary was now 13 pounds per month, less 65f for retirement, but he had more children and more expenses.[13] In 1912, they returned to the court again. Esther was now identified as a French citizen, a *rentier*, living with her brother at a good address on Rue de Rosette.[14]

Their case illustrates the limited scope of forum shopping after the legal reforms. In an attempt to create a nationality distinction between himself and his wife, for example, Jacob attempted to argue that the case should be heard by the Mixed Tribunals. This argument was rebuffed by the Cour d'appel d'Aix, which returned the case to the consular court of Alexandria. By 1912, we see two individuals with the potential to exercise diverse legal personalities who have chosen to settle for a single nationality. Accommodation and conformity was imposed on them by an appeals court, but they seem also to have accepted its terms. This may be because, in their case as in many others, consular laws of marriage seem to have managed disputes to the relative satisfaction of both European litigants and their imperial subjects.

Maltese marriages governed by British law were also a site for litigants to explore legal difference and choice of law. Because the Maltese (almost all of whom were Roman Catholic) did not practice legal divorce, estranged wives were successful in making claims on the estates of deceased husbands, even after decades of separation and subsequent remarriages.[15] Explicit claims to Maltese nationality intensified whenever Britain modified its personal-status laws. There was a marked increase in the number of separation and maintenance cases following passage of the Summary Jurisdiction (Married Women) Act of 1895, which simplified existing separation procedures and brought legal remedies within reach of middle-class families.[16] As we will see in the next chapter, Alexandria's Maltese were creative advocates for their distinct status. In a 1907 separation case, the husband (unsuccessfully) challenged the jurisdiction of the court, claiming that Maltese laws should be used.[17] Another male defendant made similar claims the next year, writing that the Married Women Act "by the way, does not apply to my case, as I am a Maltese by birth, subject to the laws of my personal status enacted by the Legislative Council of Malta and sanctioned by the Crown."[18] The British consular court showed its willingness to accommodate uniquely Maltese law by entertained a series of lawsuits to recover damages as a result of broken marriage promises, which was a particular Maltese concern.[19] Like Esther and Jacob, many Maltese who availed themselves of consular legal services found nationality a useful tool to settle marriage disputes according to laws of their choosing.

Acquisition of Nationality Through Marriage

During the early years of the British occupation, consulates were relatively lenient in extending foreign nationality to locals through marriage. Cases that would not pass scrutiny in later years were tolerated in the 1880s and 1890s. In 1891, for example, an Algerian living in Tanta applied for a registration certificate (for the first time in his life) on the same day that he married a local woman. When he died three weeks later, his wife requested French protection. The Alexandria dragoman informed her that she was only eligible for protection if she had children with her husband. She then wrote to inform the consulate that she was pregnant. Consular documents noted that she was a singer (*chanteuse*), a profession that was subject to innuendo, and it seems clear that the timing of the husband's request and marriage and the wife's pregnancy intrigued the consular staff. Nevertheless, having not yet developed rigorous practices of exclusion, they granted the woman her certificate of protection.[20]

The consulates were not universally permissive, however. The French consulate was concerned that widows, especially relatively young ones, would remarry local subjects but drift along under the protection of their first husbands. In 1881, when another local-born widow of an Algerian asked for a certificate, the dragoman made a note on her dossier cover: "Before giving her a new card, ensure that she has not remarried to a local subject."[21] The consulate must have pursued this question, for the widow presented them with a certificate of nonmarriage (duly preserved in her dossier). Consular surveillance provided an incentive for such women to stay unmarried or to remarry foreigners. Nationality was a controlled quality, and it could only be transferred under certain circumstances.

Decades later, in 1912, a widow of irregular nationality found her consulate less willing to go along with her strategic manipulation of nationality. Anissa Solal had for decades believed herself to be a Tunisian French subject, by virtue of her marriage to Nessim Rahmin Benrubi, who had been born in Sfax. After the death of her husband, however, she found that he had neglected to register with the consulate. Consular efforts to trim its lists of foreign subjects after the turn of the century disqualified him (and her) from protection; now she "could only be considered an Ottoman subject." (As we will see in subsequent chapters, foreign nationality could be lost through inactivity, with Tunisians assigned Ottoman nationality as a status of last resort.) All through her marriage to Nessim, then, Anissa had been a local subject. In an ironic twist, however, his death offered her another nationality resource to fall back on: her father, Yussuf Cohen Solal, had been Algerian. Under French law, French subjects received the nationality of their husbands, but the Ottoman nationality law of 1869 did not allow for the transfer of nationality to a wife. As a result, Anissa was duly registered as a protected Algerian subject, the nationality of her father.[22]

Anissa's escape from her husband's nationality was a rarity. Foreign and local authorities' consensus on one clear area of dominion—men over women—proved difficult to oppose. The frustrating inconsistencies of nationality could be elided by reference to the clear code of gender domination. Consider another Algerian woman's attempt to use nationality as a weapon in her divorce. Her husband, Raphaël Ben Lassine, was registered with the consulate as a French-administrated Algerian (*administré français en qualité d'algérien*). In 1908, he asked the French consul to apply the 1870 Crémieux decree (by which Algerians could become French citizens), and the consul agreed that Raphaël could become a citizen.[23] Raphaël's dossier in the registry of Algerians shows that he collected an identity certificate every year from 1891 to 1904.[24] Why did this consistent pattern of exemplary conformity to subjecthood regulations change? Why would he seek to become a citizen only in his late forties? We do not know, but in 1914, as part of a broader effort to win a favorable divorce settlement, Raphaël's wife, Esther, asked the French consular court to downgrade her husband's nationality status from citizen to subject.[25]

The basis of her argument and the advantage that she wished to gain are not made clear in the case record. The court took her case seriously but rejected her claim. It decided that the consul's 1908 decision was the correction of a previous error, which had made Raphaël a subject (*administré*) rather than a citizen. This ruling illustrates the dynamics of nationality law as practiced by the consular courts. First, it shows how marriage was often the catalyst that activated nationality. Second, it shows that jurisdiction offered the means to protect those of superior status. In the same lines that upheld Raphaël's citizenship, the court also ruled that it was incompetent to judge the case. Underlining the split between citizen and subject, it said that administrative authority (that is to say, the law that concerns *administrés*) cannot supersede civil authority, which controls the civil and personal status of citizens. Although the consular tribunal could uphold the consul's view, it was not competent to dig into the legal details of the administrative decision itself; for that, one must appeal to the Conseil d'État. Reference to this remote tribunal served to bolster protection for citizens while decreasing subjects' access to justice.

In another characteristic twist, the court fired a nonlegal Parthian shot, after all legal questions had apparently been settled. This move underlines its weakness as a *legal* institution. After ruling that it was incompetent to hear the case, the tribunal nevertheless added its opinion that the major evidence in the husband's favor was the fact that he had exercised citizenship for six years without his wife protesting. If Esther has now changed her mind, the judgment reads (a bit sarcastically), she could appeal her case before a competent tribunal, not them. Oddly, the court seemed to imply that citizenship could be determined on subjective grounds, such as her protest or lack of protest, rather than its own objective criteria. The court then noted two criteria of citizenship: having one's name on the list of voting French notables (an entirely circular criterion) and allowing one's son to be signed up for conscription and called to France for military service. Esther had been put in her place.

Nationality Miscegenation

Nationality provided a reason and a means for the global effort of white men to save white women from brown men and even to save certain brown women from certain white men.[26] One evening in January 1883, a Muslim woman named Haniya bint ʿAli Bakr went for a walk in Khatt al-ʿAttarin. She encountered an Italian named Antonio Simoni, who worked nearby. He had seen her many times before, and when he invited her to come with him to his house in Hamamil she agreed. When her brother found her four days later, Haniya did not want to leave Antonio. He also wanted to marry her. The Italian consular court brought charges against him. After a police investigation, in which she repeated her wish to continue to live with him and to marry him, Haniya was sent to the Egyptian prosecutor and remanded in preventative custody.[27] Prosecution of both parties was typical in such cases whenever mixed nationality was involved.[28]

One of the new tools that state authorities produced through their monopoly on jurisdiction was the refusal to recognize certain kinds of marriages. In 1912, amid a generalized panic in Egyptian law enforcement about the "white slave trade," Major A. Gordon Ingram, the inspector of the public security division of the Alexandria police, set the familiar fear of brown men in a new context.[29] He reported that Mohamed Amin Rifaat Zada, who already had three wives, had married an English girl (Laura) in London and was bringing her back to Alexandria.[30] "I am told by the husband . . . that he merely married her in order to have an English son."[31] This hypothesis did not make sense in legal terms—children did not follow the nationality of their mothers, husbands did not follow the nationality of their wives, and fathers did not follow the nationality of their sons. But Ingram's concern was for the English girl, who would lose her British protection and be left "to the mercy of [her husband] and the local Religious Law Courts." To enhance his claim, Ingram generalized this particular case, stating that seven hundred Egyptian students in England were trying to marry English women and bring them back to Egypt.[32] Such marriages meant a transition from secular to religious law: "the worst aspect of a marriage with an Egyptian Moslem is that the English wife loses her British nationality, and is at the mercy of her husband's caprice in the matter of divorce."[33]

In his response to Ingram's initiative, Donald Cameron, the British consul-general of Alexandria from 1909 to 1919, resisted talk of white slave traffic, "a phrase which essentially implies that the man profits by the forced prostitution of the woman." He focused instead on practical questions of protection and class. There was no question that these marriages and the divorces that often followed created a burden for the consulate, and he enumerated a list of examples: Maud Knight and her infant daughter, Enayet; Dr. Ahmed Lutfi and Dr. Daoud Hilmi, both married to English women; a 1904 case, when as consul at Port Said he refused to solemnize the London marriage of a Miss Grimes and a Mr. Neechamall because the latter was a Hindu and (apparently) had another wife in Hyderabad.[34] He also pointed out examples of happy marriages—an English woman married in Assyut twenty years earlier, and just this year "Mustafa bey Menzelawi, a wealthy landed proprietor," whose wife "seemed to be quite happy independent; . . . such a ménage may be possible if the husband is wealthy."

Cameron dwelled especially on a marriage contracted in 1909. At that time, he was asked by the governor of Alexandria whether the mother of a British girl (Beatrice Holbrook, age twenty) would consent to her marriage to a Muslim before the *qadi* of Alexandria. Cameron consulted the Foreign Office.[35] The girl's mother, resident in Britain, gave her consent and resolutely refused to be persuaded to withdraw it, arguing that her daughter must do what suited her. The mother scarcely had a choice. Beatrice had gone to Alexandria at age sixteen, in 1905, as a performer in Madam Davis's song-and-dance troupe, and her example had influenced her sister, who "having found nothing to do here for 19 months is going out to Alexandria also to earn a living in the same way." Considering the girls' limited prospects, Beatrice's marriage with Ibrahim Effendi Yakout al-Behery was probably a good outcome for her, even if he might marry another. So the consulate finally communicated her consent.

The consulate also had a way to communicate its own disapproval, however. It commonly solemnized marriages made elsewhere, endorsing them for specific legal purposes, but in this case it refused to do so. It noted that the Foreign Marriage Act of 1892 "contemplates and deals with marriage from the only point of view which is recognized by English law, namely the Christian or Monogamistic standpoint, that is to say as the union of one man with one woman to live together to their lives' end to the exclusion of all other persons."[36] It seems that the prediction of a troubled future that this note implied came to pass. In 1912, the consul sent his constable to the home of the couple, hearing that Beatrice was being badly treated by Ibrahim. This was not true, he found, but the husband was about to take a second wife. "It is doubtful whether such an arrangement can last very long," the consul stated, "but she is still a British subject."[37] Only his refusal to solemnize the marriage preserved this protection.

Polygamy and concubinage were the rubrics for refusing to solemnize marriages and for cautioning women against marrying Muslims. Once in Egypt, the English wife would enter the "harem," where she would be at the mercy of female relatives who would try to convince her husband to repudiate her. In the Holbrook case, the consul fed a vicar in London arguments with which to convince the mother to withdraw her consent: "The facility of divorce in polygamous countries and the evident misery of existence in the unwholesome atmosphere of a 'harem' are arguments which the least natural of mothers should appreciate."[38] Even sexual impropriety, which could typically be solved by marriage, was in this case not an inducement. "According to our views, if a girl has been ruined, it is generally better that she should be married to her seducer; but with Egyptian

Moslems such an arrangement may make bad worse, because the harem life would be intolerable to most English girls."[39]

In 1910, the Foreign Office revised its consular instructions on marriage, stating: "In no case should a Consular officer solemnize the marriage of a man professing a religion, or subject to a law, which recognizes polygamy or concubinage. If requested to solemnize such a marriage he should report the facts to the Secretary of State."[40] In 1912, the Foreign Office extended this control domestically, asking the Home Office to request of its marriage officers in Britain that "in cases where English women propose to marry natives of a polygamous country their attention should be seriously called to the risks involved."[41] This was not a new concern. In 1901, Lord Cromer prepared an elaborate marriage contract for use in mixed marriages. Its text, which contains a lengthy exposition of a certain vision of marriage under Islam and its risks for Christian girls, would hardly make for happy reading during a wedding celebration. The Foreign Office thought better than to give it wide publicity (as Cromer urged) but sent copies to the Home Office for use when necessary.[42] By refusing to solemnize the marriages, the consuls kept them invisible to English law; when her marriage collapsed, the girl could return to her nationality and indeed could contract a Christian marriage. The important thing in these cases was to resist the logic that nationality follows marriage: "If she applies to the Consulate it is essential that she should not have lost her British nationality by marriage in the UK."[43] Only under that circumstance could the consulate protect her.

Polygamy provided a pretext for discouraging such marriages, but sanction could be denied to non-nationals irrespective of their religion. By 1911, it appears that the British consulate had decided that the 1892 Ottoman marriage law was inadequate for foreign Christian marriages, so it performed a large number of them itself. Candidates were required to reside in Alexandria for three weeks before their wedding.[44] Many Jews were also married at the consulate, though more exotic requests, such as that of a Romanian Jew born in Zanzibar who wanted to celebrate marriage at the consulate, were refused.[45] Early in 1912, the consul in Assyut refused to solemnize the marriage of Maude Page, an English girl, with a Syrian Anglican. The prospective groom, baptized in Syria at age ten, was a communicant, and the couple had the support of their archdeacon. But if they had not already realized that, regardless of missionaries' promises, Christianity was no international brotherhood, the consul made it even more clear to them.[46]

He identified a catch-22 of jurisdiction: On the one hand, marriage at the consulate was only binding on the British girl, and he could not guarantee that they would afterward marry at the church so that the man would be bound to the contract. On the other hand, the consul could not marry the couple *after* a church ceremony because the new bride would have ceased to be a British subject.[47] The legal logic behind the refusal to solemnize Muslim marriages (to do so would extinguish foreign nationality) was thrown out in favor of a new (and false) pretext to refuse to solemnize Christian marriages (because they extinguish foreign nationality).[48]

Bigamy, Legitimate Nationality, and Objective Legal Personality

Bigamy prosecutions across borders were a mark of nationality's rise. The world of empire offered many opportunities (mostly to men) to maintain concurrent affective relationships in different contexts.[49] Nationality was a legal instrument that insisted that legal identity was transportable and objective. This premise meant that multiple, context-dependent identities became contradictions liable to resolution before the law. A husband's personal status in one setting should be the same everywhere else.

As a legal idiom, nationality diversified the bonds that marriage established between people. Empirical studies of marriage always reveal complex twists and turns, and these assumed novel forms under the sign of nationality. The mixed relationships of Violet Peradon (née Schiff) were far from unusual in an era of mobility, but their nationality effects were something new. When she died in 1898 at the age of thirty, the local authorities reported her death to the French consulate. As it turned out, and despite her reputation, she was not a French subject. The authorities needed some protector to handle her affairs, and without a positive nationality to go on, they turned to her sectarian affiliation, as represented by the Grand Rabbinate of Alexandria. The rabbinate took charge of Violet's possessions and her cadaver. Its agent found a British registration certificate among her papers and at once deferred to nationality, a superior form of affiliation. The British consulate was also unwilling to assume the burden, however. Violet had been given the registration certificate "by mistake" in the previous year, and the consulate had already disavowed her before her death.[50]

In fact, the British consulate knew Violet well. In 1895, it sentenced Robert McKay, a man she had married the year before, to one year of hard labor for bigamy.[51] McKay, a corporal in the mounted military police, married an Austrian subject named Elizabeth Battistig at the Alexandria consulate in 1886. They had two children together. In the early 1890s, while McKay was serving with the Coast Guard in the Suez Canal, Elizabeth suffered a miscarriage and fell into mental illness. "Losing heart," McKay left for England with his two young children, as well as Violet, whom he had met some years earlier in Isma'iliya. They married in Scotland. Violet claimed that although she knew that McKay lived with Elizabeth, she only discovered that they were married after they returned to Alexandria together. McKay told her, "even if she is my wife I only married her in Catholic Church and the marriage is of no value." This proved not to be the case. The consul passed a heavy sentence in Robert McKay's bigamy case "for the vindication of the law." He was incensed that McKay had stated that consular marriage was "nothing and was got up by lawyers in Alexandria and that he could snap his fingers at them all."[52] As in the case of counterfeiting, the judicial institution guarded its authority over civil marriage anxiously.

When the British consulate denied Violet its protection, it did so for legal reasons—her marriage to a British subject did not convey his nationality to her because the marriage was invalid—but also for moral reasons. At McKay's bigamy trial, his defense turned on the demolition of Violet's reputation. In court, it was revealed that she "kept a bar," the International Bar on Stagni Street, where McKay's first wife "has been several times making a disturbance." In cross-examination, recorded in a few abbreviated lines, the full extent of Violet's dubious reputation emerges:

> As an Actress, I went under Violet De Vere, my professional name. No other man's name. I know Pecci, have lived with him. I have received letters & telegrams in name of Pecci. Hired Piano in name of Peradon from a Mr. Hecks, have receipts (C). Brought a case of assault against him, he was fined a month ago . . . sang at Grande Bretagne by his request. He received 10/ per night from it, has never supported me. I have earned money for household.

The trial judge in Alexandria objected to this cross-examination; it "was directed to insinuation of charges against her character which as they were not proved amounted to an aggravation of the wrong which he had inflicted her by his act of bigamy." In a petition for remittance of his sentence sent from his prison in Malta, however, McKay continued to blame Violet: "The woman ... spread all sorts of rumours and evil things against Petitioner's wife, and filled up his head with all the evil she could against her. ... His heart and head was full with sorrow about this affair which this woman impressed upon his mind. It was then he foolishly went through the form of marriage with this woman."[53] When reviewing the case at the Foreign Office, the judicial advisor Davidson felt that Violet's character was relevant and that she was in fact an "assistant in the felony."[54] An entertainer and barmaid was not a legitimate wife and certainly generated no sympathy that would win the consulate's help.

Violet had also been married before, to a man of another foreign nationality. The rabbi's letter of 1898 shows that Violet was unable to benefit from French protection, despite her 1885 marriage to Louis Peradon, a French subject. Four days after she married him (in London) in 1885, he left as chief cook on a boat bound for Australia. She never heard from him again.[55] When she married McKay, she did so under her maiden name "because Defendant [McKay] objects to the name of a Frenchman on the Documents." In 1897, she declared that she was free to marry again, having no reason to believe that Peradon was now living—curiously, she did so at the British consulate. It seems that she lost her French status when she married McKay, even though that marriage was eventually invalidated. As so often, positive nationality was easier to lose than it was to gain. Left without a nationality, Violet's status was reduced to default local subjecthood.[56]

McKay's first wife was another lost soul. Elizabeth Battistig was twenty-four when she married into British nationality in 1886. Her mental illness began around 1894, and in 1903 she was committed to the Egyptian government's lunatic asylum at ʿAbbasiya. Doctors reported that Elizabeth suffered from "chronic mania with exaltation"; sometimes irritable and aggressive, she believed that she was the commander of an army and queen of Egypt. In 1912 and 1913, the consulate took account of her case. It cost three pounds per month to keep her at ʿAbbasiya. The Alexandria Benevolent Fund, a charitable organization associated with the consulate, had spent more than three hundred pounds on her since she had been committed. Although her husband, a military man, was not taking responsibility for her, could she not be transported away from Alexandria on a warship? Eventually, the consulate decided that it made no sense to ship her to Britain. She had never been to England and spoke no English, just "incoherent Italian and Arabic." In the end, the authorities decided to continue paying for the asylum.[57] Whereas the consulate disavowed Violet, it took responsibility for Elizabeth—legitimate marriage could be a surer source of nationality protection.

Secular Nationality and Religious Law

Extensive, expensive legal exploration of nationality was, for the most part, restricted to the wealthy. This legal wrangling was not only about money, however: a 1902 case before Alexandria's French consular court concerned control over the body of a local-born woman married to an elite French protégé. Nafissa Hanem Zuhni was born a local subject but gained French protection when she married an Algerian who enjoyed special "diplomatic" status inherited from his father, a prominent member of the ʿulama. After her first husband died, she married his brother, Shaykh Ahmad bin Sulaiman Pasha.[58] In 1902, while Ahmad was away in Cairo, Nafissa fled her marital home in Alexandria and went to live with her brother in Ramla (a suburb of Alexandria). In order to compel her return, Shaykh Ahmad called on the qadis and muftis of the Islamic courts, the local police, and the French consular courts.[59] In hearings before the French consular tribunal, Nafissa resisted foreign protection, making two arguments against French jurisdiction over her.

First, she claimed the right to exercise Muslim (rather than French) personal status. Because both husband and wife were Muslim, the French court agreed that Muslim personal-status law obtained. Since 1896, however, it was the consular tribunal and not the qadi that governed the personal status of French-administered Muslims in the Levant.[60] This new power was exercised according to French codification of Islamic law. In this case, the court referred to articles of its "Hanafi code" (both husband and wife being Hanafis), which showed that a Muslim man could indeed compel his wife to return to his home.

Nafissa's second objection held that neither she nor her husband were in fact French subjects (ressortissants). The court replied that Nafissa's name appeared in the consulate chancellery register on the pages of both her first and second husbands; under French law, wives followed the "condition" of husbands who were French citizens, subjects, or protégés.[61] The court upheld her husband's French protection and dismissed Nafissa's claim that his special protection did not extend to his wives, who could not be made to lose their original nationality. The court did not bother to respond to Nafissa's argument that it should throw out her husband's claim both because it was he who had repudiated her and prevented her from returning by his objectionable conduct and because there was no law, French or Muslim, to make a fugitive wife return to her husband.

On this basis, the French consular court upheld Shaykh Ahmad's right to compel Nafissa to return. It remained for the court to spell out the means by which he could enforce this right. This was no trifling matter, for the French consular court often failed to see its sentences carried out. Nafissa's husband had a fatwa from the *mufti* of Alexandria allowing him to use the police ("*la force publique*") to force her to return. The tribunal agreed that it could not delay her return, even according to French procedure, because Muslim law stipulated that the return be immediate. Nafissa was therefore ordered to return home at once, regardless of appeal.

Evidently, Nafissa did not comply; several weeks later, she attempted to have the judgment overturned because the means of its execution were not specified.[62] The court again ruled against her, stating that the means were multiple, not limited, and that force was not excluded. The tribunal announced that it must take into consideration procedures used in similar circumstances in the Muslim world. Correspondence on this topic with the governor of Alexandria was added to the dossier. His expert view showed that in Egypt (and in the Muslim world in general), judgments returning wives to their conjugal homes could be executed by means of constraint and even force.[63] Although Nafissa was not directly subject to this rule, under the French version of Muslim personal-status law she was subject to the norms in place in local Muslim society. The judgment was therefore confirmed.

Although Nafissa was ultimately unsuccessful in her attempt to escape her husband's control, her case shows that jurisdictions were poorly compartmentalized in marriage cases. Although every authority (including her husband) agreed on the subjecthood of women, she managed to exploit cracks in their ill-fitting legal apparatus. By refusing to comply, she quite effectively challenged regnant regimes of nationality and gender. In doing so, she raised the ire of the men who ran those regimes. Lest we presume that women benefited from any consistent consular benevolence, consider the retrospective view articulated by the French legation as the capitulations were folded up in the late 1930s: our officers "were on the receiving end of claims by women who became more harsh the less right they had to what they wanted. Indeed, this feminine logic is a common practice in the Levant. Its aim is not to discover the truth, but instead to win the given argument."[64]

Marriage (and related questions of divorce, inheritance, custody, and maintenance) was the most important trigger of nationality-law jurisprudence in Alexandria. Breakdowns in private life drove litigants into a formal legal sphere that had taken the place of local and nonstate adjudicators. Some of these litigants were reluctant to concede sovereignty on the basis of nationality, while others were eager to explore the limits of nationality-based claims. Here more than anywhere, the new legal technology of private international law struggled to corral human diversity. This chapter has shown ways that lines of gender, sect, and class revealed nationality's inconsistencies and the improvised nature of its practice.

Nationality was a legal category, but it was also a category of practice. Those for whom legal tests of contact with foreign persons or territories were inconclusive could be evaluated according to their gender or their conduct in Egypt: taxpaying, military service, liability to local justice, and so on. Typically, this test was a losing proposition for those who wished to retain foreignness. It was easier to prove contact with locals than it was to prove distance. Definite criteria of foreignness and nationality were invoked most often in the context of inheritance and marriage litigation. That these issues came to the fore during material and personal struggles in which subjects grasped for any advantage suggests the strategic rather than natural fit of these categories. This suggestion is corroborated by the fact that questions of nationality were only rarely posed in other legal contexts (though taxation was sometimes an issue, and government employment became a new area of nationality debate after the beginning of the twentieth century).

PART III
Other Nationalities

7
Europeans

‘Ali Salama al-Bayumi spent a summer morning in 1897 selling goat's milk with his mother. After lunch, he and his brother walked off to tend their goats, which were grazing near the lighthouse at the western tip of the Ra's al-Tin peninsula. Crossing an open space beside the khedive's stables, they saw a soldier leaning out a window of the British barracks. The soldier was throwing pieces of bread to girls gathered below, and the boys asked for some. The soldier told them to go away. One of the brothers threw a stone. The soldier threw it back, then picked up the rifle that he had been cleaning and placed a cartridge in its chamber. The children ran away; after the bullet hit him in the back, ‘Ali stood up and ran a few more steps, then fell down again.

Andrew Lawler, a private in the First Royal Warwickshire Regiment, quickly cleaned his rifle and replaced it on the rack. Later that day, he tossed the spent cartridge into the sea. When his commandant told him the following morning that witnesses had seen gun smoke at his window, he realized that he should confess. He explained that the cartridge that killed the boy had failed to fire in two different guns at the shooting range, and he was horrified that it had actually gone off when he shot the boy. "I have often seen other men pointing empty rifles at boys outside for fun." It was an accident.

The soldier was tried for ‘Ali's murder.[1] Sir Charles Cookson, the chief judge at the British consular court in Alexandria for almost thirty years,

was due to retire at the end of the month. He saw that the case was a deli-
cate one and cabled London asking that a replacement judge be sent. None
was available, the Foreign Office replied; he would have to postpone his
retirement.[2] ʿAli's mother and brother testified at the preliminary examination, as did the government doctors who performed the autopsy. The
khedive's valet testified that he witnessed the scene from his room across
the square, and Lawler's commanding officer explained how the confes-
sion was elicited. Lawler pleaded not guilty, and he was acquitted after a
rushed two-day trial, with the shooting ruled accidental. Consul-General
Cookson retired on schedule.

A grown man, part of the occupying army, shot a defenseless child in
the back on a whim. He went free, and his liberation was sanctioned and
delivered by an elaborate institutional apparatus designed to guarantee
to foreigners the kind of judicial protection that locals could not access.
This case displayed all the injustice of native weakness and European
strength under the rule of colonial difference. By this evidence, European and native were distinct, opposed social positions in turn-of-the-
century Egypt, separated by a host of structures: economic, religious,
racial, linguistic, and of course legal. The liberation of ʿAli's murderer
seems an inevitable product of the sham justice that marked the sharp
line of difference.

But in thousands of cases heard by British, French, and American consular courts between 1880 and the First World War, Lawler's acquittal was
almost uniquely unjust. The caricature of courts that systematically protected the colonizer from the colonized does not describe the vast bulk of
court work in this context. This is not to say (as Chang does in the Japanese
case) that nineteenth-century consular courts were especially just institutions.[3] The reason that colonial privilege could not systematically
and egregiously be deployed before the courts was that the distinction
between foreign and local, colonizer and colonized, European and native
was rarely obvious. Lawler's case was exceptional: he was clearly English,
and his victim clearly native. As a soldier, Lawler's civil standing was especially strong; ʿAli, as a poor local child, was triply disenfranchised. In most
other instances, however, the correlation of nationality and status was less
clear, or unclear; this is the nature of nationality. Foreign judicial institutions were not able to prefer their own kind because they were rarely able
to identify real foreigners and real natives.

The critical difference between Lawler and ʿAli was not one of national-ity. Lawler had a nationality, of course, and ʿAli did too, in a certain incho-ate sense. But the more complex categories of status that conditioned their interaction during the murderous episode—white European soldier of occupation versus brown poor native child—were also the categories they carried into court. Lawler's status granted him a broad warrant of impunity, if not quite immunity. ʿAli's status meant that he had no claims, beyond the merest procedural pretense, to protection or dignity by law. The puzzle is to discover how nationality reflected status differences but also reinforced and produced them.

One of the purposes of this book is to show that nationality is no natural category. To that end, this chapter and the five that follow detail six "other nationalities," other kinds of status that operated in complex and thorough ways in Alexandria. While not comprehensive—lines of caste, class, sect, gender, bondage, disability, estate, and race are not prominent—this set of statuses comprises many of the major categories at play in law and society in Alexandria. These categories can be arranged in a hierarchy: the Euro-peans treated in this chapter were at the top, then other foreigners and protégés (chapters 8 and 9), then Ottomans (chapter 11), then local sub-jects (chapter 12). Bad subjects (chapter 10) constituted a special category at the bottom. Individual lives were not predetermined by these catego-ries, of course, but in Alexandria identification status typically determined legal jurisdiction and often dictated extralegal attitudes. Lawler and ʿAli's case features an unusually wide hierarchical distance between parties. As we will see, ranking was typically less clear-cut: poor Europeans, foreign-ers, Ottomans, protégés, and locals competed for standing in the courts just as they did in the streets of Alexandria. States seeking legible status structures had an interest in foreclosing such diverse systems. As they took charge of the certification of nationality, using means described in chapters 3 and 4, nationality took first rank in status determination. At the same time, nationality's subcategories proliferated, and so too did cat-egory errors and subversion of the sort we saw in chapters 5 and 6.

This chapter describes the strongest nationality category—those who possessed the legal privilege of foreign nationality and the social power of European appearance and connections. Colonialism's characteristic irony lay just below the sound surface of this strength, however: almost every European was saddled with deficiencies of class, race, or gender.

Furthermore, as we will see in the next chapter, most foreigners were not even Europeans.[4] This chapter begins to untangle this ideal nationality archetype. The first section describes the services and privileges that elites could expect as Europeans (even if they were not European in the strict sense). The second section considers the position of poor Europeans, whose social status mitigated against the legal protections that their nationality status offered. The third section discusses people of Maltese origin, some of whom managed to "pass" as Europeans, at least in the eyes of the law. The closing section examines the language that residents of Alexandria used to describe the "Europeans" that they identified in the city's streets.

European Notables

In 1888, a contentious individual named John Colborne, harassing the British consular court over the conditions of his detention, objected to the nationality of one of the jurymen in his trial. Aristides Kaphate, he claimed, was not a British subject but a (Cephalonian) Ionian. He was thus not qualified by birth or parentage for jury duty; what was more, he lacked a competent knowledge of the English language.[5] The claim was dismissed when it was confirmed that Aristides Cavafy was English born.[6] But Colborne was undeterred and used his connections to place a question in the British parliament a year later, asking "whether British subjects have been tried at Alexandria by juries of five, often not Englishmen, but Greeks and Levantines with British passports?"[7] Consul-General Cookson answered that jurors were taken from a list, carefully revised each year, of British subjects who have competent knowledge of English. "On it may undoubtedly be found not only 'Englishmen' but Scotchmen, Irishmen, Welshmen, Maltese, and other subjects of Her Majesty of different origins, but . . . no one is put on it merely on the strength of his being in possession of a British passport, without further evidence of his nationality." There were no Greeks on the list. In its instructions to Cookson, the Foreign Office wrote that "the exact meaning of the term 'Levantine' as applied to an individual person appears to be by no means settled, but . . . if it is interpreted to mean 'belonging to or born in or resident in the Levant,' this characteristic quality does not exclude from the jury list of the Consular courts of the Levant those who in other respects come under the legal definition of 'British sub-jects.' "⁸ Despite these official allowances, Colborne's view represented the norm. Citizenship, I have argued, was a rarity in the nineteenth century. In Alexandria, a robust set of civil, political, and social rights were enjoyed by a mere handful of wealthy foreign men. These archetypal Europeans are interesting figures but have no business representing the city's social norms. They were mere exceptions.

What rights and privileges did these exceptions enjoy? As we have seen in previous chapters, they could count on consular support in their every-day lives, the backing of the law in financial and personal disputes, and protection from the perils of anonymity. Europeans working through their consulates could activate a network of advocates, even by remote control. This was the case in 1896, when George Edington, a London businessman, wrote to the consul on behalf of his wife, who was named Khadijah. Khadi-jah was the daughter of a certain ʿAbdul Hamid Bey, who had married an English woman at a church in England in 1849. The couple lived in Alexan-dria for twenty years, until Khadijah's mother returned to England with her child. She and her husband were estranged. When ʿAbdul Hamid died, how-ever, European networks rolled into action to claim his estate: an unnamed person sent the death announcement to Khadijah in London, and George wrote to the consul asking for help. He quickly received letters and advice from notables in the English community of Alexandria and met a leading Alexandria barrister on vacation in London. Eventually, even Lord Cromer himself interceded with the government on Edington's behalf. All of this help was to no avail, however; all of these contacts agreed that the will that Khadijah possessed had been superseded by a will deposited with the qadi of Alexandria, and she had no claim on the estate and should not even try. Edington could not dominate the rights of the elite Egyptian family of ʿAbdul Hamid in the way that Lawler dominated the boy he shot. There were limits to European exceptions, and rules could not be bent.⁹

Outside of such contests, however, notable Europeans could count on consular protection during times of vulnerability. A man like Henry Barker, "probably the wealthiest British Subject in Alexandria," worth between eighty and one hundred pounds sterling, received such consid-eration.¹⁰ When Barker's mind weakened late in life and his family sought to have him certified, the British consulate went to great lengths to pro-tect his interests. The consul consulted far and wide, concerned that the family was not adequately considerate of Barker. "If he finds out the steps taken, he may acquiesce in them and put himself in my hands for he is a great respecter of 'authority' and things may go quietly on as they are." Through the intervention of the British Minister in Constantinople, it was decided that he would be declared incompetent ("a lunatic") but would be informed of the proceedings.[11] This sort of concern for welfare extended to other European elites, including those visiting for work or tourism.

European notables could also count on consular protection in more odious circumstances. In 1901, Job Gammage, the manager of the Merchant Sailor Home and harbor missionary for the Church of Scotland, drugged and raped his domestic servant, Eliza Cuff.[12] When her pregnancy became apparent, he sent her to stay at a mission in Jerusalem. The missionaries sent her back to Alexandria when they heard her story, at which point Gammage threatened her with consular punishment. The case came to light because of her pregnancy, and though he was made to pay child support, Gammage was acquitted of the criminal charge of rape by a jury of his peers.[13] Gammage used the power that he held over Cuff as a man, as her employer, and as an entrenched European—when Cuff had arrived in Alexandria alone four years earlier, she was a stranger in a strange city. This case could just as well have taken place in England, where all the same conditions would have applied, and he received satisfaction from the courts. In this case, the rule of difference depended on gender and class, rather than nationality.

For the European notable few, nationality was a minor accessory in the crony privilege network that spread through the metropole, through empire, and indeed across the globe. But that accessory was the constituent element in Alexandria's jurisdiction regime, and in the hands of nonelites lacking the same suite of citizenship privileges, nationality became the primary point of engagement with the state. For nonelite Europeans, nationality meant restriction as well as privilege. A generation of scholarship has revealed the flaws and inconsistencies within the myth of personal sovereignty that European colonizers projected in the world of empire. Some studies show the class distinctions within the communities of colonizers.[14] Others point to connections between colonized and colonizer that undermine the separation on which the categories depend.[15] Still others focus on individuals who themselves embody aspects of the colonizer and the colonized.[16] This chapter confirms these critiques of the imagined European colonizer. In particular, two statuses diverged from the European ideal type in Alexandria: imperial subjects (such as the Maltese) and poor Europeans.

Poor Europeans

Wealthy foreigners were the best Europeans; poverty was the greatest threat to European status.[17] Poor subjects—both foreign and local—were always less capable of assuming the sort of civil and political rights that emerging regimes of nationality could offer. Even the rudimentary procedures of consular nationality—registration, prosecution, probate, burial— were performed with less care for the poor. The poor found it difficult to access the legal privileges granted to foreigners and were rarely able to project the social identity that wealthy archetypal Europeans found useful in Alexandrian society. As soldiers, sailors, governesses, and menial laborers, their rootlessness in Alexandria frequently left them with nowhere to turn but to the consulates, which acted as agencies of welfare and social control for the foreign communities. When subaltern foreigners committed crimes, died, or went mad, consulates stepped in to sweep up the mess and, often as not, parcel it up and send it back to Europe.

Consular staff considered distressed foreign subjects burdensome.[18] Often, consulates were obliged to pay for the burial of foreigners whose families could not themselves pay.[19] Charity was more forthcoming when formerly elite Europeans fell to poverty. Herbert James Gedge Pasha was a retired captain in the Royal Navy. In Alexandria's European society, he was called "El Liwa" (Captain) because in addition to his work triangulating the Alexandria harbor for the Ports and Lights Administration, he had commanded the khedive's yacht. He died a European notable but with a long list of debts. His huge, ceremonial funeral masked the fact that he had little more than one hundred pounds to his name when he died.[20] Most poor Europeans died intestate, and consular agents cataloged their meager estates. Auction sale summaries show how and to whom their possessions were sold.

If death brought a responsibility that could not be dodged, the appeals of living impoverished Europeans to the consulate often fell on deaf ears. Alexandria's foreign population numbered in the tens of thousands, and the consulates could not assume responsibility for all foreigners' welfare. The British consulate had a special category for the most impoverished Europeans: "distressed British subjects." These individuals were able to access certain social benefits from the consulate and its related agencies: subsistence, employment, accommodation, and especially passage home. The material situation of some of the thousands of Europeans who came to Alexandria searching for work are revealed in the estate files of those who died in Egypt. They came in poor, and many went out poor too. Workers used the consulate to help them collect wages from recalcitrant employers.[21] Women came in large numbers. Some entered the service of local elites.[22] Others served as governesses or taught English.[23] The experience of Eliza Cuff in the service of Job Gammage was far from unique. Wherever possible, consulates obliged family members (in Alexandria or abroad) to support relatives in distress.[24] For the rest, national and sectarian relief societies (which operated with the support of the consulates) provided short-term assistance. The relief and management of sailors was an old consular duty, and it persisted during this period. A typical case, in 1894, involved British sailors engaged to work on an Ottoman ship. They had been thrown off the ship at Jedda and forced to make their own way home. Their captain was picked up in Suez but jumped bail and headed for Constantinople. The consulate was left to handle the correspondence with sailors' societies in Britain and return the men home.[25] The overriding concern of consulates was to be rid of the burden of poor supplicants.

Some poor Europeans were involved in criminal activity, and here the courts shouldered the burden of social control. European mendicants and vagrants, discussed in chapter 10, were a particular embarrassment. Most poor Europeans led quiet lives, however. Foreigners worked as domestic servants of local subjects and as low- and midlevel employees of the Egyptian government. Consular support was enlisted in labor and pension disputes. Civil cases show the settling of petty debts and the activity of pawnbrokers and loan sharks.

Birth earned this subaltern European population more consideration than that afforded Algerians, Tunisians, Maltese, and other imperial subjects; for instance, the former were incarcerated in gentler prisons, and if sent home they were "repatriated" rather than "deported." Nevertheless, the material inferiority of these subaltern Europeans was apparent at consular courts run by and for notables.

Maltese Europeans

The wealthiest British subject in Alexandria at the turn of the century was a
Maltese merchant named Roberto Stabile. When he died (in Geneva) in 1914,
he left an estate worth £135,000.[26] He was not the only wealthy Maltese.
Seven others left fortunes between ten and twenty-five thousand pounds
sterling, comparing favorably with the wealthiest Britons.[27] Wealthy Maltese used consular offices as fluently as any British-born subjects to protect their property and interests. When in 1892 Stabile complained that the
local police had confiscated his shooting rifle, the British consul advocated
firmly on his behalf. He recommended Stabile to the governor of Alexandria
as a "respectable British subject," shared his outrage, and secured the punishment of the offending officers.[28] But while the British consulate showed a
pattern of solicitousness in assisting Stabile and in collecting the affairs and
corresponding with the families of impoverished Britons who died abroad,
it was less careful when dealing with the Maltese poor: by and large, they
were treated indifferently or even with a hint of disdain. A certain Paolo
Callus died falling down stairs in February 1880. Writing to the consul in
the course of the inquest, the consulate's surgeon Doctor Mackie (one of
the richest men in Alexandria) remarked: "If the Maltese continue to go off
as they have been doing lately the population will be thinned and my hand
kept well in practice in post mortems."[29] Nevertheless, the consulate knew
that it could not ignore its chief constituency; it was no accident that its
chief clerk, William Chevalier, spoke Maltese.[30]

In his description of the nineteenth-century Egyptian population,
Daniel Panzac lists the professions of European immigrants seeking their
fortune "along the banks of the Nile": "Military men, physicians, engi-
neers, technicians, merchants, artisans and adventurers."[31] If we exclude
merchants and artisans, consular records of employment show that this
list of romantic professions was far from the mainstream reality for foreigners in Egypt.

While the occupations listed in table 7.1 reveal the humble professions
of many Britons in Alexandria, it also shows the even more humble position of the Maltese. Poor Europeans could grudgingly be assumed and
admitted to European status. This was the burden necessitated by capitulatory privilege and the expanding state—anyone who was born, died, or
came to court had to have a nationality. But the Maltese were subjects of

TABLE 7.1 Professions of registered British and British Maltese subjects, 1888–1889

	Maltese	British		Maltese	British
Clerk	111	58	Painter	19	0
Carpenter	101	0	Broker	17	4
Merchant	23	56	Mechanic	17	0
Engineer	7	74	Laborer	16	0
Storekeeper	39	6	Butcher	13	0
Trader	38	3	Tailor	12	1
Blacksmith	19	0	Telegraph Clerk	0	10
			Other	189[1]	96[2]

Notes: FO 881/5968.
1 In 74 other professions.
2 In 47 other professions.

the British, not their equals. Only in Egypt were they considered European, and thus they often benefited from nationality misrecognition.

A decade and a half before ʿAli was shot by Lawler, another Arab boy died at the hands of a foreigner more typical of Alexandria's nationality complexity. One morning in October 1880, this foreigner came to collect a single piaster from the owner of an oven at Bab al-Gir. Ragab Muhammad, the oven boy (sabi furn), told the foreigner to come back later; as it was still early, he explained, no customers had come yet, and they had no money whatsoever. Upset by this response, the foreigner jostled Ragab into the fire, badly burning his arm. The local authorities sent the foreigner, a British subject, to his consulate, asking that he be detained until Ragab recovered.[32]

Six months later, after a long fight with his infected wound, Ragab died in hospital. Alexandria's governor wrote to the British consul, asking him to begin prosecuting his subject for murder. A trial date was set, and on the appointed day Ragab's mother arrived at the consular court with all of the prosecution's witnesses. The accused did not attend his trial, however; in fact, he had left Egypt months earlier. In the weeks that followed, the Egyptian authorities repeatedly asked the British consul to locate the accused and to extradite him for prosecution in Egypt. The consul resolutely refused their requests, arguing that he had no power over British subjects outside of Egypt. Ultimately, Ragab's assailant was never punished.

Thus far, the pattern of injustice is familiar. But this impunity differs from Lawler's case. Ragab's assailant, Alfredo Baldacchino, was also a child, and he was Maltese. Whereas Private Lawler was acquitted by a judicial institution willing and working to protect one of its own, Alfredo merely slipped away. In this case, the court was negligent rather than unjust. It neglected him because he was a child over whom it was unwilling or unable to assert physical control, and it neglected him because he was Maltese.

In Ragab's mother's petition to the police, Alfredo is called "*khawaga*": a title of respect that signaled foreignness.[33] From her perspective, he seemed to enjoy all of the advantages of a European. The Maltese certainly had a strong claim to foreignness in Alexandria. Maltese had been Catholic for four centuries and British subjects since the beginning of the nineteenth century. They enjoyed the same tax and legal exemptions as other "Europeans." In the great foreign-local conflagration of 1882 (a year after Ragab's death), Maltese were prominently identified as foreign, were attacked as "Europeans," and were evacuated by the British navy.

From another perspective, however, the Maltese do not appear so foreign. The Maltese were the European's other. In her recent work on European migrants in North Africa, Julia Clancy-Smith argues that Europeans must not be treated as a monolithic bloc. She uses the Maltese as a central example of a "European" community that differed from others in order to answer an important question: "Where did Europe begin and end in the nineteenth century, and who was a European?"[34] The evidence of the consular courts certainly supports her contention that their difference indicated social diversity within the European community. On one hand, a number of elite Maltese received excellent service from the consulate.[35] On the other, five Maltese were charged for every one Briton who appeared before the criminal court.[36] Higher charge and conviction rates of Maltese British subjects indicate that legal equality did not create equal conduct or equal treatment. One of the clearest measures of the standing of the communities is their share of various case types. Whereas Maltese predominate in the criminal cases, it is Britons who populate the inquest files. Careful medical attention to the cause of death of poor Europeans (suicide was strikingly common) as well as cases of European "lunacy" filled consular dossiers.[37] Suicide and madness, though not marks of distinction, were nevertheless privileges reserved largely for Europeans and the few Maltese subjects whose wealth won them special consideration.

The political division between colonizer and colonized was inescapable, but cultural factors did even more to distinguish metropolitan Europeans from Maltese. The most important of these was language. The colonialist fantasy of elite, cosmopolitan Alexandria was limited to the few thousand Europeans who spoke French, supported by a thin layer of servants with whom they communicated in pidgin French and Arabic. But non-Europeans demonstrated more basic cosmopolitanism: facility of communication. Maltese British subjects and Maghribi French subjects spoke dialects of Arabic that allowed them to live in a different world from the Alexandria of Europeans. Above all, language gave them the possibility of community with the majority of the city's population. An illiterate peddler of beans and bread appearing as a witness in an 1883 murder case could distinguish between a "European" (Italian) victim and a "Maltese" aggressor, having only heard their voices in an unlit street.[38] A Maltese house painter who died on the street in 1896 called for help in Arabic only. This proved an unfortunate choice: the Maltese witness who heard him decided not to come to his aid "because I heard no European voice."[39] Maltese, not French, may have been Alexandria's "European voice" par excellence. The historical linguist Alexander Borg suggests that Maltese was a sort of lingua franca:

> Notwithstanding its Arabic origins, Maltese itself as spoken by *colons* from Malta, not only retained its formal distance from native Arabic but also achieved to some extent the role of an intercommunal linguistic medium between various European groups (Italians, Greeks, Arabs, etc.) reserved for certain sociological situations, and Maltese *Sprachgut* became common coin among Europeans and Arabs alike.[40]

Fluency in this "common" tongue was a strong basis for proficiency in other Mediterranean languages. A great proportion of the Maltese population spoke Italian, and Maltese were often confused with Italians, coreligionists whose company they tended to prefer to that of Britons.[41] Maltese social mixing with southern Europeans further distanced them from first-class Europeans because southern Europeans were not on par with the British.

While only a minority of Maltese spoke English, many spoke Egyptian Arabic with some facility. The Maltese language is an offshoot of Arabic, most closely related to Maghribi Arabic, a fact that helps explain strong Maltese migration to Algeria and Tunisia.[42] While the Arabic spoken in

Alexandria would not have been transparent to Maltese migrants, with some experience the close linguistic relationship between Arabic and Maltese would have greatly facilitated communication. Though less proficient in the local idiom than Syrians or Maghribis (I found little evidence, for example, of Maltese literacy in Arabic), on the whole they were more fluent than other foreigners. Consular court documents are filled with accounts of Maltese in conversation with local subjects, undoubtedly in Arabic.

Migration and mobility have been characteristic of Mediterranean communities for millennia.[43] As Clancy-Smith and others have argued, migration in search of improved work and living standards, notably within the Mediterranean, was a major feature of Maltese society under British rule.[44] Despite this reputation of mobility, evidence shows that Alexandria's Maltese were more settled and better integrated than its British Europeans. An 1888–1889 census of British subjects shows that almost 95 percent of registered Maltese were born in Egypt or had been resident there before the upheaval of 1882, compared to only 70 percent of Britons. This settled population lived in families: two-thirds of registered Maltese reported dependents, compared to only half of Britons.[45] Maltese were at home in Alexandria, with families, quarters, and markets to call their own. The divide between Europeans and their subjects was expressed in patterns of settlement. There was little overlap between second-class settlement and that of first-class Europeans, who tended to settle in ʿAttarin, Manshiya, and Ramla (served by Rue de Rosette, as discussed in chapter 1). Much of Alexandria's Maltese community lived around an area near the western port known as *al-harra al-maltiya* (the Maltese neighborhood).[46] This poor and densely settled neighborhood (a consulate document from 1886 described its houses as "huts") was the setting for many Maltese cases before the consular court.[47] The dwelling described in a 1914 indecent assault case was typical: twenty-two families shared a single floor of a house, and children choked its single hallway.[48]

Identifying Europeans

Vulgar cosmopolitan encounters show how poorly the juridical lines of nationality mapped onto the social life of identification. One Thursday night in April 1886, a brawl spilled out of the Union Jack Bar onto al-Sabʿ Banat.

A Maltese man named Paolo Demeck, who had been drinking coffee across the street from the Union Jack, heard two Maltese brothers "talking against him." He crossed the street, entered the bar, and a fight began and spread; at some point, three British soldiers became involved. The brawling crowd, which contained between a dozen and thirty Maltese, fought with fists, canes, swordsticks, and knives; the soldiers used their belts as weapons. In court records, the story becomes confused. A chair was thrown from the café across the street; stones were thrown; soldiers were knocked down, got up, and were knocked down again; help was summoned; two soldiers ran off in the direction of the police station; some Maltese were held back, while others rushed forward. When the dust settled, one soldier had been stabbed three times and two others battered with sticks, stones, and chairs.[49]

Trial testimony shows that there was no agreement on the vocabulary to identify Arabs, Maltese, Europeans, and English soldiers. Most witnesses, including those best placed to interpret identities, described a fight between Maltese and English soldiers, but other versions reveal telling identification "errors." One English soldier saw Arabs and Englishmen fighting; another said the fighting was among Maltese, whom he also described as Europeans; the third said the fight was between Arabs and Europeans. A former soldier who witnessed the fight from his window described a crowd of Europeans and the presence of an Arab who helped the stabbed soldier. None of the men who described the Maltese as Europeans were ignorant of the term Maltese, as all three used it in their testimony, and one in fact noted that the crowd was speaking in Maltese.[50]

In the eyes of the police, "European" sometimes operated as a useful generic category for identification, in much the same way that "native" did for foreign authorities.[51] The Arabic vocabulary describing foreigners involved about half a dozen terms: some were geographical (*urubawi* and *ifranki* meant European) or titles of (something like) respect (*khawaga*).[52] All matters involving foreign subjects were subsumed by a single bureau, the *qalam ifranki*, at the governor's office; in these bureaucratic terms, "*ifranki*" was a more capacious term than "European." In the social description that was the currency of investigation, "European" made sense because it signaled important clues about distinction in dress, bearing, language, and habits, clues that were legible to most witnesses. Of course, when it came time to prosecute, "European" proved too general; the police had to specify nationality in order for their case to be directed to the competent authorities. The terms used for this purpose related to the subjecthood or affiliation of the individual: *tabiʿ* (subject) and *raʿiya* and *mahmi* (protected) followed by reference to the specific state of protection (*dawlat al-ingliz, fransa*, and so on). National specificity was essential to the work of the local authorities. In order to deal with a foreign witness, victim, or suspect, the police needed to contact his or her consulate. "European" was not precise enough for this purpose; synonymous with "foreigner," the term only told authorities that their powers over the subject were circumscribed. It made more sense for them to misidentify a Maltese as Italian or Greek than to identify him or her simply as European; indeed, as we saw with Violet Peradon in the last chapter, consular court files contain many such "errors."

Social impressions did not always coincide with juridical status. The local police found "European" efficient shorthand for many purposes. When Giorgio Axisa, a Maltese alcoholic, threw himself out of the window of the hotel room he shared with two Italians, the police reported the death of a "European person" (*shakhs urubawi*). A more precise description was not immediately apparent and, in any case, unnecessary to their purposes. Upon receiving the report, the translator at the British consulate could immediately specify the dead man's nationality based on the name Axisa. He elided the process of discovery by rendering *urubawi* as "Maltese" straightaway; this nationality distinction was necessary to the consulate's procedures.[53] While local authorities used both "Maltese" (*malti*) and "European" (*urubawi*) alternately and unproblematically, sometimes for the same individual, British consular officials never described their subjects as anything but "Maltese."[54] Britons were reluctant to extend European status to the Maltese. It was only by an accident of legal categories that they found themselves on the same side of the arbitrary foreign/local borderline. By other measures (race, class, and so on), that line would be drawn differently. It made practical sense for local authorities to call Maltese Europeans, but the British would never risk equating these social categories.[55]

In social encounters on the streets of Alexandria, hints of foreignness and privilege formed a subtext that conditioned every decision. The field of preponderant European legal privilege—the rule of colonial difference—was real but thin. A vaster social category of European derived from it, however. For Europeans, foreign nationality was only the beginning of status privilege, which was also enhanced by wealth, dress, health, and the licensed threat of violence. European-looking confidence men were able to draw on their foreign bearing to snare local victims.[56] The pallor and bearing of a European was an especially useful tool for those who wished to pass as officials. In 1887, an Irishman named Donald Ramsay McKenzie spent a productive day in Ziftah (in Gharbiya province). Passing himself off as an irrigation inspector, he was able to enjoy a nice meal, curse at some irrigation workers, and "borrow" ten francs from a priest, on the pretext of having lost his wallet. Through sheer coincidence, a genuine inspector passed through the village while McKenzie was there. McKenzie was arrested, and the case was referred to the nearest British Consular Agent at Tanta.[57] In fact, McKenzie had previously been charged with fraud, but those of European appearance had ample opportunity to "pass" as officials and conduct themselves with the superiority of the occupiers.

Needless to say, the alien occupiers were not a welcome presence in Alexandria. Violence between poor Egyptians and Europeans in September 1893 and Egyptian protests against the British occupation in the summer of 1895 were signs of resistance.[58] More frequently, occupiers faced "weapons of the weak."[59] As we saw in chapter 1, occupying soldiers rarely passed unnoticed. In 1905, two army captains who had served in South Africa drowned while bathing in the sea near the Beau Rivage Hotel in Ramleh. Carey drowned trying to save Stokes, and the inquest jury congratulated him on his unsuccessful rescue attempt. The crowd on the beach, "mostly natives," did not stir to help.[60] Natives could not always stand back safely from the dangerous recreation of military men. In March and April 1885, two separate groups of soldiers from the same ship set off on shooting expeditions that triggered fights with peasants.[61] Anticipating events twenty years later at Dinshawai, the natives who asked them not to trample their fields were dealt with harshly by the law. The governor of the province of Bahaira (who personally investigated an incident at Kafr al-Dawwar) issued a general directive to arrest anyone guilty of molesting Europeans on shooting parties; such behavior was a "disgrace for natives." Shaykhs, landlords, and managers of estates were to instruct their peasants to ask any such European "gently and politely" not to trespass on plantations. If he did not comply, "they are not to touch him or molest him in any manner, but they are only to try to know his name and his nationality."

Local authorities sometimes used nationality confusion against Europeans. When Ben Lipschitz, a "naturalized Australian," complained of his treatment at the hands of the local police in 1911, the British consul wrote to the commandant: "Dear Hopkinson Pasha, Would you kindly cause an inquiry to be made? The complainant seems to be a respectable person." Hopkinson's reply reveals one dimension of the complaint: "the reason he was asked to produce papers to prove his Nationality was because his name not being an English one the Police were doubtful as to the truth of his allegations."[62] In the same letter, he filed assault charges against Lipschitz on behalf of his policeman.

Europeans not stereotyped by name could often be classified on sight. The construction of new quays for the eastern harbor, completed in 1905, was the major public-works project in Alexandria at the start of the twentieth century. When workmen saw Frederick Barlow walking around the quay they were building on a December evening in 1902, his dress and behavior sent a clear signal. The next morning, an Italian worker was able to identify his body after it was dragged from the water: "I am certain that it was the same man, because when we see a well dressed man about there we look at him well."[63] Barlow was marked as elite, well dressed, European, and different from the Italian who identified his body.[64] These signs instantly confirmed the foreignness, affluence, and hence identifiability of the cadaver—it only remained for police to determine his name. The European criminal bureau (qalam al-jinayat al-ifranki) sent a formulaic letter to all consuls, informing them of the death of a European and asking them to send someone to the Government Hospital to identify the body.

This display was inconclusive, however. The British consulate felt it knew its subjects; as we saw with Henry Hampson in chapter 3, it tracked them carefully. As no British subject was missing, the body at the hospital could not be British. Having failed to identify the body by its foreignness, the authorities then proceeded based on its next most significant mark: its circumcision. The body was entrusted to the son of the rabbi of Alexandria, who buried it in the Jewish cemetery. As we have seen, the transfer of individuals of indefinite identity from national to sectarian responsibility was a frequent administrative maneuver. Days later, when the British authorities realized that an English fitter at the government railway shops was in fact missing, they had the body exhumed. Although he was not an elite man, Frederick Barlow's European body (like that of Hampson) was abruptly reclassified, both in identity and in dedication for the afterlife, when it was reburied in a Christian cemetery.

For non-Europeans, identification by nationality was typically something new. For Europeans, this status was usually already settled. The strongest and most efficacious claims to European status required no documentation. The dress and comportment of the man on the quay and other residents of Alexandria could obviate legal demonstrations of nationality. Categories of nationality, sect, class, and language were incidental tools that enabled identification of these foreigners. Identification was not the same as identity, however. Alexandrians read signals in order to place individuals in society, not to form conclusions about the essence of their being.

Alexandrians' experience of the actually existing Europeans in their midst form a critical part of this story. Histories of the colonial career of liberal individualism tend to treat it as an abstract quantity or distant force. The history of legal practice shows how the personal experience of rights differences brought about banal and concrete efforts to enhance status without reference to overarching concepts such as liberal citizenship. In this sense, the unjust privilege of Alexandria's tiny handful of sovereign European individuals and the deficient status accorded poor Europeans and "European" subjects of empire such as the Maltese were useful object lessons for the non-Europeans they encountered.

The rule of colonial difference ought to be manifest. In colonial settings such as turn-of-the-century Alexandria, the ideal European would be identified on sight, marked by dress, bearing, location in the city, and language, all of which implied possession of a bundle of special privileges. As we have seen, such persons existed, and they naturally assumed the legal role that the full exercise of their nationality offered to them. We have also seen, however, that this archetypal citizen was a rarity. In Alexandria's expanding matrix of nationality subcategories, legal status and social status were rarely a seamless match, and sociolegal category errors proliferated. The chapters that follow propose a matrix of legal identities that cover the range of a pluralist society. As soon as we identify the European ideal type and the exploitative legal relationships that it established with the rest of humankind, we find defective examples of the ideal. In the chapters that follow, we will encounter the defects, inversions, mimicries, and ironies that marked the status of the vast majority of Alexandrians.

8

Foreigners

In 1905, an Algerian subject named Zarqawi Muhammad al-Sharif persuaded a local man named Sid Ahmad Ahmad al-Habla that he was capable of alchemy. He convinced Sid Ahmad to hand over a gold coin, which Zarqawi transformed into a more substantial lump of gold. His confidence won, he was induced to hand over a large sum—fifty pounds sterling—promising a still larger gain. When Sid Ahmad looked into the crucible after the transformation, he found that his gold had disappeared altogether. Zarqawi was arrested along with two local subjects, who called themselves Haj Idris and Haj Muhammad. Zarqawi was also assumed to be a local, and all three were tried at the native courts and sentenced to six months' imprisonment. This sentence was heavy enough to warrant a gamble: after receiving it, Zarqawi revealed his Algerian nationality and was turned over to the French consular court ("*ses juges naturels*").

Zarqawi did not know how to play the French court skillfully. He obstinately denied any guilt or even knowledge of the affair and challenged a respectable witness who testified against him. This man, Maggaouiri, was a prosperous merchant with an honorable reputation. Zarqawi, on the other hand, was a mere peddler (*colporteur*) in Oriental articles. He had no shop, no commercial records, and could find no Algerian or Tunisian notable who would vouch for his character (*moralité*). Zarqawi's reputation was further compromised by his deep integration in the local community.

"In Arab milieus," the court noted, "he passes not for a merchant, as he claims, but for a sorcerer and a healer." The court called his confidence game "theft by magic spell" (*vol au sortilège*), noting that it was "a classic procedure in Egypt." Zarqawi's claim that Maggaouiri had trumped up the charges in revenge for a failed joint business venture was not credible. But despite his obvious guilt, his dissimulation of his status in Egypt, his obstinate refusal to acknowledge his actions, his affront to a respectable man, and his association with natives, in the final reckoning Zarqawi benefited from his gamble with foreignness. The French court sentenced him to four months in prison, two months less than he and his local accomplices received in the native courts.[1]

Zarqawi's transformation from local dross into foreign gold exemplifies the strange work of nationality law in turn-of-the-century Alexandria society. For his local victim, his accomplices, and the "Arab milieus" in which he lived, Zarqawi's reduced sentence was an experience of colonialism that differed radically from that produced by the British occupiers. The manifest injustice of an English soldier acquitted of the cold-blooded murder of an Arab child (described in chapter 7) was, in a certain sense, consistent with the logic and social experience of foreign military occupation. That an ordinary peddler and healer such as Zarqawi would receive the mantle of foreignness was more unexpected. Although late nineteenth-century Alexandria's social hierarchy had a top (wealthy European notables) and a bottom (Arabic-speaking indigents and bad subjects), its middle was a murky mix of overlapping characters and statuses. In one sphere, however, status was definitely measurable. The capitulations, which exempted subjects and protégés of Western powers from local jurisdiction in the Ottoman Empire, made foreignness a potent legal category. Nationality law frequently upended the hierarchies of Egypt's colonial society. Soldiers in the army of occupation, British administrators and civilians, and Maltese subjects of the British crown were assigned to a single category of nationality; so were French citizens, naturalized Algerian Jews, and Tunisian Muslims. These categories were set against counterpart nationalities enjoying capitulations: Italian, Greek, and so on. Standing outside this pageant of nationalities were local subjects, who did not have the legal personality to hold even the most inferior rank. This qualitative distinction between foreigners' varieties of nationality and locals' lack of the same was one particularity of Egypt's sociolegal complexity.

Close experience of the privilege of other imperial have-nots (such as Zar-qawi) was both galling and instructive. The example of foreign subjects' rights was an important ingredient in the development of counterpart rights of local status and of Egyptian nationality.

In his examination of postcolonial civil law in certain African countries, Mahmood Mamdani finds that subject races constitute a single field but that not all races are native.[2] The institutional distinction between citizens and subjects and between settlers and natives that he describes is similar to the distinction between Alexandria's Europeans and foreigners, down to its legal ramifications. Non-native races (such as Indians, Tutsis, and Arabs) are subjects and not settlers, and they are treated differently from settlers and natives in politics and in law. These non-native non-settlers are a burden of independence, just as Alexandria's subject foreigners were a cost associated with the benefit of the capitulations. Though authorities served them without zeal, they could not escape the ironies of their in-between status. Maltese and Maghribis could be subjugated in their native lands and excluded from the rest of the empire, but Egypt was a site of exception, a third place where they enjoyed special privileges.[3] Most such territories would be eliminated in the twentieth century in the attempt to foreclose such ironies.

Socially speaking, foreignness was so heterogeneous a position as to lose its descriptive power; only its legal meaning—as a category of nationality—retained a degree of unity. Foreign status was testable by courts and police establishing jurisdiction. Often the result of that test did not conform to the colonial stereotype: most foreigners in Alexandria were not European (just as most *colons* in Algeria were not French). In this chapter, I will use "foreigner" to describe a foreign subject who is presumed to be a non-European. Legal records afford unique insight into the lives of those born outside of Europe but who could claim European protection. Less than European but more than native, these defendants, plaintiffs, and witnesses discovered and deployed a new kind of status, best understood in terms of foreignness, to assert power in their legal struggles. But these non-Europeans—Algerians, Tunisians, Maltese, but also Indians and Persians—were "second-class foreigners" without many of the European privileges described in the previous chapter.

In the first section of this chapter, I examine the position of these imperial subjects from the perspective of the consulates that grudgingly assumed the burden of protection, which obliged them to offer these imperial subjects equivalence—if not equality—with Europeans. In the second section, I give evidence of the many advantages foreign nationality offered these non-Europeans. The third section treats foreigners who "passed" as locals, except before the law.

The Accidental Equality of Europeans and Their Imperial Subjects

Writing in 1939, the French legation in Cairo looked back with relief at the ending of the capitulations. Colonial subjects had been the worst of it: "The question of Algerians living in the Ottoman Empire, especially in Egypt and particularly concerning Jews, has over the last eighty years constituted one of the most confusing problems requiring the attention of those in the Oriental department. . . . Even specialists themselves had trouble finding their way" through the masses of contradictory rules.[4]

Algerians, Tunisians, and the Maltese discussed in the preceding chapter—all imperial subjects of capitulatory powers—are "confusing problems" similar enough to be brought together productively. Malta, Algeria, and Tunisia had exported population throughout the Mediterranean for centuries, and each of the three communities numbered about five thousand in turn-of-the-century Alexandria.[5] Each community benefited from foreign status in Egypt only because it was a colonized subsidiary of a great power. There are also useful differences within the category. The North African colonies were larger and more important to France than was Malta to the British. Approaches to citizenship and nationality differed significantly: many Algerians (and Algeria itself) became French, while few Maltese visited Britain, let alone became British. Malta was Catholic, the Maghrib mostly Muslim; sect and language divided the three colonies from their colonizers. These differences manifested themselves starkly at times: for instance, Maltese were evacuated from Alexandria in 1882, but Algerians and Tunisians were not.

The foreignness that Maltese and Maghribis exercised in Egypt was the result of an imperial accident. If Britain had not added Malta to its empire, Maltese would at best have been represented by a community agent without capitulatory powers.[6] This was the case for Tunisians before 1881 and

Algerians before the 1840s; until the French conquest, both communities were considered semi-Ottoman, hence semilocal. Britain took control of Cyprus too late for its subjects to be considered British—this was the problem of Theodore Safa, whose story opens this book. When Britain and France invaded, it was not only the inhabitants of Malta, Algeria, and Tunisia who came under imperial control: many members of the Maltese and Maghribi diasporas also became imperial subjects. The expansion of rationalized governing bureaucracies during the nineteenth century meant that an ever-larger proportion of the world's population was counted and categorized according to nationality, race, religion, and origin. Even migrants fleeing the colonizers carried their new subject status with them, and in most cases (including Egypt) it was transferred to their children. In fact, between a quarter and a third of Maltese and Maghribi heads of household in late nineteenth-century Alexandria were Egyptian born.[7] Thus a considerable number of British and French subjects in Alexandria had never set foot in the British or French empires.

When Maltese and Algerians in Egypt were subsumed into the foreign nationality of their colonizers, it was not the extension of privilege but rather the delegation of responsibility: consulates in Egypt and the Ottoman Empire were expected to control their new imperial subjects. Efforts to reform the laissez-faire system of regulation as foreign populations expanded in the middle of the nineteenth century show how untenable the system of protection had become. Despite the structural changes brought by the Mixed Courts and the British occupation, demographic pressure and imperial contradictions continued to cripple the consular system in the decades following the 1876–1882 settlement. This strain was not restricted to Britain and France but affected every capitulatory power. In Alexandria alone, tens of thousands of foreign subjects relied on their consulates for every administrative procedure. When the French occupied Tunisia in 1881, Tunisians resident in Alexandria became French subjects overnight, doubling the consulate's Maghribi constituency. The consular workload was almost unmanageable in its quantity and diversity. The social order of European empires was based on the superiority of metropolitan citizens over colonial subjects. When large numbers of citizens and subjects swamped the anachronistic capitulations system, consular officials were forced to treat all of their subjects with a sort of equality that was alien to the world of empire. Colonial hierarchies broke down as

TABLE 8.1 French subjects in Alexandria, 1882–1917 censuses

	1882	1897	%	1907	%	1917	%
French total	8,215	5,221		4,304		8,556	
French citizens		3,350	64	3,713	86	3,555	42
Algerians/Tunisians		1,871	36	591	14	1,225	14
Tunisians						640	7
Algerians						585	7
Egyptians						1,314	15
Moorish						734	9
Jews						417	5
Syrians						400	5
Other races						911	11

consular institutions, local authorities, and justice systems proved unable to maintain consistent distinctions between types of foreigners.

A legal accident accompanied this imperial accident. If a new legal system had been created at the end of the nineteenth century, the large, mixed Maltese and Maghribi communities that existed in Alexandria would never have been offered the possibility of equal treatment with Europeans and systematic superiority to locals. But the capitulations, a holdover from a time before France, Britain, the Maghrib, and Malta were colonizer and colonized, were not easily displaced. The law code that governed all British subjects (Britons, Maltese, Indians, natives of Gibraltar and the Ionian Islands, and so on) in Alexandria and the rest of the Ottoman Empire was created for that setting at the start of the nineteenth century, and it differed from law codes used elsewhere in the British Empire by treating all subjects equally.[8] Maghribis experienced the same unusual leveling of rights: French citizens and subjects were also governed by a single law. In the French case, the penal and civil codes used in Egypt and the Ottoman Empire were those used in the metropole, with only minor adjustments (for instance, serious criminal cases and appeals were referred to the Supreme Court at Aix).[9]

Of course, the colonial relationship was not displaced. Consular officials and local authorities retained powers to match the rights accessed by their subjects. They used these powers to fix second-class subjects: to define them, to manage them, to repair them, and, sometimes, as we will see, to convert them from foreign to local. Authorities used language and labels to designate second-class foreigners as clearly as possible. The French consulate divided its nationals into two broad categories: citizen and subject. Citizens were sometimes called "citoyens français" but usually "français" tout court, and their civil status was the responsibility of the chancellery. While "citizen" was a single, unambiguous label, within the broad category of "subject" the French consulate used the terms *administré*, *protégé*, and *sujet* almost interchangeably.[10] Often, the geographic origin of the subject was also specified: *sujet français indigène de l'Algérie*. In practice, the consulate distinguished between three types of subjects: Algerians, Tunisians, and those of other origins. Tunisians were sometimes called Algerian and vice versa; sometimes they were also called "French." Legal distinctions about status (between, for instance, naturalized Jews or those born in Egypt and those born in Algeria) lay behind these various categories, but the consulate's disinclination to distinguish between different categories of second-class foreigners, surprising in otherwise formulaic records, betrays a lack of attention to the second class as a whole, as well as a tendency to lump it together. The British were more specific in their categorization, perhaps because they had fewer legal categories to deal with. The proper official category employed in official correspondence was "Maltese British subject." Shorthand was more direct: "Maltese" in its most restricted sense was the operative category. As we have seen, "British" was reserved for Britons, and Maltese were systematically excluded from the category "European."[11]

Distinction between Europeans and foreigners went beyond language. The civil status of Maghribis was the responsibility of the *drogmanat* rather than the *chancellerie*, which meant that French subjects entered the consulate by different door from citizens.[12] Despite evidence of settlement and integration, consular authorities considered second-class foreigners an alienated, outsider, dangerous population.[13] The rate of criminal offenses in Maltese and Maghribi communities was higher than the rate of criminality among British and French citizens; so too was the poverty rate, population density, and the frequency of mingling with locals. Despite legal equality, court records show a pattern of distinction between first- and second-class foreigners, above all in criminal cases. At the French consular court,

French citizens were charged about as often as Maghribi subjects, but conviction rates were 56 and 70 percent respectively.[14] Within the constraints
of leveling law codes, the Europeans who ran the consular courts were able
to operate according to familiar colonial hierarchies. The systematiza-
tion of British consular justice after 1844 was in large part a response to
concerns about unruly Maltese in the eastern Mediterranean.[15] Algerians
abroad were similarly suspect in French eyes, as departure from the colony
implied opposition to the French occupation.[16] The conditions for Algerian
registration were set out in the 1830s, but few Algerians registered until
the 1860s, when other avenues of foreign protection were closed by the
regulation of 1863 (discussed in detail in chapter 9).[17] Ironically, the net
decrease in protégés entailed an increase in French subjects.

Even wealthy Maltese or Maghribis were rarely welcomed into the community of foreign notables.[18] The consular courts identified notables by
inviting them to serve as judges, assessors, or members of juries. Thus the
consular juries that judged defendants (most of whom were imperial subjects) were overwhelmingly composed of metropolitan citizens. Of the 234
British subjects called to perform this quite burdensome service between
1880 and 1914, only twenty were Maltese.[19] Exclusion was even more stark
at the French consular court during the same period: not one of the more
than one hundred members of the French colony chosen by election or
appointment to serve as assessors at the consular court was a Maghribi
subject or even a naturalized French citizen. Other paths to respectability,
such as appointment as community representative before the Municipality or the Mixed Tribunals, were also closed to the Maltese and Maghribis,
subsumed in British and French nationality. Membership in the (Protestant) Church of Scotland or in English- and French-language cultural societies was equally problematic. The bar of respectability was set quite high,
and few second-class foreigners qualified, even the most wealthy.

The French and British consulates displayed even less zeal for their
work with the poorest foreigners. Shared nationality was the cause of
absurd contact between elites and subalterns.

The room on the earthen floor of which the body was found lying was
very small and contained no furniture but a wooden bench evidently
used as a bed. There was no window, and no hole even for light or ventila-
tion when the door was shut. The seams of the door were even closed by

paper and [canvas] plastered over them. On the floor of the room near the body were two earthenware vessels used for holding fire for cooking. On these vessels there was a quantity of burnt coal on the top of which was a coffee pot without water, leading one to suppose that at the time of death these coal fires were alight and that he was boiling water to prepare a meal. The door of his small hut was found shut so that he was hermetically closed in with no means for the smoke to escape if the fires were alight. In this way death may have happened from suffocation. But, at the same time he was a very aged and decrepit looking man—as I remember well his appearance—and may have died from ordinary causes.

This description of the hut where a poor British Indian subject lived and died is drawn from a postmortem report written by James Mackie, a British consular surgeon in Alexandria. Local police found the body in the hut near Deaconesses' Hospital in Muharram Bey. A registration certificate found with the body informed the police that he was a British subject. The British consular constable caused him to be buried "after performing the rights according to the Mohamedan faith by their clergy." The burial cost 107 piasters (just over a British pound). The constable sold the hut, some lumber found around it, and a saddlebag that the man possessed the next day. The consulate retained a slight surplus of 26 piasters (five shillings).[20]

Mackie knew the dead man, whose name was Sayyid Bassim: "From the part of his face which was still undestroyed by maggots and from his clothes I recognized him as an old fakir whom I had often seen by the roadside in the poor shabby destitute looking condition of his class." It seems extraordinary that Mackie, one of the richest men in the city, would not only handle the body of this poor man but also "know" him.[21]

The Uses of Foreignness

Despite its inferiority to European status, second-class foreignness had its advantages. A young Algerian named Ibrahim Masʿud Badukh, who was charged with theft six times between 1893 and 1901, made considerable use of the ambiguities of his foreignness.[22] Most of these thefts followed a similar pattern. Badukh would drop a bag in the street, and then he and an accomplice would accuse a passerby of stealing the bag. They would move their victim into an alley and search him or her for items lost in the pretended theft. Often, Badukh would "reclaim" cash; twice, when robbing women in this fashion, he also claimed to have lost earrings. He asked to examine the woman's own earrings to see if they were his and returned them in a bag that, when opened, contained only two small pebbles. Not surprisingly, this unnecessarily complicated operation frequently ended in his arrest.[23]

Badukh's foreignness was legal, not social. Like Zarqawi, the alchemist described at the opening of this chapter, Badukh had already been convicted at the local tribunal when he first appeared before the French consular court. It is not clear how Badukh realized that he might be wise to "appeal" his six-month sentence by asserting foreign nationality, but doing so certainly proved worthwhile. He was released from his local sentence, and the French consular court, taking note of his young age, reduced the sentence to four months, minus time already served.

In the years that followed, Badukh continued to do well by his French status. He was acquitted of police charges in 1895 and 1898 because of insufficient evidence; in both cases, he managed to plant the evidence on his accomplice during the carriage ride to the station. Later in 1898, the French court sentenced him to one year's imprisonment for another theft, but that sentence was halved on appeal. He was back in court in 1900, again released because of insufficient evidence. Finally, however, his luck ran out, and he was sent to prison for two years, denounced by his Greek accomplice for the theft of cash from Mousse Chababon, a rabbi who was a British protégé.

The consular courts were intended to protect foreign subjects from arbitrary justice. Above all, this meant giving foreign defendants a fair trial. On this score, the British and French consular justice systems appear relatively equitable at the judgment phase. Most defendants lost, and few verdicts were radically skewed in favor of (or against) the consulates' own subjects.[24] In criminal cases, Maghribi accused were convicted 70 percent of the time; in civil cases with clear outcomes, Maghribi defendants lost three-quarters of the time.[25] On the face of things, then, it would appear that being summoned to the French consular court was ominous for Maghribi defendants. The same was true for European defendants, most of whom also lost. But foreign fear of arbitrary local justice focused less on false conviction than on cruel and unusual punishment. Here there is clearer evidence of systematic advantage for second-class foreigners. Badukh and Zarqawi saw their native-court sentences reduced when they changed status. French penal law was laced with attenuation mechanisms, and these were frequently invoked.[26] Although foreigners could expect few favors in the verdicts they received, they typically enjoyed lenient sentencing.

The locals with most to fear from foreigners were policemen, soldiers, and *ghafirs* (watchmen). Consular records contain hundreds of cases of aggression toward local authorities, which typically involved resisting arrest, insults, disrespect, or assault.[27] Although most foreigners who met such charges were convicted, the "fair-mindedness" of the courts produced some questionable acquittals.[28] Authorities were much frustrated by their impotence over foreigners.[29] Alfredo Baldacchino, the Maltese youth who caused the death of the local boy Ragab Muhammad, escaped to Malta after having been entrusted to the custody of the British consulate. The prefect of police in Alexandria showed his frustration in repeated, insistent letters to the British consul.[30] Decades later, little had changed. Salomon Allouch, an Algerian, had a large business exporting vegetables to Turkey. In 1912, customs agents discovered that he was defrauding the Egyptian customs administration. Confronted with the evidence, Allouch destroyed the incriminating document and was arrested. Rather than being taken to his consulate, he was placed in the local jail. How to explain this unusual procedure? He may have been concealing his status as a French protégé, but because he was well known to the customs service, this seems unlikely. Allouch may have dissimulated his French nationality because he was also facing charges for assaulting the bailiff of the Native Tribunal at Manshiya. After a night in jail, he claimed or was made to claim French protection, and the consulate granted his conditional release. Shortly thereafter, he disappeared from Alexandria. Despite the serious charges laid against him, Allouch was given cavalier treatment by the consulate and was able to make his escape. Local authorities likely took little comfort from the heavy sentences subsequently given him: he was tried in absentia, and the sentences could not be carried out.[31]

A few examples of consular duplicity in the liberation of guilty subjects probably went a long way in convincing local authorities of second-class foreigners' advantage. A Tunisian troublemaker named Muhammad Yussif Gimei was charged with assault in 1901.[32] While spending an evening at a café, he began to quarrel with the owner. Other employees intervened, then a watchman, and finally police officers; Gimei struck all of them.

The French consular court acquitted him, saying that the evidence was thin and that the version given by police agents was unreliable. In most cases, consular failure to cooperate with the police was unwelcome but forgettable. In Gimei's case it must have been infuriating. In 1899 alone, he had been convicted three times of assault on police officers.[33] That this man's word was given more weight than that of agents of the police must have added to authorities' unhappiness with the capitulations. Religious authorities shared this experience. At the end of 1912, a Maghribi book-store owner, ʿAllam ʿAttiya ʿAbdul Rahman ("El Maghrabi"), told the qadi of the Karmuz mahkama that Muslim tribunals were "unjust and arbitrary." The qadi charged him with slander. At the consular court audience, no witnesses were called, and the qadi found that his word alone was no more powerful than that of the accused, who was acquitted.[34] Again, nationality offered access to venues that reversed the order of authority.

Foreigners derived social power from their foreignness. Imperial subjects and protégés made explicit claims to impunity to police and local subjects alike. Local subjects had reason to give credence to these claims. A Maghribi like Muhammad Sultan, landlord of a tenement owned by his family waqf, was able to rebuff a lawsuit from Evangelos and Clé-anthie Plomaritis, two local subjects. Muhammad had been collecting unpaid rent when an incident occurred. Their suit for 1,200 francs (£48) claimed that he had insulted and assaulted them, triggering a hysterical episode that left Madame Plomaritis disabled. Despite the European char-acteristics of these local subjects—Greek names, Christianity—their claim was laughed out of court when a milkman testified that Madame Plomari-tis was prone to such fits whenever bills were collected.[35] Engaging with the foreign legal system entailed encounters with unknown codes and unknown practices. The courts presented considerable obstacles to locals' complaints, beginning with the need to use a foreign language and employ some sort of advocate. Individuals asking for civil damages in a criminal complaint against a French subject had to pay a deposit, for example. Only a quarter of plaintiffs who paid cautions won convictions, and those who could not pay were forced to abandon their claims.[36] Presumably many other cases were abandoned long before they reached the court.

Although the impunity consular justice sometimes offered to second-class foreigners was irritating to local authorities and opponents, it was hardly enough to cause widespread consternation. Consular courts were not a direct threat because foreigners had no right to prosecute locals before the consular courts. But the advantages that accrued to second-class foreigners extended beyond the courtroom's verdicts. The appearance or reputation of foreign nationality carried social advantage, and those who were seen as foreign were treated differently in commerce, conflict, and other kinds of interaction. Cultural behavior—dress, speech, and so on—reinforced the social power that derived from the projection of foreignness. Legal advantages lay behind this social power, but in many cases law was an unstated or even invisible presence; the social power that derived from law took on a power of its own that could endure in the absence of legal advantage.[37]

Even a slight advantage was significant, particularly to foreigners' reputation of impunity. It is perhaps a coincidence that Badukh's luck ended the first time neither victim nor accomplices were local. It is also possible that so long as his only opponents were local, foreign legal status meant that even individuals as slippery and inept as Badukh were at a clear structural advantage. Second-rate foreignness meant more than localness, which was the absence of status, the absence of standing. Local subjects feared disadvantage vis-à-vis foreign adversaries and would abandon contests or settle them on unfavorable terms. In general, the advantages of foreignness were apparent and exploited well before verdicts were issued. For this reason, its power should not be evaluated merely on the basis of the outcomes of court cases. Second-class subjects were able to win meager advantages, but these were nevertheless beyond the reach of those without foreign status. In the eyes of local authorities and local subjects, these "foreign subjects" belonged to an extensive and powerful category.

Consular court records tell us more about foreign defendants than they do about foreign plaintiffs, who had to pursue their cases before the jurisdiction of the defendant. Consular courts only heard civil and commercial cases between parties of the same nationality; cases between mixed parties (the vast majority) went to the Mixed Tribunals. The noncriminal cases left to consular courts were overwhelmingly between parties who shared more than just nationality. Very few cases arose between Europeans and second-class foreigners because of the social distance between the two groups. Cases between second-class foreigners were predominantly family disputes between husbands and wives, disputes between related heirs, and the settlement of debts and business partnerships between friends and relatives. The courts provided a useful venue for ordinary civil and commercial transactions between Maltese and Maltese or Maghribi and Maghribi.[38] When, for instance, two Maghribi merchants chose to dissolve a decades-old commercial partnership through which they had sold imported Moroccan and Tunisian wool at a shop in the Suq al-Magharba, they did so at the consular court.[39] Court records show that the case was judged in a Muslim legal idiom, using *hijri* dating.

Second-class foreigners found that the consulate could be used on and in their own terms. In areas of personal status, systematic and distinct patterns emerge from the court records, showing that Maltese were treated differently (though not necessarily worse) from Britons. This different treatment often suited litigants' purposes. For example, Maltese inheritance law entailed division of estates among a wider set of family members than was usual in British law. In the jurisdiction of the British consular courts, Maltese inheritance and marriage breakdown (particularly separation, maintenance, and custody) were settled according to the laws used in Malta. French subjects who were Muslims took personal-status cases—again, usually civil cases involving family questions—to Alexandria's *mahkama* (Islamic court).[40]

Aggressive use of the court by foreign plaintiffs intimidated foreign defendants. Withdrawal of charges is a hallmark of successful, strategic use of the courts. In such cases, complaint before the court was the catalyst for out-of-court settlement, at which point charges were withdrawn. The number of such incidents is impossible to estimate, but there was a pattern of such use by the Maltese. The moneylender Filippo Calleja used the threat of court action repeatedly and with great success to scare payment from his petty debtors.[41] The court was an auxiliary venue for the settlement of family disputes. Succession struggles would be aired in the courts but settled between family members. Even violent contests sometimes worked in the same way. In 1906, a Maltese who had been stabbed in the buttock by his brother-in-law lodged charges at the consulate. The court pursued this charge but had to abandon prosecution when, after the heat of the moment had passed, every member of the family (including the victim) refused to cooperate with the proceedings.[42] While certain Maltese litigants were undoubtedly coerced into abandoning their claims, most appear to have been satisfied to settle disputes on their own terms, using the consular court only for its catalytic effect.

Beyond the court, the consulate offered other services to Maltese and Maghribis. By the end of the nineteenth century, state and bureaucratic institutions had become a useful resource for many residents of Mediterranean cities. Registration with the consulate was necessary in order to travel with legal documents, to avoid paying local taxes, and to avoid local military service (although for French subjects, at least, registration also entailed the expectation of service in the French military). The consulate was also a useful resource for the resolution of family and financial disputes outside of court, and the consulate's clerks and janissaries often acted to resolve disputes informally.[43] Finally, the consulate offered (on an ad hoc basis, and similar to its services for poor Europeans) a rudimentary system of social services: relief for the destitute, advocacy with employers, transportation homeward, and so on.

But the consulates did their best to curtail these services for imperial subjects. In a period of expanding state and bureaucratic control, both the French and British consulates called on ethnic and religious self-service organizations to perform services for second-class foreigners that consular staff performed for first-class Europeans. Religious institutions accounted for their members, served a welfare function, and issued documents not only instead of but also parallel to states. Muslim courts and Christian churches performed civil services for non-European foreigners (issuing birth certificates, verifying poverty, maintaining registration) that consulates performed for citizens. Maltese welfare was assigned to Alexandria's Maltese Benevolent Society (a community organization), family networks, and individual members of the community, who provided relief to the destitute, paid hospital bills, and buried the dead.[44] Aid cut across national/imperial lines: the Benevolent Society was open to and run by British, Italian, and local Maltese subjects. More remarkably, considering its fear of Maltese criminality, the British consulate abdicated surveillance and even some policing to the Maltese intermediaries and the community as a whole.[45] Catholic parish priests issued certificates of birth and marriage, of course, but also identity and character references.[46] As we saw earlier, when the British authorities decided that one of their Jewish subjects was not in fact British, they referred all questions about her nationality to the rabbi of Alexandria.[47] The Jewish and Muslim communities performed similar functions for Maghribis. Registration with the French consulate depended on certificates of notoriety from community notables, who also issued certificates of destitution that liberated subjects from consular fees.

Whether they acted through community or consulate, foreigners' nationality-based rights claims offered them power over other categories of people, those with rights that were weaker still. There existed a third class of foreigners, people that second-class foreigners (Maghribis and Maltese) could expect to dominate at court. In the summer of 1886, the Persian consulate communicated a complaint against Salem Ben Hussain, a Tunisian merchant, to the French consulate. Hussain ʿAbd al-Gawad, a Persian peddler, claimed that he had met Salem at the Tunisian market on the last day of Ramadan. When Hussain refused to sell him handkerchiefs at the price he demanded, Salem beat him with a stick. Salem denied the charge, saying that he had been in his shop all day and hadn't entered the market. He called two Algerian witnesses, who testified that they had been to his shop to settle accounts with him. The peddler's two witnesses, both Persian lemonade sellers, seem to have commanded less respect than their Algerian counterparts. Salem carried the day with his own testimony. He argued that Hussain (whom he described as a "bedouin," confusing different categories of outsider) was trying to run a little number during Ramadan. Two days before the trial, he had attempted to extort twenty francs (almost a pound) from Salem by offering to withdraw his charges. (Two further witnesses testified that they'd seen the two gesturing together.) Perhaps the decisive statement was Salem's assertion that as a rich and well-known man, he had no need to busy himself with handkerchiefs. The court released him.[48]

Persians, Indians, Sudanese, Caribbeans—all were made to see the power of second-class foreigners. Europeans rich and poor, as well as their imperial subjects, might deploy the privileges of the capitulations to secure legal and social advantages. A certain number of other foreigners, rarely visible in the records, lacked the security of the capitulations treaties and the mutual-support system of the most-favored-nation clause. Because it was a Muslim state, Persia was deemed ineligible for a capitulations agreement.[49] Persian subjects were not subjects of the Ottoman sultan, however. As a result, they were caught between foreign and local legal regimes. Categorical protection was also an exception to be eliminated. For Persia, the road map was clear: recognition of sovereignty in public law and subjecthood in private law were the same project. As we will see in chapter 11, Ottomans were further along this road, having joined the community of nations in the 1850s and promulgated a nationality law in the 1860s.

The Ottoman/Persian nationality contest has been studied by Karen Kern, but a strong test case never arose in Egypt, and the problem of Persian protection went unresolved until the very different conditions of the 1920s.[50] Foreigners from subaltern states inhabited an inchoate realm of nationality-based exceptions without positive rights that awaits further study.

Passing

Maghribis were the most cosmopolitan of foreigners. Despite variations in dialect, Tunisian and Algerian immigrants were proficient users of Alexandrine Arabic.[51] The greatest language difficulty most Algerians and Tunisians faced in Alexandria was the use of French at their consulate. As we have seen, many Algerian and Tunisian French subjects were well enough integrated into the body of local subjects to be "mistaken" for locals. This association was supported by links of religion and language, as well as geographical adjacency. In 1912, an Algerian sentenced by the Alexandria Native Tribunal to three years of hard labor decided to try his luck with the French court.[52] Once he came into French jurisdiction, the orthography of his name changed from Abu Kurra to Bouguerra. Bouguerra's case record narrates the transfer of jurisdiction as follows: "The Egyptian government, which arrested this French national (*ressortissant français*) at the scene of the crime and was unable to obtain any proof of his identity, naturally considered him a local subject. Once it realized its error, it hastened to render [Abu Kurra] to the French consular authorities." The record suggests that Bouguerra was indistinguishable from a local subject, even to the local police. This may or may not have been true; he may have hidden his nationality or been ignorant of it, or the police may have chosen to ignore it so long as possible, or the question may have been considered insignificant. The position of the French authorities was entirely passive: "naturally" considered a local subject, Bouguerra needed documents and genealogy to prove that he was worthy to be punished as a French subject. Once his "true" status was clearly established, however, the rules of the game changed completely, all previous conclusions were thrown out, and the investigation began again from scratch.

For many foreigners, foreignness was an abstraction to be manipulated. Imperial governments established the rules of the game, and consulates were its local adjudicators. Despite these rules, the game was full of ambiguities that skillful players, those who understood these conditions, could turn to their advantage. The major point of ambiguity was the disjuncture between legal and social placement of the foreign/local borderline. Marked by authorities' uncertainty in labeling second-class foreigners, this disjuncture created space for a manipulation of the ambiguities of foreignness. Second-class foreigners' in-between status was regularly rehearsed in their day-to-day lives. Infrequent contact with the consulate and Europeans reminded them of their inferior rank, while more frequent interaction with the majority of Alexandria's population, its local subjects, allowed them to exercise superiority. Maltese and Maghribis were happy to exercise the privileges of foreignness and were not particularly bothered by their place within the foreign spectrum. When useful, their foreignness could be made manifest; the rest of the time, it was of little practical use.

Clancy-Smith argues that there was overwhelming confusion about the status of the Maltese community. But confusion about where to place the "hybrid" Maltese was for the most part restricted to Europeans. For most inhabitants of the city, the Maltese were not "cultural creoles," and their status was not unclear.[53] It was French citizens and Britons who were the indistinguishable mass of uncomprehending foreigners who could only be clustered under the general category of "European." Likewise, Clancy-Smith's notion that Maltese were "outcasts" depends on official European reckonings of social inclusion. In the eyes of the majority of the city's population, it was the bourgeois Europeans who were the outsiders. Maltese and Maghribis, who were able to communicate directly with most Alexandrians, were distinct and identifiable. Maltese and Maghribis who appeared before the courts were clear about the legal status they sought or exercised. They would use foreignness, imperial subjecthood, national identity, and localness so far as they were useful. To cast their strategy as "displacement," as occupation of "in-between spaces," unwittingly endorses the notion of fixed, European nationalities bounding those spaces. But for the Maltese and Maghribis, the confusion was others', not theirs.

Those foreign nationals who lived in "local" society used nationality as a tool of advantage, not identity. The story of second-class foreigners contains two narratives that are by now familiar parts of the historiography of colonialism and nationalism. The first is the story of appropriation and subversion by the colonized of the legal tools of the colonizer. This triumph, exemplified by Maghribi and Maltese use of the consular courts, leads us to the second story: the reification of community identity. Law made available categories of distinction and taught Maltese to claim Maltese distinction from Britishness. In the same way, language and settlement became reified as Maltese. Similarly, many Algerian and Tunisian French subjects were taught to claim distinction from their Arabic-speaking neighbors that went beyond the mere name "al-Maghribi."

Europeans might pass for officials, as we saw in the last chapter. Despite the Orientalist fantasies of Richard Burton, John Buchan, T. E. Lawrence, and Henri de Monfreid, they were far less likely to pass for locals. As we saw in the cases of Salomon Allouch and Ibrahim Badukh, non-European foreigners could pass as locals. These were not *mutamassirun*, the elite foreigners who Egyptianized during the interwar period. The turn-of-the-century model of foreigners' "passing" looks more like choice of venue, and the legal nationality that goes with it, by individuals whose social identity was settled. It was British and French administrators, as well as Arabic-speaking police officers, local authorities, and other foreign subjects, who were unsettled, and they fumbled to categorize Maltese and Maghribis in status contests before the consular courts.

Because consulates exerted minimal effort in administering second-class foreigners, consular records of imperial subjects and protégés were far from complete. As we saw in chapter 3, subjects were miscounted and mislabeled, and names were misspelled. Although personal names were ubiquitous in protocols of identification, they did not work as unique identifiers. The name of the inept thief described above appears in court records in every possible permutation: Ibrahim, Abramino; Masoud, Mas'oud, Massoud; Badouk, Badouh, Badoukh, Badouch. The name of a Maltese named Carmelo Buhagiar, accused before the British court, underwent a different kind of transformation in the documents reproduced in figure 8.1. When police first wrote to the consulate (in Arabic), they transliterated his name directly: *Karmilu Bukajiyar*. In the weeks that followed, opinion about how to fix his identity changed. When the police next wrote, they referred to him as *Karminu Abu Hajar*.[54] Buhagiar and Abu Hajar are in fact the same name, but the former version is unmistakably foreign, and the latter is unmistakably Arab. It is impossible to say how or

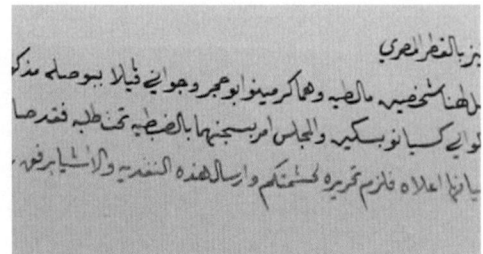

FIGURE 8.1 Two Arabic transliterations of "Carmelo Buhagiar," 1883.

Source: FO 847/6/49, with permission of the National Archives of the UK.

why this orthographic "correction" was made, but it indicates a change in the social categorization of an individual whose legal category was beyond doubt.

That local authorities often call Maltese European but that the British never do is revealing of the categories at play. For the British consulate, it made little legal difference whether they were dealing with a Briton, Maltese, or another kind of British subject, yet this detail was of considerable practical importance. For local authorities, too, the social fact that they were dealing with a foreigner of any kind seems to have been as important as the legal specification of his or her foreignness. For Maltese (and, presumably, Maghribis), who had more dealings with locals than with Britons, this order of things was useful. It showed that they were able to accrue to themselves many of the social advantages of foreignness in general, despite consular efforts to restrict them to a second (-class) category of foreignness.

Locals' immediate experience of second-class foreigners' advantage was an essential part of their desire for a different legal order. The apex of the celebrated "nationalist" revolution of 1882 was the antiforeign riots in Alexandria. Historians have neglected the essential fact that the foreigners with whom locals fought were mostly Maltese and that the fight took place in a Maltese neighborhood. Arabic-speaking Alexandrians were not fighting Maltese because they were troubled by Maltese imperial aspirations or Maltese control of the Caisse de la Dette Publique. They were fighting

Maltese because they were the immediate emblems—exemplars—of the injustice of foreign privilege. The British occupation did not settle this inequality of legal personality, nor indeed did the creation of the Native Courts. The weakness of localness remained apparent in social, commercial, and legal interactions with foreigners.[55]

The Maltese and Maghribis of Egypt depart from T. H. Marshall's classic formulation, in which citizenship begins with political rights, proceeds to civil rights, and culminates in social rights.[56] Though his model has been subject to intense criticism,[57] the primacy of political rights (at least) is firmly established in the literature on the history of citizenship. Alexandria's second-class foreigners developed a set of civil rights and even some social rights, but without any political rights.[58] Despite mistreatment and neglect, these foreigners exercised rights in Egypt that were unavailable to them in their home colonies (Malta, Algeria, and Tunisia) or in the imperial metropoles (Britain and France).[59] To some extent, this was a question of attention: imperial subjects had ready access to consular offices in Alexandria, using exactly the same channels used by citizens. These channels were unavailable in the home colonies, while migratory access to the metropole (where such channels were available) was typically closed to imperial subjects.[60] But in Egypt, these foreigners were able to use the courts not as highly constrained subjects to a colonial justice system (as was the case in the colonies themselves) but as equals under European extraterritorial laws. In Egypt, second-class foreigners took the vague raw material given to them by their colonizers and the local authority and did their best with it, which was to reconstitute it as a powerful category: foreigner. Second-class foreigners found space between first-rate foreigners and native subjects in which to exercise limited but significant power vis-à-vis colonizers and locals alike. So in one sense this is a story of triumph, of appropriation and subversion by the colonized of the legal tools of the colonizer. But the base of much identity, the sort articulated in political and cultural terms in the nationalist movements of the late nineteenth century, was actually a narrow and self-interested desire for advantage in contests of status. Alexandria's evidence shows that many individuals assumed national identification labels (such as Maltese, Algerian, and eventually Egyptian) first and foremost in order to assume civil rights and legal advantages, rather than as an expression of an upsurge of political, cultural, or national identity.

The notion that foreignness was a complex, confusing, blurred category of agency overstates the importance that second-class foreigners attached to their claim to be foreign. For Maltese and Maghribis, nationality was essentially a limited, negative claim. In terms of politics, culture, and language, "foreigner" was an identity both hollow and indistinct. Only when defined in terms of civil rights does it become a clear and meaningful category. If the Maltese and Maghribi communities of Alexandria sometimes showed the integrity of national communities, this appearance was based as much on attraction to the raw materials of extraterritorial advantage as it was on any native upsurge of nationalist feeling. This is not to mention the thousands who did not bother to register and never availed themselves of the court's facilities. Assumption of a particular category and its accouterments brought particular advantages, and it was to those advantages that foreignness gravitated.

Foreignness was above all a claim of distinction and exemption from localness. This claim was all the more important because second-class foreigners were often considered locals in social terms. For this reason, the influence of second-class foreigners upon Egyptian nationalism went beyond modeling colonial nationhood. On a more fundamental level, the civil rights exercised by these immediate foreigners created a perceived lack of counterpart rights among locals and thereby created a need for those rights. Writing in 1900, Muhammad al-Muwailihi described foreigners, from the perspective of an Egyptian *effendi* sitting in a dance hall, as "Maghribi riffraff" (*siflat al-magharaba*) and "exploiter subjects of foreign states" (*masakhkhirin min raʿaya al-duwal al-ajnabiya*) who gamed foreign protection to avoid local prosecution (in this case for pimping).[61] If Europeans were clearly oppressors in Egypt, their imperial subjects presented another face of colonial injustice. Anecdotes of impunity made for a bad reputation for whole communities of nonlocal Arabic speakers in Egypt who were believed to exploit foreign protection for nefarious ends. Certainly there was no shortage of evidence of this practice. The desire for enhanced legal standing born of outrage over the legal privileges held by undeserving social competitors had a long pedigree. As we will see in the next chapter, the rights of protégés—employees, favorites, and coreligionists of foreigners—were the subject of intense opposition throughout the

Ottoman Empire at the middle of the nineteenth century. Ottoman legal reforms of the 1860s sharply curtailed protégé numbers, but even at century's end, their reputed legal privilege constituted a nationality irritant as prominent as any Maltese or Maghribi foreigner. Evidence of local subjects disgruntled with rights inferior to their foreign and protégé neighbors suggests that a more basic narrative of the discovery of national identity might be in order.

9
Protégés

"Certainly, it seems to me if any one has a reasonable claim to British protection under all the circumstances, she has in an imminent degree. There are Greeks and other non-Britons in this city who have obtained such protection. Dear sir, is it impossible for her to obtain the same?"[1] So wrote the godfather—the protector—of Miss Margaret Ann Gowans to the British consul in Alexandria in 1906. He was trying to resolve a discrepancy between legal status and social status. The unfortunate young woman was twice orphaned: born to "Ottoman" parents, she was adopted by a British couple in her infancy and raised in Constantinople. When her adoptive parents died, she learned the secret of her birth and the fact that, despite an Anglican baptism and English education, she had no legal right to British protection. The law, when formally applied, reduced the privileges of almost every protégé (or supposed protégé) that it encountered. When Miss Gowans left Constantinople to work as a governess in Alexandria, her godfather could no longer act as her guardian. He wrote to the consul asking him, in effect, to substitute in that role. Even a few years earlier, this service would have been granted to a European as a matter of course. But at the end of the nineteenth century, laws both Ottoman and British had narrowed the range of possibilities, and consular staff struggled to translate goodwill into protection. "If you can manage to get her registered it would be a great boon to her," wrote one official to another, "but I don't myself quite see how it can be effected."

Although Miss Gowans was European in social terms, she did not qualify as foreign in legal terms. In the traditional Ottoman context, an individual in her situation might be given the status of a foreign protégé. Those enjoying capitulatory rights could take out patents of protection (*berats*) for their allies and subalterns, including employees (such as translators, clerks, guards, and servants), coreligionists, dragomans, and diplomatic and consular representatives. As Maurits van den Boogert's fine study of *beratlıs* in the eighteenth century shows, these protégés enjoyed much the same status as foreigners: they avoided many local taxes, ducked prosecution and litigation, traveled more easily, inherited estates according to favorable formulas, escaped conscription, and avoided police searches.[2] Not all protégés used protection in these ways, but some did. Gowans, for example, was particularly anxious to secure free movement between Constantinople and Alexandria. And regardless of intent, the real and imagined immunities of protégés systematically intimidated local subjects.

Protégé status was particular to the Ottoman Empire, and it became the first front in Ottoman efforts to end extraterritorial jurisdiction. In 1863, an Ottoman regulation definitively limited protégé numbers for the first time.[3] Notably, this regulation preceded the first Ottoman nationality law, issued in 1869. Under the standardizing impetus in international law that emerged during the last quarter of the century, the meaning of protection was further specified and narrowed. Its legal sense was restricted and detached from the normative general meaning of the word. It became a narrow space for outsiders who would not be counted as European or foreign in the census. Guarantees (*damanat*) were privatized (along with the guilds and corporations that used to provide them), and Ottoman protection (*riʿaya*) was formalized, as we will see in chapter 11. Only a small (and shrinking) number of people protected by a foreign government were deemed protégés; most objects of foreign protection (that is, the Europeans and foreigners treated in the preceding chapters) were now described as nationals, subjects, or citizens. Ironically, those few protégés who retained the status after 1863 demonstrated an enhanced sense of entitlement, more specific than Europeans or foreigners, deriving from the old principles of protection. As the law changed, however, these protégés found that they could no longer invoke the same robust protections they once had and that they had lost some privilege along the way. But many of the privileges of protection became incorporated into the evolving field of nationality, which became more exclusive and thus met their needs.

Questions of protection were evaluated according to two systems: moral judgment and positive law. The debate about protégés, both in the politics of the nineteenth century and in the historiography of recent years, is characterized by an uneasy blend of moral and legal arguments. The first section of this chapter considers turn-of-the-century legal definitions of protection and its practice in the eighteenth and nineteenth centuries. It then turns to the individual protection afforded consular officials who were local subjects. The third section examines broader categories of group protection, including imperial subjecthood and minority sectarian communities. In both cases, the 1880s witnessed the ending of long-established guarantees. The last section takes up background issues of moral obligation and popular anxieties about illegitimate interlopers that accompanied the turn-of-the-century abolition of protection. In closing, I discuss the endurance of old forms of protection in the new skin of nationality.

The Morality of Protection

Protection was a moral project. It was offered to recipients deemed deserving because of affinity with the protecting power, often articulated in terms of class or religion. Protégés made more sense in moral terms than they did in legal description, and the expansion of nationality law brought the waning of their status. Because of its historical resonances the category was disproportionately important for both its supporters and its detractors. For both camps, the protégé debate was a question of justice. For the former, the protégé category offered a means to protect those non-nationals who offered extraordinary services to their state. It also offered a means to help those (like Margaret Ann Gowans) who had a cultural claim on foreign status but, through accidents of law and circumstance, could not convert it into official status. In this view, it was just to reward service with protection and, indeed, to protect embattled minorities. Protection was the duty of the patron to his clients, and the protégé deserved protection in a moral sense, even if it could not always be pulled off legally.

For detractors, the figure of the protégé embodied the injustices of the capitulations: unwarranted privilege for a minority, put to harmful effect through economic and political outrages. There was no question of deserving individuals. Instead, the offense derived from imposing terms on an unwilling population. In this sense, the protégé incarnated inequalities between states. In British Egypt, the foreigner—and especially the soldier—naturally filled the shoes of the protégés of yore. Those discovering nationalist and anticolonial rhetorics found a ready scapegoat in the figure of the protégé.

In broader social histories of the Ottoman Empire, protégés are often assigned a catalytic role. Edhem Eldem makes the case that at the end of the eighteenth century, non-Muslim Ottoman subjects were a frustrated bourgeoisie expelled from or fleeing the Ottoman system into the arms of foreign protection.[4] In the nineteenth-century Syrian context, Abdul-Karim Rafeq has examined the ban on land ownership by foreigners (one of few legal disabilities apparently suffered by subjects of the capitulations), and Sibel Zandi-Sayek traces the repeal of that ban in Izmir.[5] In her study of nineteenth-century Beirut, Leila Fawaz argues that local entrepreneurs began their ascent as middlemen for Westerners, then succeeded them. In this process, consular protection was the great prize that they sought in order to protect their commercial interests. She notes that although it seemed to consuls that everyone was asking for protection, in fact only a small number received it.[6] Despite the fewness of their number, protégés played a decisive role in nineteenth-century economic, social, and political transitions.

In many ways, the idea of protection was more important than its legal actualization. This is true (as we will see) in estimates of the overall scale of the issue and also in specific individual examples. Protection was a source of intimidation, which rarely depended on the juridical substance of the claim. When, for example, a British subject assaulted a railroad conductor in 1908, the police station commander told the railway men that he could do nothing because the accused was a British subject.[7] This was completely false (and in fact the assailant was convicted), but those protected by foreign powers certainly traded on a reputation of impunity that influenced even policemen. Similar stories appeared frequently in the press: in 1892, for instance, a reader in Helwan wrote to *Al-Muʾayyad* reporting that faced with a French-born English subject assaulting a railroad employee, police were too intimidated by his protection to intervene.[8]

The contemporary literature on Ottoman history often treats protégés in quite alarmist terms. The most-cited modern academic survey of the

Ottoman protégé system describes it as "a grave threat to the existence of [the] empire."[9] Other recent scholarship offers similarly strong rhetoric, asserting that extraterritoriality was *the most* important policy consideration for successive Ottoman regimes up to the First World War.[10] Timur Kuran identifies an even more profound role for protégés; in his account, the choice of law available to non-Muslims was instrumental in the Middle East's economic underdevelopment:

> Minorities gained an advantage and Muslims started falling behind, only when the former began to exercise their *choice of law* differently, in favor of western legal systems. This flight from Islamic law, and from the laws of local minorities, took place as hundreds of thousands of Christians and Jews acquired western protection and moved their business dealings, usually in part, outside the Islamic legal system.[11]

These and similar studies cite a small set of evidence of illegitimacy (for example, only six of the 1,500 protégés in Aleppo in 1793 were legitimate), a set derived from classic Orientalist texts and polemical consular correspondence.[12] But in their rush to identify a single antagonist, these studies overlook two facts. First, as preceding chapters have shown, most protégés and foreigners were, like Margaret Gowans, people of limited means and limited importance. Second, while foreign protection was a convenient path to privileges such as choice of law, it was hardly the unique avenue of access. The protégé fixation of these recent studies betrays a lingering moral frustration.

It cannot be denied that protégés were the topic of considerable official anxiety in the eighteenth and nineteenth centuries. In general, Ottoman and Egyptian administrations were concerned about the limits that the protégé system placed on their own sovereignty.[13] In particular, they disliked the sale of patents of foreign protection (*berats*) to local subjects.[14] But close reading of the archival records show that after the middle of the nineteenth century, this concern could no longer be attributed to actually existing protégés—by the 1880s, their number was tiny. This fear of small numbers seems to confirm the moral rather than material character of the offense caused by protégés.

On the face of things, it is difficult to square the scale of this category with the worry it caused. Certainly there is little evidence to support a recent claim that there were "millions" of protégés in the mid–nine-teenth century or that "the French especially in an effort to increase their influence in Egypt, sold or otherwise granted citizenship papers" at the time of the First World War.[15] In his careful study of the Ottoman capitu-lations in the eighteenth century, van den Boogert estimates that at the end of that century the empire counted about 2,500 protégés.[16] This cor-responds to 0.01 percent of the total population of the empire.[17] The num-bers that I have collected from nineteenth-century Egypt paint a similar picture. In 1856, a total of forty-seven foreigners in Alexandria and 117 in Cairo enjoyed British protection.[18] An exhaustive consular census in 1888 shows only eleven British naturalized subject families (twenty-seven men, women, and children) and eighteen British protected subjects (thirty-two men, women, and children total) in the city.[19] We can infer from registra-tion numbers that the French consulate in Alexandria had no more than a dozen protégés during the 1880s, when the city counted a quarter of a million inhabitants.[20]

If there were so few protégés, why the concern? Both the panic over protégés and the idea of protection itself were mostly imaginary. Panics over "strangers in our midst" are, of course, a general feature of modern citizenship and migration regimes.[21] There is nothing here that resembles the supposed 1,500 illegitimate protégés of Aleppo.[22] Tightened regula-tion of status after 1863 did much to reduce the supposed fifth column of illegitimate protégés: by 1879, according to a German official's report, five hundred protégés had been dropped from German consular registers.[23]

If numbers count, it is the foreigners described in chapter 8, the thousands of Algerian French subjects and Maltese British subjects who received foreign-registration certificates each year, who should have caused most concern. Indeed, they too slipped into the shoes of the hated protégés. These "second-class foreigners" were considered of humble means, however, while protégés were believed to be wealthy. While this stereotype is inaccurate, the commodification of protection was a tangi-ble irritant. As we saw in chapter 3, protection was a thing of value: its paper tokens were traded, gifted, purchased, forged, and stolen. The lib-eral imperial doctrines of equality elaborated during the Tanzimat miti-gated against the traditional trade in protection.[24] The central injury lay in the perception of arbitrary foreign authority, however, and it was left to positive law to offer a remedy. When cases were formally adjudicated, their most striking feature was the disjuncture between the imagined and the sanctioned dimensions of protection, which is precisely the issue at play when counting protégés.

It was this persistence of unfair privilege—illegal protection—that confirmed the offensive imaginary sense of protégé status. Long after codes had been installed that were applied rigorously enough to strip the protection of those wealthy protégés foolish enough to press their legal claims to the bitter end, people who seemed deserving still won foreign protection. Stein's recent study of the malleable British protection of an ultrawealthy Baghdad Jew in interwar Shanghai elegantly illustrates the flexibility of this form of status. But Silas Aaron Hardoon, like Antun ʿAbd al-Massih, was a rare exception, too narrow a basis for her general argument that protected status "placed its holders outside the dyads of colonial subject or naturalized citizen, colonizer or colonized, Eastern or Western, European or Occidental . . . rendering them intermediary figures of imperialism whose legal status shifted over time and from place to place."[25] The stories of the few who slipped between the cracks distract us from the many more who could no longer do so as the law increasingly limited options for all except those few whose wealth the law cannot constrain.

Legal Definitions of Protection

"Protection is an institution which has no equivalent in modern Western legislation." So wrote Pierre Arminjon, a professor at the Khedivial Law School in Cairo, in 1903.[26] This statement, appearing in one of the first modern treatises on extraterritorial legal protection in the Ottoman Empire, is inaccurate. The treatise itself shows that both the general functions of protection (shielding, guarding, keeping safe) and the formal statuses of protection (protégé, protected person, *mahmi*) appear in the Western laws used to govern the Western populations of the eastern Mediterranean. But Arminjon's assertion that protection was alien to Western law is symptomatic of the broader knowledge problem that swirls around the figure of the protégé, a category that blends and blurs in both the legal work of the turn of the century and the historical work describing that period: there is great distance between the imagined dimensions of protection and its actual articulation in legal practice.

Arminjon is correct that protection goes almost unmentioned in the canonical treatises of Western international law.[27] In composing his study, he relied on manuals specific to the Ottoman context.[28] When, after Arminjon, international law had occasion to treat the question, protégés were defined (in retrospect) as exceptional. But until the later nineteenth century, when nationality became the dominant legal category of personal affiliation to states, protection was the most common category of affiliation in the eastern Mediterranean. This label corresponds to the essential function at the heart of regimes of affiliation: securing personal status under the safeguard of a powerful authority. In present-day conceptions of citizenship, the question of protection tends to be overshadowed by other concerns: rights and responsibilities, voice, and the like.[29] But the role of protection endures, especially outside the municipal context. Private international law is, in many ways, a means of assessing protection regimes. "Strong" citizenships—those of powerful countries—are strong precisely because they protect better than the "weak" citizenships of states with limited military or diplomatic capacity.[30]

In his pioneering treatise, Arminjon offers this definition: protection "is a juridical link attaching a person to a state, affording that person certain rights and advantages enjoyed by nationals of that state (*droits et avantages dérivés de la qualité de national de cet Etat*), but without granting that person nationality (*cette qualité de national*) or the personal status that goes along with it."[31] He suggests that protection can best be understood in contradistinction to nationality and subjecthood (which he considers equivalent): "the protégé remains under the power of his national sovereign, he retains his personal status (which depends on nationality), he enjoys none of the rights and owes none of the obligations that follow from the nationality of the country that protects him. He benefits to a very great extent, however . . . from the institutions and laws of the protecting state."[32] Arminjon thus suggests four measures for protection as practiced: sovereignty, personal status, rights/obligations, and access to institutions and laws. The most relevant later source, Abu Haif's Egypt-focused 1924 survey of private international law, presents a different typology, distinguishing between Ottoman and Egyptian protégés (*mahmiyun wataniyun*) and foreign protégés (*ajanib mahmiyun*); between temporary protection and perpetual, heritable protection; and between four modes of protection: diplomatic (*siyasi*), civil, religious, and legal.[33]

Nationality regimes can be divided into those that define nationality as a legal status (such as France and Germany, drawing on Roman law) and those that define it as a legal relationship depending on allegiance (such as the common-law countries).[34] Protection was clearly conceived as a relationship governed by duty, merit, and obligation. It was essentially personal. Ultimately, therefore, it is not definition but description that makes protégé status clear, both in Arminjon's study and others that followed.[35] Just as we have observed with nationality itself, the category was elaborated through concrete cases, despite jurists' urge to give it an abstract definition. In addition to dozens of unusual and rare varieties of protection that need not detain us here, these studies enumerate three main categories of protégé: consular employees, Western imperial subjects (that is, the foreigners of chapter 8), and protected religious minorities. This typology derives from legal treatises, which are based on legislation as well as published test cases. My research into everyday practices, as revealed in consular and legal records, shows that protégé status was stretched to include people who fit none of these categories.

In a recent article, Arnut Becker Lorca argues that international law became universal in the nineteenth century, when "semi-peripheral international lawyers"—petitioners in Japan, China, and the Ottoman Empire—appropriated that law to further the interests of their states.[36] While this argument certainly has its claims, especially in the field of legal history, in colonial history it reinforces the familiar bias that places the elite at the center of historical experience. In this book, I aim to consider the experiences of a broader share of the population. This approach entails considering law's influence on individuals, rather than state interests. The legal status of protégés was elaborated at the same time that international lawyers worked out the status of Egyptian and Ottoman states under public international law.[37] Many more individuals had direct experience of private international law, and the uneven but inexorable expansion of nationality and other private international law statuses is an essential feature of the universalization of international law in general.[38] But these individuals did not (as some suggest) make their own legal worlds. Instead, they became the grounds on which emerging legal orders were realized. If some protégés triumphed over circumstances, many more hit up against hard constraints, as we will now see.

The Duty to Protect Deserving Individuals

In 1883, Antonio Zananiri, a former dragoman of the British consulate at Alexandria, requested protégé status for his six sons, aged ten to thirty-five; he wanted to leave "a good protection" as their inheritance.[39] He had served the British for many decades, going back to the Syrian crisis of the 1830s; for sixteen of those years, he worked without pay. Now he wanted to capitalize in the terms of the new system on a legacy of protection he believed he had built under the old, informal system. In the old system, foreign protection operated on the basis of passive local authorities, who did not "object" or claim authority over the families of protégés. Now, however, the consul had informed Zananiri directly that he could no longer protect his adult sons. Zananiri was worried:

> After forty six years of arduous and responsible services I was surprised at receiving a notice like this, which affects my position with my equals and may injure myself and family established here for 170 years as merchants much respected. One of these results may be that if an ignorant Local Officer supposing himself to be annoyed by me and wanting revenge, he may unjestly [sic] cause an injury to my children.

As systems of affiliation became more formal, Zananiri feared the uncertain and unguaranteed position of his sons and now sought to put their protection in writing, as it "may be hereafter wanted more than before." Zananiri was well placed to anticipate change, and it came soon enough. If his request was successful, at least for a time—four sons are listed as protégés in the Returns list of 1888—the door of protection was closing.[40]

In 1888, Muhammad ʿAbd al-Munʿim, a janissary, interpreter, and sometime provisional British Consular Agent at Damietta, wrote to request "extension" of the protection that he and his father (who had done the same work for forty years) enjoyed. He cited Zananiri's precedent and noted, "I am substantial merchant of good standing, owning much property."[41] The Foreign Office suspected that Muhammad wrote only because some question about his entitlement to protection had arisen, but (as in Zananiri's case) it gave permission for the extension of protection, provided that Egyptian authorities raised no objections.[42] But Cromer, the consul-general of Egypt, then wrote that he had several objections to promoting ʿAbd al-Munʿim, chief among them that he was formerly a *cawass* (guard) for the local authorities, and they would be pained to identify him as British consular agent. It appears that ʿAbd al-Munʿim was actually removed from the rolls of British subjects.[43]

Mutual consent was the basis of the emerging principles by which nationality and its counterparts would be negotiated. States would exchange lists of protégés and would refuse to accept conversions of status unless their counterparts agreed. On the face of things, the protection afforded consular employees was a straightforward determination. The 1863 Ottoman Regulation on Foreign Consulates, also in force in Egypt, set clear limits: consulates-general could protect four translators (dragomans) or guards (*cawasses* or janissaries), consulates could protect three, and vice-consulates and consular agencies could protect two.[44] Any further protection required a specific agreement with the Ottoman government. The protection of employees hired after 1863 was personal and temporary, which is to say that it could not transfer to family members or descendants of the protégé and ended when consular employment ended.

Although the 1863 regulation clarified the status of many consular employees, it did not extinguish the old system of extensive protections. A side agreement maintained permanent and heritable protection for those who had jobs before 1863, as well as their families.[45] In practice, Ottoman and Egyptian authorities often challenged this grandfathered protection. Meanwhile, consulates often ignored the rules and extended pre-1863 protection to consular employees engaged after 1863, as well as their children.[46] This possibility was about to close, however.

The saga of Abraham Argi, an auxiliary dragoman at the French consulate in Alexandria in the early nineteenth century, illustrates the dialogue between ideas of protection and the changing laws governing protégé status. The French consulate's archival series on registration of protégés contains almost twenty files, stretching over a century and a half, concerning protection claims by Argi's extended clan. Born in Chania (Crete), Abraham provided services for the Jewish French protégés and subjects in Alexandria. Four (perhaps five) sons of Abraham lived as protégés, and consular archives contain files for at least seven grandsons and a great grandson. Many members of the family worked in finance (as *courtiers* and *changeurs*) in Alexandria as well as the smaller Delta centers of Mansura, Zifta, and Tanta.

Until the end of the nineteenth century, the Argis enjoyed comprehensive protection equivalent to other foreigners; indeed, their files
were part of the French *recensement* of Algerian subjects. But the change
that Zananiri feared hit them in 1904. In that year, the family's protection was comprehensively reexamined after the local police charged
Haim (a grandson of the original protégé) with an infraction. Like the
Algerian foreigners described in the previous chapter, Haim immediately
claimed French protection ("*s'est reclamé de la qualité d'administré Français*").[47] In light of his birth, descent, and residence—now key measures of
identification—the authorities were skeptical: Haim (like his father) was
born in Alexandria, and he had lived in the Delta town of Zifta, off the
beaten path for foreigners, for about twenty years. Following the principle that status could be discovered by mutual consultation, the Egyptian
authorities requested that the French investigate. Consular investigation
showed that Haim's father (first registered in 1849) was in fact refused
renewal in 1876 because protection was not extended to sons and grandsons of consular employees. This error (according to the side agreement
to the 1863 regulation, the family's protection should have been grandfathered) was soon circumvented: in 1880, Haim and his two brothers each
received fresh certificates of protection, which they renewed faithfully
for the quarter-century that followed.

The Alexandria consular officer charged with the 1904 investigation
admitted that the Argis' situation was certainly "irregular" according to
the Ottoman regulation of 1863, but he argued that the consulate should
try to make an exception, given the family's non-Egyptian origin and the
longstanding nature of their protection. Legally, the last of these arguments should have guaranteed continued protection, but this and other
cases show that the 1863 side agreement was not well known to many
of those who actually did the work of certifying protection. Instead, the
clerk made a moral argument suggesting that the family was foreign and
deserving of protection. In an effort to bolster the effect of his plea, the
consular agent recommended that the exceptional protection be given
only to those Argis already registered, excluding their dependents. Again,
this contradicted the side agreement. The agent noted that local authorities had never raised difficulties about this protection. Also, he noted
that the brother of Abraham (the dragoman and original protégé) had
been an *English* protégé and that that protection had been passed to his

descendants.[48] He argued that "this seems to suggest that no member of this family was ever considered a local subject." The letter closed with a warning of the "terrible (*fâcheux*) effect that loss of protection could have on this family, so long considered French protégés." The specter of an uncertain future appeared again, and they were cast as deserving of the safety France could offer.

Characteristically, the protected status of the Argis was reestablished not through positive decision but through inattention. French officials passed their findings on to the Egyptian Ministry of Foreign Affairs, which did not reply. The consulate took this silence as consent and continued to protect the whole family. Haim was able to register again, and he continued to do so until his death in 1908.[49] His widow and children took up their own protection in the years that followed. The letter of the law of protection is almost completely absent in the dozens of surviving files concerning the Argi family. It took half a century for the language of the 1863 regulation to be translated into the consular files. The earliest such reference that I have found comes in 1923, when the family's protection was definitively canceled because it was "personal and temporary." In 1939, a consular letter simply states that the family was registered in error ("*à tort*").[50]

Consulates and employees undertook all manner of improvisations to maintain protection, which was an important part of the compensation offered to local servants of foreign powers. One remedy was to invent special posts. In February 1911, Sheikh El Khoury Bey, a senior interpreter to the British Army of Occupation for twenty-eight years, was appointed honorary consular interpreter in Cairo, in order to retain his protection (it was not passed to his children, however).[51] By this time, silently maintaining protection was no longer reliable. As we will see in chapter 12, government employment became an important means of enforcing Egyptian nationality. Protection was no longer a benefit of employment; instead, nationality became a requirement for job holders. The personalization of protection described above is part of the broader movement toward "free" labor in the late nineteenth century.[52] In this process, employers (both state and private) lost many of the powers and responsibilities of legal protection over their employees. But if protection was driven from the labor market, the enigmatic status of the protégé endured in the international law of imperialism.

Categorical Protection

While employee protection became personal and temporary (mimicking jus soli), imperial protection extended to "foreign" subjects remained categorical and permanent (like jus sanguinis). Under the influence of waxing nationality laws, this contrast exposed an inconsistency in the principles governing protection. As we have seen, protection was based on relationships between a sovereign protector and a deserving individual. This economy was disrupted in the case of categorical protection, which was extended to natives of certain territories and certain sects. Arminjon argued that protection is distinguished by its individual rather than collective application and that local sovereignty is the foundation of the native protégé's personal sovereignty.[53] Categorical protection featured prominently in deep-seated, historical anxieties about local sovereignty. In these cases, the personal qualities of the individual protégés were not in question. Instead, it was a measure of the power of protecting states (mostly European) over states that did not meet the standard of civilization.

States extended categorical protection to subjects of other states in a number of ways. First, they conveyed protection to subjects of states without representation in Egypt, whether because of diplomatic rupture or size of population. During the Greco-Turkish war over Crete in 1897, for example, Greek consulates in Egypt closed. At first, France assumed protection of Greek subjects, citing its treaty right to protect subjects of unrepresented Christian countries.[54] Historically, France had protected Genoese, Tuscans, Ragusins, Romanians, and others using this provision. But writing in 1903, Arminjon noted the fading appeal of this protection: "Today, the French authorities no longer seem to want to increase the number of subjects under their jurisdiction (*justiciables*) by annexing unappealing individuals (*personnalités souvent peu intéressantes*)."[55] Britain had always contested this protection, and it did so again in 1897; eventually, Britain, France, and Russia partitioned Egypt's Greek subjects into three zones and split authority territorially. Low-ranking personnel from Greek consulates relocated to the consulates of their protecting powers for the duration of the conflict.[56] In a similar manner, from 1871 Switzerland allowed its subjects to choose German or American protection. During the First World War, German subjects in Egypt were protected by British consulates. Foreign states with tiny populations resident in Egypt that did not delegate protection to a larger power courted accusations of abuse of privilege. Brazil was the most notorious power in this regard. There were virtually no Brazilian subjects in Egypt, and its consular agents (who enjoyed protégé status) were the cause of complaint. As we saw in the last chapter, Persians were another exception.

A second and more significant way in which foreign states conveyed protection to noncitizens was through imperial expansion.[57] The previous chapter treated foreign subjects of European empire by comparing their status to that of European citizens, but their status was even more comparable to that of protégés. After the 1863 reduction in the numbers of protégés, the growth of European imperialism meant that the new influx of non-European foreigners, protected under capitulations treaties, took the place of the imagined fifth column of protégés. Although non-Arabophone, non-Muslim protégé numbers waned almost to nothing by the last quarter of the nineteenth century, their character as a suspect underclass of false interlopers was transposed onto the new group of colonial subjects. As we have seen, these foreigners often won favorable results before the courts. Their status as individuals identified as local but protected as foreign created discontent.

Whereas personal protection was a normal medium of affiliation before the rise of territorial-based nationality, afterward it became a means of treating the unusual products of regimes of exception. Territories without independence under public international law—colonies, protectorates, and the like (of which Egypt was an example)—lacked the sovereignty requisite to generate nationality and hence resorted to other forms of status. This was, for example, the case for "British Protected Persons," a status invented for particular kinds of nonsubjects that came to encompass highly differentiated territories within the empire (again, including Egypt). British protection could also be conferred upon individuals, again on exceptional grounds.[58] Certain subjects of Cypriot and Ionian origin posed such problems.[59] Stelianos Apostolides was one such protégé. This man of independent means arrived in Egypt in 1897. His nationality status was not entirely clear; like Margaret Gowans, he did not possess a definite legal claim on assistance but asserted a social right to access consular offices. He was a Greek subject, but as he later testified in the British consular court, "I have always lived in England but not from my childhood." He obviously considered his birthplace (Cyprus) peripheral to his status, but nowhere is it specified that he was a naturalized British subject. Apostolides appears

in the court records because a certain Athanase Giro, himself a British subject, convinced him to hand over two thousand pounds, to assist Giro in
his business in Aswan, supplying the army. Giro convinced Apostolides of
his bona fides through his fine appearance, his ownership of two carriages,
and his pleasant company at dinner. Apostolides did not ask for a receipt.
Under cross-examination, he was forced to admit his lack of acumen: "I
have never worked for my livelihood. . . . I have a slight idea of what business is through my intelligence. I consider myself not a fool. I have been
taken in in this case. I can't tell whether I have been taken in before." He
continued to lend small sums to Giro even after the large sum was not
repaid. Only half a year later did he seek repayment with a suit before the
Mixed Tribunals (a jurisdiction choice indicating that he was not claiming
British nationality). His criminal charge against Giro at the consular court
was dismissed.[60] Apostolides was obviously an easy mark for con men, but
his wealth also won him easy access to the British consulate.

The legislation covering such protected persons was itself confusing.
The Ottoman Order in Council of 1899 stated that " 'British subject' includes
a British protected person, that is to say, a person who either (a) is a native
of any Protectorate of Her Majesty, and is for the time being in the Ottoman dominions; or (b) by virtue of Section 15 of 'The Foreign Jurisdiction
Act, 1890,' or otherwise enjoys Her Majesty's protection in the Ottoman
dominions."[61] Many Greeks fell into these gray areas. On the French side,
members of the Algerian diaspora such as Mahri Hamawi (described in
chapter 3) posed similar problems. Tunisia was the best example in Egypt
of the wholesale transfer of protection from one sovereign to another. The
partial surveys managing the transition of Tunisians to French protection
in 1881 and 1884 became a lasting model: when Egypt and Italy signed a
treaty regulating the nationality of Libyans resident in Egypt in 1921, they
based it on the Tunisian settlement produced four decades earlier, even
using letters of notoriety as the principal proof of identity.[62]

The third category of protection, by religious categories, was an older
and murkier practice than protection by imperial categories. The protection of Christians (and their holy places) in the Ottoman Empire had been
an important prize in the Great Game. From the 1740 French capitulations
agreement, to the 1774 Treaty of Kuçuk Kaynarca that gave Russia protection over Jerusalem, to the 1861 partition of Mount Lebanon, protection of religious minorities offered an opportunity for a foreign foothold

within the Ottoman Empire.[63] But by the 1880s, when capitulatory powers no longer needed comprador coreligionists to penetrate eastern Mediterranean economies, the practice was already on its way out. Under the 1865 addendum to the agreement on protégés, religious protection was straightforward: one dragoman and one *procureur* of every foreign mission or monastery were allowed protection. This provision only applied to missions and monasteries made up of foreign subjects, however. An exception for Egypt allowing protégés for native Coptic, Catholic, and Maronite churches was destined to lapse, according to a verbal agreement, on the death of the procurers currently in the job.[64] The Tanzimat reforms had emancipated Christians and Jews within the Ottoman Empire and given them full equality under the law, so the constitutional basis for continued religious protection was absent.[65]

Yet consular files record the existence of a few individuals who did not satisfy the requirements for protection but were nevertheless classified as protégés. Mixed amid the thousands of French *drogmanat* dossiers recording the status of Algerians, Tunisians, and later Moroccans are dozens of interlopers—files of non-Algerians, non-Tunisians, non-Moroccans—who nevertheless won protection. The word "protégé" is emblazoned on the cover of these files. In 1879, a certain Daoud Hanen was given protection on the strength of an 1868 request from the Catholic archbishop of Egypt.[66] In 1880, Moise Kahla, a Greek Catholic from Damascus, requested French protection in Alexandria. In support of his claim, he presented a French passport given to him in Beirut in 1868, when he was a seminary student heading for Rome. The Alexandria consulate referred the question to its Beirut counterpart, which told them to refuse protection—the passport was issued only for the purpose of religious education, and Moise (now an apprentice pharmacist) had quit his studies.[67] Antoine Zaghikian, an Ottoman subject and policeman born in Constantinople and presumably Armenian, was protected by the French consulate until 1881.[68] Fathallah Sabbah, dragoman of the Capuchin convent at Aleppo, passed through Alexandria in 1881 and was recognized by the French consulate.[69] A certain Fadlallah Dabbas, dragoman of the Sisters of St. Joseph at Saida, received the same treatment on his visits in 1883 and 1886.[70] After the 1880s, however, this form of protection faded as religion became incidental in the designation of protégés, correlated with imperial factors as Muslims and Jews joined Christians in protection as imperial subjects.

The consular employees, imperial subjects, and minority protégés that we have encountered made claims for protection (both spurious and legitimate) under the rubric of existing laws. Even when those laws were bent and broken, they offered a structure that promised to replace the moral judgments that seemed to govern protection. But consular files reveal the persistent presence of other protégés who had no legitimate place in the new regime. Nessim Amado, a widely traveled sixty-five-year-old Jew from Rhodes, was given French protection in Alexandria in 1880 on the strength of a patent of protection issued in Izmir in 1839.[71] Nicolas Touchou, a Constantinople-born tobacco merchant, registered in 1884.[72] Shaykh Ahmad bin Sulaiman Pasha, the husband of Nafissa Zuhni whom we met in chapter 6, maintained extraordinary protection into the twentieth century. These *beratlıs* held on to their status, and their presence suggests a broader contingent of protégés lingering in protection decades after the law made it impossible.

While public panic depended on the homogenization of protégés, the evidence presented in this chapter shows the differences among them. Indeed, the panic did not hit all its targets. The Argi clan comprises precisely the sort of "illegitimate" protégés that the nineteenth-century Ottoman panic envisaged. As Jews and moneylenders, one expects them to be discriminated against by Egyptian and French consular authorities alike. In fact, however, their protection was maintained (in 1905) and even restored (in 1880), at moments when the law was applied and then rejected. This conscious disregard for the law is particularly difficult to explain at a time when other individuals were being squeezed out of uncertain protections.

If local actors managed to ignore far-off definitions of protégé status, those definitions were to win out in the end. In the 1880s, a whole variety of protection claims still passed muster. By the 1890s, these claims were significantly curtailed, and after 1900 the few remaining protégés were embattled by the rise of nationality. Delayed conversion to nationality was a sign of the incomplete incorporation of Alexandria into the international legal system that governed it in theory. The surprise of those losing status, on the other hand, was a sign of the increasingly successful expansion of the law, which broke down the vast distance between the "real" and the "imagined" senses of protection. Even in the 1880s, even the most "deserving" protégés under the old regime, whose extraordinary service to foreign powers (particularly in wartime) sometimes resulted in protection, encountered a changing environment. This was the case for a certain Tanous Khouri Schelal, a Lebanese horse trader who was given French protection in 1861 for services rendered to the French army (presumably during their landing in August 1860). When he presented his certificate of protection in Alexandria twenty years later, he was refused registration.[73]

New conditions emerged, too, that made protégé status less attractive. Docteur Basile Apostolidis, who was given French protection in 1871 in return for medical service that he rendered in Cairo, wrote to the French consulate in November 1889, renouncing this protection.[74] Other respectable Ottoman subjects, men who would previously have qualified as protégés, found new means to keep or win protection. In 1895, Gabriel Huri's name was deleted from the registers of French protégés.[75] This Beirut-born landowner, resident in Marseille, had received permission to settle in France in 1890, clearly a mark of acceptability. He did not in fact settle in France, as his business kept him in Egypt most of the year, but on the strength of this permission, he received protection certificates in 1891 and 1894. In 1895, however, the consulate decided that "admission to residence (*domicile*) [in France], especially when granted to an Ottoman subject, does not constitute a right to protection." Ten years later, he tried again, citing his French education, his business interests in France, his ongoing sentiment of attachment to France, which among other things led him to marry a Frenchwoman and to migrate, with the firm intention this time to make the most of his residence situation. His request was favorably received by the consul in Alexandria, who noted that there was no consensus on how to treat such cases. Evidently, qualitative claims of affection continued to hold weight, despite relatively clear law. This was because protection was basically moral rather than legal.

Those who dispensed and those who received protection, as well as third parties observing its workings, perceived the system in three modes: obligation, commodity, and exception. As obligation, protection was conveyed by a sovereign authority upon a deserving subject who warranted favor because of her or his loyalty or (like Margaret Gowans) vulnerability. As commodity, protection was a legal privilege with economic benefits that constituted a form of compensation for services rendered. As exception, protection was a means of managing affiliation when existing laws and procedures failed to satisfy the desires of powerful interests. While each of these modes was a usual feature of "traditional" systems of affiliation, they were at odds with emerging positive legal definitions of membership.

Recent work on "liminal" legal statuses during the twentieth century points to the flexibility of the category of protégé.[76] But the litigious cosmopolitan risks becoming a stock character in twenty-first century microhistory.[77] While approaches that insist on the creative agency of such individuals make for interesting narrative, they tend to sidestep a more profitable analytical undertaking: the structural description of the universal regime of legal identification that is a unique feature of the modern world. Protégé status was a particular Ottoman status that was foreclosed by the expansion of law in general, and nationality law in particular, at the turn of the twentieth century. The handful of protégés who remained, like the bad subjects of the next chapter, occupied the space of legal exception that was so characteristic of the colonial. The distance between them and the law brings the moral coloring of protection into focus.

The most important consular court case in Egyptian history, if we measure importance in financial terms, was likely the probate of Antun Yusuf ʿAbd al-Massih described in chapter 5. This case, which ran between 1885 and 1890, forms a pivot between the old system of protection and the new. In the end, the court concluded that an Ottoman subject could not become a member of the British community in Alexandria purely "so as to attract to himself English law."[78] But the principle asserted by the court—that nationality and protection meant more than mere legal convenience—had long been a fiction for many bourgeois protégés in Alexandria. Antun's case was thus pivotal: it contained elements of the old system (reliance on foreign courts as refuge) and of the new (protégés' sense of entitlement was disappointed).

The practice of protection was a dialogue between the uneven expansion of international law and the enduring influence of older ideas about protection. The reduction in the total number of protégés in the half-century before the First World War could not assuage the widespread concern that this status created among local subjects. Even one exception was too many, and in every case the exceptions mapped onto known patterns of racial, sectarian, class, and imperial privilege. As law expanded its embrace to grasp everyone in Egypt, protégé status mattered most to those who could not have it. This was an effect of the emerging notion of nationality, which asserted its moral neutrality and indeed derived authority from the image of impartiality and universality. But this neutrality was a fiction, and exceptions were commonplace. Even after the figure of the protégé disappeared, institutions continued to differentiate between claimants on the basis of moral obligation, and individuals demanded access to commodified status on the strength of their personal qualities.

The next chapter considers an "other nationality" still less visible in the law books and more vivid in the moral register than the protégé: bad subjects. The other side of protection was to guarantee orderly conduct. Both protégés and bad subjects were categories used by state institutions to describe individuals who were neither ethnic peers nor fellow citizens of their protectors; protégés were deserving clients, while bad subjects were necessary burdens. Like bad subjects, protégés were few in number. Though protégé numbers dwindled, a growing number of bad subjects provided new grounds for responsible authorities to express their visions of affiliation and see those visions thwarted by their unsuitable subjects.

10
Bad Subjects

One January morning in 1891, a Syrian immigrant to Alexandria was sitting in a cafe in Sikkat al-Gadida, near the city's port. He heard strange noises coming from his home, which sat above the cafe, and with the help of neighbors he set out to investigate. On the building's terrace, they discovered a man holding a purloined key and a crowbar. The neighborhood boss (*shaykh al-harra*) arrested this man, who was identified as Giuseppe Scerri, a Maltese British subject and habitual thief. Scerri had been arrested a dozen times since 1878, mostly for robbery, assault, and coining, and there can be no doubt that he was a bad man whose presence threatened the peace in Alexandria.[1] Even other criminals thought so: in 1884, a (drunken) acquaintance who stabbed Scerri in the neck explained to the police that he did it because Scerri refused to stop stealing and was "bad" (*min al-ashrar*).[2] In 1886, Scerri showed his contempt for the British consular court by attempting to fix a case against a friend arrested for assaulting a British soldier.[3] Thus the British consular court prosecuted Scerri rapidly in 1891, sentencing him to six months of imprisonment. Like most convicted Maltese British subjects, Scerri was deported to Malta to serve his sentence and warned not to return to the Ottoman Domains unless he could furnish a sizable surety (in this case £200) to guarantee his good behavior. Only a person of considerable means could gather such a sum, so the guarantee was (legally if not always in practice) a way to banish the irritant from Alexandria.[4] In a society of migrants, cash guarantees replaced the personal guarantees that were a key currency of early modern social order.[5]

The 1891 deportation was not the end of Scerri's story. He returned to Egypt in 1892 without having paid the surety, taking advantage of a loophole in enforcement: neither the British nor the local authorities had the authority or personnel in place to turn him away at Port Said.[6] Somehow he attracted British attention, and faced with his recidivism, the consulate imposed the ultimate nationality punishment: it struck Scerri's name from the rolls of British protection. In the Egyptian context, foreign status was the locus of positive legal rights. It was a distinction, and local subjecthood was the default alternative. As we saw in chapter 4, lists of names maintained in the offices of the city's foreign consulates were the site of legal rights and duties that in other contexts are called citizenship. Often, foreign status had the quality of protection—those whose names appeared on consular rolls were free from prosecution, taxation, conscription, and search at the hands of local (Egyptian and Ottoman) authorities. Men such as Scerri were burdens for the consulates, however. Although the consulates used tools of control and punishment to subdue their disorderly subjects, eventually the institutions tired of troublemakers. Expulsion was one means to make problems go away, and when this failed consulates could strip their subjects of foreign status. When Scerri's name was removed from the rolls of British subjects, he became de facto a local subject.

This practice was the inverse of forum shopping: just as foreign subjects renounced foreignness if it proved troublesome, foreign consulates could strip troublesome foreigners of their foreignness.[7] Now, the British consulate ended its cooperation with local authorities, contravening the custom of definition of subjecthood by mutual consent. Scerri's name was struck from the rolls of British protection ("*sara ismuhu mashtuban min dimna ra'aya al-inkliz*," in the words of Huri, the Maltese clerk who composed Arabic letters issued by the consulate). In a letter to the governor of Alexandria, the consul spelled out the new terms of responsibility that he had unilaterally dictated: "Should he return to Alexandria or Ottoman Dominions it will be for yourself to take such steps in the matter as you may take."[8] When Scerri was arrested once again by the police and conducted to the consulate, the consul was able to deny all responsibility: "having been struck off the list of British Subjects [Scerri] is only under the jurisdiction of local courts and the British Consulate has no longer any liability in regard to him."[9] The local authorities did not give up. They too moved to deport Scerri to Malta and asked the British consulate to pay for his passage. The consul refused, publicly, but a note on the back of a telegram shows that he directed an associate to find the funds to get rid of Scerri once again.[10]

What was the nature of the British consulate's responsibility for bad subjects such as Scerri? The institution was no panopticon; it paid attention to its bad subjects only when forced to do so. Generally speaking, consular, legal, and state institutions in Alexandria divided individuals into three separate categories: those who deserved respect, those who could be ignored (the most numerous category), and those who should be controlled. Scerri won consular attention because he caused trouble that required a settlement, and that unhappy task fell to the institution on whose rolls his name appeared.

As personal-status regimes based on state affiliation were spreading in the metropole and empire, the extension of legal status to ever-larger portions of the world's population meant the expansion of rights, but it also entailed (and indeed encouraged) enhanced mechanisms of control.[11] Mobile populations were a source of anxiety and trouble for administrators throughout the nineteenth-century world of empire, and they developed specific legal technologies designed to control social fluidity.[12] For foreign subjects in the Ottoman Mediterranean, the capitulations created and enhanced legal and social rights, and, as we saw in chapter 8, many individuals claimed rights overseas that were superior to any available at home. This apparently liberal face of imperialism had its underside, however: the bundle of rights enjoyed by foreign subjects was also the locus of restriction, as the capitulations became a leading means to control Mediterranean representatives of the "dangerous classes" familiar in other nineteenth-century settings.[13] Legal records from Alexandria show the emergence of a category of undesirable individuals called "bad subjects" in English, "*vagabonds*" in French, and "*ashrar*" or "*ashqiya*ʾ" in Arabic. The city's various legal authorities employed the category to constitute a pool of individuals who could be circumscribed and controlled.

Bad subjecthood was a category of exception in which ordinary legal reason was suspended. As Samera Esmeir and Timothy Mitchell have shown, turn-of-the-century Egypt was riddled with spaces of legal exception.[14] Bad subjecthood was not a spatial determination of exceptional jurisdiction (such as the special jurisdictions on *ʿizbas* that Esmeir and Mitchell describe) but a category affixed to certain exceptional persons who were deemed to have exceeded the claims of jus soli and jus sanguinis. This chapter probes this exception for traces of status later wrapped into the norm of nationality. Its first section reexamines the question of subjecthood, but in isolation from the imperial context that is its typical frame (including in chapter 8). The second section discusses vagrancy and vagabondage, forms of exaggerated poverty that breached standards of good conduct and became linked with "special vagabondage" offenses—narcotics and prostitution—that were marks of bad subjecthood. The third section considers those labeled bad subjects, an indelible status characterized by hopeless recidivism. Because bad subjects could not be reformed, they were subject to sanctions of deportation, exile, and loss of protection, which is the topic of the fourth section.

Subjecthood

As we saw in chapters 3 and 4, police identified foreign and local alike according to the authorities that knew and controlled them. Individuals were categorized not in the census' terms of nationality but according to their protection (*himaya* or *riʿaya*) and their affiliation (*tabaʿiya*). During the 1880s and 1890s, the vocabulary of nationality for both foreign and local insisted especially on subjecthood. Maltese, for example, were never merely "Maltese" (*malti*) but "Maltese subjects of the English state" (*malti tabiʿ li-dawlat al-ingliz*). Locals—*atbaʿ lil-hukuma al-mahalliya* (literally "subjects of the local government")—were categorized by their *shaykh*, or the headman of their neighborhood, guild, or sect, who would be able to provide more information. The British were British *subjects* (*atbaʿ li-dawlat al-inkliz*, literally "subjects of the English state"). This clear language gets to the heart of nationality as it was constructed at that time and place. Nationality was about being a subject of some protecting authority, not a citizen of a nation-state. It was about negative obligations, rather than the sort of positive rights and privileges that we associate with citizenship: free passage, or what we might think of as social rights (such as welfare) or political rights (such as suffrage). These rights were absent from the spectrum of issues with which subjecthood was concerned and were instead restricted to the elite minority.

Subjecthood had little to do with individuals and much more to do with authorities. States and other corporate bodies were assigned responsibility and given administrative power over individuals. Subjecthood had little to do with what an individual had the right to *do* and much more with the question of what one authority or another could or could not do *to* him or her. And so, in practical terms, a British subject was someone who could be prosecuted by the British consular court and could not be prosecuted or taxed by the local authorities. A local or native subject was someone who was liable to prosecution, conscription, and taxation by the local (that is, Ottoman or Egyptian) authorities. Only after individuals were assigned to the authority that controlled them could they be accurately identified.

In this context, the figure of the bad subject emerged as a stand-in, improvised strategy to deal with the most dangerous remnants of the old system of protection before the establishment of a new, universal regime. A consensus can be discerned in institutional practice according to which individuals in this defective category were treated with special suspicion and agreed-upon techniques by all of the institutions that they encountered. The bad subject was a shared, transnational category that described an undesirable class using diverse terms (*shaqi, mauvais sujet*) but treated it with the same remedies: deportation, banishment, and loss of protection. The improvised nature of the bad subject category was clear—it came up as a general, moral description and even explanation rather than a legal category or tool that entailed specific procedures.

According to received wisdom, states are rapacious: they seek to gather subjects and then to capture their labor, their tax revenue, their military service, and so on. They settle populations, map them, and count them. Populations not captured or embraced by the state are seen as a threat, and they have been the object of sustained incorporation efforts over the nineteenth and twentieth centuries. This dynamic is used to describe both successful and unsuccessful states, and historians have found peripheries and hinterlands especially revealing of the essential nature of the state.[15] While there can be little question of the general validity of this model, it does not tell the whole story. The bad subject was not the target of the greedy expansive state's appetite for population. Instead, bad subjects were undesirable, and states avoided power and responsibility over them. Whereas James Scott's rebels ran away from the state, in this case the state ran from the undesirables. It was only dragged back to assume the burden of administration by mutual obligation to other states, and it undertook a moral project of subject definition as a result.

"Bad subject" groups a cluster of other labels: recidivist (*arbab saw-abiq*), vagrant, vagabond, poor, homeless, stateless, member of the "dangerous classes," even certain bedouins. This group was the inverse of the protégés discussed in the last chapter; they were those without patrons, guarantors, or protectors. Both protection and its absence was a moral measure of individuals spelled out in social classification and legal procedure. The point of resemblance between the various forms of bad subject was state anxiety. At the end of the nineteenth century, states moved to establish universal subjecthood among the populations of the port cities of the eastern Mediterranean. This move came at a time when the system of client protection (by neighborhood and guild *shaykhs*, for instance) that had organized sociolegal control in the Ottoman Empire for centuries had been displaced.[16] In its place there emerged a new system of control, one in which the remedies employed to deal with the various bad subjects resembled one another, bolstering the category's coherence. It was a transnational and translational category. In the American context, for example, "dangerous class" was the late nineteenth-century descriptive term that "appropriately delineated for the larger society the faceless mass of people who made up the nation's paupers, tramps, and criminals."[17] In India, "thuggee" served a similar purpose earlier in the century.[18] The challenge for police was that this was not merely a criminal class but also one of poverty and homelessness, and it required a variety of approaches.

Protégé was a category that appeared in legislation, but bad subject was not. My choice to frame this chapter around bad subjects as an inferred "other nationality" therefore depends on interpretation of practice rather than reading of doctrine. Sociolegal categorization should not be limited by the law in the books. Legal historians often show practices that contradict the letter of the law, and it is also valuable to show practices (such as those concerning bad subjects) that are unreflected in the letter of the law. The evidence shows that in practice Alexandria's legal authorities showed as much consensus about bad subjects as they did about protégés. The shared stock of remedies, regardless of nationality or authority, is the basis on which bad subjects were marked. Just as they did in controlling wayward wives such as Nafissa Hanem (see chapter 6), the city's various legal institutions showed unity rather than fragmentation in dealing with bad subjects. Undesirables were assigned to a category of deficient sub-jecthood that spread across nationalities, and individuals in this defec-tive category were treated with special suspicion and agreed techniques by all of the institutions that they encountered. Undesirability began with poverty—a great threat to foreign prestige and the maintenance of orderly communities of privilege—but it was only those who combined poverty with dangerous behavior who were assigned to the common category of bad subjecthood that transcended nationality.

Vagrants and Vagabonds

In 1905, four of Alexandria's most prominent French merchants wrote to their consul to complain about Marie-Louise Dijol. This forty-two-year-old woman had been living in Alexandria for nine months. The notables claimed that she was in the habit of begging on the street (*la voie publique*) and insulting passersby. She was often intoxicated. She accosted French subjects at their homes and asked them for money and even forced her way into a private office of the Contentieux de l'État. "La fille" Dijol, as the officials called her, was unmarried. She had come to Alexandria from Greece, where she had also lived on charity; her passage had been paid by a French community glad to be rid of her. The French Traveler's Assistance Society (*société de bienfaisance*) in Alexandria offered her repatriation, but she had refused to leave. The time had come to shift this problem to another shore, and the French consular court possessed the legal means to do so: it charged her with vagrancy (*vagabondage*). Although the judgment noted attenuating circumstances—her poor state of health, a bad arm, and the difficulty she faced in correcting her behavior—she was sentenced to two months in prison and barred from residence in Egypt for a period of five years.[19]

Despite misgivings about their less-than-solid status (detailed in chapter 7), most poor foreigners were able to exercise nationality if they chose. It was only those who combined poverty with dangerous behavior who were assigned to a common category that transcended nationality. Vagrants and bad subjects were the two main faces of this common cat-egory. While the European poor, Maltese and Maghribi imperial subjects, and protégés were inferior to elite Europeans in Alexandria, they exercised a clear (if curtailed) set of distinct privileges of nationality at the British and French consulates. Legal treatment of vagrants and bad subjects was characterized by exclusion from such rights.

Vagrancy was exaggerated poverty. The term was used in a variety of ways by different authorities.[20] While in the European context vagrancy was above all an issue of labor control, in the context of Alexandria it was applied to those who lacked three things: fixed domicile, means, and regular employment. The test was clear—in order to avoid conviction, those accused of vagrancy had to show that they had a home, money, or a job. In the wake of the post-1907 recession in Egypt, for example, the twenty-year-old André Pignol was convicted after it was shown that "for several years, he traveled through different countries without ever practicing his profession of plasterer or doing any steady work."[21] This threshold of proof was quite high, and a large part of Alexandria's highly transient population (individuals such as Sayyid Bassim, the deceased British Indian subject mentioned in chapter 8) would have been hard-pressed, if charged, to provide such evidence.

In practice, however, few were charged with vagrancy, and even to these the French consular court showed some leniency. In January 1892, the French consular agent at Damanhur (a provincial town on the rail line between Alexandria and Cairo) found a penniless Frenchman named Emile Level soliciting money to buy a ticket to Cairo. The agent who arrested Level found that he had no profession and no justification for his trip to Cairo. It was also discovered that the French traveler's assistance society (*société de bienfaissance*) in Alexandria had just given him a ticket to Marseille, which he had not used. When the case came to trial, however, the Alexandria consular court ruled that Level—who had arrived from Beirut, using regular papers, only two weeks earlier—had not been in Egypt long enough to be considered habitually unemployed, and he was acquitted.[22] The local police arrested René Barbeaud as soon as he arrived at Alexandria's port in 1908 because he carried no passport or identification documents, and they charged him with vagrancy. He had just completed a five-year sentence at a French military work camp and seemed a suspicious character. The court did not convict him, however, noting that he had come to Egypt carrying four Italian livres, named his profession (*tailleur*), and stated that he had come to Egypt to work. He was not, therefore, a vagrant.[23]

If vagrancy law had been assiduously applied, the courts would have been very busy. Instead, the charges were reserved for those considered undesirable for other reasons. A demobilized soldier named Pierre Martin was one such undesirable. He was able to show some residence, some employment, and some means, but the court was determined to convict him. He had lived for a year in Alexandria, working a week here and a week there, sometimes as a shoemaker and sometimes an agricultural laborer, but never consistently enough to please the court. He possessed nine shillings—more than many Alexandrians—but this did not constitute "means." He spent some of his time at a residence called the Hotel Favorite and took some of his meals there, but this too was inadequate: "passing residence in a furnished room of a cheap hotel where rooms are rented in common" did not constitute residence. A large part of Alexandria's foreign population would also have failed this sort of test, but Martin's real undesirability lay elsewhere: he was found in possession of a list of addresses and a draft letter of mendacity, which the court believed proved the true source of his means.[24]

Vagrancy law was a useful pretext to be rid of troublesome mendicants and disruptive and embarrassing foreigners, such as Martin and Marie-Louise Dijol. Vagrancy was a flexible charge, easily proven. It could be adapted to many purposes. It could be applied to those with irregular professions, such as a French subject named Gaston Bardot: in 1913, this Cairo resident "informed the Court that he was a juggler, that he could get no employment in Egypt and that he then commenced performing upon the streets; that as this appears to be against police regulations, he was in consequence arrested by the local police. He stated further that he had only been arrested once before and that was for deserting from the French Army." He was sentenced to be deported (though his deportation was put off because he informed on an American who had broken into his own consulate).[25] Not all vagrants were beggars, but mendicancy was a social irritant that ordinarily triggered criminal charges of vagrancy. When Ernest Alexis Loutz, a French-protected Swiss citizen, was charged with vagrancy in 1899, the court made it clear why he was being charged: "investigation has proven that Loutz begs in an ongoing fashion, both in the street and at private homes, and that he has more than once abused the charity of those who took an interest in his case, lied to them about his identity or escaped them when they attempted to repatriate him. His history is deplorable, and wherever he has gone, he has left the impression of a dangerous vagrant." A letter from the Société Suisse de Secours de Caire, making similar allegations, was also entered into evidence.[26] There existed in the imaginations of consular officials (and to some extent in reality) a Mediterranean vagrancy welfare circuit. This circuit parallels (and sometimes overlaps) the circuits of labor migration, theater entertainment, and radicalism described in recent literature.[27]

Vagrants were troublesome because of their poverty but also because of their mobility. As we saw in chapters 3 and 4, state efforts to identify and classify populations in Britain, France, and (by the end of the nineteenth century) the Ottoman Empire and Egypt using censuses, identification documents, and taxation records emphasized place over personality. Territory was surveyed, and individuals were fixed according to origin and residence. Foreigners' displacement was the source of certain anxiety in this system, but regulations such as the capitulations organized foreign populations to general satisfaction. Vagrants were more threatening. The nexus of police and judicial control depended on place. Neighborhood authorities monitored residents and held them accountable for their behavior. Those without residence lived outside of this system, and that act alone rendered them dangerous in the eyes of authorities, especially in troubled times. This combination of unemployment and international transience was characteristic of those convicted of vagrancy. In two 1908 cases, French subjects were arrested by local police while camping on fields or empty land (*terrain vide*) outside of town.[28] Both were deserters from military service—a key duty of nationality—and one had previously been expelled from Italy. But it was the nature of the space where they had settled—unplanned and unregulated—that caused the local police to intervene and constituted the strongest evidence of their guilt.

Critically, vagrancy was a crime reserved for Europeans: thirty-three of the thirty-four individuals charged with *vagabondage* by the French consular court between 1889 and 1914 were French or Swiss (and the only non-European charged, a Tunisian, was named Victor).[29] Vagrancy law can be considered a social-welfare procedure, a legal mechanism by which the consulate settled problems in the European community. There were certainly non-European foreign mendicants, but they would not beg of Europeans; these burdensome imperial subjects were consigned to the informal authorities of the neighborhoods where they lived and were ignored by the consulate. Maltese, Algerian, and Tunisian communities were left to their own devices.

Criminal Bad Subjects

Vagrants were only one variety of a broad, generic category that police, consulates, and judicial institutions applied to foreign subjects who were not merely poor but undesirable. Bad subjects who were not vagrants could not be measured against a limited set of definite criteria. Instead, the resemblance between those assigned to the category reflected an operational reality shared by institutions concerned about recidivism, career criminals, and bad company. As we saw in chapters 3 and 5, the criminal activity that caused consular and government administrators in Alexandria most anxiety during the 1880s and 1890s was not murder, violence, theft, or even political sedition but counterfeiting and forgery of official documents. Individuals who committed these crimes were immediately considered bad subjects, received the most severe prison sentences, and were almost always deported.

During the first decade of the twentieth century, a number of other crimes became associated with bad subjecthood. Living from the proceeds of hashish or prostitution was considered a form of nonemployment; the French court prosecuted prostitutes and procurers who could not show the source of their income under the rubric of "special vagrancy" (*vagabondage spécial*). A Maltese British subject named Pasquale Magri was arrested four times in four months in 1909 for running hashish dens. Magri was a fluent user of Alexandria's jurisdictional complexity. He changed the location of his operations frequently, sometimes using foreign-owned premises (which local police could not raid without the presence of a consular agent), while at other times using buildings owned by local proxies. He hired Italian subjects to hang out in front of his "cafés" and obstruct police raids. Again and again, evidence disappeared before authorities could enter Magri's shops. Finally, the police and the British courts resorted to weak, deductive evidence to prosecute him. Referring to his "idle life" (*vie oisive*), they asserted that because he "has never worked in our city" in the four previous years, he was a suspicious character and must be selling hashish.[30]

Sophistry of the sort used to charge Magri was untenable except when all authorities concerned agreed to believe in it. Of course, the authorities did this all the time: the system of devolved jurisdiction depended on it. In certain instances, bad character was elevated from personal description to legal explanation. When a Maltese father and son who ran a grog shop frequented by suspicious characters were murdered in 1880, the Alexandria police and the British consulate struggled to name any single suspect. The police attributed the deaths to the bad character of victims. In the final police report, they were described as "dishonest men" (ʿadmai al-istiqama): "it appears that their death was the result of their association and secret dealings with [unknown] persons."[31] The police identified Egyptian, bedouin, Austrian, Maltese, and Italian suspects in their murder. Keeping bad company (mauvaise fréquentations) was a common characteristic of bad subjects; bad subjects of any nationality had more in common with one another than with their own compatriots.

Subjecthood was about the nature of the person, and this nature (particularly in the case of bad subjects) could rarely be changed. In 1896, a sixteen-year-old boy named Ahmad was arrested with three other boys. They were carrying twelve white metal spoons, three pairs of scissors, and a can of conserves stolen from a merchant's shop. Ahmad, an Algerian French subject born in Alexandria, was the youngest of this gang. He was sentenced to two months in prison.[32] In the eight years that followed, the French consular court found him guilty six more times (three times for assault, three times for theft), and he spent a total of four years in prison.[33] Ahmad's series of convictions exemplified the problem of bad subjects. He was identified as a recidivist on his second conviction, and the court treated him accordingly, yet his behavior became increasingly serious: theft of conserves escalated to assault for hire. According to official and consular logic, bad subjecthood was a fixed characteristic, a state of being, the sort of thing that nationality was becoming. Authorities rarely believed that bad subjects such as vagrants could be reformed. Bad subjects were usually recidivists (though most recidivists were not bad subjects).[34] Young recidivists were considered particularly dangerous. The court observed Ahmad's behavior with a sense of its inevitable progress: "the fact that he hired his services to commit this terrible assault shows once again the sort of life that Ahmad Ahmad al-Maghribi leads."[35] His final conviction involved an elaborate assault on a police officer.

He began by throwing stones, but when chased onto the terrace of a house, he began to hurl vessels of ordure onto his pursuers. Finally, he asked for a knife with which to kill the police officer.[36] After this case, the young man disappeared from the court records—whether he died, was reformed, or left Alexandria, the consulate and police were relieved to be rid of him.

Ahmad was not the only bad young man. In the year of his disappearance (1903), a fifteen-year-old Tunisian subject named Isma'il 'Abd al-Hamid al-Sayyid al-Waziri began a similar career at the court. Its low point came when he stole the watch of the consulate's gardener from the desk of the consulate's guard.[37] In 1899, when he was sixteen years old, Mohammad Ghima was convicted four times of assaulting police while intoxicated.[38] Three similar charges followed, and in 1906 he attacked Haj Yusuf Hussain Ghima (probably his father) when he refused to give him money, shoving his head into a plate of beans that he was eating.[39] Whereas young vagrants could be forgiven disorderly behavior (in two separate 1904 cases, minors were found to be vagrants but were acquitted given their youth, with their fathers held civilly responsible), young bad subjects were considered less malleable.[40] Prison could not change the nature of a bad subject.

Banditry and brigandage, objects of special security anxieties and procedures worldwide, were also in the purview of bad subjecthood.[41] Banditry (qat' al-tariq) was an exceptional crime in the Islamic legal tradition—it was one of five hadd crimes, classified as an offense against God as well as public order. By the 1880s, this crime had been removed from shar'i jurisdiction in Egypt, but it retained its Islamic gravitas in the state courts.[42] In Egypt during the first decades of British occupation, the great domestic demographic and policing concern was the nomadic population on Egyptian territory.[43] By their placelessness, foreign vagrants and Egyptian bedouins—unruly, uncontrolled, unsettled—endangered authorities' efforts to rationalize their subject populations.[44] They were assigned to a common field of spatial anxiety, and authorities addressed spatial solutions to both problem populations. Bedouins were to be settled or at least fixed to a narrow range of space. If settlement was about establishing a link between people and place, the prescribed remedy for vagrancy—deportation—was an attempt to pull the broken links between person and place out by their roots.

From Deportation to Loss of Foreign Protection

If the consulates and local authorities distinguished between the poor, European vagrants, and foreign and local bad subjects in legal argumentation, in practice they resorted to a single solution for the disruption they caused: deportation. Ann Stoler and many others have argued that poor foreigners compromised the standing of pure foreigners in empire.[45] Deportation constituted an admission that the problems created by problem subjects were intractable given the available resources. The consulate and associated national benevolent societies provided temporary relief but quickly shifted the poor to the metropole or to another place in the Mediterranean. And as we have seen, undesirables could also be shifted to Alexandria from Greece, Italy, Istanbul, and other ports. Foreign consulates in Alexandria frequently used deportation (here labeled "repatriation") to eliminate the problems created by poor foreign subjects. Welfare provisioning for Europeans and foreigners was dispensed by private sectarian aid societies, but this emerging nationality privilege was sponsored by consulates. By removing a subject from the territory, institutions sought to eliminate an irritant. For those convicted of vagrancy, deportation entailed a ban on return (*interdiction de séjour*), in this case, to Egypt, for a period of five to ten years.

Deportation was a common technique used to deal with the needy in Britain and France, and it seemed a natural fit for poor foreigners in Egypt.[46] Deportation was also used for imperial subjects, such as five Tunisian paupers repatriated on the same ship in 1881.[47] Three penniless young Frenchmen who disembarked at the Alexandria harbor in 1911 were immediately slated for repatriation by the consulate. While awaiting their ship, they were housed at a home for retired sailors (*asile des vieillards*). They robbed one of the residents of the home and fled. When captured, their implausible story included a plan to support themselves by "selling Japanese spiders in Cairo"; inexplicably, this seems to have convinced the French tribunal to drop vagrancy charges, but the men were convicted of theft.[48] Foreign subjects classified as "lunatics" were also sent away from Alexandria in order to maintain the integrity of the community. British subjects convicted of serious offenses in Alexandria (sentences of three months or more) were sent to prison in Malta (echoing the transportation of criminals from Britain to Australia).

Deportation was equally popular with local authorities. At the beginning of the 1890s, Egypt's secret police produced photo cards of foreign
deportees from Port Said.[49] These young men were identified by name, age,
physical description, national type (in my small sample, every one is Greek
[*yunani al-jins*]), and criminal type: recidivist bad subject (*min arbab al-
sawabiq al-ashqiya*). The Egyptian police routinely requested that consulates
send recidivists and other bad subjects away from Alexandria, and consulates often complied. The letter they wrote concerning Pasquale Magri, the
Maltese seller of hashish described above, was typical: "As this individual
lives the life of an outlaw (*vit toujours en dehors des règlements et de la Loi*),
and is a perpetual cause of trouble for public peace and security, I would
be much obliged if you would give the necessary orders so that this wretch
(*triste personnage*) can be expelled from the country (*Pays*)."[50] Pasquale was
sent away, but for certain bad subjects deportation was less than definitive.
Vincenzo Buhagiar was first deported from Alexandria to Malta in 1874.
In the mid-1880s, he returned to Alexandria, engaging in repeated acts of
fraud, theft, and counterfeiting. In each case, local authorities could only
enumerate Buhagiar's previous convictions and ask once again that he be
removed from the country after trial: "As Vincenzo's previous offenses are
numerous, it is hoped that you will agree, after his trial, to banish him as a
protection from his bad conduct (*tabʿidihi li-l-amn min shururihi*)."[51] He was
duly sent away, but he returned to Egypt again and again. For such a bad
subject, unsuccessful territorial banishment was followed by banishment
from protection.

Removal of consular protection was relatively rare, and it was reserved
for bad subjects such as Giuseppe Scerri, whose story opened this chapter,
or Vincenzo Buhagiar, who could not be controlled through deportation.
Sebastiano Gambin was typical of the bad subjects encountered by the
courts. This Maltese young man (nineteen years old) was a habitual thief
and always seemed to carry a crowbar. He was arrested in February 1891
while breaking into a matchmaker's storeroom of sulfur. Consul Cookson held him for two months, but despite repeated letters and personal
requests, he was unable to induce anyone to press charges and was obliged
to release him.[52] Only a month later, he was charged with another theft
and sentenced to one year of hard labor in Malta.[53] After he was released,
he returned to Alexandria and began thieving again. He was sentenced to
another six months in Malta, and this time he was asked to provide a £50

surety (a large sum for a poor man) as a guarantee of future good behavior. Gambin could not pay and was therefore "deported from the Ottoman Dominions," which is to say that he was ordered not to return to Alexandria once his sentence was complete. When he was arrested yet again, having returned to Alexandria and to his old ways, the consul decided on a different strategy. Cookson informed the governor of Alexandria that Gambin "has been sentenced to one months imprisonment [for defying the deportation], and at the expiration of that period to be struck off the register of British subjects. He will therefore then be handed over to be dealt with as local subject."[54]

Gambin was clearly a recidivist, but his crimes were relatively minor—in one case, for example, he was charged for the theft of a blanket. Cookson reasoned that the young man showed signs of becoming a habitual criminal, and even his widowed mother wanted him sent away from the bad company he kept in Alexandria.[55] If he was worthy of losing registration, many others might also have been. The British consulate shifted responsibility for this consistent troublemaker entirely into local hands at exactly the moment that other British administrators were working at the interior ministry to get Egyptian crime under control.[56] Perhaps the left hand did not know what the right hand was doing. It is also possible that the consular court considered the range of options that formal and informal empire offered for dealing with Gambin and decided that the means offered by the local authorities in Egypt would be most efficacious. But when Gambin was sent to the consulate from the Caracol Labban charged with breaking and entering yet again, the consulate changed course. Although Gambin was a British subject when he committed the crime, he was still under a deportation order. The British consular court gave him a sentence for breaking deportation, then handed him over to the local police to be tried for the theft, totally washing its hands of him. The final document in Gambin's file is a receipt from the police acknowledging that he had been delivered into their custody after serving his one-month sentence. British archives hold no further evidence of prosecutions but show that he was still alive and visible to the authorities two decades later, when he received one-third of his mother's £72 estate.[57]

Nineteenth-century Mediterranean port cities are often depicted as fluid societies in which people of different cultures and religions lived side by side in vibrant harmony. A growing literature questions the validity of this image, arguing that cosmopolitanism is a chimera.[58] This chapter supplements these arguments, which express skepticism about the positive mosaic, with evidence of the sort of vulgar cosmopolitanism described in chapter 1, which shows the danger and undesirability of mobility, fluidity, and diversity. The poverty and danger of these port cities is the subject of a useful literature.[59] This chapter focused on the legal mechanisms used to address undesirable members of the foreign population of Alexandria: practices of deportation and denationalization that operated in the broader context of the spread of nationality. While nationality and the courts were important tools for advocacy and protection, they could also be used for control and exclusion. The same authorities that jealously protected favored subjects cooperated in order to define and prosecute undesirables. The universalization of nationality was in large part an effort to eliminate the jurisdictional cracks in which protégés and undesirables alike found refuge.

Consular court records are among the few sources that record the history of subaltern, impoverished Europeans and colonial subjects (Maltese, Algerian, Tunisian) in the world of empire. Case files from French, British, and Egyptian archives show the ways that consulates dealt with indigent, quarrelsome, recidivist, and transgressive subjects. A foreign-local consensus emerged about the characteristics of bad subjects, and the local authorities would often call upon consulates to expel undesirables from Egyptian territory. Sometimes, the consulates obliged; in other cases, foreign undesirables were stripped of their foreignness (their consular protection). These foreigners were made into locals, which became the default status of those without foreign protection. Then as now, however, efforts to make undesirables disappear exposed the flaws and contradictions in a "universal" citizenship regime predicated on nationality.

The category of bad subject reminds us of two neglected facets of modern nationality. First, regimes of universal legal personality were (and are) not straightforward liberal instruments. Diverse examples, from Tanzimat Mount Lebanon to Nazi Germany, show that the very legal instruments that extend rights that appear to protect certain minorities can be used to control them, just as they create other kinds of minorities (such as the bad subjects) who are excluded from liberal rights.[60] Second, figures such as the bad subject take their place in alternate histories of individual rights that feature figures and categories that were subsequently curtailed or submerged. Histories of this sort offer a means to think beyond narratives of Western liberalism's inevitable triumph.[61]

Vagrants were a standard concern in European states and port cities worldwide, and criminologists were engrossed with the challenge of reforming bad subjects in the late nineteenth and early twentieth centuries. Similarly, incarceration, deportation, repatriation, and exile were common remedies for such undesirables. In Alexandria, it is clear that a pluralist legal regime organized according to discrete communitarian, national, ethnic, and sectarian spheres always produced exceptions. Consulates, the very institutions that promoted the strictest definitions of nationality as an either/or status, agreed in practice to consign rebels to a common category and to exclude them from Alexandria. Sound national affiliation demanded more than just clear proof of identity. Material stability and social responsibility were also required. The poor and the disobedient, from the consular perspective, created problems akin to the less-than-foreign individuals who could claim only tenuous protection. The privileges of foreignness—freedom from taxation, freedom from prosecution, and inviolability of domicile—could not properly be exercised by bad subjects and vagabonds. Vagabonds had no domicile and no potential for taxation. Bad subjects, meanwhile, were too free from prosecution. Vagabonds and bad subjects of all nationalities (foreign and local) formed a special category of transnational subject, excluded (like the stateless) from the universal regime of legal personality.

Exile is intimately related to foreignness. Today, the foreigner is often cast as a defective, excluded figure.[62] In the Ottoman Mediterranean of the nineteenth century, however, the foreigner was whole and privileged. Exile *to home* and loss of foreign status were the strongest tools that the consul possessed to control his privileged community. Whereas in Europe the banished vagrant or troublemaker was simply shifted to an equivalent jurisdiction, in Egypt his or her legal identity was transformed by geographical displacement. Poor Europeans and Algerian, Tunisian, and Maltese imperial subjects lost social and legal privilege when they were removed from Egypt. Those whose names were struck from the consular rolls became locals, an even more radical transformation of status. And so in this way the figure of the deficient subject reinforced distinctions—not between communities but between those who exercised the pseudocitizenship rights associated with universal regimes of nationality (of which consular protection was an embryo) and those who were not part of that system. This is, as many scholars have shown, the use of outsiders: they are the exception that makes the rule.

Local subjects, meanwhile, were immune from such means: They had no home country to which they could be deported and no nationality to lose. But local status was not entirely void and without form. As part of their effort to join the community of nations, the Ottomans established a legal framework for Ottoman nationality in 1869 and worked to flesh it out in the decades that followed. If international law was to be a universal regime, every state had to build its component of the interlocking whole. The next chapter explains the Ottoman contribution to this project.

11
Ottomans

The "Italian Chronicle" section, in the inside pages of the June 11, 1897, edition of *L'Imparziale* ("a political daily paper, the only one designated for publishing announcements and judicial edicts of the Mixed Court of first instance of Cairo") contained the following note:

> On a recent evening during the show at Carlo Felice Theater, Mohamed Bey Rachad of Alexandria, a rich 45 year old Egyptian currently resident at the luxurious Hotel Isotta, attempted to commit an obscene act upon a 15 year old boy, a student at one of Genoa's schools, in the box where he was seated. The boy reported the act, and the bey was conveyed to prison and his case referred to the judicial authorities.

A week and a half later, the Egyptian Ministry of Foreign Affairs sent the Italian representative this exquisitely pained request for information:

> Insofar as one of the presidents of the Native Magistrate's Courts bears the name Mahmoud Bey Rachad, and this man is currently on holiday in Europe, my colleague the Minister of Justice would be very relieved to know if the individual of whom this article speaks has no relationship with the Magistrate who has such a similar name. . . .

Wishful thinking. Several individuals were embarrassed here: the bey in question (who left Genoa in haste and shame), the minister of justice, and the minister of foreign affairs. But which nation was assigned the shame? The letter from the prefect of Genoa shows that as far as the Italians (in Italy) were concerned, the bey was an Ottoman subject.[1]

This episode manifests a conundrum of Egyptian nationality at the turn of the twentieth century: when translated into human terms, the veiled, inconsistent sovereignty regime in Egypt offered unconvincing answers to pressing questions of affiliation and belonging. This effect was a result of the questions asked, which were newly universal, modular, personal, and legally significant. Everywhere in the world, regimes struggled to synthesize answers. In Egypt, as in many other spaces and as for many other populations, the available answers were barely plausible. The Ottoman state was better able to generate responses. It possessed institutional tools—such as its ministries and its network of embassies and consulates—and legal tools—a long series of foreign treaties as well as domestic legislation such as the Nationality Law of 1869—to support this legitimization work. This work was a central focus for Sultan Abdulhamid II. But the human weight of the empire's erstwhile and waning provinces was an unending source of difficult problems.

Egypt generated an especially complex matrix of Ottoman statuses. Outside of the Ottoman dominions, in places like Genoa, Egyptians and Ottoman subjects from elsewhere in the empire shared the same nationality de jure. De facto, the answers were more complex. Later on in the summer of 1897, three Egyptian merchants resident in Guatemala, seeking to regularize their status, claimed British protection. The British ambassador informed London, as well as the Egyptian and the Ottoman authorities; none, it seemed, was in a position to meet the merchants' needs.[2] If foreign cases produced gray areas of imperial and state jurisdiction, domestic cases were even less clear. Although natives of Egypt seemed to assume Ottoman subjecthood in Istanbul and elsewhere in the empire, Ottomans in Egypt could not expect a clear-cut determination of status.

In the last decade and a half, historians of the Ottoman Empire have dramatically recast our understanding of the nature of the empire in its provinces, demonstrating the flexible, locally conditioned, and often ephemeral nature of the imperial presence in each provincial setting.[3] Egypt has not played a role in this revision. There are some good reasons for this omission: although Egypt remained a part of the Ottoman Empire until the First World War, Istanbul's direct influence over its erstwhile province waned dramatically over the course of the nineteenth century. By the time Britain invaded and occupied Egypt in 1882, few remnants of direct control remained. With rare exceptions, historians agree that Egypt was, for all intents and purposes, independent of the Ottoman Empire by the last quarter of the century.[4]

Legal-history approaches suggest otherwise, however, and point to the global significance of the Egyptian example. The Charkieh case of 1873 remains a leading international case of state immunity.[5] An 1872 collision on the Thames between the Khedive Isma'il's ship *Charkieh* and a Dutch steamer raised a new question: Was the khedive an independent sovereign and thus immune from suit? The British High Court of Admiralty denied the khedive's claim, ruling that he was a "subject prince" because Egypt was an Ottoman province (by *ferman*), its army part of the Ottoman army, its taxes raised in the name of the Ottomans. It had no separate right to send ambassadors and consuls (*jus legationis*), and it had no flag. If the khedive's standing vis-à-vis the Ottomans was a productive question for international lawyers, the standing of his subjects over the decades that followed would provide further fodder for lawyerly reflection, as this chapter will show.

The conventional narrative of Egyptian/Ottoman separation deserves reexamination on both theoretical and empirical grounds. Theoretically, the new literature on Ottoman provincialism is part of a broader reconceptualization of empire that aims to confront the normative position of the European experience.[6] This reconceptualization has drawn on new empirical data concerning the varieties of forms of membership, political and otherwise, occasioned by empire.[7] Ottoman history, for its part, is beginning to develop a theoretical framework to talk about the complexities of its membership regimes.[8] This chapter argues that differences between Ottoman subjects' membership in their state and European and American archetypes of citizenship reveal contours of the global phenomenon of nationality. In particular, the Ottoman example shows that membership is often a sparse regime that should not be imagined to be greater than the sum of its parts. The first section of this chapter questions the idea that Egypt was independent of the Ottoman Empire before the turn of the century and outlines the demographic and institutional presence of Ottomans

in Egypt. The second looks at citizenship laws and practices of nationality, applied to Ottomans and Egyptians alike. The third section examines
evidence from law courts for enduring Ottoman nationality in Egypt. The
fourth section discusses a rise in Ottoman assertions of nationality control during the Second Constitutional Period. The conclusion argues for
the exemplary merits of the apolitical model of Ottoman citizenship found
in British Egypt.

Post-Ottoman Egypt?

Ironically, the British occupation of Egypt in 1882 and the Veiled Protectorate that followed did much to enhance notions of Egypt's national independence. During the early years of the occupation, the situation of Egypt
vis-à-vis the British and Ottoman empires was characterized by two fic-
tions. Public discourse pretended that the Ottomans retained a measure
of control over Egypt and that Egypt retained a measure of independence
from Britain. In official correspondence, Egypt was carefully and consistently referred to as *al-qutr al-misri*, the "Egyptian region," and other safe
synonyms of "region," such as *taraf* and *diyar*.[9] In the interests of pragma-
tism, oppositional political strategy was structured around opposition to
British imperial control. The nationalist discourse that emerged in the
1890s appeared to instrumentalize (or even marginalize) Ottomanism in
order to address the British.[10]

A whole literature endeavors to define Ottomanism; it is by no means
unusual that this identity should fail to fit Egyptians exactly.[11] If Ottoman
nationality, the central concern of this chapter, had its legal articulation
in 1869, it is a mischaracterization to describe it as citizenship. Ottoman
nationality was formulated for foreign consumption and had no primary
municipal effects. Subjecthood was the concept of membership in common usage during the nineteenth century, not as the Arabic/Ottoman
term *tabiʿiya/tabiiyet* (which derives from *tabiʿ/tabi*, meaning subject, e.g.,
of a state or sovereign) but as the older *reaya*, for "flock" or "subjects."[12]
The relationship of shepherd (the Ottoman sultan) and flock (his subjects)
was based on notions of protection and loyalty rather than sovereignty
and allegiance. It is on this basis that more recent scholarship argues that
as late as 1905, "in the final analysis, the majority of Egyptians considered

themselves to be Ottoman subjects," and those interested in forging an independent Egypt pursued a policy of de-Ottomanization as a result.[13] By the turn of the twentieth century, as the older concept of subject-hood became brittle with the weight of state expansion, Ottomanism was increasingly defined as Islamic, with the enthusiastic moral and material support of Egyptians during the Italo-Turkish war over Libya (1911–1912) the last great sign before the First World War of Egypt's Ottoman affiliation.

The institutional history of Ottoman nationality in Egypt remains to be written. But accounts of Ottomanism that privilege political debates offer few resources to understand the lives of tens of thousands of Ottomans living in Egypt who did not identify as "locals." If the manner in which these individuals were controlled and served by Ottoman authorities is unclear, even their numbers in the decennial census (table 11.1) are confusing.

Daniel Panzac has produced several studies of the population of nineteenth-century Egypt in which he displays careful critical faculties. His suspicion of uneven growth rates, for instance, leads him to depart radically from the census figures of Egypt's aggregate population.[14] But where foreigners are concerned, his work is enthralled by the census and its nationality categories and content to trace a smooth growth rate for the foreign population, ignoring the fact that Ottomans appear and disappear from the census figures.[15] In 1882 and 1897, they are counted as local subjects; in 1907 and 1917, they are foreigners and are divided into the sub-categories listed in table 11.2.

Though these numbers are inconsistent, it is clear that there were large numbers of subjects to manage using the tools of identity documents, inheritance rulings, and marriage registration. Bureaucratic structures supported the rights claims of Ottomans in Egypt centered around Gazi Ahmed Muhtar Pasha, the Ottoman high commissioner in Egypt from 1885

TABLE 11.1 Ottomans in Alexandria, 1882–1917 censuses

	Absolute number	% of population
1882	5,169	2.2
1897	14,306	4.5
1907	21,827	6.6
1917	11,384	2.6

TABLE 11.2 Ottomans in Alexandria and in Egypt, 1907 and 1917 censuses

	Alexandria 1907	Egypt 1907	Alexandria 1917	Egypt 1917
Turks	8,953	27,591	3,549	8,471
Arabs	61	440	90	386
Armenians	2,762	7,747	1,827	7,760
Greeks			2,005	4,258
Jews			427	1,243
Syrians	10,051	33,947	2,795	7,728
Other races	691	951		
Total Ottomans	21,827	69,725	11,384	30,797

to 1908.[16] Muhtar Pasha's irregular position meant that Ottoman offices, like those of the British, were labeled with euphemisms. Muhtar's function involved a great deal of political and diplomatic work, as detailed in Aimee Genell's study.[17] But his office also performed bureaucratic work on behalf of Ottoman subjects resident in Egypt. The extraordinary Ottoman mission in Egypt (*mısır fevkalade komiserliği*) was headquartered in Cairo in the Ismaʿiliya Palace on Masr al-ʿAtiqa Street, boasting an administrative staff of seven in 1896.[18] There were also bureaus in other major cities: there was a *mutasarrif* in Alexandria, and in 1907, Port Said's office was large enough to have its own passport agent.[19] Often described as an inert symbol of a fallen empire, Muhtar was in fact the superintendent of the legal status of Egypt's sizable Ottoman population. Their demands of him, recorded in the files of the Ottoman archives, show the practical workings of decades of administrative labor. As was the case for nationality in general, money and marriage were the chief occasions for nationality work. The inheritance of Greeks and Bulgarians deceased in Egypt were returned to their heirs in the empire.[20] At times, as in the 1910 death of Dimitri Yvanidi in Alexandria, the work entailed careful examinations of nationality.[21]

The flow of subaltern and notable subjects between Egypt and the Ottoman Empire meant a large volume of routine work of this sort. Subaltern subjects felt the physicality of national jurisdiction. A prisoner transfer undertaken just before the British occupation shows how tightly bound were the Ottoman and Egyptian states at that point. The prisoner in question (a Maltese British subject named Giovanni Callus) had been convicted of theft by the British consular court in Alexandria and sentenced to five years of penal servitude in Malta. In the course of the investigation, it was discovered that in 1870 Callus had escaped from the "Central Turkish prison" in Istanbul, where he was serving another five-year sentence for theft. Before he could begin his sentence in Malta, he had to complete his sentence in Istanbul.[22]

Negotiations over the transfer reveal the complex relationship between empire, autonomous province, and capitulation powers. Initially, the Ottoman police requested the prisoner from the Egyptian foreign minister, by way of their own (Ottoman) foreign minister. The British consul-general in Alexandria (who had custody of Callus) refused this Egyptian intermediary, stating that the prisoner would only be handed over to local authorities upon a "properly attested [direct] request from the Ottoman authorities." Eventually, Callus was transferred following an Ottoman request to the British consul in Istanbul, which was then conveyed to the British consulate in Alexandria, which then transferred the prisoner to the Egyptian police, who transferred him to the British prison in Istanbul, whence he was transferred to Turkish prison. The Egyptians could not sit at the bargaining table, but they could pass messages and, of course, the prisoner himself.

After the occupation, the Egyptian state was represented in Istanbul by a *kapı kethüdalık* in Istanbul that performed functions comparable to the Ottoman high commission in Egypt. It served warrants from the Egyptian courts on individuals resident in the Ottoman domains.[23] It also verified the nationality status of suspects apprehended in Egypt, such as a Romanian subject in 1914.[24] This office persisted until the time of the First World War. And the Ottoman interior ministry also dealt directly with the Egyptian authorities, in a manner not unlike that of other foreign states. Often, these dealings concerned passports: inquiring about fees for Syrians returning from America in 1889, for example, or responding to an 1893 Egyptian request for Ottoman passport regulations.[25] A file from 1902 contains a number of letters concerning passport errors requiring rectification.[26]

The counterpart administrative offices were part of a system that differentiated between Ottomans and Egyptians. In his diary of a trip to London in 1886, the celebrated Syrian writer Jurji Zaydan devotes many pages to the headaches faced by Syrians passing through Port Said on their way to Europe.[27] He recounts that the local government required any

Syrian sailing for Europe to provide evidence of moral rectitude (*annahu min atayib al-nas wa anna siratahu hasana ila akhirihi*).[28] In order to show that he was no "bad subject," Zaydan spent days running from office to office, procuring forms, signatures, seals, and stamps. He spent two days in the company of the *shaykh* of the Syrian community (*shaykh al-shawam*) of Port Said, who acted as his fixer. He certified Zaydan's standing and guided him through the maze of police, quarantine, and municipal officials who also needed to sign Zaydan's papers. The *shaykh* was paid ten francs for his troubles. It was the steamship company that enforced this exit control for Syrians by demanding the certificate before issuing their tickets. Zaydan's text bristles with impatience, which was a common experience for Syrians caught in Egyptian bureaucracy.[29]

Egypt's cities were visited by travelers from all over the world, and if Jurji Zaydan's experience was novel it was certainly not unique—technologies of mobility control were in an active testing phase all over the world, from South Africa to India to Hong Kong to San Francisco. Mobility controls were also in place in Syria, whence Zaydan came, and other parts of the Ottoman Empire. But the hassle he faced as a traveler was temporary. The legal and bureaucratic situation of Ottomans resident in Egypt entailed considerably more complications. Most—but not all—of the thousands of Egyptian residents recognized as Ottoman subjects de facto were Christians of Syrian or Greek origin. Legally, these individuals worked with a provisional nationality in a world where national status was gaining substantial new importance. As the next chapter will show, newspapers from the time reveal that they were the locus of considerable nationality anxiety. They were claimants of local privilege as well as targets of local discrimination. Certainly their status as locals-who-were-not-locals (echoing the foreigners passing as locals of chapter 9) brought with it considerable bureaucratic hassle.

Much of Muhtar's work was political, of course. While Britain drew most nationalist political fire, the Ottoman Empire remained *the* key referent for Egypt's elite political and intellectual culture, even as late as the turn of the century. Egyptians were active observers of, and indeed participants in, the Ottoman reform movements of the early twentieth century. Egypt was a site of exile for Syrian journalists, Young Turks, and other opponents of the regime, but it was not merely an inert foreign land.[30] This political work could take on a nationality dimension. An example from the late

1880s shows the distance between the Ottoman self-image and its realizable power. Jean Broussali was an Egyptian-born Armenian law student in Paris during the 1880s.[31] From Paris, he agitated publicly concerning the Ottoman treatment of Armenians. The Ottoman ambassador in Paris did everything in his power to stop him, eventually contacting a certain Fourens, perhaps in the French Foreign Ministry, who threatened Broussali with expulsion. By 1888, with Broussali's activity unchecked, the embassy discovered that he was no longer studying but was receiving a stipend from the "Mission des élèves égyptiens à Paris." It asked the Porte to follow up this question with its representatives in Egypt. The khedive's government replied that Broussali had never received such a pension. In June 1888, the ambassador discovered—to his great surprise—that Broussali had naturalized as a French citizen. France had always refused to naturalize without Ottoman permission, he argued.[32] The French minister was embarrassed, saying that it was the fault of the justice minister, but reported that there was little he could do now. The Ottoman minister pressed his demands, suggesting the naturalization be canceled. They discovered then that when Broussali had requested naturalization in 1887, he had relied on the Persian subjecthood he had declared when requesting domicile in 1884. But when asked, the Persian ambassadors in Paris and Constantinople stated that they had no idea who Broussali was. This episode shows two ways in which Ottoman sovereignty was frustrated. First, Egypt was in a real sense out of its reach, and the Ottoman state had little recourse when facing uncooperative attitudes on the part of Egyptian and European officials. Second, it was clear that misdirection was a danger of the incomplete subjecthood practiced by second-tier states such as the Ottomans, Egypt, and Persia. Broussali moved quite effectively between these statuses without ever being called to account. For the Ottomans, in this case at least, Egypt was as out of reach as Persia or France.[33]

Citizenship Laws and Nationality Practices

There was no real element of political participation in turn-of-the-century Egyptian citizenship. Western archetypes of citizenship are therefore ill-fitting models. French and American visions of membership in the nation-state find no counterpart.[34] None of the terms of Marshall's classic civil-political-social citizenship typology fully apply.[35] Instead, liberal imperialism's ugly underbelly was on display: for most Egyptians, membership meant only labor in the planned national cash-crop economy, an economy focused on foreign debt payments. The state made much of its authority through law, however. Although few Egyptians can be considered rights-bearing subjects, the law began to offer them new possibilities of civil standing.

The first Ottoman nationality law was published in 1869, but Egypt did not have its own nationality law until 1926. As a result, during the 1890s heyday of Egyptian nationalism, Egyptians who traveled abroad, used the law courts, or responded to census questions could only represent themselves as Ottoman citizens. A 1900 Egyptian decree-law concerning the attribution of nationality and distinguishing (for the first time) between Egyptians and Ottomans was no nationalist watershed, either.[36] It was enforced gradually and inconsistently; even the new Egyptian passports issued after 1889 (figure 3.4) were printed not in Arabic but in Ottoman Turkish and French. Evidence of nationality practice poses two problems for the traditional narratives of Egyptian independence from Ottoman control: first (according to censuses and legal sources), the Ottomans were consistently identified as locals rather than foreigners until 1907. Second (according to census and noncensus evidence, such as law-court practice, passports, and political agitation), the Egyptians were persistently identified as Ottoman.

Gianluca Parolin's recent survey of citizenship in the Arab world exemplifies the contradictions produced by a purely textual reading of Egyptian nationality.[37] According to this understanding, Ottoman nationality began with the first code of nationality in 1869. Parolin describes this legislation as a reaction to the capitulations. In order to curb abuse of this foreign privilege (including by Ottoman-born subjects exploiting loopholes), the Ottoman sultan finally asserted his right to approve all changes of nationality. The Ottoman nationality law functioned as a code of naturalization rather than of citizenship: it granted no intrinsic rights. Its articles concerned only questions of acquisition of nationality, which largely followed jus sanguinis principles.[38] (The 1900 Egyptian nationality law, which fits on a single page of the state's official journal, is also exclusively focused on acquisition. Clearly, membership was about jurisdiction rather than rights.)

Despite Parolin's legalistic reading of citizenship, he seems compelled to tell a story that goes beyond statute.[39] He offers assertions about Egyptian nationality that depart from the evidence he presents: at some indeterminate point after 1869, a sense "of 'indigenous nationality' (al-raʿawiya al-mahalliya) emerged" in the Ottoman provinces, including Egypt.[40] "By the end of the 19th century, the Egyptian indigenous nationality was fully shaped," he goes on to argue.[41] "By the turn of the 20th century, Arab lands—where religious affiliation was the only known form of membership beyond the kin group—suddenly witnessed the rise of two new forms of secular membership, an overarching Ottoman nationality and a local indigenous one."[42] And again: "Indigenous nationality only complemented Ottoman nationality, the latter being conditional to the former . . . and the Egyptian was treated internationally as an Ottoman subject."[43]

In the context of an otherwise well-ordered study, this welter of assertions points to a breakdown in categories: archetypes of Western citizenship fail to account for certain varieties of non-Western experience. The "full shape" of nineteenth-century "indigenous nationality" that Parolin invokes cannot have been essentially legal (there was no Egyptian nationality law) or political (there were no political rights). Nor did "indigenous nationality" reside in the domain of civil citizenship rights—in the Ottoman context, these had been articulated much earlier, in the 1839 Gülhane rescript and its Tanzimat cousins.[44] Nor were Egyptians, who traveled on their "own" passports by 1899, simply treated internationally as Ottoman subjects. Religious and kin-group membership, meanwhile, were not the "only known forms" of membership: professional and neighborhood associationalism was extensive in Egypt.

As we will see, it was the details of implementation that defined the nationality law. For Ottoman nationality administrators, the most useful provision of the 1869 law was the requirement that all nationality changes be authorized by imperial irade. In the decades that followed, officials could fall back on this rarely observed procedure to object to most nationality changes as the need arose. In 1890, the consular section of the Ottoman Foreign Ministry saw an opportunity to assert its authority in Egypt. Ottoman subjects of Greek origin claimed Greek nationality when arriving at the Egyptian border in order to avoid paying Ottoman taxes.[45] Ottoman subject formation had traditionally circulated around the question of taxation, and payment of tax was taken as a sign of subjecthood. Reaya were, quite simply, those who paid taxes, and the *askeri* elite were those who received that surplus.[46] Tax exemption was the "most important marker of legal status in the Ottoman Empire."[47] Thus it is entirely consistent that taxation status would be a central marker of the new nationality. At the same moment, the Egyptian government was engaged in debates with Greeks resident in Egypt over nationality questions, concerned that Egypt had become a key site for nationality change and document fraud. Greeks made these claims based on documents issued by local mayors in Greece, who were the ones to certify nationality by entering names in *municipal* registers. They had a reputation of doing so in return for electoral support. The Ottomans sought to have the Egyptian government accept Ottoman certification of Greek nationality documents. They offered to certify the seals and signatures of these documents, rather than their contents, in order to discover fraud.

Foreign Ministry bureaucrats discovered that the Ottoman law forbidding Ottoman subjects from changing nationality with an authorizing *irade* had never been published in Egypt. They took the opportunity to publish the law and create a nine-month grace period (February 1 to November 1, 1890) during which Greeks in Egypt could register with their political agency, after which the Greek agency would furnish the Egyptian government with a list of all of its subjects resident in Egypt. After November 1, any claimant not on the list would be considered a local (Ottoman) subject. The imperial government had no doubt that those who raised difficulties did so in bad faith. "Real" Greeks would have no difficulty proving their nationality; as for the others, "from the first examination of any such case, any difficulty that arises must suggest that the claimed nationality is illegal." Again, it was the Ottomans who would certify the validity of the mayors' certificates.

The problem was not that nationality was easy to get or to change in Egypt but that official documents attesting Greek nationality were too easy to get in Greece. The Ottoman authorities urged the Egyptian authorities to create a united front in verifying these documents according to a single set of criteria. In doing so, they asserted a degree of sovereignty over Egypt, in the form of certification expertise. Every form of nationality had its own system of attestation. The Greek system was far more decentralized than most and was therefore subject to corruption, for instance by local officials looking for votes. The Ottoman authorities asserted their unique ability to verify the genuineness of the seals and signatures on these local documents and hoped that the Egyptians would accept their validations.

This "solution" did not address the key problem, which was that competent local officials were issuing valid documents for invalid reasons, and it did not explain why the Ottomans could evaluate the validity of the documents better than Egyptian officials. (There was a broader context in which Greeks were a proxy for sovereignty struggles with Egypt. In 1889, for instance, the Ministry of Finance sought to settle complaints by Greek sponge fishers that it had licensed who were prevented from fishing in Egyptian waters.)[48]

Sometimes, of course, the stories of foreign naturalization are straightforward and clear. An Ottoman-born man named Stephen Mirzan migrated to Boston in the late 1850s and naturalized in the United States. He returned to Alexandria in 1864, working as a broker and a propagandist for the khedive. In 1879, following the loss of khedivial sponsorship, Mirzan murdered a lawyer who was acting as an agent for the khedive. He was tried by the American consular court in Alexandria and sent to Albany, New York, to serve his sentence. Although it never made any claim over Mirzan, the Ottoman Interior Ministry kept itself informed of this case involving its erstwhile subject.[49]

More typically, the status of Egyptian courts and of Ottoman nationality in Egypt was far from clear. This was especially true within the empire itself. In the summer of 1886, provincial officials in Aleppo wrote to the imperial Justice Ministry about the case of Shamly Ibrahim.[50] This Ottoman subject had been on the losing end of a commercial case before the Mixed Tribunals in Alexandria. He was sentenced in absentia, and the authorities wondered whether and how they were to execute the sentence. (It is not clear how the executing warrant was conveyed to Aleppo.) Was he to be treated as a local subject procedurally? The Justice Ministry referred the question to the judicial office of the Foreign Ministry, which patiently explained the terms of the Mixed Tribunals treaty signed a decade earlier. Yes, sentences of the Egyptian Mixed Tribunals were executable in the Ottoman domains, the same as any other sentences from Egypt's "local tribunals," after minor procedural adjustments. Citing an 1872 letter from the sultan to the khedive, in which he agreed to the establishment of the Mixed Tribunals, the legal bureau advised that the tribunal was a legitimately *Ottoman* institution. In this sense, it should have been incompetent to try Shamly Ibrahim because as an Ottoman he was not a foreigner. But it was he, and not the Ottoman authorities themselves, who ought to have argued to have the case dismissed. Therefore, the authorities in Aleppo should proceed to execute the judgment. If this advice was realistic, it blurred many lines of legal principle. Not least of these was the fact that jurisprudence defined Ottomans as foreigners for the purposes of the Mixed Tribunals.

In 1889, the Alexandria Mixed Court of Appeal ruled that if a local wife had acquired foreign nationality through marriage but without getting permission of the Ottoman state per the 1869 laws, she would still be considered foreign unless the Ottoman government contested her nationality.[51] This ruling fit a broad tendency in Mixed Tribunals jurisprudence not to press cases of nationality undisputed by governmental authorities, which is to say that the court refused to entertain private disputation of nationality. Hence its ruling in 1890 that nationality is sufficiently established by registration in consular registers; if another nation disputes the question, it becomes a diplomatic matter on which the Mixed Tribunals cannot rule.[52] In the same year, it ruled that the Ottoman Bank was subject to mixed jurisdiction.[53]

It was plain that Egypt was no longer Ottoman in the eyes of the Mixed Tribunals, but Ottoman status lingered in other law courts and venues. If pressed to define their status, local subjects had no recourse but the Ottoman nationality law of 1869.[54] Ottoman protégés (raʿaya) in Egypt occupied the same contested space as Greek Egyptians, French Algerians, and British Maltese. On the street, many Ottomans were identified as foreign. An Ottoman assailant who stabbed a British sailor in 1883 was sent for prosecution at the Greek consulate, which promptly returned him to the local authorities.[55] As mentioned in chapter 3, the French protection of Mahri Hamawi was challenged when the local authority discovered that he carried a passport issued by the *shaykh* of the Syrian community, an Ottoman.[56] Fifteen years later, Alexandrians such as a grog-shop owner who signed his inquest deposition in Hebrew still bore the ambiguous label "*rayah*" (*raʿiya*).[57]

Ottoman and Egyptian in Court

As we have seen, the de jure local status of Ottomans was ignored in the jurisprudence of the Mixed Tribunals, Egypt's prestige legal venue. Without a consistent general definition of Ottoman status in Egypt, this jurisdictional flexibility spread to the Native Courts, consular courts, and beyond. In Ottoman-Egyptian practice, nationality was the aggregate of many minor claims or assertions. Tracking these assertions is difficult precisely because each one is relatively unimportant (and certainly apolitical) in its moment. Yet occasionally the records reveal self-identifications that ring strange, and these merit our attention. In September 1908, we find Hussain ʿAbd al-Latif, a Muslim "commission agent" (that is, a wheeler-dealer) in the delta town of Dissuq, identifying himself in an affidavit as an "Ottoman subject" and in an earlier letter as a "local subject."[58] By 1908, these categories were incommensurate in statute and census. So was this self-identification deliberate or careless? Hussein disappears from the archive after this trial, but the "error" suggests that, even in legal documents submitted to a court, the distinction between Ottoman and Egyptian was often elided.[59] But if these technicalities were of minor importance for some litigants, for others they were determinative. This was especially true of wealthy men such as Antun Yussuf ʿAbd al-Massih, whose story was told in chapter 5. Even during their occupation of Egypt, the British repeatedly affirmed Ottoman legal sovereignty. Following a 1908 question in British parliament, for example, consular legal authorities determined that Ottoman law applied to real property in Egypt.[60]

The case of Nicola Adamidis shows the capaciousness others could attribute to Ottoman nationality. He was born in Ottoman territory to a Greek father in 1838. He moved to Cairo in 1859, then to England in 1865, where he was naturalized three years later. In 1870, he asked the secretary of state for a certificate allowing him to live outside the United Kingdom for more than six months without losing naturalization. He received this certificate but did not take the necessary oath before returning to Egypt in 1874. He lived in Alexandria for the rest of his life, where he was a member of the Greek Orthodox Church and "identified himself actively with the Greek Community and their charitable societies. But he registered himself at the British Consulate as a British subject and was always so regarded."[61] His estate papers included a British passport issued in Alexandria in 1905, for travel for Europe.[62] He was perhaps aware of the tenuousness of his British protection and foreign status and so made sure to carry a document to ease his travel.

Adamidis was a very wealthy man—his estate totaled twenty-four thousand pounds. After he died while visiting Athens in July 1906, his heirs (a brother and seven nieces and nephews) asserted Adamidis's British nationality. They did this because, like the heirs of ʿAbd al-Massih, they stood to inherit more if Adamidis was a British subject. His will satisfied the terms of Greek law as well as that of the Orthodox Patriarchate (the law in Turkey relating to Ottoman subjects belonging to Orthodox church), but it was invalid under English law. His relatives stood to inherit more of his estate under intestacy law than they did under the terms of the will. Unfortunately for them, the British judge who heard the case ruled that Adamidis "was without a nationality. He had ceased to be a British subject and we have it in evidence that he was no longer a Greek subject." It did not matter whether he was Greek, Egyptian, or Turkish domiciled, because the will was recognized under all three laws. Posthumously, Adamidis lost the British subjecthood and protection that he had always practiced while alive. He had lived his whole life under consular protection, and his name featured in all consular lists of subjects.[63] Only after intense judicial scrutiny (and his own death) was his identity made to appear multiple and problematic and his British status ruled false.

The contest over the nationality of Adamidis's dead body was all about money, but the question of foreignness was not only material. Through all of this time, Ottoman was the default nationality for those who needed something more than local status. It was not the grounds for positive rights but rather the status of last resort. This was the case of Miss Margaret Ann Gowans (described in chapter 9), a girl living in Istanbul who lost her birth parents (nationality unknown, but presumed Ottoman) and her adoptive parents (British). She was sent to work in Alexandria, where she was treated as an Ottoman subject, despite the best intentions of the British consulate to give her British protection.[64] It was also the case for the Tunisian-born Jew named Nessim Rahmin Benrubi described in chapter 6, who failed to register at the French consulate when he moved to Egypt. When his widow sought Tunisian French subject status in 1912, she was told by the French consular court that her husband, by failing to register with the French consulate in Egypt, had become an Ottoman subject.[65] At the same time, numerous cases exist of Algerians and Tunisians receiving foreign protection even after holding Ottoman passports.[66]

A Late Reassertion of Ottoman Nationality Law

In 1909, the Ottoman legal authorities embarked on a redefinition of the 1869 nationality law.[67] In an explanatory note, they argued that "every problem of nationality has greater importance and delicacy for the

Ottoman empire than for any other place," and "nationality matters have acquired a completely exceptional form and nature as regards public international law, due to the well-known effects of ancient agreements." Therefore they set out to reformulate the 1869 Ottoman nationality law, including necessary corrections and additions. Although this project was unrealized, it measured a rising interest in international legal work that accelerated after 1908. The Ottoman defense of sovereignty during the second constitutional period extended into the domain of nationality law. In 1911–1912, for example, the Foreign Ministry engaged in an extended contest with the German embassy over the nationality of Selim Butrus (Pierre) Anhoury.[68] Anhoury, recently deceased, had been the German consul in Damietta since 1881, and before that (from 1867) he was a dragoman at the German consulate in Alexandria. His nationality became a contentious issue during his succession.[69] The legal bureau insisted on its traditional argument that any change of nationality required the explicit approval of the Ottomans. They defended this position against counterarguments about passage of time, customary practice of international law, and the implications of the Ottoman-issued exequatur investing Anhoury with the consulship. They went so far as to suggest that the "Pierre" Anhoury described in this *ferman* as a German subject was not the same person—legally if not corporeally—as Selim Butrus Anhoury, who was and remained an Ottoman subject. In doing so, the Foreign Ministry insisted on its territorial right, per the 1869 law, to approve every change of nationality: "other than the specified legal form, no document [*acte*] can bring about loss of nationality; if it is claimed that the Egyptian Authorities knew the Ottoman origins of the deceased, their silence at or after agreement does not take the place of Imperial Authorization required by Ottoman legislation . . . the [Egyptian] authorities have no right to settle questions of nationality or to permit or recognize loss of Ottoman subjecthood." The *Note Verbale* even contains the unusual argument that before 1869, Ottoman nationality was governed by the shariʿa: in 1867, Anhoury and his family received Prussian subjecthood, "but the [German] Imperial Embassy must know that at that date, questions of nationality were governed by Shariʿa law, which does not allow loss of Ottoman nationality."

It is difficult to account for the Ottoman administrators' persistence in this apparently distant and private affair. Their extensive correspondence closes with a plea that Germany stop protecting the heirs of Selim Anhoury and stop intervening in their disputes in Egypt. In 1911, the census bureau gave approval for the Interior Ministry to consent to the wish of a certain Ibrahim Pasha to change his nationality from Ottoman to German.[70] A few years later, in wartime, the Foreign Ministry was dealing with the forced conversion of Muslim foreigners to Ottomans.[71]

With the outbreak of the First World War, questions arose concerning the status of Egyptians resident in the United Kingdom. Until Ottoman sovereignty over Egypt was extinguished in December 1914, these Egyptians were officially classified as enemy aliens. The Home Office and the Foreign Office worked with the police to regulate this population, many of whom were students. They were given identification cards giving name, age, the educational institution and police station where they were registered, and stating that they were "of Egyptian nationality" (a legal status that did not exist), their "family . . . domiciled in Egypt," and that they had "never served the Turkish government in either civil or military capacity; and [were] not hostile to the Allies."[72]

The Ottoman Empire did not manage to produce "a different shade of colonialism" in Egypt. Just as we have seen with French Algerians, British Maltese, Greeks, and even Persians, nationality was a diffuse domain for the projection of sovereignty. States could—and did—pose more and more nationality questions, more and more insistently, but the answers available were rarely complete or comprehensive. Ottoman and Egyptian nationality legislation were acts of translation performed for Western diplomatic audiences. For ordinary subjects, both Egyptian and Ottoman, what mattered was application of the law through their use of mobility control, identification documents, the census, taxation, military service, arrest and search, legal standing at law courts, and so on. Syrians resident in Egypt— and Ottoman officials themselves—found that they could do little with nationality status. As we will see in the next chapter, Ottoman appeals for rights as Egyptians were largely ineffective. Often, their situation served to define Egyptian nationality, just as Ottoman nationality helped to define European nationalities.

The unusual situation of Egypt in the history of empire has received some consideration in terms of international politics and public international law, but its position in the emergence of private international law has rarely been explored. Ottoman subjects were an uneasy fit in the

Egyptian legal regimes, which distinguished between foreigners meeting the standard of civilization (nationals of capitulatory states) and those from "uncivilized" states such as Iran, Japan, and China.

The Ottoman Empire succeeded, by the middle of the nineteenth century, in becoming a member of the community of nations. In terms of public international law, treaties brought it into the fold of the civilized. This membership was incomplete in practice, and the terms of Ottoman standing could easily be reshuffled. Nevertheless, the Tanzimat effort to meet the standard of civilization appeared to have been crowned with success. Indeed, the Hamidian state displayed a high degree of state capacity in certain areas: the generation of symbolic capital, the practice of surveillance, the colonization of outlying territories. Recent scholarship has used these and other signs of strength to argue that the reforms of the nineteenth century were successful in a certain sense. While these arguments are somewhat convincing, they can be balanced with tangible signs of incapacity. The situation of Ottomans in Egypt shows that the colonizing reach of the Ottoman Empire certainly exceeded its grasp.

The Ottomans fell short of equality with Western powers in the realm of the Egyptian capitulations. As signatories of capitulatory treaties, states as obscure as Brazil and Belgium had their say on the composition of the Mixed Courts and the constitution of the diplomatic community in Egypt. Britain, the occupying power after 1882, maintained its capitulatory standing alongside its domination of Egypt in practice. The Ottoman Empire did not manage to win standing of this sort, however. Whereas the minor capitulatory powers and Britain managed to generate and regenerate legal garments to cover the irregularities of their extraterritorial rights in Egypt, the Ottomans could not find a format to exert their power. This was not for lack of trying. Just as many individual subjects came to appreciate the limits of the emergent system of nationality during the 1880s, so too did states. The Ottoman Empire was surprisingly resilient in its assertion of sovereignty over Egypt. Decades after ceding hereditary control to Mehmet Ali, and years after the British occupation of Egypt, Constantinople continued to expect some degree of control over persons tied to its erstwhile territory. That expectation was disappointed.

A rich literature describes the inescapable, formative power of Western rationality (especially in the form of historicism) over any study of the non-West.[73] This literature is pessimistic, in a certain sense: this hegemony is insurmountable, and in any case it is hardly practical to dismantle the whole edifice of Western thought. The task of the postcolonial scholar is instead to explore and articulate the ramifications of this bias, to assist the unsteady progress of scholarship rather than clear the ground for some new project.[74] While early studies of postcolonial citizenships focused on political agency in the context of nationalist struggle, more recent scholarship finds that the political focus leaves little place for life as ordinarily lived in the postcolonial world. Postcolonial scholarship has instead emphasized the legal dimensions of citizenship.[75]

The privileging of politics immediately engenders problems in any empirically informed study of citizenship. Perhaps reframing political citizenship as a relatively rare practice within the broader field of citizenship is a useful move in explaining political citizenship itself. If we can hold in check romantic efforts to identify cosmopolitan citizenship in the Ottoman past, the gray areas of imperial nationality described in this chapter can figure as a typical global practice; banal affiliation traces a (and perhaps the) ordinary course of nationality.[76] In these cases, consistency ceases to be a goal of international law. This core characteristic of international legal practice is still with us. Tens of millions of stateless persons and undocumented migrants show that international law is comfortable with inconsistent jurisdiction, just as we see in Ottoman Egypt.

12

Locals

In 1898, six Egyptian residents of Syrian origin launched a judicial appeal to have their names entered in the register of Egyptian voters (*dafatir al-intikhab*).[1] This appeal could hardly have been motivated by a desire for political voice: the effective voice of a single voter in elections for Egypt's Legislative Council was negligible, and the council itself ("not intended to legislate, but rather to advise about legislation") was similarly powerless.[2] While this claim for voting rights was ostensibly political in nature, the case was actually about social standing and civil rights.[3] The Ottoman nationality law of 1869 met the needs of Egyptians and non-Egyptian Ottomans alike when they were outside of the empire, but it offered no means of distinguishing Egyptians for domestic purposes. In the closing years of the century, the Egyptian domestic regime created new restrictions on those defined as non-Egyptian. But in the absence of any law defining Egyptian nationality or governing its attribution or loss, local subjects seeking to define or redefine their status in Egypt sought stand-in instruments. In this instance, the Election Law (*qanun al-intikhab*) of May 1, 1883, was appropriated as a definition of membership.[4]

The first article of the law was usefully ambiguous: the right to vote was given to "any Egyptian from amongst the subjects of the local government" (*kull misri min raʿiyat al-hukuma al-mahalliya*).[5] The 1898 case turned on the interpretation of this article and, more specifically, on the term (*lafza*) "Egyptian" (*misri*). We have seen that subjecthood (*raʿiya*) was a potent description of individual affiliation to states. The Tanzimat transformation of this status culminated in the 1869 nationality law. Until 1883, however, the distinction between the status of Egypt (which was an "exceptional province" [*eyalat-i mümtaze*]) and other provinces did not extend to the Egyptians themselves. Article 1 of the Election Law of 1883 thus became a baseline for subsequent lawyerly definitions of the precedent pedigree of Egyptian nationality. But "*misri*" proved a mirage, at least as far as rights were concerned—voting rights without voting are only the most evident example of its false-front function. Far more significant, this chapter will argue, was the anodyne term "local" (*mahalli*), which was the common term used to describe the government and its subjects.

In describing locals and foreigners, scholars are confronted with the same quandaries of specificity and universality that complicated legislative, census, identification, and justice work. Ehud Toledano uses "insider" and "outsider" as generics that function something like "local" and "foreign."[6] Elsewhere, he uses "native Egyptians" for Arabic speakers.[7] Harold Tollefson uses "inhabitants" for "native," perhaps mimicking government use in reference to residents.[8] Alexander Kitroeff uses "minority" to describe foreigners in his study of the Greeks in Egypt, implying the existence of a majority of (homogenous) "Egyptians," before settling on ethnicity as the category of social distinction.[9] Nancy Reynolds has emphasized the cultural register, distinguishing between *baladi* and *ifrangi*.[10] The accuracy of each of these generic terms, like the categories specified in the five previous chapters, must depend on faithful attention to the varied and changing uses historical actors found for them.

Local status—the protonationality of the majority of Alexandria's residents—was the product of a legal dialectic. As we have seen, the capitulations generated the broad category of foreigner through exemptions from local taxation, conscription, prosecution, and search. The foreigner was he who was not local. The local, in turn, became an empty signifier holding the place of the nonforeign. Over the decades of the British occupation, state and society began to lend positive meaning to this default label. The "local" was at first an absence existing only to endorse the status of the rights-bearing foreigner, in much the same way that the status of humans could be defined by the status of nonhuman others.[11] In time, however, the local began to figure as the opposite of the foreign, especially as foreign subjects who lost protection sought to define their new status. The "nationalist revolts" of 1882 and 1919 bookend the rise of an explicit Egyptian nationalism that began to propagate rights claims for Egyptians that mimicked the terms of foreign subjecthood. A collective generic sense of a local counterpart to foreign national communities began to emerge under the signs of *ahli* (native) and *watani* (national), terms that gradually acquired political force. In a small but growing number of cases of contested nationality, individuals were categorized as Egyptian subjects in much the same way that foreigners might be identified by nationality.

Of course, local nationality was never really the same as foreign nationality. While anticolonial claims on behalf of natives and nationals are a familiar theme in histories of the turn of the century, the quiet, parallel, distinct development of localness (*mahalliya*) as a set of strategic legal practices was equally significant. Meanwhile, "Egyptian" (*misri*) became as meaningful in the nationalist register as it was powerless in the legal register. It was a concept that organized a cause and became the rallying cry of Ahmad ʿUrabi, Mustafa Kamil, ʿAbdullah Nadim, Muhammad Farid, and other nationalists. Yet the unity that the term "*misri*" projects was ephemeral and rhetorical, and the label never delivered on its promises (and in many ways has yet to do so). Actionable, appreciable rights were (and are) secured under other headings. This chapter examines those headings. First it explores the local context. Among "ordinary Egyptians" on the streets of Alexandria, no one spoke of Egyptians. Instead, people were described in terms of settlement or origin: town dwellers, peasants, bedouins, and so on. Meanwhile, those who needed a collective identifier for Egyptians used not "*misri*" but "*ahli*" (native), "*watani*" (national), and "*mahalli*" (local). The second section of the chapter looks at negative definitions of localness, that is, localness as the absence of state protection. The third section considers the last decade of the nineteenth century, when the six Syrian-Egyptian litigants felt nationality constraints and raised their legal claim. After the turn of the century, certain individuals began to assume local status as a locus of rights. In the fourth part of the chapter, I consider an individual who effectively navigated the spaces between local status and a thoroughgoing Egyptian nationality that could be imagined but did not yet exist.

Identification Without Identity

When Alexandria's authorities needed to identify locals, they used subnational social categories. In the 1880 case of quail purchased with counterfeit coins introduced in chapter 5, the British consul wrote to the governor, asking him to summon the following personalities to court: "the Bedwee Oghele Ebn Moussa, Manoli Keeper of a liquor shop, Bassiouni Soleyman, porter, Aly Daoud Cook at Attarin, Mr. Galli officer of the Caracol el Labban." On this list, the consul employed categories of identification that were usable: name, profession, and residence, the very categories that (as we saw in the opening chapters of this book) appear in police records. Locals had few means of participation in the identified world of the foreigner. The local witnesses in this case were illiterate people who did not possess seals and were unable to certify the transcripts of their testimony. The officers of the caracol certified the depositions of certain witnesses, while the victim, ʿUqila ibn Musa (who was given false coins by a Maltese to whom he sold a large number of quails), scratched a mark on his testimony.[12] None of these locals could assert subjecthood in legal terms understood by the foreign consulates. When the foreign consulate needed them as witnesses, it identified them according to local convention.

When ʿUqila testified, he identified himself by residence, *shayakha*, and occupation. But he was most clearly identified as bedouin: the consul's letter described him as "Bedwee," and even the Maltese counterfeiter called him "*ya ʿarabi*" and "*ya shaykh*." Bedouin was one of five precise categories that Alexandria's police employed to describe and differentiate between local subjects during the closing decades of the nineteenth century. As we have seen in previous chapters, specific descriptions of protection and nationality made sense because they signaled critical information used in interactions between locals and foreigners. The language used to describe locals differed, however: Until the beginning of the twentieth century, its signals had little to do with state or nation. Police categories bore the mark of practicality: they were about identification, not identity. Five general labels helped investigators track individual subjects to their home or source of protection.

Ibn al-balad, the first of these labels, was the term for a city dweller. In folk use, the term means "real" Egyptians, as opposed to foreigners, peasants, or rulers, and in certain contexts it means Cairene.[13] In legal use at the turn of the twentieth century, however, the term was often used to specify urban origin. *Balad* meant city or region, and one version of "Alexandrian" was *balad-hu iskandariya*. Not all inhabitants of a city were considered its sons, however. In the early nineteenth century, North Africans, Syrians, Yemenis, and Sudanese were excluded from the category, which was based on ancestry rather than place of birth.[14] During the 1840s, census takers divided the local population of Alexandria along native/newcomer lines. Local-subject migrants to Alexandria (*aghrab*) formed the majority; natives of the city (*ahl al-iskandariya*) made up only a quarter of all locals.[15] This distinction endured, although nationality classification systems such as the census did not always reveal it. In his careful attempt to use court records to describe local society in mid-nineteenth-century Egypt, Toledano identifies the numerical core of Egypt's "anything but homogenous" population as those "born and bred in Egypt . . . Arabic-speaking, Muslim, uneducated, and poor."[16] When this group was given a collective classification, its urban component was most often considered *abna' al-balad* on the basis of residence alone, an identifier sufficient for legal needs.[17]

A second term, *fallahi*, designated a farmer or peasant. While this category made up the bulk of Egypt's population, *fallahin* were a minor presence in Alexandria's police records. This is because most *fallahin* migrants were rapidly assimilated as town dwellers.[18] *Fallahi*, when used in Alexandria, indicated a newcomer. The distinction between settled foreigners and newcomers described in chapter 1 was at least as important for their local-subject counterparts. *Fallahin* who remained in the countryside also played a critical role in the nationalist identity construction of a normative (urban) Egyptian subject, as Michael Gasper has shown.[19] Those who visited the city stood out, and as we have seen these newcomers were often easy marks for urban scam artists.

A third label, *ibn ʿarab* (plural *ʿurban* or *awlad ʿarab*), was the term for nomads or bedouin. In police use, the category sometimes also comprised sedentary families descended from nomadic tribes.[20] Although nomadic, *ʿurban* were often associated with place. The bedouin who lived and circulated in the environs of Alexandria were called "nomads of Alexandria" (*ʿurban iskandariya*). In police records, the label *ʿarabi* often bears an implication of lawlessness, and it was not unusual to find *ʿurban* associated with foreign bad subjects.[21] The bedouin minority played an even more critical role in the construction of an Egyptian identity, in both nationalist and

nationality terms. They were an *imperio in imperium*, defined under different census terms and governed by different laws and different institutions
from the rest of Egyptians.[22] In fact, they might even be considered a different nationality, as a 1904 article on the "bedouin capitulations" demonstrates.[23] Bedouins appeared as collectivities long after urban and peasant
subjects were individuated. In this they resemble other Ottoman tribal
populations, as well as "natives" elsewhere in the world.[24]

A fourth term, *barbari*, designated those who originated from the south
of Egypt. This category was sometimes assimilated with "Sudanese" or
"Nubian" and sometimes distinguished from it. The term could be accompanied by, or replaced with, reference to dark skin or enslaved status.[25] The
incorporation of this group into the Egyptian state and Alexandrian society and the assimilation of many of them into local subjecthood is a topic
that historians have only begun to reveal.

Finally, we have a series of qualifiers and honorifics that function differently from the preceding labels. The police category *ra'iya* (literally
"protected") often reflected a minority sect. Some of these were Ottoman subjects; others were protected by the local government (*al-hukuma
al-mahalliya*).[26] Certain local subjects, especially non-Coptic Christians and
Jews, might also be titled *khawaga*, a term with its own lines of differentiation that rarely involved legal nationality.[27] *Effendi, bey, pasha, hanem*,
and other titles designated local subjects who possessed the protections of
rank, power, notability, and/or wealth.

In the eyes of the police, local subjects were never simply Egyptian.
They were identified using one of these five categories and according to
other specific traits of occupation, residence, family, or sect. The practical, everyday typology mapped onto census categories.[28] The 1882 census
offers a baseline indication of certain administrators' sense of social categories and shows their uneasiness with a unified, generic local subject.
As we saw in chapter 4, the broadest distinction was between "settled
natives" ("real Egyptians," those from other parts of the Ottoman Empire,
and Sudanese) and "bedouins" (semisedentary or nomadic). These categories do not correspond at all points to the five categories of practice used
by the Alexandria police, but the absence of a cumulative count of local
subjects in the census is telling.

Until the end of the nineteenth century, national categories such as
"Ottoman" or "Egyptian" were of little use to local authorities. The 1840s

divide between local and foreign was between those under the control of the authorities (*dakhil al-hukuma*) and those outside their control (*kharij al-hukuma*), and later in the century this divide still obtained, but those under government authority now belonged to one of the five categories described above.[29] The generic term "local subject," as a comprehensive, collective category that combined and subsumed all of the above types, was called into being to serve a different purpose from those of the police. At first, it was used primarily by foreign powers uninterested in the distinction between different kinds of nonforeigners or in police work or access to local subjects. Just as outsiders were described generically as "Europeans," anyone without foreign protection could be described as "native" and assigned to the protection of local authorities without any further investigation; it was up to the police to identify them with greater precision.

In 1887, an Italian policeman trying to remember the date of a shooting recalled that it occurred on a Sunday when "*they* were celebrating Bairam." At the time of the incident, the streets were crowded: "There were people of all nationalities round about."[30] The policeman's language insists on difference. "Nationality" is a universal, commensurate category to which anyone can belong, but it only designates difference. The Muslims, meanwhile, are the plain other, the third party, "they." The simple categories that the policeman used to describe this mixed crowd confirm the segmentation of the vulgar cosmopolitan crowd described in chapter 1. Some in the crowd had faces—nationalities—and others were faceless natives. They appear as the strongest of all generic collective nouns: the third-person-plural pronoun "they." Throughout this book, I have argued that categories of affiliation must be evaluated first for practical purposes of identification. Whatever identity meaning they might contain is obscure and of little retrievable value. This is especially true of the generic category "local," which was rendered using four different terms.

Mahalli (literally "local") was an external and administrative term, one never used by the locals to describe themselves. Typically, it appeared in a construct about subjecthood: *tabiᶜ lil-hukuma al-mahalliya* ("subject to the jurisdiction of the local government.") The term's great advantage was that it managed to circumlocute the problem of Egypt's status under public international law. The government was always "local," not "national" or "native." The anthropologist Farha Ghannam describes the local as a produced space that is (quoting Appadurai) "an inherently fragile social achievement" and obliterated by globalization.[31] In this case, the local was a more durable compromise that functioned until overrun by the logic of the modular nation-state.

Watani (literally "national") was more challenging in this regard, as the term contained the seeds of anticolonial ideas. The girls playing in front of the barracks from which Lawler shot ʿAli, for example, were called *watani-yat* in the interrogation transcript; the term was translated as "native."[32] Perhaps it was the implicit nationalism of *watani* that made it the least frequently used generic term for local. The term was not used to label public institutions. Neither was a third term, *misri* ("Egyptian"). This term was used in certain legal settings as a spatial and administrative designation. The label "Egyptian" on the 1899 passport (figure 3.4) was applied to the khedive, not to the state or its people. Of course, both *watani* and *misri* were gathering strength in the nationalist register, but their use in the register of identification and protection remained limited.

The most used term was *ahli*, a multivocal term in common use in many Arabic-speaking regions before the nineteenth century.[33] Initially a descriptor of convenience, the term was invested with more and more meaning in the Egyptian legal context after the British occupation. In the 1880s, local authorities only used it as a generic, collective term to describe local subjects when writing to foreign authorities. A local subject was called *shakhs min al-ahali*, literally meaning "one of the native folk." In a letter to the British consul in November 1880, for example, the police referred to bedouins (*awlad al-ʿarab*)—the group least integrated into the Egyptian state—as "natives" (*ashkhas min al-ahali*).[34] The general significance of the term was bolstered in 1883, with the creation of the Native Tribunals (*mahakim ahliya* and not *mahalliya*).

Social (as opposed to administrative) users continued to prefer more specific language, and the meaning of *ahli* was sometimes contested. In correspondence concerning the case of the counterfeit payment for quails mentioned above, the term *ahali* was reserved for city dwellers and accentuated the contrast with the *ʿarab* bedouin. ʿUqila was called *al-ʿarabi* or *shakhs ʿarabi* by police and witnesses and "bedouin" by the Maltese "keeper of a liquor store." When he saw that something was amiss he called on "two Arabs" (*ibnain ʿarab*), then went in search of the police. Nonbedouin locals involved in the case, on the other hand, were called *ashkhas min al-ahali*.[35]

While this word choice did not deny the local status of the bedouin, it did nothing to assert their commonality with city dwellers.

The notions of foreign and local that developed in Alexandria between 1880 and 1914 developed this tension between the specific and the generic. On the one hand, as we saw in chapter 4, the 1917 census enumerated a sixty-five-way taxonomy of foreign and local. Just as this extensive vocabulary of specificity reached its pinnacle, however, people in Alexandria began increasingly to fall back on simple generic terms such as *ahli* for social description. Samera Esmeir's and Timothy Mitchell's recent explorations of humanity and universalism in colonial Egypt suggest that discourses of commonality and equality are inseparable from practices of distinction.[36] Legal status generated counterpart generic categories—foreign and local—that took on social meaning. This social meaning, in the years that followed, found political articulation in the form of nationalism, and local nationality became a positive legal status.

By 1914, it was possible to invoke a sense of local or Egyptian that included both *ibn al-balad* and *ibn ʿarab*.[37] What changed during this period? Not the social relations between urban and rural dwellers, between those from the north and those from the south, or between the sedentary and the nomadic (or formerly nomadic); even today, the divide between these groups is clear and enduring.[38] A new register of identity emerged, one that had not existed before, wherein city dwellers, *fallahin*, and nomads were one. This was the register of nationality, a new way of answering "who are you?"

Nationality Without Protection

During the 1880s, localness was still a condition of nonbeing from the perspective of foreign legal institutions. In her examination of the "concept of the foreign," Rebecca Saunders fixes the character of the foreign, in a present-day context, as negative, deficient, and pathologized. Foreigners are objects of xenophobia, living a constant state of loss of home. The native, the local—home—is their opposite.[39] In late nineteenth-century Alexandria, however, it was the local that was "pathologized, improper, and impure." Foreigners were whole, possessing a broad range of rights and privileges. Those without foreign protection were unidentified and consigned to local status. To engage foreigners in Alexandria's courts, "natives" had to employ new vocabulary; it made little sense for them to describe themselves according to the five subcategories enumerated above. Instead, they learned to mimic the modular nationality that foreigners deployed before the law. Ariel Salzmann's argument that Ottoman legal citizenship was reactive and derivative is also true of Egyptian citizenship, which was in fact doubly derivative.[40]

As we saw in chapter 10, consulates occasionally stripped the most troublesome of their bad subjects of consular protection. In so doing, they rendered the bad subject void of nationality, which translated directly and by default into local status and populated Egypt with the sort of subjects a state might wish to avoid. It was not only the outrages of bad subjects that caused such transformations. Certain false steps in tax payment, military service, or legal proceedings could trigger foreign-to-local conversion through administrative decision. Consulates were often content to use evidence of local status to deprive their imperial subjects of protection. Muhammad bin ʿAli Yahya was born in Algiers, but his 1883 application for protection was refused when the *drogmanat* learned that he had paid local taxes for fifteen years.[41] Vita Beniada was struck off the consular rolls in 1885 after he was convicted for theft by the Native Tribunal and did not contest its competence.[42] Consular courts were reluctant to read these acts as positive steps of affiliation with the local authorities rather than as renunciation of foreign status. The consulates reserved positive criteria of affiliation for other foreign nationalities.

Certain individuals lost foreign status without realizing it or changing their civil practices. In 1880, ʿUmar bin Yaʿqub was surprised to discover that he had lost his French protection in the late 1860s, and was considered a local subject by the Egyptian government.[43] He wrote to the consul in an attempt to change or even to deny this situation:

> For the last dozen years, I have had the honor and the advantage, as an Algerian subject, to enjoy French protection. Just over a month ago, I learned from the Prefect of the Alexandria police that this protection had been taken away (*rétiré*), and that I found myself under (*soumis à*) local authority. The surprise of this news is made more painful because I have absolutely no idea what could have caused this step to be taken. I always sought to be faithful and submissive before the French authority

to which I was subject. Son of an Algerian and born on French soil in Algeria, I . . . have the greatest interest, on foreign soil, in keeping a nationality for which I feel affection, and which honors me as much as it is precious to me.

The obsequious language of his plea is not unusual, but the extra evidence that he later adduces is rather more striking: "The occasional difficulties I have had in my commercial life have always been submitted to French juris-diction. Last March, when I was once again summoned before the French consular tribunal, I respectfully followed its decision. I can show you a copy of the judgment, if necessary." 'Umar was the victim of a nationality gap: he suffered the costs of foreignness (in that he was liable to consular court jurisdiction) but not its benefits (he was denied French protection).

Protection had its own economy, and Egypt was being drawn into its world market. Just as nationality, subjecthood, and foreign protection could be traded on for social and legal leverage, it could be fabricated, challenged, withdrawn, or muddled. In the absence of formal, universal determinants of status, accidents (of birth and migration, religion and sec-tarianism, and so on) stepped in wherever gaps existed. Many of those who fell through the gaps between foreign and local struggled to assert a posi-tive status. In so doing, these migrants were at the vanguard of nationality practice in Egypt, in much the same way that (at the turn of the century) foreign workers formed the vanguard of labor organization and Levantine migrants formed the vanguard of political radicalism.[44]

Local authorities contested claims to foreign nationality with increas-ing frequency in the years after 1881, complementing the consulates' growing desire to purge their rolls of questionable subjects. Together and over decades, they winnowed away at the mass of unidentified inhabitants of Alexandria. This process had unintended consequences. The consul-ate's use of civil rights and procedures to measure status sowed the seeds of positive recognition and positive definition of local status. Eventually, the possibility emerged for local status that was not just the absence of citizenship, protection, or affiliation but the possession of certain rights. This was true of individuals, of dual nationals, and of a few whole com-munities. When foreign authorities recognized local civil procedures that triggered the loss of foreign protection, they enacted a sort of recognition of Egyptian public sovereignty. This transition from absence to opposite to counterpart was by no means a smooth progression, however. As local status was being defined in distinction from foreigners, it also required a distinction from Ottomans and Syrians.

The Uses of Localness

In the spring of 1896, the nationalist rhetorician Mustafa Kamil gave a speech in Alexandria to an assembly of eight hundred in which he urged the city's patriots to continue their hospitality toward Europeans who were friendly to the nationalist cause. He described a moderate nationalist position that focused on British evacuation and showed respect toward the English, which he contrasted to the extreme and insulting posture of antioccupation activists that he called "intruders" (*intrus/dukhala'*).[45] These "intruders," he argued, were dividing the Egyptians, cutting them off from the Europeans. They were the true "mortal enemy," and sincere patriots should battle against them with pen and word.[46] He did not specify who these intruders were, but his call for support of Khedive ʿAbbas Hilmi makes it clear that he intended the Syrian press.[47] In the days after the speech, Syrians of the city showed that they understood it to mean them.[48] Fifteen months later, Mustafa Kamil returned to the subject in another Alexandria speech, specifying that he meant only certain Syrians, "a gang known to all, who had turned their back on their own land and repaid Egypt's hospitality with ingratitude and hate."[49] These men attack the khedive and the sultan in the same breath, attempt to divide Copts and Muslims, and spread the message that the Egyptians "are a savage and fanatical people that wishes to annihilate all Europeans."[50]

This culture of rejection was the background for the 1898 judicial appeal cited at the beginning of the chapter. The six appellants argued that the mere fact of residence in Egypt rendered any Ottoman subject an Egyptian: "*kull ʿuthmani misri bimujarrad tawattanihi bimisr.*" Furthermore, they argued that they had been treated as Egyptians by various wings of the local government: they paid tax, held employment, and so on—the same civil practices that defined the emerging distinction between locals and foreigners.

The court used a more complex definition of "Egyptian civil and political nationality" (*al-jinsiya al-misriya al-madaniya al-siyasiya*) in order to measure the claim. It held that Ottoman dominion (*haqq al-siyada*) over Egypt did not entail unity of nationality. According to this reading, Mehmet Ali played a decisive role in the creation of Egyptian nationality. He wrested from the Ottomans the special privileges that transformed Egypt from a province like any other (*wilaya ghair mumtaza*) into a nation possessing jurisdiction over its own nationality (*ikhtisasiha bi-jansiyatiha al-wataniya*).[51] Since that time, Egypt had enjoyed a set of privileges (*imtiyazat*) that distinguished it from the rest of the empire and made it a nation (*umma*) with an independent government: it wrote its own laws, appointed its own officials, raised its own army, and had an independent law-court system. For these reasons, Ottomans residing in Egypt did not automatically become Egyptian "because the privileges (*imtiyazat*) and rights that were given to the Egyptian and gave him a civil and political national nationality (*jinsiya wataniya madaniya wa siyasiya*) proper to him were not granted to other Ottomans." Therefore, "after the granting of [these] privileges to Egypt, no Ottoman settling (*tawattana*) in Egypt can be considered Egyptian unless he takes on (*iktasaba*) the Egyptian nationality."

The court then asserted the encompassing quality of this nationality, which treats various types of subjects equally. Anyone living in Egypt (*mustawtinan misr*) at the moment that Mehmet Ali won the province its special privileges was Egyptian. This included both the territory's original inhabitants (*al-ahali al-asliyin*) and those who came to Egypt with Mehmet Ali in the first half of the nineteenth century.[52] The administrative status of Egyptian was extended to all such residents, "without regard to religion (*diyana*) or nationality (*jinsiya*)." The use of *jinsiya* here is puzzling, coming as it does in a definition of what makes up the Egyptian *jinsiya*. This apparent circularity suggests that the term itself was in flux; as late as 1898, it could mean "nationality" (in the overall sense of the judgment) and "ethnic type" (in the specific sense of this sentence). While the former sense was ascendant, it was not established: this judgment, like other articles that would appear in the press over the next decade, carried the title "What Is Egyptian Nationality?"

The answer comes in the long list of modifiers: civil (*madani*), political (*siyasi*), national (*watani*). These adjectives were necessary to specify the new meaning being attributed to *jinsiya*. The arguments of the appellants offer further evidence of the definitional work in process. The litigants and the court sought to embody nationality in specific practices. The question of franchise was merely pretextual and did not reappear after the opening lines.

But other civil claims—the familiar trio of state rights of taxation, conscription, employment—feature prominently.

The court invoked a particular set of "universal" legal norms concerning nationality that reveals its concept of the nature of the Egyptian state. Nationality is a natural right of an independently governed state.[53] It is a contract binding an individual to his nation (*umma*). The contract depends on the assent of the government, however, which "is not compelled to consider any person a member of its community (*fard min afradiha*) without its consent (*ridaha*)." The individual, on the other hand, must hold one (not two or no) nationality. He or she cannot acquire or lose a nationality by any means except the explicit consent of the government, which is not compelled to accept any particular request for nationality. Thus birth, residence, payment of taxes, military service, and state employment in Egypt are each specifically excluded as positive criteria for naturalization.[54] We have already seen that it was precisely these practices that were used to determine the line between local and foreign. The rhetoric used by the court was absent from documents produced in administrative offices.

Thus nationality remained a context-specific determination. Where was an Egyptian not an Ottoman? Istanbul was one site outside Egypt where the identification of Egyptians qua Egyptians, rather than Ottomans, was sometimes desirable. As early as 1899, as we saw in chapter 3, there was an Egyptian passport that was distinct from the Ottoman passport. It seems likely that Egyptian residents or travelers in Istanbul used the office of the *kapı kethüdası* for certain bureaucratic procedures, just as Ottomans in Egypt used the office of Gazi Muhtar Pasa. But within Egypt, a new momentum began to build that created rights for locals by identifying and then excluding "non-Egyptians."

It appears that the earliest blanket restriction on non-Egyptians came about in 1890, when candidates for employment in the State Railways were obliged to present a certificate of Egyptian nationality.[55] (Significantly, there was no standard format for such a certificate. As late as 1909, regulations specified that candidates for the Police and Administration School should present certification of Egyptian nationality on stamped paper signed by two government functionaries.[56] This specification suggests that use of such certificates was relatively uncommon.) Educational institutions were reserved for Egyptians—the Ecole Normale Khedivial was founded in 1895 to train teachers "of Egyptian nationality," and a free girls' school founded in 1908 was reserved for those possessing Egyptian nationality.[57] In al-Muwaylihi's 1907 satire *Hadith ʿIsa bin Hisham*, one of the reasons why an effendi might quit his job (along with conduct and poor French) was *wataniya* ("nationality" or "nationalism")—notably, this was a new joke that the author added subsequent to his 1898 serialized version of the same scene.[58]

The exclusion of non-Egyptians from state employment was not applied in all wings of the administration, however. Article 10 of the 1901 version of the employment decrees first promulgated in 1895 and 1897 stated that Ottoman subjects born in Egypt and residing there, as well as Ottoman subjects resident in Egypt for at least fifteen years, were "considered as Egyptians."[59] This article formed part of the 1898 appellants' claim, but it was rejected on the principle that one ministry's regulation cannot alter a more fundamental law (such as the Elections Law).

The legal resolution of the rejected appeal came in 1900, when the Egyptian government published its first nationality law in the pages of its official journal.[60] This brief decree clarified attribution of Egyptian nationality to Ottoman subjects born or long resident in Egypt, such as the appellants in the 1898 case. The law is too short to tackle any but the specific issues raised by the appellants and thus seems to be written in reaction to the case. Most significantly, the last article of the implementation regulation released the next day states that those who win Egyptian nationality in this way do not automatically receive the right to vote but must apply for it separately.[61]

This decree accompanied a number of other court judgments that defined an ever-larger purview for Egyptian nationality. One of these cases concerned Antonio Magri, a Maltese bad subject involved in the 1880 quail-and-counterfeit case (he also features in chapter 5). The British consulate had withdrawn its protection from Magri, and so it was the Native Court of Appeal that issued a decision confirming its jurisdiction over him. Its reasons are instructive and established precedent cited in many subsequent verdicts: law is territorial, and the Egyptian state has jurisdiction over everyone in its territory, regardless of nationality. That said, treaty and custom have established a number of exceptions, but these exceptions are strictly limited, and the presumption is local jurisdiction. Therefore Magri became a local subject once he lost the British consular exception.[62] A similar logic applied in a set of four cases in 1900 and 1901 asserting jurisdictions over Moroccans in Egypt.[63]

Arabic speakers (including Christians and Jews) from the Ottoman Empire and French colonies in North Africa who could not provide substantial, documentary proof of foreign nationality were consigned to local status in theory, but they discovered it one by one, if ever at all. For many of these individuals, nationality was not (yet) an active question. Indeed, the nationality of those for whom the question was posed differed starkly from the nationality of those who were never asked. It was rare that poor Arabic-speaking Muslims or Copts born in Egyptian territory encountered a circumstance in which they were called upon to identify themselves as local subjects. Those who were aware of their localness did not face circumstances that challenged that affiliation. Even descendants of immigrants, such as Alexandria's large Maghribi community of the eighteenth century (*magharba*) or the *barabira* from the south, were considered different but not foreign.

It was those who might possibly claim to be foreign who most risked becoming positively identified as local subjects. In this, they resembled the Maltese and Algerian foreigners described in chapter 8, who had to accentuate their legal subjecthood because their social character did not announce their foreignness. An 1888 circular from the minister of the interior instructed provincial governors that "no one can be considered a foreign subject until this status has been duly established and acknowledged." But this apparently sweeping change was not for everyone: "This rule is exclusively applicable to Greeks and those protégés not of foreign origin. Thus, for example, an individual of French, Italian, or English origin is easily recognized; because his nationality is not in doubt, there is no need to demand that he proves his foreign status."[64] Non-Arabic speakers from the Mediterranean, such as Greeks from Cyprus, and Margaret Ann Gowans, the adopted Ottoman child described in chapter 9 who lost foreign nationality when she was orphaned, were faced with this fact.[65] On several occasions, reconfiguration of empire brought about wholesale conversions of nationality. For half a century, while Britain controlled the Ionian Islands, Ionians formed a significant segment of the British subject population in the Ottoman Empire.[66] An eighth of British residents convicted at the Alexandria consular court in 1845–1846 and 1851–1855 were Ionian.[67] But when Britain transferred the Ionian Islands to Greece in 1864, this group of foreign subjects was jettisoned. Some became Greek subjects, but many faded into the background of localness.[68] These individuals were treated with more sympathy by consulates, and the burden of proof of foreignness was lighter, but still they became locals. Like the Syrians, these erstwhile foreigners discovered nationality only when called on to articulate it in legal terms around the turn of the century.

Nationality law contained large gaps through which erstwhile foreigners sometimes slipped. Alexandria's social mosaic was riddled with incommensurate legal categories. As nationality law tightened, nationality gaps became more dangerous. Contrary to popular belief, the consuls could not distribute foreign nationality to whomever they chose. Forum shopping, which had been common at midcentury, decreased dramatically after the pivotal period of legal change (1875–1885) identified in the introduction to this book. While the consulates rarely resisted local claims over foreign subjects, they were more reluctant to release subjects who wished to quit foreignness in order to win advantage. To do so entailed acknowledging positive criteria of local status, which foreign powers were reluctant to extend. The Greek/British/Ottoman Nicola Adamidis, discussed in the previous chapter, was described by the British consular court as "without a nationality." In this way, it resisted positive criteria of local nationality.

When it was necessary to describe local status in positive terms, the court resorted to Ottoman nationality, which of course was sophistry in the Egyptian context. In the throes of a 1908 divorce, Emanuele Sorati's wife Annette used the British consular courts to force her husband to make support payments for their children. When he saw that the consulate was taking her side in the dispute, Sorati attempted to duck its authority. Sorati's Ottoman father and Maltese mother brought their family from Beirut to Alexandria in the boom years of the 1860s. Both parents died within a few years, and Emanuele was placed in an orphanage. He was registered as a British subject during the 1870s, evacuated with other British subjects in 1882, and took up British subjecthood again on his return to the city. He now wrote to the British consul informing him of his decision to quit British protection: "despite my devotion to the glorious Union Jack, which I have always sought to honour in my conduct, today I reaffirm my Ottoman nationality, which I was made to abandon without reason." Sorati's polite attempt to exercise patriotic rhetoric recalls ʿUmar bin Yaʿqub's letter quoted earlier; those who sought to change status did well to keep their future options open through flattery. But Sorati was unable merely to sidestep jurisdiction. The British consul rejected his attempted nationality conversion and forced him to pay.[69]

Another way in which foreigners became local was through the rejection of dual nationality. Egyptian government employees who had the possibility of claiming foreign protection, even if they had never exercised it, were forced to renounce any such claim. In 1913, two Tunisian public employees, both lawyers with the native court system, were informed by the Egyptian Ministry of Justice that they would lose their positions if they did not confirm Egyptian nationality by renouncing French protection. This did not appear to pose a problem, as neither man had ever requested a registration certificate, used the court, or considered himself a French subject. One had even paid the *badaliya*, a special tax to exempt his son from serving in the Egyptian army.[70]

But the ironies of colonialism were many. The same French consular administration that worked so zealously to purge its rolls of inadequately documented subjects now refused to release these men who wished to quit French protection: "On ne change pas de nationalité par un si simple acte! [One cannot change nationality just by writing a letter!]." French administrators proceeded at a glacial pace, and one lawyer wrote again and again, to the Alexandria consul, to the French minister in Cairo, and even to the President of the Republic in France. Meanwhile, pressure from the local government mounted. His last letter said that he had been given eight days by his bosses to produce a certificate of single nationality. The Alexandria consul referred the question to the government of Tunis, which told him that the applicable law (from 1861, before the French invasion) did not allow Tunisians to take another nationality. On this basis, the consul refused to remove the men's names from the roster of protégés.[71] It seems certain that the men lost their jobs.

Foreign and local authorities evaluating nationality after the turn of the century cited the legislation of another era. The Egyptian minister of foreign affairs referred to the 1869 Ottoman Law of Nationality for the conditions governing change of nationality. The French administrator of Tunis, meanwhile, cited an 1861 beylical decree and wrote that the government of the Tunisian protectorate was not disposed to authorize Tunisians to acquire a foreign nationality, "wishing to maintain the arrangements (*dispositions*) of the article." Reference to law codes of a previous administration was convenient for colonizing authorities: it bolstered their claim to benevolent rule, as demonstrated by continuity with and respect for previous arrangements. In the same instant, the laws were only partially applied, bolstering the authority of the colonizers. The beylical decree of 1861, invoked to deny acquisition of Egyptian nationality, could equally be used to prohibit the acquisition of French nationality, but this application was of course never contemplated. The response of the Tunisian resident met the needs of the French authorities in Egypt, who used it as the point of reference in future requests from Tunisian subjects to abandon French protection. But the Ottomans no longer controlled Egypt, and the bey did not have power over Tunisia. Recourse to the legislation of abrogated states confirmed the isolation and peculiarity of the consulates' nationality discourse. Only the First World War would overturn its conservative legislative base.

Not surprisingly, fine distinctions between categories of nationality were elided in most everyday practice. Above all, it was consular officials who chose to impose the letter of the law on occasion, often to the bewilderment of their subjects. Tunisians seeking to renounce French nationality in 1913 in order to maintain jobs with the Egyptian government were treated to a lesson in nationality law. Although the two Tunisians discussed above were lawyers, in their requests they conflated French protection with French naturalization. French officials haughtily dismissed their request on the basis of category error, stating that there had been no record of any *naturalized* subjects by that name. They did not bother to address the real import of the request to become local or to look for the men's names in the *drogmanat* lists. In this case, confusion about foreign status prevented subjects from enjoying all of its benefits while exposing them to many of its costs.[72] The local government sought in this way to make itself orderly and to give its state bulk. The local lawyers produced by such a maneuver in 1913 were exactly the type of national coveted by the new state.

Locals Beyond the Law

Nationality had consequences for those struggling with police, courts, tax collectors, or employers. But most Alexandrians had no occasion to discover nationality. Even for those who did, nationality was incidental rather than constant. To be refused consular registration was not necessarily the decisive end of foreignness. While one official avenue was closed, others—those that did not depend on documents or courts—remained open, and many of those refused protection already conducted themselves as foreigners. The conditions of nationality changed over time, and one generation's wishes were not necessarily shared by the next. Individuals themselves, not officials, could also sever the bonds of protection and identification by nationality.

Many foreigners, once registered with a consulate, never practiced legal foreignness again. In their social behavior, they did little to distinguish themselves from locals. The many instances of mistaken identity before the courts enumerated above hint at a broad field of foreigners rarely troubled by questions of national status. Authorities mistook foreigners for local because they had no reason systematically to ask questions of nationality. Alexandrians who generally conducted their social lives as locals or without reference to nationality but who resorted to foreign status when necessary were less foreign than local. When they presented themselves to the consulate, it was not an act of return to identity after a charade of localness. It was, rather, incidental use of a strategic tool. It is not easy (nor perhaps even appropriate) to determine whether such individuals were locals becoming foreign or foreigners becoming local.

Shaykh Ahmad ʿAbduh was a Tunisian French subject under the jurisdiction of the French consular court of Alexandria. He was an ʿalim who presided over marriages, issued death certificates, and mediated disputes, all based on his status as a member of the ʿulama.[73] One reason that the capitulations system complemented the millet system that governed religious minorities so well was that foreign status tended to coincide with Christianity or Judaism: Muslims were rarely foreign subjects. The status of Muslims from Algeria, Tunisia, and India was a fresh challenge to the Ottoman legal system in the middle of the nineteenth century, when imperial subjecthood took on new salience. The dilemma of Muslim foreign status was brought into focus by people like Shaykh Ahmad, a contrarian whose persistent disrespect for Egypt's clerical classes taxed the legal resources of French consular justice.

ʿAbduh's first visit to the French consular courts of Alexandria came in 1893, after he insulted Muhammad Bakhit, the qadi of Alexandria, at the city's Islamic court (mahkama).[74] ʿAbduh called the qadi something like a "troublemaker" (the case record says "grand querelleur," noting that the name is very insulting in Arabic). Prosecutors sought to cast this insult as an affront not merely against a respectable individual but also against the Egyptian state he claimed to represent. The court found, to its regret, that the *qadi* could not be considered a public official but noted that "even if he cannot be considered a public authority (*ayant le caractère de fonctionnaire public ou agent de l'autorité*) under French law . . . he still deserves all respect and dignity, especially from his co-religionists, because of the religious and judicial powers (*attributions*) given him by the Egyptian Government." ʿAbduh was convicted of private affront and given a small fine.

In seven subsequent cases, the affront was cast as professional rather than personal.[75] According to an Egyptian government decree dating to 1880, only state-designated agents could issue official certificates.[76] ʿAbduh had no such authority, and again and again local subjects found to their surprise that burials and marriages that he certified were considered invalid. The governor of Alexandria was terribly irritated by this behavior but had no direct suasion over the foreign *shaykh*. The governor complained repeatedly to the French consul, who dutifully attempted to put an end to ʿAbduh's activity. Again and again, ʿAbduh lost these legal contests. He received prison terms of two months, three months, and finally, in 1899, one year.

The French court needed to perform two kinds of translation to deal with ʿAbduh. In an act of linguistic translation, the French court weighed questions of Islamic religious authority between litigants who spoke no French.[77] In an act of legal translation, the French consular courts found ways to frame the Egyptian government's needs in French statutes.[78] French legal codes provided especially powerful remedies for private challenges to public authority. Shaykh Ahmad's French subjecthood made him an easy target for such prosecutions, and his own attitude to the court contributed to his liability.[79] In French legal terms, the twenty-eight-year-old hothead's 1893 insults to the *qadi* became "defamation," and his performance of clerical duties without official certification (without being a *maʾdhun*) became "usurpation of public duties." The *shariʿa* and consular courts agreed on a mode of action toward a troublesome individual: they would prosecute him for operating outside official channels. In so doing, they made use of significant (and similar) recent changes to each legal system. The French justice system, through its work in Algeria, had developed means to accommodate and implement a formalized, officialized version of Islamic law as state law for minorities. The expanding Egyptian state, meanwhile, was performing precisely the same operation with the Islamic law of the majority. Both systems, then, were able to stigmatize Ahmad's independence as an affront to the new order.

It took years for lawyers, judges, and litigants to arrive at a practical consensus on the reform. After the string of convictions culminating in his 1899 prison sentence, ʿAbduh too learned its uses. It was a dozen years before his next appearance before the French consular court, but he did not cease performing the functions of a Muslim cleric: the charges he faced in 1912 were identical to those that led to his previous convictions. This time, however, he learned to satisfy the letter of the law and avoided conviction. In previous cases, he was convicted because he claimed to be licensed by the *mahkama* to approve marriages; now he did not make that claim but continued his activity all the same. He found clients who were uninterested in (or unaware of) the *mahkama*'s sanction and the state sanction that went along with it. Under these conditions, neither Egyptian nor French authorities could now find any effective French legal rubric for their charges against him. Although French law did not recognize the private certification the *shaykh* issued, neither did it forbid it.

Ahmad's activity was doubly troublesome: it rankled not just the French consular court but also the Egyptian state, which had been working since 1880 to assume control over the personal-status regulation of Muslims, which was until then the jurisdiction of relatively autonomous ʿulama. Both France and Egypt had codified and assimilated Islamic law and made formerly independent *qadis* and *muftis* into public servants during the nineteenth century. Ahmad's foreign status allowed him to operate as local ʿulama had previously. Ironically, it was a "foreigner" who was able to maintain traditional, "local" religious practices long after the modernizing Egyptian state moved to absorb them. Franco-Egyptian inability to change Ahmad's behavior once he mastered the new system shows the limits to the reach of the apparently "universal" rule of law in the modern state. A maverick such as Ahmad, who would probably have been controlled through discretionary justice in an earlier system, exploited rigid structures of status to avoid sanction, thereby exposing the new limits to the reach of the newly fused system.

Socially, ʿAbduh's foreignness was useless to him. The dozens of Muslim locals whose marriages he certified had no interest in his foreign status and were almost certainly unaware of it. ʿAbduh himself was curiously attentive to the French courts, however. The French consular court was a relatively impotent institution rarely able to elicit cooperation. Unlike many French, foreign, and local subjects, however, ʿAbduh displayed a willingness to play by the court's rules. He always appeared in court when summoned, and he was one of very few losing defendants ever to appeal his conviction to the Supreme Court at Aix (in France).[80] Such scrupulous conformity to the rules of the French legal system is difficult to explain, especially in one so willing to challenge the established order of authority. While the cursory records of the French consular court offer little insight into ʿAbduh's obedience, they show that it paid off in the end. ʿAbduh eventually learned to skirt French and Egyptian authority in such a way as to enjoy all of the benefits and none of the costs of foreign protection, all while practicing "local" Islamic authority in a way that local subjects could not. Like the members of the Hadrami diaspora that Engseng Ho has described, ʿAbduh was able to become "native" in Egypt while retaining his diasporic privileges.[81] He was an object of official anxiety because the legal procedures he performed eroded the very grounds on which the emerging Egyptian state sought to stake its claim to sovereignty.

In 1911, the *Al-Ahram* daily published a lengthy letter to the editor under the title "Who Is a Real Egyptian, and What Is Egyptian Nationality?"[82] The article attacks the ignorant Egyptians who, whenever they argue with an Egyptian of Syrian origin, call him *dakhil* (interloper) or *gharib* (stranger). The author presents a cosmopolitan vision in which everyone has a right to belong. Discrimination contradicts laws of religion, society, and politics, the author argues; history shows that everyone has a right to be at home on the territory where he or she lives. But the law is an auxiliary in this article, a trick that catches xenophobes. The cosmopolitan vision denies social reality.

   Recent studies of subject formation present the idea that Egyptians could only talk about themselves as Egyptians by using the modern, universal, national, legal logic of Enlightenment rationalism taught by European colonizers.[83] When posed by the colonizer, the question "what is an Egyptian?" allowed only two modalities of response: civilized or backward. These studies are convincing, but to dwell on the specifically colonial logic of subject formation falls short of the broadest significance of the process. A large and useful literature demonstrates that both colonizer and colonized were bound to a single logic, which certainly articulated identities in an ineluctable manner.[84] This book has argued, however, that this process of colonial subject formation was less than comprehensive. The logic of nationality was partial, its use was strategic and incidental, and its sovereignty could be cast off. The nostalgic discourse about cosmopolitanism springs in part from a laudable wish to escape categories of nationality and enter a world of equality.[85] The bourgeois and inflated terms of this discourse make it inaccessible to most and historically inaccurate. But a similar egalitarian agenda can be pursued with the critical tools offered by the idea that categories of nationality and subjecthood, even at the height of empire, were less than universal and less than constant.

Epilogue

Egyptians in the Era of Universal Nationality

B y the middle of the twentieth century, nationality was enshrined as a universal right. Article 15 of the 1948 Universal Declaration of Human Rights asserted that "(1) Everyone has the right to a nationality. (2) No one shall be arbitrarily deprived of his nationality nor denied the right to change his nationality."[1] This right was the product of a vision in which nation-states formed a global web that guaranteed and dispensed justice to all humanity. Already in 1929, as evidence of the international coherence of the system, the Carnegie Endowment for International Peace could publish a comprehensive collection of the nationality laws of some eighty-six states and territories.[2] A quarter-century later, coincident with the 1954 Convention on Stateless Persons, the United Nations issued its own massive multistate set of "laws concerning nationality."[3] In this vision, the fabric of humankind was a pointillist painting without gaps, each human a clear perfect point of nationality.

The postwar order of commensurate states in a postimperial international community provided the palette for these points. But were these nationalities truly comparable? Scholars have shown that these states were incommensurate as regards sovereignty and other elements of public international law, but the incommensurate nature of their membership regimes has not received the same attention.[4] The formal equality of states in the postwar system of public international law implies the formal equality of their nationals, but some states—and some nationals—are more equal than others, as nationally differentiated visa rules make clear.[5] Just as the domestic emancipations of the nineteenth century enabled discrimination on the basis of race, religion, and gender, the international-rights regimes of the twentieth century license and naturalize discrimination on the basis of nationality.

But if, as this book has argued, nationality rose from one status among many to become the indispensable identification label by the time of the First World War, where has it disappeared to today? Within a few decades of its endorsement as a universal right, nationality faded from view for two reasons. First, its distinct role has been subsumed by nationalism and citizenship; indeed, "citizenship" and "nationality" became synonyms. Second, the midcentury assertion of universal nationality (signaled in the UDHR) "settled" the nationality question in a way that has thus far been largely invisible to critique. But the international system of identification and protection by state affiliation was not a necessary development. The contests of sociolegal status in turn-of-the-century Alexandria reveal its contingent origins and provide materials to critique its present practice. Above all, this book shows how apparently uniform status regimes can conceal persistent discrimination by asserting universal rights without delivering them.

This epilogue considers the effects of the naturalization of nationality in the years after 1914. In the first section of the chapter, I discuss universal nationality as a global phenomenon emerging during the interwar period. If, as I have claimed, nationality was one of many possible categories of affiliation before 1914, its triumph after the war canonized a smaller set of "other nationalities": the stateless, the refugee, the colonial subject, the foreigner, and the minority. The second section surveys a number of moments in twentieth-century Egyptian history when the new logic of nationality became increasingly manifest, as Egypt implemented global nationality norms. In the third section of the chapter, I show how the "other nationalities" discussed in this book were rejected or assimilated by the postcolonial, postextraterritorial republic of Egypt after the 1950s. In the concluding section, I consider what we can know about those in the past who answered the question "who are you?"

The Era of Universal Nationality

If nationality was an increasingly potent mantle before the First World War, it was not yet indispensable. Nationality was enshrined as a universal category only during the interwar period. It was part of a raft of new universals: along with nationality, the categories humanity, citizenship, and nation-statehood each emerged as vehicles for claims to voice, power, and rights that invoked universal principles. These were constituent elements of a global system governed by international law in which there was a place for every person and every community and each assumed its place.

Now that nation-state nationality was, in theory, available to all, alternate forms of affiliation were pathologized. But as the prewar roster of "other nationalities" homogenized and contracted under the sign of the universal, new "others" filled the gap. From an international perspective, the three most important "others" in the interwar period were statelessness, refugee status, and colonial subjecthood. As Hannah Arendt showed many decades ago, these three nationality effects were necessary exceptions that bolstered the standing of the national citizen.[6] From a domestic perspective, the prominent "others" were the foreigner (largely consistent with its prewar meaning) and the minority (a newly salient category). These positions, too, helped bolster the universal promise of nationality, as efforts to attenuate alien and minority disabilities implied the plenitude of full membership. Of course, universality was an aspirational logic rather than an empirical fact. Recent studies of human rights have attended to the misleading rhetorical force of universalist claims and the elisions they produce. In studies of the nation-state, however, the role of the universal is less prominent.[7] But the nation-state's various modularities derive much of their authority from their universalist claims. It is the necessary condition for the either/or logic that gives nationality its warrant.

As this book has shown, modern subjectivities developed at a number of scales simultaneously. Scholars such as Foucault, Scott, and Mitchell emphasize the power of the state. The role of nonstate collectivities—from international and nongovernmental organizations to anticolonial movements to transnational religious and ethnic communities—in creating modern subjectivities has attracted increasing attention.[8] Others argue persuasively for the salience of empire throughout the twentieth century and into the twenty-first.[9] The role of the ordinary individual in the formation of modern subjectivities—the personal and practical characteristic of nationality that I identify in the introduction—is less well understood. This book, which traced the emergence of nationality through thousands of individual contingencies, tells a story that complements rather than supplants other scales of subject formation. The interplay between claims at the individual scale and collective claims became increasingly complex over the course of the twentieth century. In the interwar period, policy makers saw fit to efface the practical fact that nationality status came into being on an individual basis, preferring to define it as a collective category. It was a period when—for good and ill— all manner of collectivities and groups were being conjured in the space between individual rights and state laws. French authorities in Egypt, for instance, sought in 1939 to "do away with capitulatory, which is to say individual, forms of protection, leaving only protection by common right, which in our case means protection conferred collectively, due to their origin, on natives of France's possessions or dependencies."[10] As Samuel Moyn has argued, those engaging in nationalist and anticolonial struggles also chose collective rather than individual idioms to make their rights claims during the early and mid-twentieth century.[11] But these collective claims were underpinned by the new notion that every individual had a place in the international legal system.

The five major exceptions to universal nationality (the stateless, the refugee, the colonial subject, the foreigner, the minority) have attracted much scholarly attention. Paradoxically, the focus on these exceptions has tended to shore up the standing of an (imagined) universal national citizen. Scholarly focus on categorical distinctions such as the lines between subject and citizen or national and stateless persons tends to endorse rather than interrogate the normative image of Western citizenship. Meanwhile, normative concepts of liberal citizenship and human rights provide a vocabulary for decolonization centered on equality and domestic rights. Projects about "conscripts of modernity," even as they reveal many of the contradictions of modern citizenship, ultimately critique its shortcomings rather than the principle itself. These views are not dissimilar to the Carnegie/UN vision, by which statuses on the short list of nonstandard "other" nationalities were defined as precarious positions requiring remedy. In every case, there is a presumption of some normative nation-state membership that is whole and complete. One consequence of a literature on citizenship dominated by political rights, domestic focus, and equality is the failure to appreciate the discriminatory work that nationality performed in the twentieth century.

In a prominent comparative survey of statelessness and citizenship, for example, Linda Kerber situates citizenship as a rule for which statelessness is a tributary exception. While this normative position may make some sense in the narrow context of the United States in the twentieth century, its universalist assumptions are less convincing. In the early twentieth century, national affiliation was far from universal, even for those whose allegiance was clear-cut. Even in the United States, nationality was a novelty for most of the population. The United States is one of a few particularly strong states where a really complete story of nineteenth-century citizenship can be told, but even this story ignores the majority. Kerber's fine tour of subsidiary statuses is persuasive in showing how the stateless make the citizen, but it suggests that the important thing about statelessness is that it helps us understand citizenship.[12]

What would be the analytical effect if the disenfranchised, the stateless, who are the heart of Kerber's article, were cast as the rule? Certainly this would shift the focus closer to the median sampling I urge in the introduction to this book. Kerber dwells on statelessness as a means of illustrating the fearsome power of the state, but another, less bleak view is possible: the state is not all, and many live perfectly viable stateless lives, even in strong states. A more capacious definition of statelessness would include subsidiary statuses everywhere in the same field as full-blown American citizens. There is considerable space between Kerber's two poles of statefulness and statelessness for those who identify with states only in limited contexts. For every individual fleeing or ignoring or refusing the state in a borderland or a Zomia, there were others living oblivious to the state in centers like New York, San Francisco, or Alexandria.[13]

For emergent states and their interlocutors, internal and external sovereignty were entangled. Nation-states were rarely content preaching only to their own choir but sought legitimacy in the higher international realm. Although the doctrinal link between internal and external sovereignty was clear, Prasenjit Duara has argued that internal sovereignty was above all a promise (if not a realization) of equal citizenship to transcultural peoples on peripheries newly incorporated into the national territory. If equality

of citizens was a formal international requirement, its domestic operation was rather more complicated to realize.[14] And the confusion between
external rights (questions of nationality) and internal rights (questions of
citizenship) was intensified by certain prominent shortcomings of universal nationality.

In the early twentieth century, nationality was a leading topic in international law textbooks, treatises, and journals. The most complex problems
of private international status turned on nationality. Law reviews reported
on cases from around the world, tracing the progress of jurisprudence in
the field.[15] Nationality was a key site in the legal transition from empire to
nation-state, and the elimination of extraterritorial jurisdiction—a main-
stay legal technology in the age of empire that became untenable in the era
of universal nationality—was a major aim in China, Japan, Turkey, Egypt,
and elsewhere.[16] As the conflicts of laws were resolved, however, questions
of nationality gradually faded from prominence. The disappearance of
nationality from legal discourse is a sign of the category's triumph. By the
1980s, nationality was no longer a major topic of private international law.
When nationality surfaced, it was most frequently a problem of corporate
rather than human personality. As we have seen, nationality was never an
important topic of domestic law (although in this regard it was unusually
present in the Egyptian context). Over the course of the twentieth century,
it was consigned to a minor role in the associated fields of immigration
law and refugee law. The triumph of universal nationality was so complete
that it disappeared from the law. But though the law bounded nationality
rigidly and clearly, in practice people were by no means respectful of this
doctrine. The contextual, temporary, strategic uses of affiliation that this
book describes endured in the postwar order.

As citizenship and nationality became bound as synonyms after midcentury, the distinct function of nationality was obscured. According to
a Eurocentric view, subjecthood (the affiliation that nationality came to
embody after the First World War) was meant to be succeeded by citizenship.[17] Citizenship was a key aim of decolonization struggles.[18] But even
in states possessing the capacity to dispense civil and social and political
rights (states such as France), this succession was far from inevitable. If
(again following Moyn) we agree that the post–Second World War international order "conceded the sovereignty of nations more than the prior
experiment at international organization of the interwar years did," the

question of different state capacities to take up rights becomes key.[19] Often, a status called citizenship functioned (and still functions) like nationality: bare affiliation. But citizenship is also a difference machine—that is its nationality function, and we are surprised that citizenship is exclusionary today only because we forget that it includes nationality. Although nationality has been subsumed in citizenship, its function as the legal locus of the global rule of colonial difference has endured.

Egypt in a World of Nationalisms and Citizenships

Britain declared martial law in Egypt and extinguished Ottoman sovereignty at the start of the First World War. In Turkey, the capitulations were seen as defective remnants of an outmoded international system, and they were abrogated by the Ottomans in October 1914: "The Imperial Government has adopted as a basis of its relations with the other powers the *general principle of international law*."[20] These moves changed the de jure status of Egypt under public international law and of its residents under private international law. International law offered no principles for the legal reconstitution of a post-Ottoman Egypt, and Ottoman nationality law remained in force there (if not in Turkey). Although the legal ruptures of wartime provide the pretextual end date of this book, Egypt's postwar history is littered with other prominent milestones (1922, 1937, 1948, 1956, 1967) with nationality effects. Each of these moments forms a point of passage in the subsequent development of Egyptian membership.

The 1920s produced a new settlement, in which anticolonial nationalism defined the medium of Egyptian belonging. This surge in collective politics inaugurated a period of explicit elite nationalism that has attracted sustained historical attention.[21] Historians have constructed counternarratives around gender, religion, and economics, setting these factors up as rivals to and interrogators of effendi nationalism.[22] While productive in many ways, this framing serves to naturalize Egyptian nationality, and the nonelite domestic communities that sought to build other collective identities have largely escaped scholarly attention.[23] The isolation of most Egyptian historiography from its broader regional context precludes most questions about the universal reach of Egyptian nationality or its commensurate relationship with other nationalities.[24]

In 1922, the United Kingdom issued its unilateral declaration of Egyptian independence. By this point, it appeared that the distinction between foreign and local had been clarified to the extent that Britain could reserve for itself "the protection of foreign interests in Egypt and the protection of minorities." These two categories—foreign and minority—became the authorized "others" that the rule of colonial difference required. Already in 1923, the Cairo penal court ruled that "the foreigner (ajnabi) is anyone who is not a local (watani)."[25] This ruling came in the context of a decision that the stateless must be considered foreigners.

Meanwhile, the nonforeign, majority remnant continued to assume the more positive form that it had begun to take on in the prewar period. After the turn of the century, nationalism was a constant concern for the British administration. In 1919, quite large numbers of Egyptians exercised their political voices not merely through the domestic unrest of that year but also through the proxy international votes (tawkilat) that thousands gave to the Wafd delegation to Versailles. But outside of this anticolonial moment and the effendiya class, self-identification in terms of Egyptian nationalism was infrequent, inarticulate, incidental, and ineffective. For most nonforeign residents of Alexandria, little could be won or even communicated through self-identification in national terms. As everywhere, the outward garment of nationality—modular, equal, equivalent—concealed the domestication of the rule of colonial difference. The advent of a common nationality did not end the inferior status of peasants, women, nomads, southerners, Copts, and others, but it helped conceal those tensions. Writing in the mid-1920s, Abu Haif asked, "should personal status be determined by nationality, domicile, or religion?"[26] This question marks the stark distinction that had emerged between newly rival systems of legal classification. As Duara shows for the transnational Chinese population in the early twentieth century, appeals to race and culture did not require agreement on the meaning of those terms. Egyptians, like Chinese, were building nationalist concepts that had not existed before, putting the national in transnational for external as much as internal reasons.[27]

On May 31, 1926, the Egyptian government published its first complete nationality law. Local subjecthood, which I described in the previous chapter, provided many of the ingredients for the Egyptian nationality enshrined with the decree-law of 1926. By this time, the universalist pressures of the international community had already made a protonationality of local status.

The Wilsonian project as adapted at Versailles produced a number of strange statelike objects from the remnants of empire. If a certain number of these objects, such as the mandates and protectorates of the Middle East, did not conform to the normative vision of public international law, all of them confirmed its teleology. Egypt was no exception; it was bound on the path to independence, and its residents were on the path to citizenship. Typical of modern law, the content of this inexorable progress was less important than its external form. So long as some Egyptians could present their credentials of nationality in the international arena, the universal requirement was satisfied.

Other nationalities were folded into the local, in problematic ways. Some former protégés and Ottomans experienced status changes as old systems of explicit privilege were bent by the leveling of legal status. But, as we have seen, this process began long before the 1920s. As early as the 1860s, privilege migrated along lines of nationality. In the interwar period, Egypt's privileged nationals worked to remake their privilege within the context of domestic citizenship. The politics of Egypt's so-called liberal age were marked by this domestication. In *Egypt Under the Khedives*, Robert Hunter argues that the first "Egyptian" nationalists were state employees who learned this self-description for professional reasons.[28] These elites wielded the resources of the state in their own interest. Nationalism expanded along the stolid avenue of self-interest; to claim otherwise is to exaggerate and misread its terms. In Partha Chatterjee's formulation, for example, nationalist elites develop a subsidiary and protected role for their subalterns in advance of the anticolonial and postcolonial political projects.[29] Nationality was taken up relatively late in the process. The rights and privileges it offered went to elites first, of course, but only after the category came into being. And they did not only target the political rights of elected representation and an end to imperial/colonial government that dominate discussions of nationalist and independence struggles in colonized states. Marshall's civil and social rights receive relatively less attention, but in early twentieth-century Egypt citizenship was a manner of using the state to win benefits.

Education and government employment were two local practices that taught the vocabulary of Egyptian nationality in order to receive and maintain position. The minority of the Egyptian population that enrolled in or graduated from school (and formed the core of the *effendiya*) understood their place in the state structure. Government workers, such as the two law-yers of Tunisian descent described in chapter 12, were obliged to proclaim their Egyptian nationality in the years before the First World War. Beyond these two fields, however, the benefits of local status were often more obscure than its costs, counted above all in terms of taxation and conscrip-tion. Chapter 7 relates the stories of two mothers who lost their sons to for-eigners and attempted to win justice (and compensation) by means of local status. Self-identifying as locals for perhaps the first time, they engaged local authorities and the consular courts. Their endeavors failed, and what-ever claims the local authorities made on their behalf were ineffective. The mothers observed the success of their foreign counterparts, and it seems possible that they may have drawn lessons from this encounter.

A focus on political rights claims privileges groups and effaces the inclu-sion and exclusion of individuals, a process that I have argued is essential to the establishment of the modern nation-state. Elizabeth Thompson's landmark monograph on citizenship in modern Middle Eastern history argues that citizenship in a colonial context is best defined in plain terms of law and engagement.[30] This is as true for British-occupied Egypt as it is for the French mandates in Syria and Lebanon, which are the focus of her study. But Thompson's study of colonial citizenship goes well beyond this simple definition. While she argues (accurately) that citizenship is made by contact with the state through its agents, she seems to contradict this assertion with an overriding emphasis on policy and social movements rather than everyday experience as the shaper of citizenship.[31] The basis on which Thompson excludes peasants from her account (they "did not mount organized movements of their own during the period of French rule, and so did not participate as distinct players in the construction of citizenship)" suggests that social groups must be organized in order to be distinct and in order to be involved in the construction of citizenship.[32] The evidence presented in this book suggests instead that the decisions and initiatives of *individuals* to accede to group membership were a key to the construction of nationality in Egypt and the citizenship forms that fol-lowed on from it. Of course, the interwar Syrian organizations Thompson studies possessed a character of their own that is not the same as that of their individual members. Organizations, like states, entice membership and mold members' identities; as we have seen, Alexandrians learned to shape their identities (when necessary) to the requirements of authorities.

Thompson's view that nonorganized peasants were nonparticipants in debates over citizenship creates serious difficulties in her discussion of "subaltern citizens" because it obliges her to consider only "subaltern movements" to the exclusion of individuals.[33] The movements she identifies under this rubric seem to lose their subalternity: although women, youth, labor, and Islamist populism are subaltern categories, the organizers of these movements (who form the basis of her evidence), as well as the notion of a "well-developed subaltern consciousness," were more elite than subaltern.[34] The rank and file of these movements are for the most part absent from Thompson's account, such that their identification with the movement may be an instance of the misrecognition I described in chapter 1. In his study of labor communities in turn-of-the-century Egypt, John Chalcraft argues that "the key to the cabbies' success was almost certainly the connection to nationalist politics."[35] But connection is not identification; without direct evidence, the movement neither demands nor deserves the nationalist mantle. The nationalist-striker link was certainly clear to Britain, as Chalcraft's press evidence of fear of wider unrest shows, but that does not make it real for the strikers themselves. It was an instance of circumstantial identification.

Thompson distinguishes colonial citizenship from the mainstream citizenship discussed in most of the literature. By isolating the colonial experience, she particularizes it and prevents it feeding back into conceptions of metropolitan citizenship. The evidence presented in this book shows that local subjects, second-class foreigners, and poor Europeans shared many similar experiences before local and foreign authorities. The essence of that experience was differentiation, and this characteristic of nationality persists beyond the contexts and eras of colonial citizenship. It is necessary to dissolve binary distinctions between colonizer and colonized, between pre- and postcolonial, if international history is to yield its most productive insights.[36] Nationality has faded from view because we have uncritically assumed that when its most acute forms were consigned to the past, its most acute functions disappeared. This was not the case.

Egypt After Extraterritoriality

Elie Simhun was born in Haifa in 1905.[37] His father Ibrahim, born in Jerusalem, was of Algerian origin. When Elie was one year old, his father and mother moved with him to Egypt, presumably attracted by an economic bubble (soon to burst). Ibrahim set up shop as a merchant in the town of Mit Ghamr in Daqahliya province. It was not until eight years after the family came to Egypt that he registered with the French consulate as a French national. By this time, his business had failed, and he was working as the assistant rabbi of the town. The record is then silent until 1934, when the family's 1914 registration as French nationals was struck down at the request of the Egyptian government. As was often the case, nationality lay dormant for decades until activated (or deactivated) by some incident. In this case, Elie's brother Salomon somehow drew the attention of state authorities, who pointed to a rule that all rabbis must be Egyptian nationals.[38] The French consulate canceled their protection after it verified that Ibrahim was a rabbi, and the whole Simhun family lost its nationality. Elie faced an additional blow. Although he lost French protection, the Egyptian Ministry of Public Health, where he worked as a doctor, fired him in 1935 because it considered him a foreigner.[39]

The French Foreign Ministry archive at Nantes contains a massive collection of registration dossiers generated for Algerian and Tunisian subjects living in Egypt. As described in chapter 3, each dossier concerns a single individual and his or her dependents, their work to establish nationality, and the certification that they used when their status was questioned or activated in legal or administrative contests. It is an archive of individuals. Taken together, these many instances of claim and documentation comprise waves of nationality purges and transfers. In the period after the First World War, they form a paper counterpart to the territorial population exchanges, in Turkey and Greece, the Soviet Union, Germany, Palestine, and elsewhere that sorted population by newly defined nationality statuses.[40] In the registration dossiers, the group character of such nationality rationalization is less evident. Yet it emerges through the repeated interrogation of individuals by instances of the state asking "who are you?" in a spirit of surveillance rather than hospitality.[41] The dossiers answer this question in familial streams that flow into a broader course of nationality, often stretching over a century or more.

Elie Simhun reactivated his nationality question in October 1948, presumably in reaction to the conditions he faced in Egypt after its war with Israel. He hired a lawyer who reexamined his case and argued that his French nationality should be restored. The lawyer produced a set of five arguments invoking Ottoman and French law. Although none of these was successful, the consulate discovered a successful argument of its own: Elie was Algerian by birth because when he was born in 1905 his father had been registered as such in Haifa. This view (of dubious merit) was upheld by the French Foreign Ministry, and his French nationality was restored. Elie moved permanently to France in 1950.

This revised position derived from a French ministerial study of 1939 (mentioned above) concerning the "cleansing" (*assainissement*) of protection and registration status in Egypt.[42] This document was an attempt to draw a line under the irregularities and the abuses of the past, eliminate false protection, and proceed on the basis of "true allegiance" (*allégeance propre*). It appeared in the year that France ratified the capitulations-ending Montreux agreements and the Second World War began. The study expresses relief at the clarification that would end negotiations over nationality status and render it purely a question of domestic law. When Montreux was signed, there were seven types of French *ressortissants* in Egypt: French citizens, French subjects (notably Algerians), protégés from protectorate countries (notably Tunisians and Moroccans), *protégés ès-qualités* (dragomans and janissaries, consular agents, and procurers and dragomans of religious institutions—the remnant of the 1863 regulation), special protégés (Bayonnais, Polish, Romanian), other protégés (Swiss, etc.), and Syrian and Lebanese *administrés*. All except the first were aberrations to be managed into oblivion, and (though there remained only fifty French protégés in Egypt and probably no more than two or three hundred foreigners in total) the study gave detailed thoughts about the nature of these "other" statuses.[43] Citizenship, on the other hand, no longer required the least explanation. It was natural, and it was contiguous with nationality.

The curtailing of foreign economic and legal privileges, and the threat to foreign wealth that went with it, meant that 1937, when the negotiations to end the capitulations concluded with the Montreux agreements, was a nationality turning point. The native employees of foreign consulates (consular agents, dragomans, and janissaries of consular and religious institutions) who were protected in limited numbers after the 1863 decree lost their foreign protection in 1937.[44] The foreign nationalities envisaged in the reserved point of the 1922 independence declaration were Europeans, and the consulates worked to cleanse that status.

The Montreux agreements focused on the elimination of extraterritorial privilege for this limited list of European subjects. Many foreign subjects found that the new order displayed a rigidity that, when tested, no longer guaranteed protection to those of suitable class.

Elie Simhun's story describes one path that some "other nationalities" of the turn-of-the-century system—Europeans, foreigners, protégés—followed as Egypt's nationality landscape was transformed in the foreign exoduses (either through departure or naturalization) after the wars of 1948, 1956, and 1967. It was these decades that most permanently altered the nationality demographics of the country, as French, British, Jewish, and Greek residents left the country or became Egyptian. Protected imperial subjects able to substantiate standing were channeled into the legal status of Western nationality and (crucially) citizenship. The consequence of the sorting—and the solution to the nationality problem—was resettlement. Foreigners such as Elie followed the path many Europeans had already pursued, as postcolonial logic managed nationality differences in persons (and indeed property) by sorting. The European and foreign residents of Egypt described in chapters 7 and 8 and their descendants were the objects of the exclusion that the universalization of nationality always entails. The European, previously defined most powerfully by social rather than legal codes, became a more specifically legal category.

Lest we assume that the process was unidirectional, however, we must also consider how Egypt absorbed foreigners, Ottomans, and protégés who did not meet the standards for foreign nationality. These individuals were cast in the tragic yet picturesque role of fading cosmopolitan minorities, particularly in Alexandria. Bad subjects become a domestic problem and were internally banished in the exceptional space of prisons. One underlying verity did not change, however: "The republic of virtuous equals turned out to require the rejection of the non-virtuous."[45] Equality presented a paradox, as we also see in the case of religious minorities: when status is clarified and guaranteed, its scope is often reduced. For many bourgeois protégés, Egyptian nationality was as good as no nationality at all. As we saw in chapter 8, their foreign status had been primarily legal. As the "passing" of thousands of Arabic-speaking, Egyptian-born individuals who were well integrated into local society yet were able to claim legal protection as foreigners dwindled during the interwar cleansing of nationality rosters, the category itself transformed from a legal to a cultural description—*khawaga, mutamassir.*[46] The figure of the foreigner was translated into the nationalist register, and xenophobia became a political rallying point. The *dakhil* (interloper) was no longer a foreign national but an Egyptian subject who did not deserve that status because of identity constructs of ethnicity, sect, or descent. The exoduses of the 1940s, 1950s, and 1960s confirmed this logic. Nationality disappeared from view as the domestic population was homogenized—it became a question that was no longer asked. Debates about citizenship access in the domestic arena for sectarian and ethnic minorities are divorced from a genealogy that includes nationality exclusions. But of course those exclusions have not gone away. They have merely ceased to be recognized.

"Who are you?" The response to this question is contextual, not absolute. It is a question of identification rather than identity. How would local subjects in British-occupied Alexandria have responded to this question? The evidence this book presents suggests that responses depended in large measure on who was asking the question. The same evidence suggests a pattern of change. In 1880, few nonforeigners in Alexandria volunteered a self-description as "native subject," and fewer still used the term "Egyptian," because these terms did not identify the respondent in a meaningful way. By 1919, certainly, but even by 1914, many called themselves Egyptians. The language of self-description changed as Alexandrians developed new vocabularies that they employed, when necessary, in order to respond to shifting social and administrative structures and the new goods they could dispense if a satisfactory answer was given.

As the state expanded, this question was asked more and more frequently. Policemen who asked the question expected identification that was practical rather than merely descriptive. They needed to know name, neighborhood of residence, and profession, while the doctors and clerks of the local authority determined age and antecedents. Police identified foreign and local alike according to the authorities that knew and controlled them. Egypt's laws evolved in order to clarify the process of official identification, offering tests of affiliation and the promise of an absolute and universal answer to the question "who are you?" But as we have seen in the preceding chapters, even when this system functioned as intended, legal self-definition by nationality remained highly context specific. Census takers fixed modalities of response: their forms required that individuals identify themselves in terms of place of residence, gender, age, nationality, profession, and household size. Later, other fields were added: literacy, religion, and so on. But for most of the population, these official questions came infrequently: every ten years from census takers and occasionally but not repeatedly from tax collectors and military recruiters. As a result, the answers given had only incidental significance.

Alexandrians worked to fit themselves into the most advantageous slot in systems of identification and classification. This was equally true of foreigners and locals; as Khaled Fahmy has argued, foreignness did not imply special fluency with the law.[47] Many Alexandrians found the best answers ignored the vocabularies of foreign and local authorities. Again and again, we have seen that local authorities and foreign consulates alike had important limits to their reach. Individual Alexandrians were able to exploit ambiguities of the foreign/local divide to their best advantage by bolstering or changing status and by disregarding the authorities altogether. For the broader part of Alexandria's population, who had little contact with officialdom and even less with the literate world of the *effendi*, "Egyptian" bore little meaning and was of even less use. In order for Egyptianness or local subjecthood to mean something to this population, they had to find their own uses for the labels. These labels became effective in the context of rights, particularly those claimed in moments of contest, especially with those foreign nationals already articulating counterpart rights. Consular court records offer abundant evidence of this sort of response, which is related to but separate from the official responses just described. Strategic localness, like the categories of official and newcomer described in chapter 1, was rooted in doing rather than being. It was "nationality without nationalism."[48] For many Alexandrians, questions of national affiliation were so rare as to be irrelevant. Some of these non-nationals were simply citizens of the city, but many more—newcomers, subalterns, and so on—were not even that. Living outside of the universe of nationality, these individuals could only ever be misidentified, their bodies labeled on the basis of arbitrary details. In such cases, authorities misread and amplified signals of national status, revealing once more the indeterminate basis of such identity markers, which in any case "are always mistaken."[49]

Universal identification by nationality is both new and ordinary. By new, I mean that it is not a tradition passed down from forefathers but rather a response (often arbitrary) to relatively recent rules and administrative questions. By ordinary, I mean that for many in Alexandria (and elsewhere) nationality originated as a banal response to a bureaucratic demand for classification rather than the call of the blood for membership in the *patrie* or *watan* of ancestors. Individuals learned to self-identify by nationality when it won them benefits. The aggregation of millions of decisions to assign individuals to groups was critical to the construction of nationality. Legal description was highly context specific. As an analytical category, citizenship and nationalism do not allow us to consider the ascription of individuals to national groups without privileging political rights. Those rights are critical, certainly, but if we want to talk about the figure of the citizen in Soviet history, for example, or the postcolonial citizen, or the female citizen, or the citizenship of the poor, the category as it stands demands that we describe citizens first in terms of their *lack* of rights, which is a weak place to start. Although the struggle over political rights has dominated the historiography of the late nineteenth and early twentieth centuries, it has not been necessary to bracket the political in order for civil and social and legal rights to dominate this study. Political struggle is almost absent from consular court archives. On this evidence, Egyptians struggled to make their voices heard not at Whitehall, at Government House, or in palaces in Cairo and Istanbul but on the streets of the city and at the local police station. Some Alexandrians sought the vote, certainly, but many more sought to avoid punishment or to assign it to their enemies, to enforce decisions, to collect money, to marry and divorce, to move through the world. As historical curiosity and political need drives us to ask how individuals joined nations and nations made up our world, we can draw on their vocabularies of membership to understand the silences in our own.

Notes

Introduction: Nationality Grasped

1. As Lawrence Stone has noted, stories that begin with crime are not limited to its terms: "People hauled into court are almost by definition atypical, but the world that is so nakedly exposed in the testimony of witnesses need not be so. Safety therefore lies in examining the documents not so much for their evidence about the eccentric behavior of the accused as for the light they shed on the life and opinions of those who happened to get involved in the incident in question." Lawrence Stone, "The Revival of Narrative," *Past and Present* 85 (1979): 22.

2. Similarly, individual stories can distort the terms of identity by amplifying nonexemplary examples. Eighteenth-century examples include Linda Colley, *The Ordeal of Elizabeth Marsh: A Woman in World History* (New York: Pantheon, 2007); Emma Rothschild, *The Inner Life of Empires: An Eighteenth-Century History* (Princeton, N.J.: Princeton University Press, 2011); William Dalrymple, *White Mughals: Love and Betrayal in Eighteenth-Century India* (New York: Penguin, 2004). For the nineteenth century, see Julia A. Clancy-Smith, *Rebel and Saint: Muslim Notables, Populist Protest, Colonial Encounters (Algeria and Tunisia, 1800–1904)* (Berkeley: University of California Press, 1994). For the twentieth century, see Sarah Abrevaya Stein, "Protected Persons? The Baghdadi Jewish Diaspora, the British State, and the Persistence of Empire," *American Historical Review* 116, no. 1 (2011): 80–108.

3. Many classic studies of the nation focus on the literate: Benedict Anderson, *Imagined Communities: Reflections on the Origin and Spread of Nationalism*, rev. and extended ed. (London: Verso, 1991); Homi K. Bhabha, ed., *Nation and Narration* (London: Routledge, 1990). This is equally true of studies of Arab and Egyptian nationalism:

1. Gershoni and James P. Jankowski, *Egypt, Islam, and the Arabs: The Search for Egyptian Nationhood, 1900-1930* (New York: Oxford University Press, 1987). The dominant postcolonial critique of the nation, meanwhile, endorses that ideational construct by treating the nation as an artifact of Enlightenment rationality to be vanquished: for example, Antoinette M. Burton, ed., *After the Imperial Turn: Thinking with and Through the Nation* (Durham, N.C.: Duke University Press, 2003). Elsewhere, Burton asks, "who needs the nation?" (*At the Heart of the Empire: Indians and the Colonial Encounter in Late-Victorian Britain* [Berkeley: University of California Press, 1998], 13). The answer she offers labors under the abstraction of search for terms in description of "culture's" role in creating choice (ibid., 15). If, as Chatterjee argues, "we have all taken the claims of nationalism to be a political movement much too literally and much too seriously," its nature as a cultural construct has also been exhausted. Partha Chatterjee, *The Nation and Its Fragments: Colonial and Postcolonial Histories* (Princeton, N.J.: Princeton University Press, 1993), 5.

4. On this question, see Saba Mahmood, "Religious Freedom, the Minority Question, and Geopolitics in the Middle East," *Comparative Studies in Society and History* 54, no. 2 (2012): 418–446.

5. The discourses of the diffusion of modern state power have been carefully cataloged in Michel Foucault, *Discipline and Punish: The Birth of the Prison* (New York: Vintage, 1995); James C. Scott, *Seeing Like a State: How Certain Schemes to Improve the Human Condition Have Failed* (New Haven, Conn.: Yale University Press, 1998); and Timothy Mitchell, *Colonising Egypt* (Cambridge: Cambridge University Press, 1988).

6. Fariba Zarinebaf, *Crime and Punishment in Istanbul, 1700-1800* (Berkeley: University of California Press, 2011); Ussama Makdisi, *The Culture of Sectarianism: Community, History, and Violence in Nineteenth-Century Ottoman Lebanon* (Berkeley: University of California Press, 2000), chap. 4; Sibel Zandi-Sayek, *Ottoman Izmir: The Rise of a Cosmopolitan Port, 1840-1880* (Minneapolis: University of Minnesota Press, 2012).

7. For an early twentieth-century study of this pathway, see Max Weiss, *In the Shadow of Sectarianism: Law, Shi'ism, and the Making of Modern Lebanon* (Cambridge, Mass.: Harvard University Press, 2010).

8. Lauren A. Benton, *Law and Colonial Cultures: Legal Regimes in World History, 1400-1900* (Cambridge: Cambridge University Press, 2002); Lauren A. Benton, *A Search for Sovereignty: Law and Geography in European Empires, 1400-1900* (Cambridge: Cambridge University Press, 2010); Antony Anghie, *Imperialism, Sovereignty, and the Making of International Law* (Cambridge: Cambridge University Press, 2005).

9. See, for example, Susan Pedersen, "Getting Out of Iraq—in 1932: The League of Nations and the Road to Normative Statehood," *American Historical Review* 115, no. 4 (2010): 975–1000.

10. State typologies that look to map the range of experiences include Mark Hewitson and Timothy Baycroft, eds., *What Is a Nation?: Europe, 1789-1914* (New York: Oxford University Press, 2006).

11. This focus on the practice of international law on the human scale draws in part on the international law critiques of Nathaniel Berman and of David Kennedy, for

instance, in "International Law and the Nineteenth Century: History of an Illusion," *Nordic Journal of International Law* 65 (1996): 385–420.

12. Anderson, *Imagined Communities*, 4, passim. The term is frequently misused. One of the few texts in Middle East history to grapple with nationality, for example, offers this original definition: "Nationality, in the sense of ethnic-national identity, drew its essence from the religious-communal experience in the millet, while citizenship—a secular concept—was determined by territory." Kemal H. Karpat, "Millets and Nationality: The Roots of the Incongruity of Nation and State in the Post-Ottoman Era," in *Christians and Jews in the Ottoman Empire*, ed. Benjamin Braude and Bernard Lewis (New York: Holmes & Meier, 1982), 1:141.

13. Compare Weis's somewhat dated distinction between "politico-legal" nationality and "historico-biological" nationality, which does much of the same work. Paul Weis, *Nationality and Statelessness in International Law*, 2nd ed. (Alphen aan den Rijn: Sijthoff & Noordhoff, 1979), 3.

14. On this distinction, see also Alfred Boll, *Multiple Nationality and International Law* (Leiden: M. Nijhoff, 2007), 57–60.

15. Weis, *Nationality and Statelessness*, 4–5. A similar reading, also from the period immediately following the Second World War, appears in Maximilian Koessler, " 'Subject,' 'Citizen,' 'National,' and 'Permanent Allegiance,' " *Yale Law Journal* 56, no. 1 (1946): 62–63. As will become clear in chapter 2, there is no universally applicable definition of nationality. In the Russian context, for example, nationality is equated with ethnicity, and in the American context it is equated with citizenship. But definitions from international law form a suitable foundation for this book's investigation.

16. Boll, *Multiple Nationality*, 58–59.

17. For a useful brief scan of legal studies for historians, see Jane Burbank, *Russian Peasants Go to Court: Legal Culture in the Countryside, 1905-1917* (Bloomington: Indiana University Press, 2004), 9.

18. Koessler, " 'Subject,' 'Citizen,' " 69. Those purposes are located above all in the area of private international law. That field of law is concerned with disaggregate units, typically persons or corporations, whose nationality or domicile can be defined. Significantly, private international law is called "conflict of laws" in the Anglo-American tradition; it approaches ambiguity of nationality as a problem to be resolved. This focus on managing conflict between statuses prefigures many of the concerns of contemporary citizenship theory. For an examination of this question with respect to multicultural citizenship, see Karen Knop, "Citizenship, Public and Private," *Law and Contemporary Problems*, no. 71 (2008): 309–341.

19. Anderson, *Imagined Communities*, 5.

20. Nationality corresponds to the locus of civil rights in T. H. Marshall's classic study of citizenship, which distinguishes among civil, political, and social practices and places them in a chronological progression. T. H. Marshall, *Citizenship and Social Class, and Other Essays* (Cambridge: Cambridge University Press, 1950). While many have criticized this scheme for its rigidity, the template remains useful in distinguishing categories of rights.

21. ʿAbd al-Hamid Abu Haif, *Al-Qanun al-Duwali al-Khass fi Awruba wa Masr* (Cairo: Matbaʿat al-Iʿtimad, 1924).

22. William J. Novak, "The Legal Transformation of Citizenship in Nineteenth-Century America," in *The Democratic Experiment: New Directions in American Political History*, ed. Meg Jacobs, Julian E. Zelizer, and William J. Novak (Princeton, N.J.: Princeton University Press, 2003), 97.

23. Koessler ("ʿSubject,' ʿCitizen,' " 61) dates its emergence (as Fr. *nationalité* in the *Dictionnaire de l'Académie Française*) to 1835. On the eighteenth-century origins of the nation, see Anderson, *Imagined Communities*.

24. Gianluca Paolo Parolin, *Citizenship in the Arab World: Kin, Religion, and Nation-State* (Amsterdam: Amsterdam University Press, 2009), 25–28. If recent scholarship contests this chronology by pointing to the persistence of religious belonging, as far as nationality is concerned it seems mostly correct.

25. Talal Asad, *Formations of the Secular: Christianity, Islam, Modernity* (Stanford, Calif.: Stanford University Press, 2003); Talal Asad et al., *Is Critique Secular? Blasphemy, Injury, and Free Speech* (Berkeley: Townsend Center for the Humanities, University of California, 2009); Keith David Watenpaugh, *Being Modern in the Middle East: Revolution, Nationalism, Colonialism, and the Arab Middle Class* (Princeton, N.J.: Princeton University Press, 2006).

26. Chatterjee, *The Nation and Its Fragments*.

27. Frederick Cooper, *Citizenship Between Empire and Nation: Remaking France and French Africa, 1945–1960* (Princeton, N.J.: Princeton University Press, 2014); Mahmood Mamdani, *Citizen and Subject: Contemporary Africa and the Legacy of Late Colonialism* (Princeton, N.J.: Princeton University Press, 1996).

28. The French "*nationalité*" is particularly susceptible to elision with "citizenship." See Dominique Schnapper, *Community of Citizens: On the Modern Idea of Nationality* (New Brunswick, N.J.: Transaction, 1998). For a single-nation account of nationality, see Patrick Weil, *How to Be French: Nationality in the Making Since 1789* (Durham, N.C.: Duke University Press, 2008). For an exemplary French African debate, see Cooper, *Citizenship Between Empire and Nation*, 354–357.

29. Edward W. Said, *Culture and Imperialism* (New York: Knopf, 1993); Frederick Cooper and Ann Laura Stoler, eds., *Tensions of Empire: Colonial Cultures in a Bourgeois World* (Berkeley: University of California Press, 1997).

30. Kok-Chor Tan, *Justice Without Borders: Cosmopolitanism, Nationalism, and Patriotism* (Cambridge: Cambridge University Press, 2004); Will Kymlicka, "Territorial Boundaries: A Liberal Egalitarian Perspective," in *Boundaries and Justice*, ed. David Miller and Sohail H. Hashmi (Princeton, N.J.: Princeton University Press, 2001), 249–275.

31. Anghie, *Imperialism, Sovereignty, and the Making of International Law*; Arnulf Becker Lorca, "Universal International Law: Nineteenth-Century Histories of Imposition and Appropriation," *Harvard International Law Journal* 51 (2010): 475–552.

32. Article 15 of the Universal Declaration of Human Rights: "(1) Everyone has the right to a nationality. (2) No one shall be arbitrarily deprived of his nationality nor denied the right to change his nationality."

33. John C. Torpey, *The Invention of the Passport: Surveillance, Citizenship, and the State* (New York: Cambridge University Press, 2000), 121. A similar idea, in similar language, appears in Rogers Brubaker, *Citizenship and Nationhood in France and Germany* (Cambridge, Mass.: Harvard University Press, 1992), 22.

34. Giorgio Agamben, *State of Exception* (Chicago: University of Chicago Press, 2005). For Egypt, see Samera Esmeir, *Juridical Humanity: A Colonial History* (Stanford, Calif.: Stanford University Press, 2012).

35. On statelessness and refugees, see Hannah Arendt, *The Origins of Totalitarianism*, new ed. (New York: Harcourt Brace Jovanovich, 1973); Linda K. Kerber, "The Stateless as the Citizen's Other: A View from the United States," *American Historical Review* 112, no. 1 (2007): 1–34; Margaret R. Somers, *Genealogies of Citizenship: Markets, Statelessness, and the Right to Have Rights* (Cambridge: Cambridge University Press, 2008); David S. Weissbrodt and Clay Collins, "The Human Rights of Stateless Persons," *Human Rights Quarterly* 28, no. 1 (2006): 245–276. On dual nationality, Unni Wikan, "Citizenship on Trial: Nadia's Case," *Daedalus* 129, no. 4 (Fall 2000): 55–76.

36. The idea of modularity, invoked in Anderson, *Imagined Communities*, is developed in Manu Goswami, "Rethinking the Modular Nation Form: Towards a Sociohistorical Conception of Nationalism," *Comparative Studies in Society and History* 44, no. 4 (2002): 770–799. This book responds to her call for particular histories of modularity.

37. See especially the forum "Liberal Empire and International Law" in *American Historical Review* 117, no. 1 (2012); Peter Sahlins, *Unnaturally French: Foreign Citizens in the Old Regime and After* (Ithaca, N.Y.: Cornell University Press, 2004); Laurent Dubois, *A Colony of Citizens: Revolution and Slave Emancipation in the French Caribbean, 1787-1804* (Chapel Hill: University of North Carolina Press, 2004).

38. Adam McKeown, *Melancholy Order: Asian Migration and the Globalization of Borders* (New York: Columbia University Press, 2008), chap. 2.

39. On women, see Candice Lewis Bredbenner, *A Nationality of Her Own: Women, Marriage, and the Law of Citizenship* (Berkeley: University of California Press, 1998); Joan Wallach Scott, *Only Paradoxes to Offer: French Feminists and the Rights of Man* (Cambridge, Mass.: Harvard University Press, 1996). On empire, see Alice L. Conklin, *A Mission to Civilize: The Republican Idea of Empire in France and West Africa, 1895-1930* (Stanford, Calif.: Stanford University Press, 1997); Gary Wilder, *The French Imperial Nation-State: Negritude and Colonial Humanism Between the Two World Wars* (Chicago: University of Chicago Press, 2005); Julian Go, *American Empire and the Politics of Meaning: Elite Political Cultures in the Philippines and Puerto Rico During U.S. Colonialism* (Durham, N.C.: Duke University Press, 2008). On exclusion, see McKeown, *Melancholy Order*; Gérard Noiriel, *The French Melting Pot: Immigration, Citizenship, and National Identity* (Minneapolis: University of Minnesota Press, 1996).

40. See especially Kennedy, "International Law and the Nineteenth Century."

41. McKeown, *Melancholy Order*, 5.

42. A rich and growing literature makes this dynamic history clear. See, especially, Boğaç A. Ergene, *Local Court, Provincial Society, and Justice in the Ottoman Empire: Legal Practice and Dispute Resolution in Çankırı and Kastamonu (1652-1744)* (Leiden: Brill, 2003); Leslie Peirce, *Morality Tales: Law and Gender in the Ottoman Court of Aintab*

(Berkeley: University of California Press, 2003); Dror Ze'evi, "The Use of Ottoman Shariʿa Court Records as a Source for Middle Eastern Social History: A Reappraisal," *Islamic Law and Society* 5, no. 1 (1998): 35–56.

43. On the question of distance and jurisdiction in eighteenth-century Egypt, see James E. Baldwin, "Islamic Law in an Ottoman Context: Resolving Disputes in Late Seventeenth/Early Eighteenth-Century Cairo" (Ph.D. diss., New York University, 2010); Alan Mikhail, *Nature and Empire in Ottoman Egypt: An Environmental History* (Cambridge: Cambridge University Press, 2011).

44. For an example of nearly correct mischaracterization of capitulations, see Alexander Kitroeff, *The Greeks in Egypt, 1919-1937: Ethnicity and Class* (London: Ithaca, 1989), 2–3. It is an aim of this book to qualify his suggestion that the capitulations unified foreign national communities through "common civil rights and privileges" (3).

45. The use of the term "millet" to refer to sectarian minorities and the system governing them is a nineteenth-century innovation. See Benjamin Braude, "Foundation Myths of the Millet System," in *Christians and Jews in the Ottoman Empire: The Functioning of a Plural Society*, ed. Benjamin Braude and Bernard Lewis (New York: Holmes & Meier, 1982), 1:69–87.

46. Maurits H. van den Boogert, *The Capitulations and the Ottoman Legal System: Qadis, Consuls, and Beratlis in the Eighteenth Century* (Leiden: Brill, 2005).

47. On rhetoric, see Makdisi, *Culture of Sectarianism*. On institutions, see Avi Rubin, *Ottoman Nizamiye Courts: Law and Modernity* (New York: Palgrave Macmillan, 2011).

48. Representative works include Khaled Fahmy and Rudolph Peters, "The Legal History of Ottoman Egypt," *Islamic Law and Society* 6, no. 2 (1999): 129–135; Khaled Fahmy, "Justice, Law, and Pain in Khedival Egypt," in *Standing Trial*, ed. Baudouin Dupret (London: I. B. Tauris, 2004), 85–115; Rudolph Peters, "State, Law, and Society in Nineteenth-Century Egypt," *Die Welt des Islams* 39, no. 3 (1999): 267–272.

49. Omar Cheta, "Rule of Merchants: The Practice of Commerce and Law in Late Ottoman Egypt, 1841–1876" (Ph.D. diss., New York University, 2013).

50. Britain's first Ottoman Order in Council (only a few pages in length) appeared in 1844 and had its legislative basis in the Foreign Jurisdiction Act, 1843 (6&7 Vict. C. 94). France's Law of May 28, 1836, laid out criminal and civil procedures for the consular courts in the Ottoman empire. See Alexandre J. H. de Clercq and Charles de Vallat, *Guide pratique des consulats* (Paris, 1880), 2:386.

51. Michael J. Reimer, *Colonial Bridgehead: Government and Society in Alexandria, 1807-1882* (Cairo: AUC, 1997), 143; Eileen P. Scully, *Bargaining with the State from Afar: American Citizenship in Treaty Port China, 1844-1942* (New York: Columbia University Press, 2001).

52. Two accounts detail the negotiations that led to the settlements: Jasper Yeates Brinton, *The Mixed Courts of Egypt*, 2nd ed. (New Haven, Conn.: Yale University Press, 1968); Byron Cannon, *Politics of Law and the Courts in Nineteenth-Century Egypt* (Salt Lake City: University of Utah Press, 1988).

53. Will Hanley, "The 1876–83 Reform and Its Implementation: Many Institutions or One?" in *New Approaches to Modern Egyptian Legal History*, ed. Khaled Fahmy and Amr Shalakany (Cairo: AUC, forthcoming).

54. In Ottoman domains, in contrast, Ottoman courts had territorial jurisdiction over all crimes.

55. Italy's Foreign Office archives await indexing (or rather funding to hire indexers) but offer a good number of items from the Cairo embassy. American consular employees in Egypt weeded their collections heavily in the 1950s before shipping the crates to Washington but sent along dozens of case dossiers. The uncertain status of Ottoman subjects in Egypt extends to their records, which are concentrated nowhere but are available in glimpses at the Ottoman archives in Istanbul. I do not know Greek, and my inability to work with the records of this largest foreign minority creates a blank space in this study.

56. Two recent dissertations reveal a great deal about the definition of the state of British Egypt under law: Matthew Ellis, "Between Empire and Nation: The Emergence of Egypt's Libyan Borderland, 1841–1911" (Ph.D. diss., Princeton University, 2012); Aimee M. Genell, "Empire by Law: Ottoman Sovereignty and the British Occupation of Egypt, 1882–1923" (Ph.D. diss., Columbia University, 2013).

57. On Izmir, see Zandi-Sayek, *Ottoman Izmir*; Hervé Georgelin, *La fin de Smyrne: du cosmopolitisme aux nationalismes* (Paris: CNRS, 2005); Marie-Carmen Smyrnelis, *Une société hors de soi: identités et relations sociales à Smyrne au XVIIIe et XIXe siècles* (Dudley, Mass.: Peeters, 2005). On Istanbul, see Cem Behar, *A Neighborhood in Ottoman Istanbul: Fruit Vendors and Civil Servants in the Kasap İlyas Mahalle* (Albany: SUNY Press, 2003); Edhem Eldem, Daniel Goffman, and Bruce Alan Masters, *The Ottoman City Between East and West: Aleppo, Izmir, and Istanbul* (Cambridge: Cambridge University Press, 1999). On Salonica, see Meropi Anastassiadou, *Salonique, 1830–1912: une ville ottomane à l'âge des Réformes* (Leiden: Brill, 1997); Mark Mazower, *Salonica, City of Ghosts: Christians, Muslims, and Jews, 1430–1950* (New York: Vintage, 2006). On Tunis, see Julia A. Clancy-Smith, *Mediterraneans: North Africa and Europe in an Age of Migration, C. 1800–1900* (Berkeley: University of California Press, 2011).

58. The classic American articulation of the law-in-practice approach to legal history is Hendrik Hartog, "Pigs and Positivism," *Wisconsin Law Review* (July/August 1985): 899.

59. But see Brinkley Morris Messick, *The Calligraphic State: Textual Domination and History in a Muslim Society* (Berkeley: University of California Press, 1993); Anne Marie Clément, "Fallahin on Trial in Colonial Egypt: Apprehending the Peasantry through Orality, Writing, and Performance (1884–1914)" (Ph.D. diss., University of Toronto, 2012).

60. For "intractable problem," see Clancy-Smith, *Mediterraneans*, 5, 19.

61. Robert W. Gordon, "Critical Legal Histories," *Stanford Law Review* 36 (1984): 109. On constitutive theory, see also Alan Hunt, *Explorations in Law and Society: Towards a Constitutive Theory of Law* (New York: Routledge, 1993), 301–333.

62. Robert W. Gordon, " 'Critical Legal Histories Revisited': A Response," *Law and Social Inquiry* 37, no. 1 (2012): 208.

63. The "ordinary Egyptian" has been the totem of several recent studies that pursue their quarry using the vernacular press and the peasant subject. See, for example, Ziad Fahmy, *Ordinary Egyptians: Creating the Modern Nation Through Popular Culture*

304 INTRODUCTION: NATIONALITY GRASPED

(Stanford, Calif.: Stanford University Press, 2011); Michael Ezekiel Gasper, *The Power of Representation: Publics, Peasants, and Islam in Egypt* (Stanford, Calif.: Stanford University Press, 2009).

64. But see, for example, the nationalism-dominated contents of collections such as Geoff Eley and Ronald Grigor Suny, eds., *Becoming National: A Reader* (New York: Oxford University Press, 1996).

65. This point is also made in Engin Fahri Isin, "Citizenship After Orientalism: Ottoman Citizenship," in *Citizenship in a Global World: European Questions and Turkish Experiences*, ed. Fuat Keyman and Ahmet Icduygu (London: Routledge, 2005), 31–51.

66. Linda Bosniak, *The Citizen and the Alien: Dilemmas of Contemporary Membership* (Princeton, N.J.: Princeton University Press, 2006), 1.

67. Ariel Salzmann, "Citizens in Search of a State: The Limits of Political Participation in the Late Ottoman Empire," in *Extending Citizenship, Reconfiguring States*, ed. Michael P. Hanagan and Charles Tilly (Lanham, Md.: Rowman & Littlefield, 1999), 5; Isin, "Citizenship after Orientalism," 44.

68. For an extended development of this argument, see Will Hanley, "Grieving Cosmopolitanism in Middle East Studies," *History Compass* 6, no. 5 (2008): 1346–1367. For Alexandria, see Reimer, *Colonial Bridgehead*; Robert Ilbert, *Alexandrie, 1830–1930: histoire d'une communauté citadine*, 2 vols. (Cairo: IFAO, 1996).

69. Francesca Trivellato, *The Familiarity of Strangers: The Sephardic Diaspora, Livorno, and Cross-Cultural Trade in the Early Modern Period* (New Haven, Conn.: Yale University Press, 2009); Engseng Ho, *The Graves of Tarim: Genealogy and Mobility Across the Indian Ocean* (Berkeley: University of California Press, 2006); Sebouh David Aslanian, *From the Indian Ocean to the Mediterranean: The Global Trade Networks of Armenian Merchants from New Julfa* (Berkeley: University of California Press, 2011); Clancy-Smith, *Mediterraneans*; Ilham Khuri-Makdisi, *The Eastern Mediterranean and the Making of Global Radicalism, 1860–1914* (Berkeley: University of California Press, 2010); E. Natalie Rothman, *Brokering Empire: Trans-Imperial Subjects Between Venice and Istanbul* (Ithaca, N.Y.: Cornell University Press, 2012).

70. Benton, *Law and Colonial Cultures*; Benton, *Search for Sovereignty*; Anghie, *Imperialism, Sovereignty, and the Making*.

71. On Don Pacifico, see Abigail Green, "The British Empire and the Jews: An Imperialism of Human Rights?," *Past and Present* 199, no. 1 (2008): 175–205. On Koszta, see Zandi-Sayek, *Ottoman Izmir*, 194. On Joris, see Turan Kayaoğlu, *Legal Imperialism: Sovereignty and Extraterritoriality in Japan, the Ottoman Empire, and China* (Cambridge: Cambridge University Press, 2010), 2–3.

72. It shares this character with other Ottoman provincial sites, which have been the subject of a lively recent literature. See Jens Hanssen, Thomas Philipp, and Stefan Weber, eds., *The Empire in the City: Arab Provincial Capitals in the Late Ottoman Empire* (Würzburg: Ergon in Kommission, 2002); Marc Aymes, "Provincialiser l'empire: Chypre et la Méditerranée ottomane au XIXe siècle," *Annales* 62, no. 6 (2007): 1313–1344; Dina Rizk Khoury, *State and Provincial Society in the Ottoman Empire: Mosul, 1540–1834* (Cambridge: Cambridge University Press, 1997); Karen M. Kern, *Imperial*

Citizen: Marriage and Citizenship in the Ottoman Frontier Provinces of Iraq (Syracuse, N.Y.: Syracuse University Press, 2011); Makdisi, *Culture of Sectarianism*.

73. On the concept of trans-imperialism, see Rothman, *Brokering Empire*; Aslanian, *From the Indian Ocean*, 66–67.

74. Wilder, *French Imperial Nation-State*, 6.

75. "Quelle contradiction n'y-a-t-il pas pour les Alliés à se réclamer du principe des nationalités un peu partout dans le monde, et notamment dans les Balkans, en vue de démembrer l'empire austro-hongrois, et non pas en Égypte, où se débat la plus vieille nationalité du monde!" Jacques Berque, *L'Égypte, impérialisme et révolution* (Paris: Gallimard, 1967), 322.

76. Brubaker, *Citizenship and Nationhood*.

77. Weil, *How to Be French*, 4.

1. Vulgar Cosmopolitanism

1. On these settings, see Valeska Huber, *Channelling Mobilities: Migration and Globalisation in the Suez Canal Region and Beyond, 1869–1914* (Cambridge: Cambridge University Press, 2013).

2. The National Archives of the UK: Foreign Office (FO) 847/11/11. A similar brawl that occurred several months earlier is described in chapter 7.

3. A typical linguistic contortion, from the testimony of George Kearley: "un autre homme qui était dans la buvette m'a dit 'ne parlez pas comme cela' en anglais."

4. "Aqulu ʿan ma ashhadu bihi li-llah taʿala. . . . wa hadha hasabama ashahdu bihi wa-llah taʿala khair al-shahidin."

5. This is a challenge for authors of popular histories such as Philip Mansel, *Levant: Splendor and Catastrophe on the Mediterranean* (New Haven, Conn.: Yale University Press, 2011).

6. Misidentification was even part of the arguments of the accused: he claimed that the object witnesses saw in his hand was not a knife but a "Maltese cigar."

7. Age was not part of this series of questions; it was determined by the police doctor (*hakim*). The presence or absence of prior offenses (*sawabiq*) was always noted as well.

8. Length of residence also determined elite standing. Ilbert's chronicle of the Alexandria of (business) notables argues that a single set of elite families controlled the city from the 1860s to the 1930s. Robert Ilbert, *Alexandrie, 1830–1930: histoire d'une communauté citadine* (Cairo: IFAO, 1996), 1:278, passim.

9. James C. Scott, *Seeing Like a State: How Certain Schemes to Improve the Human Condition Have Failed* (New Haven, Conn.: Yale University Press, 1998), 53.

10. The conviction (but not the sentence) is alluded to in a letter about the problem of Maltese crime, particularly knife crime. See FO 78/3955/37 (Burrell to FO, September 6, 1886).

11. Scott, *Seeing Like a State*.

12. Will Hanley, "Grieving Cosmopolitanism in Middle East Studies," *History Compass* 6, no. 5 (2008): 1346–1367.

13. On the political implications of celebrating diversity, see David Harvey, *The Condition of Postmodernity: An Enquiry Into the Origins of Cultural Change* (Oxford: Blackwell, 1989); Daniel T. Rodgers, *Age of Fracture* (Cambridge, Mass.: Harvard University Press, 2011).

14. Some of the resonances of the French word *vulgaire* apply. This use of cosmopolitanism is not unique; for use of "cosmopolitan" in reference to slave-populated societies in Southeast Asia, for example, see James C. Scott, *The Art of Not Being Governed: An Anarchist History of Upland Southeast Asia* (New Haven, Conn.: Yale University Press, 2009), 90.

15. For a related argument from an earlier period, see Khaled Fahmy, "Towards a Social History of Modern Alexandria," in *Alexandria, Real and Imagined*, ed. Anthony Hirst and Michael Silk (Aldershot: Ashgate, 2004), 281–306; Khaled Fahmy, "For Cavafy, with Love and Squalor: Some Critical Notes on the History and Historiography of Modern Alexandria," in ibid., 263–280.

16. Political philosophers are currently engaging cosmopolitanism in such a critical manner. Significant recent collections include Daniele Archibugi, ed., *Debating Cosmopolitics* (London: Verso, 2003); Gillian Brock and Harry Brighouse, eds., *The Political Philosophy of Cosmopolitanism* (Cambridge: Cambridge University Press, 2005); Diane Morgan and Gary Banham, eds., *Cosmopolitics and the Emergence of a Future* (Basingstoke: Palgrave Macmillan, 2007); Pheng Cheah and Bruce Robbins, eds., *Cosmopolitics: Thinking and Feeling Beyond the Nation* (Minneapolis: University of Minnesota Press, 1998); Steven Vertovec and Robin Cohen, eds., *Conceiving Cosmopolitanism: Theory, Context, and Practice* (New York: Oxford University Press, 2002). The Ottoman example is invoked reflexively and inaccurately in much of this writing, and historians have a responsibility to give these philosophers more accurate material to work with.

17. Charles Taylor and Amy Gutmann, *Multiculturalism: Examining the Politics of Recognition* (Princeton, N.J.: Princeton University Press, 1994), 25.

18. This is true of thinkers as different as Appiah, Kymlicka, and Benhabib.

19. Michael Haag, *Alexandria: City of Memory* (New Haven, Conn.: Yale University Press, 2004), 17.

20. Ibid., 23.

21. Maya Jasanoff, "Cosmopolitan: A Tale of Identity from Ottoman Alexandria," *Common Knowledge* 11, no. 3 (2005): 406.

22. Haag, *Alexandria*, 18. Note the nostalgic continuity with antiquity. Transpose this paragraph to the context of apartheid South Africa, and see how it looks.

23. This approach is exemplified, in the Middle Eastern context, by a collection of essays that successfully opens out the history of previously neglected dimensions of Middle Eastern society: drinking, prostitutes, prisons, poverty, madness, migrants, entertainers: Eugene L. Rogan, ed., *Outside In: On the Margins of the Modern Middle East* (London: I. B. Tauris, 2002), 3. The collection categorizes marginality as a subunit of history from below, of "grassroots or non-elite social history."

24. Michel Foucault, *Power/Knowledge: Selected Interviews and Other Writings, 1972–1977* (New York: Pantheon, 1980), 96.

25. Haag, *Alexandria*, 17.

26. Jennifer Robinson, *Ordinary Cities: Between Modernity and Development* (London: Routledge, 2006).

27. This puzzle of placing antiquity in the present animates present-day research and publishing agendas, too. The activities of the Centre d'Etudes Alexandrines are particularly interesting in this light.

28. Two Egyptians working on the history of Rue de Rosette, with an eye to its preservation, are Mohamed Awad, who runs the Alexandria Preservation Trust and the Alex Med research group at Alexandria's Bibliotheca, and ʿAlaʾ Khalid. See his "Al-shariʿ al-kabir [The Great Street]," *Amkenah*, no. 7 (2006): 7–52.

29. Haag, *Alexandria*, 14. I will pass over the racial, gender, and religious subtexts of this passage. Note, however, Haag's treatment of the natives' clothing: the "galabiyya," that garment of Oriental languor, goes undefined, while the "hejab" (a term in relative common use in the sort of English writing that refers to galabiyyas) is meticulously and redundantly described: a veil of ignorance? Note also how he implicates the reader in his lament: "your curiosity . . . your wish . . ."

30. I am grateful to Shauna Huffaker for this observation, which she developed in the course of her research on the late Mamluk and early Ottoman history of Darb al-Ahmar, a neighborhood of Cairo.

31. Nefertiti Takla's forthcoming dissertation is a close study of this case. See also Yunan Labib Rizk, "The Women Killers," *Al-Ahram Weekly*, no. 434 (June 17, 1999); Shaun T. Lopez, "The Dangers of Dancing: The Media and Morality in 1930s Egypt," *Comparative Studies of South Asia, Africa, and the Middle East* 24, no. 1 (2004): 98–99.

32. FO 847/27/2.

33. This planning is detailed exhaustively in Ilbert, *Alexandrie*.

34. These maps are available online at http://archnet.org/publications/10217.

35. For a published historical collection of Alexandria's maps, see Gaston Jondet, *Atlas historique de la ville et des ports d'Alexandrie* (Cairo: IFAO, 1921). The outstanding collection of maps of Alexandria, however, is housed at the Centre d'Etudes Alexandrines in Alexandria, curated by Cécile Shaalan.

36. Engin Fahri Isin, *Being Political: Genealogies of Citizenship* (Minneapolis: University of Minnesota Press, 2002).

37. FO 847/27/2.

38. FO 847/35/13.

39. Ministère des Affaires Étrangères, Centre des Archives Diplomatiques de Nantes (CADN), Fonds Alexandrie: Jugements (AJ) 524/#9.

40. CADN-AJ 533/p36. The year 1903 was also the first of government regulation of automobiles. See Municipalité d'Alexandrie, *Lois, décrets, arrêtés et règlements intéressant la municipalité d'Alexandrie, 1890–1920* (Alexandria: Société de Publications Égyptiennes, 1920).

41. The July 16, 1913 Interior Ministry regulation of automobiles was printed in *al-Waqaʾi al-Misriya* (WM) 110, September 29, 1913, and in Municipalité d'Alexandrie, *Lois, décrets, arrêtés et règlements*, 556–581. Articles 17–26 are about driving licenses (though cars too were to be licensed). Drivers were to be over eighteen years of age and without a conviction for drunkenness in the last year (article 55 also concerns drunk driving, which must have been a problem). There was a fee of ten piasters (two shillings), but no exam: permits were about monitoring who was driving, not the quality of driving.

42. CADN-AJ 533/p86.

43. Elizabeth Thompson, *Colonial Citizens: Republican Rights, Paternal Privilege, and Gender in French Syria and Lebanon* (New York: Columbia University Press, 2000), 181, passim in part IV. Evidence from Alexandria suggests that the introduction of new technologies, which she discusses in some detail, may involve a sharper articulation of class practices than she describes.

44. On the contemporary development of the omnibus service in Istanbul, see Zeynep Çelik, *The Remaking of Istanbul: Portrait of an Ottoman City in the Nineteenth Century* (Berkeley: University of California Press, 1993), 90–96.

45. CADN-AJ 537/p57b. One month later, the accused was given a six-month sentence for beating a French actress who was passing through Alexandria. The sentence was not carried out, as he had already left the city. CADN-AJ 537/p62.

46. CADN-AJ 538/p47b.

47. CADN-AJ 533/p72b.

48. CADN-AJ 531/1901/#4.

49. CADN-AJ 536/p28.

50. He was also acquitted after a café fight in November with another local subject. It appears that he lost his job at some time after this rash of prosecutions; he was selling motors as a mechanic in 1908. These four counts are recorded in CADN-AJ 531/1900/#53 and 531/1900/#56. Lacoste appeared subsequently in an assault case (CADN-AJ 531/1900/#62) and a commercial case involving the sale of an engine (CADN-AJ 535/p68).

51. Such unruly foreigners were the raison d'être of the consular courts.

52. CADN-AJ 534/p126b.

53. For a powerful discussion of the category of human in Egypt during this period, see Samera Esmeir, *Juridical Humanity: A Colonial History* (Stanford, Calif.: Stanford University Press, 2012).

54. CADN-AJ 520/#23. The fine was five francs.

55. Juan Ricardo Cole, *Colonialism and Revolution in the Middle East: Social and Cultural Origins of Egypt's 'Urabi Movement* (Princeton, N.J.: Princeton University Press, 1992), 190–212.

56. The official reports of alarmist European consuls, which provide much of Cole's evidence, tend to confirm this interpretation. But one must be concerned by the narrow evidentiary basis of Cole's argument, which is based on twelve "Euro-Egyptian" conflicts, drawn from all parts of Egypt, spanning more than two decades of time (ibid., 202–203). Furthermore, the overarching rubric of the crowd is problematic: some of these "crowds" counted only three members.

57. FO 847/2/51.
58. CADN-AJ 534/p66b.
59. FO 847/35/13.
60. CADN-AJ 536/p133.
61. FO 847/6/49.
62. FO 847/18/2.
63. Cole, *Colonialism and Revolution*, 203.
64. See, for instance, the discussion of Egyptian drama involving the blackface Nubian character Osman ʿAbd al-Basit in Eve Troutt Powell, *A Different Shade of Colonialism: Egypt, Great Britain, and the Mastery of the Sudan* (Berkeley: University of California Press, 2003), 188–195.
65. FO 847/14/39.
66. Samuel Moyn, "The Universal Declaration of Human Rights of 1948 in the History of Cosmopolitanism," *Critical Inquiry* 40, no. 4 (2014): 367.

2. Keywords

1. On the role of "mandarin law" in sociolegal history, see Robert W. Gordon, "Critical Legal Histories," *Stanford Law Review* 36 (1984): 57–125.
2. Eric Lohr, *Russian Citizenship: From Empire to Soviet Union* (Cambridge, Mass.: Harvard University Press, 2012); Yuri Slezkine, "The USSR as a Communal Apartment, or How a Socialist State Promoted Ethnic Particularism," *Slavic Review* 53, no. 2 (Summer 1994): 414–452; Francine Hirsch, *Empire of Nations: Ethnographic Knowledge and the Making of the Soviet Union* (Ithaca, N.Y.: Cornell University Press, 2005).
3. Identification documents of the 1930s listed facts of birth: name, time and place of birth, authorized domicile, and nationality. Slezkine, "Communal Apartment," 224.
4. Lohr, *Russian Citizenship*, 3.
5. Key studies of this phenomenon include Ami Ayalon, *Language and Change in the Arab Middle East: The Evolution of Modern Political Discourse* (New York: Oxford University Press, 1987).
6. Story was a justice of the U.S. Supreme Court from 1811 to 1845. Wheaton, also an American, was a globally influential scholar of international law. The most pertinent section of Savigny's work is volume 8 of his *System des heutigen römischen Rechts*, translated by William Guthrie as *A Treatise on the Conflict of Laws, and the Limits of Their Operation in Respect of Place and Time*, 2nd ed. (Edinburgh, 1880). Westlake held the Whewell Professorship of International Law between Henry Maine and Lassa Oppenheim. Dicey's most famous work, on British constitutionalism, was followed by his *A Digest of the Law of England with Reference to the Conflict of Laws* (London: Stevens, 1922).
7. Mancini was a founding member of the Institut de droit international in 1873. His essay *Della nazionalità come fondamento del dritto delle genti, prelezione al corso di dritto internazionale e maritime* (Torino, 1851) was especially influential in the Egyptian

context, cited almost a century later in ʿAbd al-Hamid Abu Haif, *Al-Qanun al-Duwali al-Khass fi Awruba wa Masr* (Cairo: Matbaʿat al-Iʿtimad, 1924), 9; and in Mahmoud-Zaky Salem, *La doctrine de Mancini sur la nationalité et son application au droit égyptien* (Dijon: Bernigaud et Privat, 1923).

8. Lassa Oppenheim, *International Law: A Treatise*, 2nd ed. (London: Longmans, 1912), 362–424.

9. Frederick Cooper, *Colonialism in Question: Theory, Knowledge, History* (Berkeley: University of California Press, 2005), 7–9.

10. For a parallel argument about the legacies of imagined genealogies in human rights law, see Samuel Moyn, *The Last Utopia: Human Rights in History* (Cambridge, Mass.: Belknap, 2010).

11. Benedict Anderson, *Imagined Communities: Reflections on the Origin and Spread of Nationalism*, rev. and extended ed. (London: Verso, 1991); Mark Hewitson and Timothy Baycroft, eds., *What Is a Nation?: Europe 1789–1914* (New York: Oxford University Press, 2006); Homi K. Bhabha, ed., *Nation and Narration* (London: Routledge, 1990); E. J. Hobsbawm, *Nations and Nationalism Since 1780: Programme, Myth, Reality*, 2nd ed. (Cambridge: Cambridge University Press, 1992); Ernest Gellner, *Nations and Nationalism* (Ithaca, N.Y.: Cornell University Press, 1983); Anthony D. Smith, *Nationalism and Modernism: A Critical Survey of Recent Theories of Nations and Nationalism* (London: Routledge, 1998).

12. Raymond Williams, *Keywords: A Vocabulary of Culture and Society* (New York: Oxford University Press, 1985), 213.

13. This dominant adjectival sense makes it impossible to compare "national" meaningfully with counterparts such as "citizen" over time using word-frequency software like Google's n-gram viewer.

14. Maximilian Koessler, " 'Subject,' 'Citizen,' 'National,' and 'Permanent Allegiance,' " *Yale Law Journal* 56, no. 1 (1946): 66–67.

15. Williams, *Keywords*, 213.

16. Koessler, " 'Subject,' 'Citizen.' " See also qualification of this reading, based on Roman origins, in Alfred Boll, *Multiple Nationality and International Law* (Leiden: M. Nijhoff, 2007), 65.

17. Quoted in Boll, *Multiple Nationality*, 71. See also Paul Weis, *Nationality and Statelessness in International Law*, 2nd ed. (Alphen aan den Rijn: Sijthoff & Noordhoff, 1979), 5–6.

18. For this use, see especially Hirsch, *Empire of Nations*; Slezkine, "Communal Apartment."

19. Boll, *Multiple Nationality*, 60.

20. Williams, *Keywords*, 213.

21. Intriguingly, the assembly of all French-citizen residents of a nineteenth-century Ottoman or Egyptian city was called "*la nation*" and invested with local political authority.

22. See, for instance, Ministère des Affaires Étrangères, Centre des Archives Diplomatiques de Nantes (CADN), Fonds Alexandrie: Recensement—Algériens (RA) 50/1275.

23. Weis, *Nationality and Statelessness*, 7–9.

24. Ami Ayalon suggests that *umma* succeeded *milla* to designate the nation-state community in the last quarter of the nineteenth century. These are sociopolitical terms

for collectivities rather than legal terms for individuals, however. Ayalon, *Language and Change*, 19–24, 51–52.

25. D. A. Cameron, *An Arabic-English Vocabulary for the Use of English Students of Modern Egyptian Arabic* (London, 1892), 310.

26. Ibid., 9, 228, 270. More unusual, experimental terms could also be added to this list. My student Phillip Holmes discovered the use of the term ʿunsuri for "national" in a 1916 issue of the Meccan weekly *al-Qibla*.

27. Ibid., 32.

28. In 1892, Cameron translated *jinsiya* as "sex, specification, origin" and *jins* as "species, kind, sex." Ibid., 48. See also Marwa Elshakry, *Reading Darwin in Arabic, 1860-1950* (Chicago: University of Chicago Press, 2013).

29. Gélat's translation of *tabiiyet*, the term used in the 1869 Ottoman law, is "*nationalité.*" Philippe Gélat, *Répertoire général annoté de la législation et de l'administration egyptiennes*, 5 vols. (Alexandrie: J. C. Lagoudakis, 1906).

30. A useful compendium of laws is Richard W. Flournoy and Manley O. Hudson, eds., *A Collection of Nationality Laws of Various Countries, as Contained in Constitutions, Statutes, and Treaties* (New York: Oxford University Press, 1929); see also United Nations, *Laws Concerning Nationality* (New York: United Nations, 1954).

31. On French nationality in general, see Patrick Weil, *How to Be French: Nationality in the Making Since 1789* (Durham, N.C.: Duke University Press, 2008); revising Rogers Brubaker, *Citizenship and Nationhood in France and Germany* (Cambridge, Mass.: Harvard University Press, 1992).

32. It followed on the Naturalization Act of 1872.

33. For background, see Randall Hansen, "The Politics of Citizenship in 1940s Britain: The British Nationality Act," *Twentieth-Century British History* 10, no. 1 (1999): 67–95.

34. Brubaker, *Citizenship and Nationhood*; Derek Benjamin Heater, *A Brief History of Citizenship* (Edinburgh: Edinburgh University Press, 2004); Andreas Fahrmeir, *Citizenship: The Rise and Fall of a Modern Concept* (New Haven, Conn.: Yale University Press, 2007). But note also the restraint of a scholar like Aristide Zolberg, who refrains from stretching the meaning of "citizen" beyond its historical senses.

35. This is the formulation of T. H. Marshall, *Citizenship and Social Class, and Other Essays* (Cambridge: Cambridge University Press, 1950).

36. This genealogy is traced in J. G. A. Pocock, "The Ideal of Citizenship Since Classical Times," *Queen's Quarterly* 99, no. 1 (Spring 1992): 35–55. The fact that this particular genealogy seems necessary in order to explain the modern concept may be a sign of European insecurity in a global context.

37. For a critique of this blind spot in the political philosophy of Rawls, see Kok-Chor Tan, *Justice Without Borders: Cosmopolitanism, Nationalism, and Patriotism* (Cambridge: Cambridge University Press, 2004).

38. This distinction emerged shortly after the French Revolution. Laurent Dubois, *A Colony of Citizens: Revolution and Slave Emancipation in the French Caribbean, 1787-1804* (Chapel Hill: University of North Carolina Press, 2004).

39. Notably Linda K. Kerber, "The Stateless as the Citizen's Other: A View from the United States," *American Historical Review* 112, no. 1 (2007): 1–34; Linda Bosniak, *The Citizen and the Alien: Dilemmas of Contemporary Membership* (Princeton, N.J.: Princeton University Press, 2006); Kunal M. Parker, *Making Foreigners: Immigration and Citizenship Law in America, 1600-2000* (Cambridge: Cambridge University Press, 2015).

40. Koessler, "'Subject,' 'Citizen,'" 63.

41. The question of global citizenship, for which this distinction does matter, is not relevant to this study.

42. Weis, *Nationality and Statelessness*, 5–6.

43. George Cogordan, *Droit des gens: la nationalité au point de vue des rapports internationaux*, 2nd ed. (Paris, 1890), 7.

44. American historians of citizenship often display insularity in this respect. For instance, Kerber, "Stateless as the Citizen's Other."

45. Weil, *How to Be French*, 6.

46. Gianluca Paolo Parolin, *Citizenship in the Arab World: Kin, Religion, and Nation-State* (Amsterdam: Amsterdam University Press, 2009), 23.

47. Ayalon, *Language and Change*, 44–45.

48. Roger Allen, *A Period of Time: A Study and Translation of Hadith ʿIsa Ibn Hisham by Muhammad al-Muwaylihi* (Reading: Ithaca, 1992), 303; Muhammad al-Muwaylihi, *Hadith ʿIsa ibn Hisham, aw fatrah min al-zaman* (Cairo: Kalimat, 2013), 185. This phrase was added subsequent to the original newspaper version; see Muhammad al-Muwaylihi, *What ʿIsa Ibn Hisham Told Us, or, A Period of Time*, trans. Roger Allen, (New York: New York University Press, 2015), 2:26–27.

49. Ayalon, *Language and Change*, 48–50.

50. Parolin, *Citizenship*, 23. Similarly, Boll observes that the rights focus of much contemporary citizenship discussion differs from the acquisition-and-loss focus of the Roman citizenship regime with which modern citizenship is often aligned. Boll, *Multiple Nationality*, 65.

51. Ayalon, *Language and Change*, 53.

52. Ironically, however, the category does not help much to elaborate the distinction between *jus sanginus*, the membership that flows from birth, and *jus soli*, those rights that derive from territorial residence.

53. *A New English Dictionary on Historical Principles*, 1st ed. (1906), cited in "native, n." *OED Online* (Oxford University Press, 2014), at 3a.

54. Williams, *Keywords*, 215. For an exploration of the related concept indigeneity, see Renisa Mawani, "Specters of Indigeneity in British-Indian Migration, 1914," *Law and Society Review* 46, no. 2 (2012): 369–403.

55. "native, n." *OED Online* (Oxford University Press, 2014), at 5d.

56. Mahmood Mamdani, *Citizen and Subject: Contemporary Africa and the Legacy of Late Colonialism* (Princeton, N.J.: Princeton University Press, 1996), 48.

57. The influential 1881 Algerian *Code de l'indigénat* is one of many legal uses of this term, though it came into common use from the 1840s. Julia A. Clancy-Smith,

Mediterraneans: North Africa and Europe in an Age of Migration, C. 1800–1900 (Berkeley: University of California Press, 2011), 90, 98.

58. By the last quarter of the nineteenth century, foreign authorities typically communicated with Egyptian authorities in French. Most examples of European use of Arabic occur in correspondence with rural provinces. In a letter of April 9, 1885, from the British Consular Court to the Mudir of Beheira, the English "natives" was translated as *"anfar min al-ahali."* The National Archives of the UK: Foreign Office (FO) 847/10/31.

59. The *Majmuʿa rasmiya li-ahkam al-mahakim al-ahliya* was published with the English title *Official Bulletin of the Native Tribunals* from 1900 to 1924 and as the *Bulletin officiel des Tribunaux indigènes* from 1900 to 1936. After 1937, it was issued as the *Bulletin officiel des Tribunaux nationaux et mehkemehs.*

60. Cameron, *Arabic-English Vocabulary*, 12.

61. Online *OED*, "naturalized, adj."

62. Koessler, " 'Subject,' 'Citizen,' " 64. This distinction recalls rights-based distinctions between citizens and nationals.

63. Originally, the contrast with foreign was most striking: denizen combines the prefix *dans-* (within) with the suffix *-ein*; "foreign" merely substitutes the prefix *for-* (*OED*). In this sense, denizen and citizen were largely synonymous, distinguished from foreigners or strangers. More recently, however, denizen is contrasted with counterpart forms of membership with fuller rights. Its technical meaning involves disability: "in the law of Great Britain, an alien admitted to citizenship by royal letters patent, but incapable of inheriting, or holding any public office" (*OED*). In this sense, denizen and citizen mean different things.

64. On the denizen, see Caitlin Anderson, "Britons Abroad and Aliens at Home: Nationality Law and Policy in Britain, 1815–70" (Ph.D. dissertation, Cambridge, 2004).

65. Cameron, *Arabic-English Vocabulary*, 310. This term would come to mean "citizen" in the twentieth century.

66. Weis, *Nationality and Statelessness*, 10.

67. Abu Haif, *Al-Qanun al-Duwali al-Khass*, 96–97.

68. Ibid., 89–96, drawing on Dicey and Westlake.

69. Martti Koskenniemi, *The Gentle Civilizer of Nations: The Rise and Fall of International Law, 1870–1960* (Cambridge: Cambridge University Press, 2002), 114–115.

70. Online *OED*, "foreign, adj. and n."

71. Austin Sarat, Lawrence Douglas, and Martha Merrill Umphrey, eds., *Law and the Stranger* (Stanford, Calif.: Stanford University Press, 2010), 7–10.

72. Recent histories of early modern foreigners elaborate this point. For example, see Peter Sahlins, *Unnaturally French: Foreign Citizens in the Old Regime and After* (Ithaca, N.Y.: Cornell University Press, 2004); Lohr, *Russian Citizenship*, 11.

73. For more discussion of the term extrality, see Eileen P. Scully, *Bargaining with the State from Afar: American Citizenship in Treaty Port China, 1844–1942* (New York: Columbia University Press, 2001).

74. Online *OED*, "expatriate, v."

75. This distinction is drawn in article 9 of the Mixed Tribunals code and article 15 of the Native Courts code. For detailed discussion, see Ramzi Sayf Rizq Allah, *Tanazu' al-Ikhtisas bain al-Mahakim al-Ahliya wa al-Mahakim al-Mukhtalita* (Cairo: Matba'at Fath Allah Ilyas Nuri wa Awladihi, 1938), 92–104.

76. Quoted in Ayalon, *Language and Change*, 52.

77. Muwaylihi, *Hadith 'Isa ibn Hisham, aw fatrah min al-zaman*, 56; Muwaylihi, *What 'Isa ibn Hisham Told Us*, 132. For the publication history of this serialized book, see the translator's preface in *What 'Isa ibn Hisham Told Us*, xviii–xxvii.

78. "Imtiyazat al-'urban bi-Masr: asluha wa masiruha," *Al-Hilal* 14 (1904): 212–214.

79. See further discussion in chapter 12.

80. Weis, *Nationality and Statelessness*, 4.

81. Williams, *Keywords*, 209.

82. Hannah Weiss Muller, "An Empire of Subjects: Unities and Disunities in the British Empire, 1760–1790" (Ph.D. dissertation, Princeton University, 2010).

83. Notably, Mamdani, *Citizen and Subject*.

84. Library of Congress News Releases, "Analysis Reveals Changes in Declaration of Independence," July 2, 2010, http://www.loc.gov/today/pr/2010/10-161.html.

85. Cameron, *Arabic-English Vocabulary*, 103. Presumably he meant *ri'aya*.

86. FO 847/18/14.

87. HBM Consulate-General, Alexandria to Governor of Alexandria, December 12, 1892, in FO 847/22/52.

88. Cameron, *Arabic-English Vocabulary*, 68. It is not entirely accurate to equate *ri'aya* and *himaya*, however, as in Julia A. Clancy-Smith, *Rebel and Saint: Muslim Notables, Populist Protest, Colonial Encounters (Algeria and Tunisia, 1800–1904)* (Berkeley: University of California Press, 1994), 210.

89. For example, Julia Clancy-Smith (*Mediterraneans*, 5) refers to southern European migrants to Tunisia inaccurately as "diplomatic protégés." Diplomatic protection was in fact a much narrower field. See Linda Frey and Marsha Frey, *The History of Diplomatic Immunity* (Columbus: Ohio State University Press, 1999).

90. Boll, *Multiple Nationality*, 88.

91. Koessler, " 'Subject,' 'Citizen,' " 68–69.

92. Ayalon, *Language and Change*, 48.

3. Papers

1. Drawing on Fichte, Jane Caplan describes a paradoxical undertaking of this sort in " 'This or That Particular Person': Protocols of Identification in Nineteenth-Century Europe," in *Documenting Individual Identity*, ed. Jane Caplan and John C. Torpey (Princeton, N.J.: Princeton University Press, 2001), 49.

2. The National Archives of the UK: Foreign Office (FO) 847/1/3.

3. This right fits the "civil rights" scheme of T. H. Marshall, *Citizenship and Social Class, and Other Essays* (Cambridge: Cambridge University Press, 1950).

4. Khaled Fahmy, *All the Pasha's Men: Mehmed Ali, His Army, and the Making of Modern Egypt* (Cambridge: Cambridge University Press, 1997), 106.

5. Similarly, sponsorship by a *kefil* was a requirement for migrants to Izmir in the middle of the nineteenth century. Sibel Zandi-Sayek, *Ottoman Izmir: The Rise of a Cosmopolitan Port, 1840-1880* (Minneapolis: University of Minnesota Press, 2012), 87. On the *kefil* in eighteenth-century Istanbul, see Fariba Zarinebaf, *Crime and Punishment in Istanbul: 1700-1800* (Berkeley: University of California Press, 2011), 132–133.

6. Life without a guarantee involved a certain degree of curtailed social rights, but as Egypt's population became more mobile during the nineteenth century, it resembled less and less the sort of social death that in a previous epoch entailed living on the outskirts of towns because no neighborhood would accommodate a stranger.

7. On Egyptian demography, see Omnia S. El Shakry, *The Great Social Laboratory: Subjects of Knowledge in Colonial and Postcolonial Egypt* (Stanford, Calif.: Stanford University Press, 2007).

8. John Torpey's study of passports, which focuses on documents for movement, offers a simple three-way distinction between international passports, internal passports, and identity cards. *The Invention of the Passport: Surveillance, Citizenship, and the State* (New York: Cambridge University Press, 2000), 158–167. This rather narrow set of types privileges the role of the state (as does Torpey's study as a whole). Leo Lucassen offers a more sophisticated typology for the study of documentary practice, distinguishing between eight kinds of documents: travel, work, certificates of nationality, "identification documents," population registration, military passports, miscellaneous, and (crucially) no identification. He usefully traces shifts in their use in Amsterdam registrations between 1850 and 1905, drawing on a sample of more than two thousand items. Leo Lucassen, "A Many-Headed Monster: The Evolution of the Passport System in the Netherlands and Germany in the Long Nineteenth Century," in *Documenting Individual Identity*, ed. Jane Caplan and John C. Torpey (Princeton, N.J.: Princeton University Press, 2001), 247.

9. In each case (and in the six lists in the notes that follow), I am listing the earliest instance I have encountered of a standard format reused by the same authority in later years and (sometimes) other locations. The representative examples are an 1863 *"Certificato di Nazionalita e Residenza"* issued by the United States consulate general in Egypt (USNA 84/350/17/23/4/1/16), an 1868 "Naturalization Certificate" issued by the British secretary of state (FO 847/36/1), an 1869 *"Certificat d'Immatriculation"* issued by the French consulate in Suez (Ministère des Affaires Étrangères, Centre des Archives Diplomatiques de Nantes [CADN], Fonds Alexandrie: Recensement— Algériens [RA] 54/1536), an 1873 *"Certificat de Nationalité Algérienne"* issued by the French consulate in Damascus (CADN-RA 46/1001), an 1879 *"Certificat d'Inscription"* issued by the French consulate in Alexandria (CADN-RA 46/1006), an 1883 *"Certificat (d'Indigence et de Residence)"* issued by the Algérie commissariat de police (FO 847/6/52), an 1884 "Certificate of Registration" issued by the British consulate in Alexandria (847/21/21), an 1887 *"Certificat de Nationalité"* issued by the French vice-consulate in Jaffa (CADN-RA 53/1461), an 1893 *"Certificato di Nazionalita'"* issued by

the Italian consulate in Alexandria (Archivio Storico del Ministero degli Affari Esteri, Rome (ASMAE) Cairo 51/40), a 1903 "Duplicate Foil of Certificate of Registration" issued by the British consulate in Alexandria (FO 847/49/3), a 1910 *"Certificat de Nationalité, Recensement des Algériens"* issued by the French consulate in Alexandria (CADN-RA 51/1327), and a 1913 "Certificate of Registration of American Citizen," issued by the United States consulate in Constantinople (USNA 84/350/11/19/4/4/28).

10. Although passports are the most well-known form of identification today, they were not particularly dominant or powerful a century ago. The representative examples are an 1861 *"Passe"* issued by the French consular agency in Haifa (CADN-RA 54/1457), an 1867 "Passport" issued by the British consulate in Alexandria (FO 847/3/19), an 1873 *"Passeport"* issued by the French consulate in Palestine (CADN-RA 46/1054), an 1883 *"Mürur Tezkeresi"* issued by the Ottoman state (CADN, Fonds Alexandrie: Recensement – Tunisiens [RT] 72/307), an 1883 *"Passaporto"* issued by the Italian Foreign Ministry (ASMAE Cairo 38/8), an 1893 *"Passe"* issued by the French consulate in Cairo (CADN-RA 51/1327), an 1895 pass letter issued by the French consulate-general in Syria (CADN-RA 54/1553), a 1901 *"Permis de Voyage"* issued by the French Département de Constantine (CADN-RA 54/1553), a 1901 *"Mürur Tezkeresi dahiliye mahsusdur"* issued by the Ottoman state (CADN-RA 54/1531), and a 1907 "Passport" issued by the British consulate in Tripoli (Syria) (FO 847/46/11).

11. Andreas Fahrmeir, *Citizenship: The Rise and Fall of a Modern Concept* (New Haven, Conn.: Yale University Press, 2007), 2. Eric Lohr defines "citizenship" as "a status denoting membership in a country, usually documented with a passport." *Russian Citizenship: From Empire to Soviet Union* (Cambridge, Mass.: Harvard University Press, 2012), 3. For more on the mobility/residence distinction, see Will Hanley, "Papers for Going, Papers for Staying: Identification and Documentation in the East Mediterranean," in *A Global Middle East: Mobility, Materiality, and Culture in the Modern Age, 1880-1940,* ed. Liat Kozma, Avner Wishnitzer, and Cyrus Schayegh (London: I. B. Tauris, 2014).

12. The representative examples are an 1883 *"Acte de naissance"* issued by the Mairie of Oran (CADN-RA 53/1457), an 1884 *"Nüfus Tezkeresi"* issued by the Ottoman Interior Ministry (CADN-RA 53/1497), an 1886 "Birth certificate excerpted from the register of births" (*tadhkira wilada mustakhraja min daftar al-wiladat*) issued by the Egyptian government (CADN-RA 56/1922), an 1899 extract from the marriage register of the British consulate at Alexandria (FO 847/44/6), a 1909 *"Kashf rasmi"* issued by the Egyptian government (FO 847/42/17), a 1912 *"Certificat de Décès"* issued by Egypt's Agence Sanitaire (FO 847/48/35), a 1912 *"Extrait de Naissance"* issued by the Inspectorat Sanitaire of the Municipality of Alexandria (CADN-RA 53/1413), a 1913 *"Déclaration de Décès"* issued by the Public Health Service of the Municipality of Alexandria (FO 847/50/50), a 1913 "Burial permission" issued by the British consulate of Alexandria (FO 847/50/50), a 1914 "Death certificate" (*mulakhkhas shahadat wafah*) issued by the Egyptian government (FO 847/52/30), and a 1914 excerpt from the death register of the British Consular Court in Alexandria (FO 847/51/15).

13. The representative examples are an 1881 "Malta Prison charge" issued by the British Consular Court in Alexandria (FO 847/3/16), 1885 prisoner photo cards

produced by the Egyptian Secret Police (Dar al-Watha'iq al-Qawmiya, Cairo [DWQ]), an 1888 *"Matricule générale de la Déportation"* issued by the Algerian state (CADN-RA 50/1262), an 1893 "Death Report" issued by the constable of the British consulate in Alexandria (FO 847/23/9), a 1911 "Receipt of Patients on Admission" issued by the ʿAbbasiya Mental Hospital of the Egyptian government (FO 847/47/12), a 1913 *"Formule de consignation d'un prévenu étranger à son Consulat / urnik taslim muttaham ajnabi li-dar qunsulatihi"* issued by the Alexandria Police (National Archives of the United States, College Park, Maryland [USNA] 84/350/11/19/4/4/3), a 1914 "Notice of Death" issued by the British Consular Court in Alexandria (FO 847/51/15), and a 1914 *"Certificat Médical d'Aliéné"* issued by the Services Sanitaires of the Egyptian Interior Ministry (FO 847/52/38).

14. The representative examples are an 1863 *"Congé de Libération"* issued by the 3me Régiment de Tirrailleurs Algériens (CADN-RA 54/1536); an 1882 *"Tadhkira Hurriya"* (liberation certificate) issued by the Qalam ʿItq Raqiq, Alexandria (posted at *Dhakira Misr al-Muʿasira* [http://modernegypt.bibalex.org/], on file with author); an 1898 *"Etat signalétique et des services"* issued by the Atelier de Travaux Publics of Bougie, Algeria (CADN-RA 54/1553); and a 1912 excerpt from the registers of births and deaths of the British Board of Trade (FO 847/48/35).

15. FO 847/48/35.

16. See, for instance, the case of Ahmad ʿAbduh, described in chapter 12. This cleric issued marriage and death certificates that were unrecognized by the Egyptian government, to the great chagrin of certain of his clients.

17. The representative examples are an 1883 extract from a Catholic marriage register in Malta (FO 847/6/52); a 1902 baptism certificate from St. Catherine's Church, Alexandria (FO 847/31/6); a 1906 certificate of legitimacy from the St. Catherine's parish (FO 36/4); a 1909 *"Certificat"* of identity from the Communauté Israélite à Alexandrie (FO 847/42/17); and a 1911 baptism certificate from Malta (FO 847/48/13).

18. For examples of such creased documents, see CADN-RA 46/1008, 47/1148, 48/1167, 48/1200, 49/1244, 50/1254, 51/1336, CADN-RT 70/114, 71/284.

19. Forgeries and false stories that prove to be true deserve more study. For other examples, see Will Slauter, "Le paragraphe mobile. Circulation et transformation des informations dans le monde atlantique du XVIIIe siècle," *Annales. Histoire, Sciences sociales* 2, no. 6 (2012): 363–389.

20. Port Said's records were too poorly kept to disprove this story, but he was convicted of falsifying the signature of a public officer. CADN, Fonds Alexandrie: Jugements (AJ) 536/p176.

21. CADN-AJ 536/p102b. Merillan is likely the "friend" who provided a false document to a deserter from the French army tried during the same month: CADN-AJ 536/pp98b, 100b, 104.

22. Andreas Fahrmeir, "Governments and Forgers: Passports in Nineteenth-Century Europe," in *Documenting Individual Identity*, ed. Jane Caplan and John C. Torpey (Princeton, N.J.: Princeton University Press, 2001), 232.

23. See further discussion of this document in Hanley, "Papers for Going," 186–190.

24. See Martin Lloyd, *The Passport: The History of Man's Most Travelled Document* (Stroud: Sutton, 2003), 97–107. See also the interesting description of French practices of physical identification in Martine Kaluszynksi, "Republican Identity: Bertillonage as Government Technique," in *Documenting Individual Identity*, ed. Jane Caplan and John C. Torpey (Princeton, N.J.: Princeton University Press, 2001), 123–138.

25. In 1882, the French consulate recovered a passport issued in Algeria for travel to Mecca, which had been sold for one franc for fraudulent use (CADN-RA 47/1332). Forgery was a concern throughout the Mediterranean. For a description of a 1913 scandal involving false British identification documents held by Maltese in Tunisia, see Mary Dewhurst Lewis, "Geographies of Power: The Tunisian Civic Order, Jurisdictional Politics, and Imperial Rivalry in the Mediterranean, 1881–1935," *Journal of Modern History* 80, no. 4 (2008): 36–37.

26. CADN-AJ 536/p181.

27. A parallel can be made with anxieties about counterfeit currency, discussed in chapter 5.

28. On Jedda, see Ulrike Freitag, "The City and the Stranger: Jeddah in the Nineteenth Century," in *The City in the Ottoman Empire: Migration and the Making of Urban Modernity*, ed. Ulrike Freitag (Abingdon: Routledge, 2011).

29. For a sketch of symbolic competition between empire and republic, see Philip G. Nord, *The Republican Moment: Struggles for Democracy in Nineteenth-Century France* (Cambridge, Mass.: Harvard University Press, 1995), 190–217. CADN-RA 46/1030 contains a counterpart document from 1850, an Algerian passport "au nom du R̶o̶i̶ Peuple," on which the royal coat of arms has also been crossed out.

30. For comments on incomplete and erroneous population registration in early nineteenth-century France, see Gérard Noiriel, "The Identification of the Citizen: The Birth of Republican Civil Status in France," in *Documenting Individual Identity*, ed. Jane Caplan and John C. Torpey (Princeton, N.J.: Princeton University Press, 2001), 31–33. He argues that these "failings" epitomize the rift between central planners and the population.

31. This term is used in Caplan, "This or That Particular Person."

32. Kathryn Burns, *Into the Archive: Writing and Power in Colonial Peru* (Durham, N.C.: Duke University Press, 2010), 33.

33. Ahmad ibn Muhammad al-Tahawi, *The Function of Documents in Islamic Law: The Chapters on Sales from Tahawi's Kitab al-Shurut al-Kabir*, trans. Jeanette A. Wakin (Albany: SUNY Press, 1972).

34. Fahmy, *All the Pasha's Men*, 106. Note that these passports used the village rather than the central state as their pole of reference; those who were found out of order were returned to the care of their local shaykh.

35. James C. Scott, *Seeing Like a State: How Certain Schemes to Improve the Human Condition Have Failed* (New Haven, Conn.: Yale University Press, 1998), 65.

36. An index-card collection preserved in the French consular archives shows one system used to manage ambiguity.

37. Geographic designations could also be ambiguous. The classic problem was Tarablus, the name of two prominent cities close to Egypt.

38. CADN-RT 69/69–73.
39. On the waning of the guilds in Egypt, see John T. Chalcraft, *The Striking Cabbies of Cairo and Other Stories: Crafts and Guilds in Egypt, 1873-1914* (Albany: SUNY Press, 2004).
40. Başbakanlık Osmanlı Arşivi, Istanbul (BOA) DH.SN.THR 15/4.
41. For an example of this certificate, see CADN-RA 48/1200.
42. Jane Burbank, *Russian Peasants Go to Court: Legal Culture in the Countryside, 1905-1917* (Bloomington: Indiana University Press, 2004), 12–13.
43. There is little evidence, for example, to support the claim that "the French especially in an effort to increase their influence in Egypt, sold or otherwise granted citizenship papers" at the time of the First World War. Michael Haag, *Alexandria: City of Memory* (New Haven, Conn.: Yale University Press, 2004), 17.
44. I examined 350 of the two thousand Algerian dossiers that the French consulate produced between 1873 and 1915, and four hundred of the 1,700 Tunisian dossiers produced between 1881 and 1917.
45. The dossiers of dozens of non-Algerian, non-Tunisian protégés were integrated into the Algerian series. Moroccans became a fourth important division during the First World War. For eight hundred files on individual Moroccans, see CADN, Fonds Alexandrie (FA) 100–6, 273, 275: "Recensement des protégés français. Marocains—Dossiers nominatifs" (1914–50). More than four hundred dossiers on Lebanese French subjects are contained in CADN-FA 99, 264, 270: "Recensement des protégés français. Libanais—Dossiers nominatifs" (1925–45).
46. Patrick Weil, *How to Be French: Nationality in the Making Since 1789* (Durham, N.C.: Duke University Press, 2008), 245. He here refers to birth certificates and declarations of marriage and naturalization in the *Journal officiel* during the interwar period.
47. CADN-RA 46/1050.
48. 119 unnumbered dossiers, of a total of 348 dossiers.
49. This series does not seem to be held with the rest of the Alexandria records in Nantes; it has probably been discarded. "Dossier 19 des personnes renvoyées de la protection, année 1880" is mentioned in CADN-RA 46/1072.
50. CADN-RA 46/1060, 1079.
51. See, for instance, the case of Mahri Hamawi (discussed below), in which the French court was compelled to admit that one of two contradictory passports issued by French officials was in error (CADN-AJ 516/#36).
52. CADN-RA 49/1227.
53. CADN-RA 48/1163.
54. For an example, see CADN-RA 46/1057.
55. Sixteen of 350 Algerians and fifty-seven of four hundred Tunisians.
56. The British consulate delegated similar duties to the Catholic clergy of the Maltese diocese. See, for example, the identification document issued by a Maltese priest in FO 847/36/4.
57. He also refused to recommend certain individuals: see, for instance, CADN-RT 71/261. On status rearrangements in Tunisia itself, see Mary Dewhurst Lewis,

Divided Rule: Sovereignty and Empire in French Tunisia, 1881–1938 (Berkeley: University of California Press, 2013).

58. The forms were printed especially for use in Alexandria, but the agent's entries did not conform exactly to expectations. He ignored the French side of the form, writing only in Arabic. He also provided additional information about religion and regional origin within Tunisia that appeared to have no place in *drogmanat* procedure.

59. Their names were Saʿid Mahni Dahman, Salih ʿAli Timlist, Salim Badr al-Din, and ʿAbd al-Hamid Ghurbal.

60. Five members of the Firmoun clan received certificates on October 19, 1880, for example (CADN-RA 46/1066–9). See especially the family tree that they presented to the consulate, preserved in folder 1068. See too the Agri family, protégés who registered a month later (46/1073–5; see also 321/291, 50/1278).

61. FO 847/42/5: "This certificate must be Renewed in January mext [*sic*] Questo Certificato deve essere Rinnovato al prossimo Gennaio."

62. The incommensurate relationship between local and foreign is discussed in chapter 8.

63. CADN-RA 49/1249.

64. FO 847/28/16. Her case is also discussed in chapter 6.

65. Lewis, "Geographies of Power," 22. Lewis draws the quotation from an 1886 circular issued by the resident-general concerning taxation.

66. BOA BEO 1001/75058.

67. FO 847/22/52.

68. I have not managed to identify the "mirka" tax.

69. See his application for status in CADN-RA 46/1057.

70. CADN-AJ 516/36.

71. The author hints at this: "statelessness is no longer easily measured only by the presence or absence of a passport." Linda K. Kerber, "The Stateless as the Citizen's Other: A View from the United States," *American Historical Review* 112, no. 1 (2007): 31.

72. For a similar case from the same period, in which an Algerian woman was given a month to prove her identity and apparently never returned to the consulate, see CADN-RA 46/1062.

73. This was the case with Shaykh Ahmad ʿAbduh, a Tunisian cleric discussed in chapter 12.

74. Fahrmeir, *Citizenship*, 2.

75. FO 847/27/17.

76. BOA MKT 2210/139.

77. FO 847/12/34.

78. Scott, *Seeing Like a State*, 83.

4. Census

1. Ann Laura Stoler, *Along the Archival Grain: Epistemic Anxieties and Colonial Common Sense* (Princeton, N.J.: Princeton University Press, 2009).

2. With exceptions, as we will see. The Egyptian census of 1848 was a review in which the population was known and not anonymous.

3. Benedict Anderson, *Imagined Communities: Reflections on the Origin and Spread of Nationalism*, rev. and extended ed. (London: Verso, 1991).

4. For example, Robert Ilbert, *Alexandrie, 1830-1930: histoire d'une communauté citadine*, 2 vols. (Cairo: IFAO, 1996), which contains dozens of pages of census tables.

5. See the detailed table in Will Hanley, "Foreignness and Localness in Alexandria, 1880-1914" (Ph.D. diss., Princeton University, History, 2007), 273-274. A majority of the scholars not cited in that table simply adopt the Egyptian census figures.

6. On the long history of subnational censuses in South Asia, see Sumit Guha, "The Politics of Identity and Enumeration in India C. 1600-1990," *Comparative Studies in Society and History* 45, no. 1 (2003): 157.

7. Wendell Cleland, *The Population Problem in Egypt: A Study of Population Trends and Conditions in Modern Egypt* (Lancaster, Penn.: Science Press, 1936), 15.

8. See, for example, the National Archives of the UK: Foreign Office (FO) 78/3332/ Judicial #7 (Cookson to Granville, April 11, 1881).

9. On the 1885 and 1907 Ottoman censuses, see Cem Behar, "Sources pour la Démographie Historique de l'Empire Ottoman. Les tahrirs (dénombrements) de 1885 et 1907," *Population* 1-2 (1998): 161-178; Cem Behar, "Qui compte? Recencesements et statistiques démographiques dans l'Empire ottoman du XVIe au XX siecle," *Histoire and Mesure* 13 (1998): 135-146. See also İpek K. Yosmaoğlu, "Counting Bodies, Shaping Souls: The 1903 Census and National Identity in Ottoman Macedonia," *International Journal of Middle East Studies* 38, no. 1 (2006): 55-77.

10. The files of the Interior Ministry's Sicill-i Nüfus İdare-i Umumiyesi contain many administrative checks on the registration status of individuals. See, for example, Başbakanlık Osmanlı Arşivi, Istanbul (BOA) DH.SN.THR 25/25 (1911) and 49/77 (1914).

11. These records were kept at the office of the *drogmanat*, as opposed to the chancellery, which handled the civil affairs of French citizens.

12. Ministère des Affaires Étrangères, Centre des Archives Diplomatiques de Nantes (CADN), Fonds Alexandrie (FA) 458-61: "Fichier des Protégés français Algériens et Tunisiens."

13. Cards from later years are also marked M for Moroccan and I for Israelite (i.e., Jew).

14. For a discussion of names and identification, see Jane Caplan, "'This or That Particular Person': Protocols of Identification in Nineteenth-Century Europe," in *Documenting Individual Identity*, ed. Jane Caplan and John C. Torpey (Princeton, N.J.: Princeton University Press, 2001), 58, passim.

15. This naming practice worked better in smaller towns. A bad subject in Damanhur, for example, was known by his agnomen of al-Maghribi (CADN, Fonds Alexandrie: Jugements [AJ] 534/31).

16. British consulate files often bear marginal notes showing alternate spellings of names, in an effort to track down individuals. Similar experimentation was probably a standard practice at all consulates.

17. Derived from enclosure in Cookson to Fawcett #10 (November 14, 1887) in FO 78/4115, "Respecting the working of the compulsory registration of British Subjects in the Ottoman Dominions." See table in Hanley, "Foreignness and Localness," 285.

18. FO 881/5968. This document contains similar censuses for every Ottoman and Egyptian city where the British operated a consulate. The quality of return varies from place to place.

19. See, for instance, a letter from the Egyptian Foreign Ministry to de Martino, Italian chargé d'affaires #686 bis, dated September 23, 1899, asking for proof of the Italian protection of a certain Francis Tadros of Damietta, "*d'autant plus qu'il n'avait pas été inscrit en 1883 sur la liste des protégés italiens.*" Archivio Storico del Ministero degli Affari Esteri, Rome (ASMAE) Cairo 113/5.

20. This treaty is reproduced in Filib Jallad, *Qamus al-idarah wa-al-qadaʾ*, 3rd ed. (Cairo: Matbaʿat Dar al-Kutub wa-al-Wathaʾiq al-Qawmiya, 2003), 2:296–300. The transfer of Tunisia into French hands also created upheavals in the protection system in Tunisia itself. For this counterpart to the process described here, see Mary Dewhurst Lewis, "Geographies of Power: The Tunisian Civic Order, Jurisdictional Politics, and Imperial Rivalry in the Mediterranean, 1881–1935," *Journal of Modern History* 80, no. 4 (2008): 791–830.

21. CADN, Fonds Alexandrie: Recensement – Tunisiens (RA) 50/1279–80.

22. Dar al-Wathaʾiq al-Qawmiya, Cairo (DWQ). I have not seen these cards myself and do not know their current archival location. I have images of seven of them, however, and my comments are based on this small sample.

23. The entry in the fields for case number and date of sentence is typically "unknown," suggesting a lack of information sharing between the judicial and prison services. It is also notable that the place of the sentence is always recorded, suggesting that individuals were indexed by the geographical location of the sentence, rather than by its paper location (recorded in number and date). This suggests a reliance on human rather than paper recording. Compare Ottoman penal servitude registers from the eighteenth century, which listed names, "background," and details of their crimes; contemporary surveillance records listed name, father's name, marital status, and guarantors. Fariba Zarinebaf, *Crime and Punishment in Istanbul: 1700–1800* (Berkeley: University of California Press, 2011), 73–74, 128–130.

24. BOA Y.PRK.ESA 17/3. Most were on military or educational missions.

25. This is the case, for instance, in the most substantial of all histories of Alexandria: Ilbert, *Alexandrie, 1830–1930*; see, e.g., 759.

26. The only essay that explores the mentality of census takers to any degree (focusing especially on the methodology of the 1917 census) is Roger Owen, "The Population Census of 1917 and Its Relationship to Egypt's Three Nineteenth-Century Statistical Regimes," *Journal of Historical Sociology* 9, no. 4 (1996): 457–472. As far as the purely statistical studies are concerned, the best critique (and the best job of catching irregularities, such as the presence of Sudanese in local population counts [28]) is Justin McCarthy, "Nineteenth-Century Egyptian Population," *Middle Eastern Studies* 12, no. 3 (1976): 1–39.

27. This oft-repeated verdict was probably first expressed in Cleland, *Population Problem*, 6–9. Justin McCarthy and Daniel Panzac each correct the 1882 census by extrapolating population growth from other censuses and thereby bolster their endorsement of the 1897 and 1907 censuses.

28. Justin McCarthy, the leading historical demographer of the Middle East, states plainly that "the censuses taken in Egypt after 1897 were the best population records in the Middle East." *Population History of the Middle East and the Balkans* (Istanbul: Isis, 2002), 273.

29. Direction du Recensement Egypt, *Recensement général de l'Égypte, 15 Gamad Akher 1299 / 3 mai 1882* (Cairo, 1884), section 1, 15: Alexandria district 1: 667 foreign men and 494 foreign women do not total 1,121 foreigners; Alexandria district 3: 8,635 foreign men and 9,104 foreign women do not total 18,039 foreigners.

30. The sum of foreigners and locals in Alexandria exceeds the total population by 17, while the sum of foreigners and locals for all of Egypt falls 25,428 short of the total population.

31. Demographic history can benefit from accounting errors in much the same way that certain postcolonial historians employ convoluted, defamiliarizing writing styles to challenge their readers to reflect on the meaning behind the text.

32. Roger Owen ("Population Census") makes a similar argument about the incommensurate nature of three different "statistical regimes" that preceded the 1917 census.

33. This social scientific project would be extended, in the years that followed, with the establishment of the Egyptian archives and the production of national histories at the behest of the state. See Yoav Di-Capua, *Gatekeepers of the Arab Past: Historians and History Writing in Twentieth-Century Egypt* (Berkeley: University of California Press, 2009). The best description of counterpart projects to give the Ottoman Empire symbolic legitimacy is Selim Deringil, *The Well-Protected Domains: Ideology and the Legitimation of Power in the Ottoman Empire, 1876–1909* (London: I. B. Tauris, 1998).

34. Egypt, *Recensement général 1882* section 1, 5. See also introduction, 24–26.

35. This was also the case in Tunis, which even had a "shaykh of outsiders" (*shaykh al-barraniya*). Julia A. Clancy-Smith, *Mediterraneans: North Africa and Europe in an Age of Migration, C. 1800–1900* (Berkeley: University of California Press, 2011), 39.

36. Egypt, *Recensement général 1882*, sec. 1, 20.

37. Egyptian Foreign Ministry to Manzoni, October 18, 1906 (ASMAE Cairo 110/7b).

38. ASMAE Cairo 110/7b. These rules were subject to negotiation with the consulates, and the Mixed Court did not pass any law; a decree of January 31, 1889, stated that it did not have jurisdiction over those who refused to respond to the census.

39. The 1917 census is the only one for which methodology was recorded. See the analysis in Owen, "Population Census."

40. Quoted in Daniel Panzac, "Alexandrie: évolution d'une ville cosmopolite au XIXe siècle," *Annales Islamologiques* 14 (1978): 195.

41. Kenneth M. Cuno and Michael J. Reimer, "The Census Registers of Nineteenth-Century Egypt: A New Source for Social Historians," *British Journal of Middle Eastern Studies* 24, no. 2 (1997): 204–205.

42. Quoted in McCarthy, "Nineteenth-Century Egyptian Population," 9.

43. Compare the opposite situation, described in Zarinebaf, *Crime and Punishment*, 80.

44. In a recent essay, Robert Mabro makes a rare attempt to resolve this quandary by describing three national groups: Egyptian locals, "foreign nationals," and "foreign nationals plus non-Egyptian locals," a category that includes Sudanese, Ottomans, Greek Egyptians, and the like. Robert Mabro, "Alexandria 1860–1960: The Cosmopolitan Identity," in *Alexandria, Real and Imagined*, ed. Anthony Hirst and Michael Silk (Aldershot: Ashgate, 2004), 248. This approach has the virtue of acknowledging this semiforeign, semilocal group and giving it a name and numbers, but it does not demystify the complication created by a set of nationalities that were equally treated by census takers but overlapping and incommensurate in practice.

45. Egypt, *Recensement général 1882*, sec. 1, 11.

46. Ibid., introduction, 25. Arabic introduction, page *kaf*.

47. Ibid., sec. 1, 9.

48. Michael Haag, *Alexandria: City of Memory* (New Haven, Conn.: Yale University Press, 2004), 16–17.

49. Ian Hacking, "Making Up People," in *Reconstructing Individualism*, ed. Thomas C. Heller and Christine Brooke-Rose (Stanford, Calif.: Stanford University Press, 1986), 223.

5. Money

1. Dar al-Watha'iq al-Qawmiya, Cairo, Dabtiya Iskandariya (DWQ-DI) 739/450.

2. *"ashadd al-jaza' adaban lahu wa ʿairatan li-ghairihi."*

3. See, for instance, the testimonies of Abdou Bahran and Aly Mohammad in the National Archives of the UK: Foreign Office (FO) 847/16/7.

4. Yitzhak Nakash, "Fiscal and Monetary Systems in the Mahdist Sudan, 1881–1898," *International Journal of Middle East Studies* 20, no. 3 (1988): 378.

5. Charles Philip Issawi, *The Economic History of the Middle East, 1800–1914: A Book of Readings* (Chicago: University of Chicago Press, 1975), 522–524.

6. Viviana A. Rotman Zelizer, *The Social Meaning of Money* (New York: Basic Books, 1994), 13.

7. Roger Owen, *The Middle East in the World Economy, 1800–1914* (London: I. B. Tauris, 1993), xiii.

8. FO 847/2/47.

9. FO 847/6/49.

10. Ministère des Affaires Étrangères, Centre des Archives Diplomatiques de Nantes (CADN), Fonds Alexandrie: Jugements (AJ) 523/#77.

11. FO 847/2/63.

12. FO 847/3/16.

13. FO 847/4/4.

14. FO 847/5/6.

15. FO 847/16/7.

16. Eric Tagliacozzo, *Secret Trades, Porous Borders: Smuggling and States Along a Southeast Asian Frontier, 1865–1915* (New Haven, Conn.: Yale University Press, 2005).

17. Details contained in FO 847/18/16, a conviction for a subsequent offense. He was a stone-cold liar: "q How can you deny having sold counterfeit coins in face of the fact that I yesterday sent him to you to buy some and witnessed at a distance the sale which effectively took place, you took from him 13 f for 13 counterfeit new ten piastres pieces? R He has not come, I did not see him and no sale took place."

18. See, for instance, CADN-AJ 591/#34 (1884), in which an "*ourvier doreur*" earned 12f per day.

19. My comprehensive survey of DWQ-DI between 1880 and 1884 turned up dozens of such cases.

20. See, for instance, the swindling case of Zarqawi (CADN-AJ 534/58b), described in chapter 8, and a very similar case from 1908 (CADN-AJ 535/99b).

21. FO 847/2/63.

22. See, for instance, the description of two-franc coins in FO 847/2/63.

23. FO 369/291, FO 369/369.

24. E. J. Hobsbawm and T. O. Ranger, eds., *The Invention of Tradition* (Cambridge: Cambridge University Press, 1983), 281. This compared to stamps. Benedict Anderson, *Imagined Communities: Reflections on the Origin and Spread of Nationalism*, rev. and extended ed. (London: Verso, 1991); Selim Deringil, *The Well-Protected Domains: Ideology and the Legitimation of Power in the Ottoman Empire, 1876–1909* (London: I. B. Tauris, 1998).

25. Zelizer, *The Social Meaning of Money*. Note, however, that she does not argue from the perspective of the state.

26. D. C. M. Platt, *The Cinderella Service: British Consuls Since 1825* (London: Longman, 1971), 139–140.

27. FO 847/48/40.

28. His sons did not agree to maintain the business after his death. Liquidation of these precarious loans was too complex and costly to undertake, so one son bought the other brothers' shares. See FO 847/50/32, FO 847/52/39.

29. In a 1912 financial case, both the plaintiff and the respondent killed themselves: FO 847/47/18, FO 847/48/2, FO 847/48/15.

30. See FO 847/9/11 and especially FO 97/617.

31. Most of the details in this sketch are drawn from the arbiter's report, contained in FO 847/9/1.

32. FO 847/29/3.

33. Relevant studies of the later nineteenth century include Iris Agmon, "Recording Procedures and Legal Culture in the Late Ottoman Shari'a Court of Jaffa, 1865–1890," *Islamic Law and Society* 11, no. 3 (2004): 333–377; Iris Agmon, *Family and Court: Legal Culture and Modernity in Late Ottoman Palestine* (Syracuse, N.Y.: Syracuse University Press, 2006); Avi Rubin, "Ottoman Judicial Change in the Age of Modernity: A Reappraisal," *History Compass* 7, no. 1 (2009): 119–140; Avi Rubin, *Ottoman Nizamiye Courts: Law and Modernity* (New York: Palgrave Macmillan, 2011).

34. The case represents an earlier exploration of the citizenship debates examined in Sarah Abrevaya Stein, "Protected Persons? The Baghdadi Jewish Diaspora, the British State, and the Persistence of Empire," *American Historical Review* 116, no. 1 (2011): 80–108.

35. See citation in judgment notes, FO 847/36/1, discussed in chapter 11. The judge applied the same reasoning to Adamidis's attempts to join the British and the Greek communities in Alexandria.

6. Marriage

1. This is apparent even in the title of classic treatises: Joseph Story and Melville Madison Bigelow, *Commentaries on the Conflict of Laws, Foreign and Domestic: In Regard to Contracts, Rights, and Remedies, and Especially in Regard to Marriages, Divorces, Wills, Successions, and Judgments*, 8th ed. (Boston, 1883). Egyptian legal scholars also focused on the question: for example, see W. R. B Briscoe, "Marriage with Foreigners," *Law Magazine and Review: A Quarterly Review of Jurisprudence* 37 (1912): 129; Abd El Hamid Moustapha Bey, "De la forme du mariage des étrangers en Egypte," *L'Egypte contemporaine* (1918): 311–329. Briscoe was a leading barrister before the British consular courts in Egypt. At the French consular courts, marriage accounted for at least 241 of 2,113 hearings between 1880 and 1914; succession accounted for 138 hearings in the same period. At the British consular courts, marriage was the principal subject in 49 of 1,472 case files preserved for the 1880–1914 period, while probate and succession was the subject of 617.

2. Partha Chatterjee, "The Nationalist Resolution of the Women's Question," in *Recasting Women*, ed. Kumkum Sangari and Sudesh Vaid (New Brunswick, N.J.: Rutgers University Press, 1990), 233–253.

3. Ann Laura Stoler, *Carnal Knowledge and Imperial Power: Race and the Intimate in Colonial Rule* (Berkeley: University of California Press, 2002).

4. Ministère des Affaires Étrangères, Centre des Archives Diplomatiques de Nantes (CADN), Fonds Alexandrie: Recensement – Algériens (RA) 35/79; see esp. registration book (Suppl. 197).

5. In CADN, Fonds Alexandrie (FA) Suppl. 200 no. 239, her parents are listed as Moise Gandour and Rachel Menace.

6. CADN-RA 53/1467.

7. CADN, Fonds Alexandrie: Jugements (AJ) 524/#38. Jacob earned 12 pounds per month, so this was a large share of his salary.

8. CADN-AJ 524/#54.

9. CADN-AJ 525/#3.

10. CADN-AJ 525/#18, 525/#40, 526/#4.

11. CADN-AJ 529/1896/#21, 529/1896/#24. See also no. 83 in the "Registre des actes de l'état civil" (November 18, 1896).

12. CADN-AJ 534/p37.

13. CADN-AJ 536/p12b.

14. CADN-AJ 537/p100b.

15. See, for example, the National Archives of the UK: Foreign Office (FO) 847/42/26, FO 847/46/5.

16. None of the separation suits aims for divorce, which in any case would have been impossible for Roman Catholic Maltese.

17. FO 847/38/33.

18. FO 847/39/37. He had no chance to test his assertion, as his wife failed to appear at the court hearing, and the case was adjourned. 46/21 is a similar case.

19. For example, see FO 847/19/13.

20. CADN-RA 50/1280; see also 50/1279 for husband's documents.

21. CADN-RA 46/1041.

22. CADN-AJ 537/p8. This opinion was supported by precedents from the Alexandria consular tribunal and from the Supreme Court at Aix: " . . . la loi ottomane ne contient aucune disposition attribuant la nationalité de son mari à la femme étrangère qui épouse un sujet ottoman, une française contractant mariage avec un sujet ottoman reste française; que telle est la jurisprudence de ce tribunal (notamment jugement du 4 juillet 1890) confirmée par la cour d'Aix (7 novembre 1907)." The precedent case referred to is CADN-AJ 525/35 (*Vito Bey Hekekian c. Djemille Linant de Bellefonds*, July 4, 1890). For another case in which the consulate seemed relieved to find that a widow was of Algerian origin, see CADN-RA 46/1094. For a case in which a British-protected widow explores nationality switching, see FO 847/44/6.

23. Presuming that he thereby fulfilled requirements of decree of October 7, 1871, on "la justification de l'indégénat [*sic*]."

24. CADN-RA 50/1270. Consul Girard closed the dossier with a note on the cover: "immatriculé le 6 janvier 1908 sur le registre des citoyens français en vertu du décret du 24 octobre 1870 après justification de l'indigénat algérien de son père."

25. CADN-AJ 538/p171.

26. The classic treatments of this phenomenon are not centrally concerned with law. Gayatri Chakravorty Spivak, "Can the Subaltern Speak?" in *Marxism and the Interpretation of Culture* (Urbana: University of Illinois Press, 1988), 271–313; Robert Young, *Colonial Desire: Hybridity in Theory, Culture, and Race* (London: Routledge, 1995); Stoler, *Carnal Knowledge*.

27. Dar al-Wathaʾiq al-Qawmiya, Cairo, Dabtiya Iskandariya (DWQ-DI) 735/6.

28. See similar cases in Mario M. Ruiz, "Intimate Disputes, Illicit Violence: Gender, Law, and the State in Colonial Egypt, 1849–1923" (Ph.D. dissertation, University of Michigan, 2004).

29. On the white slave–trade panic, see Diane Liga Robinson-Dunn, *The Harem, Slavery, and British Imperial Culture: Anglo-Muslim Relations in the Late Nineteenth Century* (Manchester: Manchester University Press, 2006), 130–135; Harold Tollefson, *Policing Islam: The British Occupation of Egypt and the Anglo-Egyptian Struggle Over Control of the Police, 1882–1914* (Westport, Conn.: Greenwood, 2000), 122–124, 155. For a prosecution that adopted this frame, see FO 847/52/43.

30. The girl would be "decoy[ed] . . . into a life that can only be characterised as slavery." The resonance with early modern slaving raids is clear. For examples of that imaginary literature, see Linda Colley, *Captives: Britain, Empire, and the World, 1600–1850* (London: Jonathan Cape, 2002).

31. Ingram to Hopkinson, May 8, 1912, in FO 891/6.

32. The British consul-general in Alexandria was skeptical about this assertion. Hopkinson, the commandant of the Alexandria police, stated that Ingram's suspicion was based on a recent surveillance trip to England and Scotland, during which he had mixed with Egyptian students, as well as on two couples he had met on the ship back to Alexandria. Hopkinson to Cameron, May 18, 1912, in FO 891/6.

33. FO 891/6.

34. See 1912 correspondence concerning this case in FO 369/210. Eventually, he sanctioned the marriage, basing his decision largely on the groom's class (i.e., wealth).

35. FO 369/210/38795.

36. Langley to Cameron #22 of December 8, 1909, in FO 369/210/43749. In its consultations, the Foreign Office advisors cited as precedent a similar recent case from Constantinople.

37. Cameron to Grey #24, November 11, 1912, in FO 891/6.

38. Cameron to Islington Parish, October 12, 1909, in FO 369/210/43749.

39. Cameron to Grey #24, November 11, 1912, in FO 891/6. As evidence, Cameron reported that three female English domestic servants had recently complained to him of intolerable food, sanitation, and language in "harems."

40. FO Circular 524/10 on January 19, 1910, adding to General Instructions, chapter XXX [i.e., 30], new section 24a.

41. Foreign Office to Home Office 21185/12 of May 20, 1912, in FO 891/6.

42. A copy of this form can be found in FO 369/291/30164 (Marriage between Egyptian & British Woman, 1910).

43. The information that follows comes from FO 891/6 (Marriages: loss of right to protection by British women marrying Egyptian Moslems, 1912). One of the folders contained within this box bears the title (now crossed out) "undesirability of marriages between . . ."

44. See many such requests in FO 369/369 (1911).

45. FO 369/369 (1911).

46. On the inferiority of converts and Oriental Christians, see Heather J. Sharkey, "Empire and Muslim Conversion: Historical Reflections on Christian Missions in Egypt," *Islam and Christian–Muslim Relations* 16, no. 1 (2005): 43–60; Ussama Makdisi, *Artillery of Heaven: American Missionaries and the Failed Conversion of the Middle East* (Ithaca, N.Y.: Cornell University Press, 2008); Gauri Viswanathan, *Outside the Fold: Conversion, Modernity, and Belief* (Princeton, N.J.: Princeton University Press, 1998).

47. Correspondence in FO 369/210. Archdeacon Ward of St. Mark's Anglican Church in Assyut appealed to the Alexandria consul as well (" 'Nothing without the Consul' has always been my view in all such matters"), but he was rebuffed.

48. The nationality-defense logic extended even to an Austrian woman whose marriage to a British man was refused by Cameron, who doubted her divorce after a previous marriage. FO 369/290/21470 (1910).

49. See, for instance, the cases described in Stoler, *Carnal Knowledge*.

50. FO 847/28/16. See also discussion in chapter 3.

51. FO 780/296. The case in Alexandria was one of the rare instances when lawyers played a prominent role in argumentation. For the most part, their interventions concerned procedural matters. The arguments for the defense that the marriages were not proved fell on deaf ears. The sentence was confirmed by the Supreme Court at Constantinople.

52. FO 78/4768/Consular #5 (Cookson to FO, January 29, 1896).

53. FO 78/4773.

54. FO 78/4768/5.

55. A "stranger" told her he saw him in Marseilles in 1887.

56. After her death, her brother Thomas Scarff, a corporal in the Dorset Regiment stationed in Dorchester, tried to claim her meager property (apparel, photos, two pawn tickets). His service in the British military did not benefit her.

57. FO 369/461/26997, FO 369/561/9226. Elsewhere, her name is spelled Buttieg and Battestig. For further details on the five British subjects in the asylum, see FO 847/52/56.

58. For more details on this case, see the extended discussion in Kenneth M. Cuno, *Modernizing Marriage: Family, Ideology, and Law in Nineteenth- and Early Twentieth-Century Egypt* (Syracuse, N.Y.: Syracuse University Press, 2015), 185–204. For a taste of the wrangling over her first husband's estate following this remarriage, see an announcement published by Nafissa in *Al-Ahram* on September 29 and its retraction in the same pages on October 18, 1892. Thanks to Hussein Omar for finding these articles. Shaykh Ahmad's consular registration dossier, along with those of his father and brothers, can be found in CADN-RA 49/1205–1212.

59. CADN-AJ 532/p37. See also CADN-RA 50/1269, Nafissa's consular registration dossier. For more on obedience and cohabitation, including the finding that such cases constituted 5 percent of marriage-related cases in a shariʿa court sample from turn-of-the-century Daqahliya, see Kenneth M. Cuno, "Disobedient Wives and Neglectful Husbands: Marital Relations and the First Phase of Family Law Reform in Egypt," in *Family, Gender, and Law in a Globalizing Middle East and South Asia*, ed. Kenneth Cuno and Manisha Desai (Syracuse, N.Y.: Syracuse University Press, 2009), 3–18; Judith E. Tucker, *In the House of the Law: Gender and Islamic Law in Ottoman Syria and Palestine* (Berkeley: University of California Press, 1998).

60. This change is detailed in an article titled "Nos Protégés Musulmans," from *La Réforme* (August 1896), which is enclosed in CADN-FA 109, in the folder titled "Questions relatives au statut personnel des protégés et catholiques sujets locaux."

61. A further issue revolved around the marriage of children of her first husband to those of her second (for control of family wealth, it seems)—these were being settled by the "competent jurisdiction." Also, she signed a document (*takharruj*) that was recognized by court.

62. CADN-AJ 532/p43b.
63. In his letter #16 of April 24, 1902, the governor cited a khedival decree to this effect, which is certainly that 1897 Egyptian civil procedure code discussed in Cuno, "Disobedient Wives," 10–11. As Cuno argues, the right to compel return was an innovation—before 1897 the most severe sanction for departure was loss of maintenance. Clearly, the five-year-old procedure code was transmitted into the French system in the guise of "advice" about "local practice."
64. Archives d'outre mer, Aix-en-Provence (AOM) Fond Ministériels 1AFFPOL/1294 (Extraits d'une note de la Légation de France au Caire en date du 8 juillet 1939).

7. Europeans

1. The National Archives of the UK: Foreign Office (FO) 847/27/8.
2. FO 78/4869 (Cookson telegram to FO, June 23, 1897; FO telegram to Cookson, June 24, 1897).
3. Richard T. Chang argues that the consular courts in late nineteenth-century Japan issued fair verdicts in the overwhelming majority of cases. Richard T. Chang, *The Justice of the Western Consular Courts in Nineteenth-Century Japan* (Westport, Conn.: Greenwood, 1984).
4. One product of the more universal and exclusive nationality regimes that developed after the First World War, however, was the European local subject. The 1917 census listed "Greek" Egyptian nationals, for example.
5. FO 78/4153 (Colborne to Burrell, August 9, 1888).
6. FO 78/4153 (Burrell to Colborne, August 11, 1888).
7. Question from Sir Walter Foster. Hansard HC Deb 6 August 1889, vol. 339, c. 540.
8. FO 78/4249 (Salisbury to Cookson, August 7, 1889).
9. FO 847/26/20.
10. He was himself a representative of a minor power, acting as consul general in Egypt for Norway.
11. FO 847/36/6.
12. FO 847/31/5.
13. Frank Heraldson, George I. Souand, Cumboviz Rall, Henry Reiss, and Fred Peck.
14. For example, David Arnold, "European Orphans and Vagrants in India in the Nineteenth Century," *Journal of Imperial and Commonwealth History* 7, no. 2 (1979): 104–127; Ann Laura Stoler, "Rethinking Colonial Categories: European Communities and the Boundaries of Rule," *Comparative Studies in Society and History* 31, no. 1 (1989): 134–161.
15. Frederick Cooper and Ann Laura Stoler, eds., *Tensions of Empire: Colonial Cultures in a Bourgeois World* (Berkeley: University of California Press, 1997); Catherine Hall, *Civilizing Subjects: Colony and Metropole in the English Imagination, 1830–1867* (Chicago: University of Chicago Press, 2002); Gary Wilder, *The French Imperial Nation-State: Negritude and Colonial Humanism Between the Two World Wars* (Chicago: University of Chicago Press, 2005).

16. The best of this work includes Gauri Viswanathan, *Outside the Fold: Conversion, Modernity, and Belief* (Princeton, N.J.: Princeton University Press, 1998). For a critique of work that labors under notions of hybridity and cosmopolitanism, see my "Grieving Cosmopolitanism in Middle East Studies," *History Compass* 6, no. 5 (2008): 1346–1367.

17. Ann Laura Stoler, *Carnal Knowledge and Imperial Power: Race and the Intimate in Colonial Rule* (Berkeley: University of California Press, 2002); Hilary Beckles, "'Black Men in White Skins': The Formation of a White Proletariat in West Indian Slave Society," *Journal of Imperial and Commonwealth History* 15, no. 1 (1986): 7.

18. See the discussion of the category of distressed British subjects in Caitlin Anderson, "Britons Abroad and Aliens at Home: Nationality Law and Policy in Britain 1815–70" (Ph.D. dissertation, Cambridge, 2004).

19. See, for instance, FO 847/25/23, in which the family of the deceased Maltese custodian of St. Catherine's Convent appeals to charity to pay for his burial.

20. FO 847/50/33.

21. FO 847/18/12, in which an attempt to collect back wages for a deceased seaman, but also a wish to get money for his family from Oddfellows, was denied because he died serving under a foreign flag (on an Egyptian ship).

22. FO 847/18/30.

23. FO 847/26/3. In this case, a British woman hired to teach English to the child of a wealthy family lost her job and board after a fight with her employers. She was sent to Trieste by Cookson, getting her away and out of trouble.

24. See, for instance, FO 847/40/62 (1908), in which a mother complained that her husband leaves only six piasters per day for her children's food and medicine and has left nothing for the last three days. The family is hungry, she reported, and she has had to sell clothes for medicine. The next year, she sued *in forma pauparis* for separation, complaining that her husband was now giving her only one and a half piasters per day. The court ruled in her favor, but with little consequence.

25. FO 847/24/40.

26. FO 847/51/11. He was junior partner to Edward Cumbo.

27. These men were Moise Nahum (FO 847/33/5), Frederick Giglio (847/30/9), Theodore Cumbo (847/33/3), Themistocle Axisa (847/46/16), Albert Guttieres Pegna (847/45/38), Amabile Grech (847/48/26), and Edward Camilleri (847/48/24).

28. FO 847/21/34. There was a corresponding set of wealthy Maghribis. Because succession cases of French subjects were not systematically forwarded to the consular court, I have a narrower picture of the material circumstances of the Maghribi community. Nevertheless, certain cases display the extent of Maghribi wealth. For example, the estate of Haj ʿAbd al-Salam al-Sallami, a protégé living in Tanta who died in 1888, amounted to half a million francs (£25,000). Ministère des Affaires Étrangères, Centre des Archives Diplomatiques de Nantes (CADN), Fonds Alexandrie: Jugements (AJ) 527/#7/p115, 528/#4, 529/#35. The archives of the French consulate's chancellery hold abundant succession files, which I did not have time to study.

29. FO 847/1/31.

30. FO 847/22/50.

31. Daniel Panzac, "The Population of Egypt in the Nineteenth Century," *Asian and African Studies* 21 (1987): 27. Elsewhere, Panzac is even more explicit about this social model, in which the wealthy lead, the poor follow, and the foreign minority dominates society. Daniel Panzac, "Alexandrie: évolution d'une ville cosmopolite au XIXe siècle," *Annales Islamologiques* 14 (1978): 211, 215.

32. FO 847/3/17.

33. On the term *khawaga*, see Robert Mabro, "Alexandria 1860–1960: The Cosmopolitan Identity," in *Alexandria, Real and Imagined*, ed. Anthony Hirst and Michael Silk (Aldershot: Ashgate, 2004), 248–249; Jean-Luc Arnaud, "Des Khawaga au Caire à la fin du XIXe siècle: éléments pour une définition," *Egypt/Monde Arabe* 11 (1992): 39–46.

34. Julia A. Clancy-Smith, *Mediterraneans: North Africa and Europe in an Age of Migration, C. 1800–1900* (Berkeley: University of California Press, 2011), 8.

35. A memoir of well-to-do Maltese European life in Egypt after the turn of the century is Anna Cachia and Pierre Cachia, *Landlocked Islands: Two Alien Lives in Egypt* (Cairo: AUC, 2000).

36. My preliminary count.

37. In colonies of settlement, suicide and lunacy are considered symptoms of frontier society. See Bernard Bailyn, *The Peopling of British North America: An Introduction* (New York: Knopf, 1986), for instance, on these phenomena as markers of seventeenth- and eighteenth-century British North America's character as a frontier of Europe.

38. FO 847/6/49.

39. FO 847/26/5.

40. Alexander Borg, "Language," in *Malta: Culture and Identity*, ed. Henry Frendo and Oliver Friggieri (Malta: Ministry of Youth and the Arts, 1994), 41. See also Alexander Borg, "On Some Mediterranean Influences on the Lexicon of Maltese," in *Romania Arabica*, ed. J. Ludtke (Tubingen: Gunter Narr, 1996), 129–150.

41. Language was a key issue in nationalist debate in Malta: nationalists were divided into Anglophile and Italianate parties. Maltese nationalism was connected to the early twentieth-century renaissance in Maltese language and literature. Language is a familiar engine of nationalism; in the Maltese case, however, the debate featured an unusual imperial dimension. During the nineteenth century, middle-class opponents of English rule and cultural dominance clung to the Italian language and the Catholic religion, abandoning Maltese as backward. The proponents of Maltese language renewal, on the other hand, embraced pro-English nationalist politics. As writers worked to formalize Maltese, politicians debated the elimination of "foreign" elements, particularly Italian vocabulary and constructions. The influence of these debates upon the Maltese community in Egypt is difficult to discern, yet it forms an essential feature of the Maltese attraction to and repulsion from identification with Britain. *Encyclopedia of the Languages of Europe* (Oxford: Blackwell, 1998), 317; Henry Frendo, "National Identity," in *Malta: Culture and Identity*, ed. Henry Frendo and Oliver Friggieri (Malta: Ministry of Youth and the Arts, 1994), 14–15.

42. For a discussion of the Maltese language, see "Malta" in *Encyclopedia of Islam* 2. In 1837, the British consul in Alexandria suggested that linguistic affinity meant Maltese migrants preferred Arabic-speaking regions to Turkish-speaking regions of the Ottoman Empire. Charles Archibald Price, *Malta and the Maltese: A Study in Nineteenth-Century Migration* (Melbourne: Georgian House, 1954), 89.

43. Clancy-Smith, *Mediterraneans*; Ulrike Freitag, ed., *The City in the Ottoman Empire: Migration and the Making of Urban Modernity* (Abingdon: Routledge, 2011); Akram Fouad Khater, *Inventing Home: Emigration, Gender, and the Middle Class in Lebanon, 1870-1920* (Berkeley: University of California Press, 2001); Claude Moatti and Wolfgang Kaiser, eds., *Gens de passage en Méditerranée de l'antiquité à l'époque moderne: procédures de contrôle et d'identification* (Paris: Maisonneuve & Larose, 2007).

44. The Maltese population, numbering 150,000 during the 1880s, was one of the most densely settled in the world. During the second half of the century, the Maltese islands were home to the British fleet in the Mediterranean and the center of intensive British investment. Employment in the British navy and administration offered intermittent relief to only some of the islands' underemployed, however. See Price, *Malta and the Maltese*.

45. FO 881/5968.

46. See, for example, FO 847/45/33.

47. FO 847/11/8.

48. FO 847/52/47. It appears that this sort of house was distinguished from the *okelle*, a shared house for more affluent tenants.

49. FO 847/11/16, 847/12/45, 78/3955/37 (Burrell to FO, September 6, 1886). This brawl occurred several months before the fight described in the opening pages of chapter 1.

50. Of course, their use of the term could have been in response to cross-examination, as it came in the later part of their testimony.

51. There is an example of such use in FO 847/2/63.

52. *Ajnabi*, the most frequent term for foreigners today, does not appear in the court and police records. Another term, *jins* (type or genus), invoked category or even ethnicity. For example, local authorities classified a Maltese as *malti al-jins* in FO 847/18/16.

53. FO 847/30/5.

54. FO 847/11/8. In similar cases only one month apart, two different category practices are employed by the local authorities: a Maltese who attacked an Italian and was pursued by Arabs is consistently called "European," even after his identity has been established; in another case, a Maltese who attacked an Arab is consistently identified as "Maltese." FO 847/3/20 and 3/27. See also FO 847/2/51. In official correspondence with the consulate, local authorities often used a direct Arabic translation of the official category "Maltese British subject" (*shakhs malti raʿiyat il-inkliz*). See, for example, FO 847/2/47.

55. Uncertainty about nationality was relatively common. See, for instance, a brawl in which witnesses struggled to define who was doing the fighting—Maltese, Italians, Greeks, or others (FO 847/35/13)—or a case against an individual who was

considered British, then rejected by the consulate, then demonstrated definitively to be British once his real name was established (FO 847/40/75, with additional files in FO 847/40/64).

56. See, for instance, the cases of Charles Helfield, who worked confidence numbers in Rome, Alexandria, Cairo, and Port Said. The Alexandria consular court sentenced him to three months in prison for taking money from the inspector of the Alexandria port by promising to see that his son found a place at the Scotch School. Helfield possessed a set of purloined official stamps that he used in his rackets. FO 847/29/30.

57. FO 847/15/42.

58. See Harold Tollefson, *Policing Islam: The British Occupation of Egypt and the Anglo-Egyptian Struggle Over Control of the Police, 1882-1914* (Westport, Conn.: Greenwood, 2000), 104.

59. James C. Scott, *Weapons of the Weak: Everyday Forms of Peasant Resistance* (New Haven, Conn.: Yale University Press, 1985).

60. FO 847/35/14.

61. FO 847/10/30, 847/10/31.

62. FO 847/46/8.

63. FO 847/32/7. Barlow died from a gunshot, not drowning. Patrolmen had seen a shot flash on the beach at night. Though they had no orders to investigate, they kept sharp watch and eventually found the body, but no revolver. In the morning, the caracol commander had the body photographed and inspected the guns of the coastguardsmen who found it. The British inquest into Barlow's death was very searching regarding police procedures, suspicious that the guardsmen shot him or pilfered the body. It was decided that the police had performed correctly, though, and the death was ruled a suicide.

64. For similar findings on clothing and identification, see Clancy-Smith, *Mediterraneans*, 58–59.

8. Foreigners

1. Ministère des Affaires Étrangères, Centre des Archives Diplomatiques de Nantes (CADN), Fonds Alexandrie: Jugements (AJ) 534/pp55, 57b, 58b.

2. Mahmood Mamdani, "Beyond Settler and Native as Political Identities: Overcoming the Political Legacy of Colonialism," *Comparative Studies in Society and History* 43, no. 4 (2001): 651–664.

3. For an example of exclusion in the British context, see Renisa Mawani, "Specters of Indigeneity in British-Indian Migration, 1914," *Law and Society Review* 46, no. 2 (2012): 369–403.

4. Archives d'outre mer, Aix-en-Provence (AOM) Fond Ministeriels 1AFFPOL/1294 (Extraits d'une note de la Legation de France au Caire en date du 8 juillet 1939).

5. Seven thousand Maltese were evacuated from Alexandria in 1882, and the number of Maltese in Alexandria in 1885 was estimated at four thousand. Charles

Archibald Price, *Malta and the Maltese: A Study in Nineteenth-Century Migration* (Melbourne: Georgian House, 1954), 137, 230. The 1888–1889 consular census counted 1,960 Maltese (National Archives of the UK: Foreign Office [FO] 881/5968), and the 1907 Egyptian census counted 3,416 Maltese. Foreign offices in London and Paris issued occasional demands that imperial subjects be counted, but these were half-heartedly applied in Alexandria. Consulates often complained about the burden of administrating imperial subjects and were happy to count only those who turned up to be registered. As a result, population figures in the 1888–1889 census of British subjects and its French counterparts are underestimates. Registered subjects may have constituted one-fifth to one-third of the total subject population. For more details on counting, see chapter 4.

6. Before Napoleon's invasion in 1798, Malta was an enemy of the Ottoman Empire. It was also a small state. For both reasons, it had signed no capitulation agreement, despite the importance of its contacts with the eastern Mediterranean.

7. Based on a count of census and registration figures in FO 881/5968, CADN, Fonds Alexandrie: Recensement—Algériens (RA) 46–51; and CADN, Fonds Alexandrie: Recensement—Tunisiens (RT) 69–73. Adult children of Maltese and Maghribis did not normally register until they set up their own household or their parents died. For this reason, it is likely that more than half of the entire adult population of Maltese and Maghribis was Egyptian born.

8. This law code, made up of Orders in Council (beginning with that of June 1844), was updated in the course of the century but not replaced.

9. Unlike the Maltese, certain categories of Maghribis were granted French citizenship, and the legal status of North African subjects was a major concern for French colonial administrators.

10. Sometimes, however, one would be crossed out and another substituted. Note that about thirty French citizens are labeled "*sujets français*" in the records of the consular court. I have yet to establish the reason for this apparent extra category. Shifting nomenclature parallels the changing names of registration certificates.

11. In an Arabic deposition from 1880, for instance, a soldier called his Maltese assailant a "European" (*shakhs urubawi*). S. F. Huri, the consulate's translator, faithfully rendered the term "European" the first time he encountered it. When it appeared a second time, he translated it as "Maltese," which was both a correction and a specification. FO 847/2/51. See FO 847/36/11 for another case of a victim calling the Maltese accused a "European."

12. The administrative distinction between citizen and subject was more obvious than the judicial distinction: they used different consular offices but the same court.

13. And further. Consular fears of subjects' criminality stretch back to the early nineteenth century. Criminality was associated with mobility—not the respectable mobility of first-class foreigners (holidays at home, employment transfers) but that of the poor.

14. It is impossible to evaluate conviction rates for the British consular court using extant records. British officials preserved various dossiers of evidence but no

systematic record of outcomes; French officials preserved comprehensive records of hearings and outcomes but no dossiers of evidence.

15. This attitude is in evidence in Price, *Malta and the Maltese*. Subjects of the Ionian Islands were also a source of concern.

16. French consular officials developed elaborate tests of loyalty that they used to establish the worthiness of Algerian subjects; more on this in chapter 8.

17. AOM Fond Ministeriels 1AFFPOL/1294 (Extraits d'une note de la Legation de France au Caire en date du 8 juillet 1939). The rules governing Algerian registration were the capitulations of the Dey of Algiers of October 5, 1830, and the detailed instructions concerning the protection of Algerians in the Levant of the Department of Foreign Affairs of January 1, 1834.

18. Maltese notable families certainly existed in greater numbers than the twenty families estimated by Price, *Malta and the Maltese*, 148.

19. These assessors were chosen by lot from a list of individuals designated as respectable by the consular staff. Jury duty demanded fluency in English, a fact that may have influenced the number of Maltese invited to serve.

20. FO 847/23/9.

21. It is also extraordinary that Bassim was in possession of a British registration certificate. Clearly he found some use for foreign nationality.

22. CADN-AJ 527/#35/p97, 528/#46, 530/#16, 530/#23, 531/#28, 532/#25.

23. During the carriage ride to the police station, he routinely attempted to hide the stolen goods on the person of his accomplice, and they always accused each other.

24. The documents preserved by the British consular court rarely indicate case outcomes, so it is impossible to consider in any systematic way the ultimate fate of cases involving Maltese plaintiffs or defendants. French cases do offer this possibility.

25. These figures are based on a preliminary count of 244 cases with clear outcomes, involving clearly identified Maghribi defendants.

26. A third of sentences invoked article 486 of the Code Pénal, which reduced sentences for any manner of attenuating circumstances. After a law permitting suspension of sentences was introduced in 1899, it was applied to one-fifth of sentences. This estimate is based on my own count of sentences. The sentence-suspension law is article 1 of the Loi du 26 mars 1891.

27. French law carried special penalties for those who committed crimes (especially assault and insults) against government agents on duty.

28. Of seventy-five such cases against Maghribis during the period in question, sixty-two ended in convictions.

29. It is not irrelevant that police and religious officials were important to the Egyptian nationalist movement, which fed in large part on resentment of foreign privilege.

30. FO 847/3/17.

31. Allouch was sentenced to eighteen months in prison for the assault, and the fraud case was referred to the Supreme Court at Aix. CADN-AJ 537/p65, 537/p93.

32. CADN-AJ 532/#21.

33. CADN-AJ 530/#3, 530/#17, 531/#56. He was sentenced to terms of eight days, three months, and six months in prison.
34. CADN-AJ 537/p119.
35. CADN-AJ 537/p91b.
36. See CADN-AJ 534/pp10, 10b, 13, in which plaintiff doesn't appear to pay caution or to support the consulate's prosecution, which is abandoned.
37. This is why claims to foreignness, even by those without such status, were so desirable. Those who lost their foreign status in legal challenges had as much or more social power to lose as they did legal power.
38. The British court tried a dozen such cases each year, and the French about fifteen.
39. CADN-AJ 521/#6.
40. As we will see, the consular court was often enlisted to contest or enforce *mahkama* decisions.
41. FO 847/17/16, 847/17/22, 847/24/22, 847/29/5, and others.
42. FO 847/36/7.
43. See, for example, FO 847/39/30.
44. For examples, see FO 847/22/47, 29/11 (naming "Mr. Inglott" as a benefactor), and 36/2. The British consulate provided some support, too, compelling the Maltese government to pay for relief of impoverished Maltese and paying relief for Egyptians born of Maltese origin out of Foreign Office funds.
45. Investigating an unidentified body, Constable Whitfield writes, "I sent for Mr. Mirabita who knows many Maltese in Malta and also Mr Themistocle Axisa to find out whether he was any relation of theirs or whether they could throw any light as to who he was" (FO 847/30/5). In a case of indecent assault on a little girl in Port Said, the consul reports the justice of the crowd: "I heard that shortly afterwards the Maltese had arrested the prisoner" (FO 847/22/39).
46. FO 847/36/4 contains an interesting Italian-language document confirming the identity of a Maltese British subject. The Maltese priest who produced the document marked it with the seal of the "colonia maltese," claiming quasi-official status.
47. FO 847/28/16.
48. CADN-AJ 521/#58; 553, pp. 3–4.
49. The capitulatory powers refused to recognize Persia as a member of the body administering the Mixed Courts.
50. Karen M. Kern, *Imperial Citizen: Marriage and Citizenship in the Ottoman Frontier Provinces of Iraq* (Syracuse, N.Y.: Syracuse University Press, 2011).
51. One of the greatest colloquial poets of early twentieth-century Egypt was in fact a Maghribi, Bayram al-Tunisi. Born in Alexandria in 1893, he came to prominence during the First World War. His postwar banishment from Egypt and circuit of exile between Tunisia, France, and Syria mirrors the odysseys of hundreds of other Maghribis. His brilliant use of the local idiom is a token of Maghribi fluency. See Marilyn Booth, *Bayram al-Tunisi's Egypt: Social Criticism and Narrative Strategies* (Oxford: Ithaca, 1990).

52. The local sentence, for beating causing death, was immediately set aside, and the Algerian was sent to Aix on charge of unintentional homicide. I have been unable to discover the verdict of the trial at Aix. CADN-AJ 538/p42, Cour d'Appel d'Aix archives, Archives Départementales des Bouches-du-Rhône, Centre d'Aix-en-Provence (CAA) 2u2 392.

53. Julia A. Clancy-Smith, *Mediterraneans: North Africa and Europe in an Age of Migration, C. 1800–1900* (Berkeley: University of California Press, 2011), 8, 48–53.

54. FO 847/6/49. Note that Buhagiar's first name is misspelled by the scribe or officer who recognized his surname's Arabic roots. The first name remained foreign gibberish, the accurate spelling of which was unnecessary.

55. This was not merely an urban phenomenon. Maltese and Maghribi colonies in villages and towns were if anything more egregious in their insistence on privilege: e.g., the Tunisian Mekaoui clan in Bichbiche. CADN-AJ 534/p118, 536/p28, 537/p76.

56. In T. H. Marshall, *Citizenship and Social Class, and Other Essays* (Cambridge: Cambridge University Press, 1950), notably applied to the context of the French mandates in Syria and Lebanon in Elizabeth Thompson, *Colonial Citizens: Republican Rights, Paternal Privilege, and Gender in French Syria and Lebanon* (New York: Columbia University Press, 2000), 113.

57. It has been shown that such progress is never inexorable, for instance, and that it suffers reverses.

58. The civil rights that they lacked (jury duty, sitting as assessors, and so on) are somewhat political, in that they involve voting.

59. A partial list of these rights includes provision of a prosecutor, trial by jury (of metropolitan citizens), appeal, and the right to prosecute (citizens), right to a formal inquest, passports, welfare, and oversight of inheritance. In the Maghribi case, the right to appeal to the Supreme Court at Aix was only offered to Algerians and Tunisians outside of Algeria and Tunisia. In the Maltese case, lines of division between the Foreign Office and Colonial Office were complicated by this situation.

60. This closure was often a question of transportation. See Radhika Viyas Mongia, "Race, Nationality, Mobility: A History of the Passport," *Public Culture* 11, no. 3 (1999): 527–555.

61. Muhammad al-Muwaylihi, *Hadith ʿIsa ibn Hisham, aw fatrah min al-zaman* (Cairo: Kalimat, 2013), 222.

9. Protégés

1. National Archives of the UK: Foreign Office (FO) 847/36/13.

2. Maurits H. van den Boogert, *The Capitulations and the Ottoman Legal System: Qadis, Consuls, and Beratlis in the Eighteenth Century* (Leiden: Brill, 2005).

3. The fundamental law governing protégé status in the late nineteenth century was the *Règlement relatif aux consulats étrangers d'août 1863*, along with its 1865 addendum. These are reproduced in Pierre Arminjon, *Étrangers et protégés dans l'Empire ottoman* (A. Chevalier-Maresq & cie, 1903), 325–330.

4. Edhem Eldem, Daniel Goffman, and Bruce Alan Masters, *The Ottoman City Between East and West: Aleppo, Izmir, and Istanbul* (Cambridge: Cambridge University Press, 1999), 194.

5. Abdul-Karim Rafeq, "Ownership of Real Property by Foreigners in Syria, 1869 to 1873," in *New Perspectives on Property and Land in the Middle East*, ed. Roger Owen (Cambridge, Mass.: Harvard University Press, 2001), 175–240; Sibel Zandi-Sayek, *Ottoman Izmir: The Rise of a Cosmopolitan Port, 1840–1880* (Minneapolis: University of Minnesota Press, 2012).

6. Leila Tarazi Fawaz, *Merchants and Migrants in Nineteenth-Century Beirut* (Cambridge, Mass.: Harvard University Press, 1983), chap. 7.

7. FO 847/40/75.

8. *Al-Mu'ayyad* (Cairo) 796, September 28, 1892.

9. Salahi R. Sonyel, "The Protégé System in the Ottoman Empire," *Journal of Islamic Studies* 2, no. 1 (1991): 57.

10. Feroz Ahmad, "Ottoman Perceptions of the Capitulations, 1800–1914," *Journal of Islamic Studies* 11, no. 1 (2000): 9, 18; more generally (and consistently) Turan Kayaoğlu, *Legal Imperialism: Sovereignty and Extraterritoriality in Japan, the Ottoman Empire, and China* (Cambridge: Cambridge University Press, 2010).

11. Timur Kuran, *The Long Divergence: How Islamic Law Held Back the Middle East* (Princeton, N.J.: Princeton University Press, 2011), 171, also 198. Kuran attributes violence against minorities in 1860, during the First World War, and so on to resentment of their economic position; even intercommunal animosities in the twenty-first century are an effect. Ibid., 189, 208.

12. The Aleppo figures are taken from H. A. R. Gibb and Harold Bowen, *Islamic Society and the West: A Study of the Impact of Western Civilization on Moslem Culture in the Near East* (London: Oxford University Press, 1967), 310–311. For further critique of this figure, see van den Boogert, *Capitulations*, 85.

13. Britain came to appreciate the significance of these limits after it assumed control of Egypt in 1882. For decades to follow, it pursued the abolition of the capitulations system that it had previously supported.

14. The best study of this phenomenon is van den Boogert, *Capitulations*.

15. Richard S. Horowitz, "International Law and State Transformation in China, Siam, and the Ottoman Empire During the Nineteenth Century," *Journal of World History* 15, no. 4 (2004): 461, citing Soussa; Michael Haag, *Alexandria: City of Memory* (New Haven, Conn.: Yale University Press, 2004), 17.

16. van den Boogert, *Capitulations*, 92.

17. Bruce McGowan reports a total population of 25 to 32 million in 1800. Halil Inalcik and Donald Quataert, eds., *An Economic and Social History of the Ottoman Empire, 1300–1914* (New York: Cambridge University Press, 1994), 646.

18. "Returns to Foreign Office Circular dated April 15, 1856 of Persons enjoying British Protection in the Levant," Foreign Office Confidential Print (FO 881/768).

19. "Returns of British-Protected Subjects in the Ottoman Dominions, 1887–89," Foreign Office Confidential Print 5968, July 1890 (FO 881/5968). Port Said reports only two of each (though Gustafux Adolphus Eoll, a Swedish Protestant missionary, had eleven children).

20. Certificates of protection expired at the end of every calendar year and had to be renewed after January 1. Of the six "Protégé Certificates" that the French consulate in Alexandria issued to Faridé Asfar between 1883 and 1889, the highest numbered was 10. This meant that by June 17, 1885, when the certificate in question was issued, only nine other French protégés had registered in Alexandria. Ministère des Affaires Étrangères, Centre des Archives Diplomatiques de Nantes (CADN), Fonds Alexandrie: Recensement—Algériens (RA) 48/1152.

21. The literature on American citizenship makes this abundantly clear. Linda Bosniak, *The Citizen and the Alien: Dilemmas of Contemporary Membership* (Princeton, N.J.: Princeton University Press, 2006).

22. But although Boogert and I dismiss this account, our counts do not directly contradict it: the Aleppo situation was outrageous because the claimants were illegitimate, whereas our counts only consider the legitimate.

23. *Archives Diplomatiques* XIV (1885), 152, reported in Arminjon, *Étrangers et protégés.*

24. On equality and its discontents, see Ussama Makdisi, *The Culture of Sectarianism: Community, History, and Violence in Nineteenth-Century Ottoman Lebanon* (Berkeley: University of California Press, 2000).

25. Sarah Abrevaya Stein, "Protected Persons? The Baghdadi Jewish Diaspora, the British State, and the Persistence of Empire," *American Historical Review* 116, no. 1 (2011): 85.

26. Arminjon, *Étrangers et protégés*, 261.

27. Prominent examples include George Cogordan, *Droit des gens: la nationalité au point de vue des rapports internationaux*, 2nd ed. (Paris, 1890); Ludwig von Bar, *The Theory and Practice of Private International Law*, trans. G. R. Gillespie, 2nd ed. (Edinburgh, 1892); John Westlake and Alfred Frank Topham, *A Treatise on Private International Law: With Principal Reference to Its Practice in England* (London: Sweet & Maxwell, 1905); Albert Venn Dicey and Arthur Berriedale Keith, *A Digest of the Law of England with Reference to the Conflict of Laws* (London: Stevens, 1922).

28. His major sources are M. Féraud-Giraud, *Traité de la juridiction française dans les échelles de Levant et de Barbarie*, 2nd ed. (Paris, 1886); Francis Rey, *De la protection diplomatique et consulaire dans les échelles du Levant et de Barbarie* (Paris, 1899); and especially Clunet's *Journal du Droit International* (1874–). He depends primarily, however, on the legislation text itself.

29. This literature is too large to mention, but this oversight is particularly notable in works such as Engin Fahri Isin, *Being Political: Genealogies of Citizenship* (Minneapolis: University of Minnesota Press, 2002).

30. The "strong" and "weak" typology appears in Charles Tilly, "The Emergence of Citizenship in France and Elsewhere," in *Citizenship, Identity, and Social History* (Cambridge: Cambridge University Press, 1996), 223–236.

31. Arminjon, *Étrangers et protégés*, 262.

32. Ibid., 263.

33. ʿAbd al-Hamid Abu Haif, *Al-Qanun al-Duwali al-Khass fi Awruba wa Masr* (Cairo: Matbaʿat al-Iʿtimad, 1924), 197–198.

34. Paul Weis, *Nationality and Statelessness in International Law*, 2nd ed. (Alphen aan den Rijn: Sijthoff & Noordhoff, 1979), 29–30.

35. Notably, James Harry Scott, *The Law Affecting Foreigners in Egypt as the Result of the Capitulations, with an Account of Their Origin and Development* (Edinburgh: W. Green and Sons, 1908); Gérard Pélissié du Rausas, *Le régime des capitulations dans l'Empire ottoman*, 2nd ed., 2 vols. (Paris: A. Rousseau, 1910); Philip Marshall Brown, *Foreigners in Turkey; Their Juridical Status.* (Princeton, N.J.: Princeton University Press, 1914); Abu Haif, *Al-Qanun al-Duwali al-Khass.* See also a study that preceded Arminjon: Rey, *De la protection diplomatique et consulaire dans les échelles du Levant et de Barbarie.*

36. Arnulf Becker Lorca, "Universal International Law: Nineteenth-Century Histories of Imposition and Appropriation," *Harvard International Law Journal* 51 (2010): 475–552.

37. Protection as construed in private international law should not be confused with protection as it appears in public international law of the late nineteenth and twentieth centuries: one state's "protectorate" over another, for instance in the form of French and British mandates after the First World War under the League of Nations. See Abu Haif, *Al-Qanun al-Duwali al-Khass*, 198.

38. For an outline of this argument, see Will Hanley, "Statelessness: An Invisible Theme in the History of International Law," *European Journal of International Law* 25, no. 1 (February 2014): 321–327.

39. Details from FO 78/3581 (Cookson to Granville #44, June 7, 1883).

40. The Foreign Office approved Zananiri's petition "conditionally on a reconsideration of the question should their right to British Protection be disputed by the Egyptian Government." FO 78/3581 (FO to Cookson #46, July 2, 1883). Zananiri's estate was handled by the British consulate (FO 847/26/6). His six sons are all but absent from the consular files thereafter, but FO 847/131 (Estate of J. Zananiri, 1935) may well be the estate of his son Joseph.

41. FO 78/4153 (Cookson to Salisbury #30, November 30, 1888).

42. FO 78/4153 (FO to Alexandria #3, 1889).

43. The file contains reference to a final note from Baring, not included, which presumably ended ʿAbd al-Munʿim's protection. His name does not appear in the list of protected persons produced the next year (FO 881/5968).

44. Arminjon, *Étrangers et protégés.*

45. Ibid.

46. This was the case of Alexandre Hanna Dimitri, son of a protégé in Damietta, in 1880 (CADN-RA 46/1080).

47. CADN-RA 46/1074. Haim was particularly assiduous in renewing his protection. His consular dossier shows that he renewed his certificate every year, without fail, from 1880 to 1904.

48. This appears to be correct information: many Argis appear in the registers of the British consulate of Alexandria.

49. His 1907 registration certificate is found in his widow's dossier (CADN-RA 56/1712).

50. CADN-RA 441/1175. Even at this late date, however, red herrings continued to emerge. A 1946 explanation of the cancellation stated that the family had no right to *"sujétion algérienne,"* a status which was never mentioned at any previous point.

51. FO 369/369.

52. Compare Adam McKeown, *Melancholy Order: Asian Migration and the Globalization of Borders* (New York: Columbia University Press, 2008).

53. Arminjon, *Étrangers et protégés*, 261.

54. Article 32 of the 1740 French-Ottoman capitulations treaty.

55. Arminjon, *Étrangers et protégés*, 271.

56. Ibid., 268–269.

57. Here the public international law sense of protection, discounted in note 37 above, applies.

58. Weis, *Nationality and Statelessness*, 18–20.

59. Consider Theodore Sava, discussed in the introduction, or Nicola Adamidis, discussed in chapter 11.

60. FO 847/28/15.

61. Ottoman Order in Council, 1899.

62. Dar al-Wathaʾiq al-Qawmiya, Cairo (DWQ) 0075–018655. Thanks to Matt Ellis for sharing this information with me.

63. Selim Deringil, *Conversion and Apostasy in the Late Ottoman Empire* (Cambridge: Cambridge University Press, 2012).

64. See the *Règlement sur les consulats étrangers* of August 1863, along with its addendum of December 20, 1865.

65. On emancipation and its discontents, see Makdisi, *Culture of Sectarianism*.

66. CADN-RA 46/1016.

67. CADN-RA 46/1053.

68. CADN-RA 46/1063.

69. CADN-RA 46/1098.

70. CADN-RA 48/1169. He and his wife traveled with two servants and a cook.

71. CADN-RA 46/1045.

72. CADN-RA 48/1168. The file gives no justification beyond an 1882 registration certificate from Cairo.

73. CADN-RA 46/1076.

74. CADN-RA 46/1099.

75. CADN-RA 50/1275.

76. Notably Stein, "Protected Persons?"; Mary Dewhurst Lewis, *Divided Rule: Sovereignty and Empire in French Tunisia, 1881-1938* (Berkeley: University of California Press, 2013).

77. For instance, Ziad Fahmy, "Jurisdictional Borderlands: Extraterritoriality and 'Legal Chameleons' in Precolonial Alexandria, 1840–1870," *Comparative Studies in Society and History* 55, no. 2 (2013): 305–329.

78. See citation in judgment notes, FO 847/36/1. The judge applied the same reasoning to Adamidis's attempts to join the British and the Greek communities in Alexandria.

10. Bad Subjects

1. This from a charge sheet enclosed in the National Archives of the UK: Foreign Office (FO) 78/4392 #13 (Cookson to Salisbury, March 25, 1891), which lists four prison sentences.
2. FO 847/8/33.
3. FO 847/11/16.
4. FO 847/19/11. For another example of administrative pretext as means of exclusion, see studies of the requirement that British subjects arriving in Vancouver must arrive after an uninterrupted voyage, effectively excluding South Asian immigration: Radhika Viyas Mongia, "Race, Nationality, Mobility: A History of the Passport," *Public Culture* 11, no. 3 (1999): 527–555; Renisa Mawani, "Specters of Indigeneity in British-Indian Migration, 1914," *Law and Society Review* 46, no. 2 (2012): 369–403.
5. On guarantees in eighteenth-century Istanbul, see Fariba Zarinebaf, *Crime and Punishment in Istanbul: 1700–1800* (Berkeley: University of California Press, 2011), 78, 92, 132–133. On guarantees for laborers in mid–nineteenth century Egypt, see Ehud R. Toledano, *State and Society in Mid-Nineteenth-Century Egypt* (Cambridge: Cambridge University Press, 1990), chap. 10.
6. For vivid descriptions of arrivals in Port Said, see Valeska Huber, *Channelling Mobilities: Migration and Globalisation in the Suez Canal Region and Beyond, 1869–1914* (Cambridge: Cambridge University Press, 2013).
7. In the present day, loss of citizenship does not always lead automatically to a clear alternative status. See further discussion of this point in chapter 13.
8. FO 847/19/11. This stark statement only appeared in the draft letter, however; the final text left this conclusion implicit.
9. Cookson to Gould, telegram of July 2, 1892, enclosed in FO 874/19/11.
10. FO 847/19/11. The note on the back of the telegram of July 2, 1892, reads "Mr Ghandoor, this man must be sent off first opportunity to Malta from SS funds or permanent allowance. CC."
11. On this topic, see Adam McKeown, *Melancholy Order: Asian Migration and the Globalization of Borders* (New York: Columbia University Press, 2008); Jane Caplan and John C. Torpey, eds., *Documenting Individual Identity: The Development of State Practices in the Modern World* (Princeton, N.J.: Princeton University Press, 2001); John C. Torpey, *The Invention of the Passport: Surveillance, Citizenship, and the State* (New York: Cambridge University Press, 2000); Clifford D. Rosenberg, *Policing Paris: The Origins of Modern Immigration Control Between the Wars* (Ithaca, N.Y.: Cornell University Press, 2006).
12. On vagrancy, see Lionel Rose, *Rogues and Vagabonds: Vagrant Underworld in Britain, 1815-1985* (London: Routledge, 1988); Aravind Ganachari, " 'White Man's Embarrassment': European Vagrancy in Nineteenth-Century Bombay," *Economic and Political Weekly* 37, no. 25 (June 22, 2002): 2477–2486; A. L. Beier and Paul Ocobock, eds., *Cast Out: Vagrancy and Homelessness in Global and Historical Perspective* (Athens: Ohio University Press, 2009).

13. For example, Louis Chevalier, *Laboring Classes and Dangerous Classes in Paris During the First Half of the Nineteenth Century* (Princeton, N.J.: Princeton University Press, 1981); Andrew J. Major, "State and Criminal Tribes in Colonial Punjab: Surveillance, Control, and Reclamation of the 'Dangerous Classes,'" *Modern Asian Studies* 33, no. 3 (1999): 657–688.

14. Samera Esmeir, *Juridical Humanity: A Colonial History* (Stanford, Calif.: Stanford University Press, 2012); Timothy Mitchell, *Rule of Experts: Egypt, Techno-Politics, Modernity* (Berkeley: University of California Press, 2002). They draw especially on the work of Giorgio Agamben, *State of Exception* (Chicago: University of Chicago Press, 2005).

15. James C. Scott, *The Art of Not Being Governed: An Anarchist History of Upland Southeast Asia* (New Haven, Conn.: Yale University Press, 2009). Scott shifts the focus from the state to the unincorporated people but preserves the essential dynamic of state absorption. The large and varied body of literature is the global articulation of a perspective on marginality and governmentality in which Foucault looms large. Representative examples include Resat Kasaba, *A Moveable Empire: Ottoman Nomads, Migrants, and Refugees* (Seattle: University of Washington Press, 2009); Kenneth Pomeranz, *The Making of a Hinterland: State, Society, and Economy in Inland North China, 1853–1937* (Berkeley: University of California Press, 1993).

16. John T. Chalcraft, *The Striking Cabbies of Cairo and Other Stories: Crafts and Guilds in Egypt, 1873–1914* (Albany: SUNY Press, 2004).

17. Eric H. Monkkonen, *Police in Urban America, 1860–1920* (Cambridge: Cambridge University Press, 1981), 87.

18. See, for example, Tom Lloyd, "Thuggee, Marginality and the State Effect in Colonial India, circa 1770–1840," *Indian Economic and Social History Review* 45, no. 2 (2008): 201–237.

19. Ministère des Affaires Étrangères, Centre des Archives Diplomatiques de Nantes (CADN), Fonds Alexandrie: Jugements (AJ) 534/p48b.

20. Vagrancy was not itself an offense at the British consular courts, but it was a misdemeanor (*délit*) under the French penal code and Egyptian criminal law (which was derived from French law). Under the French penal code, vagrancy carried a three- to six-month sentence as well as a five- to ten-year ban on residence (*interdiction de séjour*).

21. CADN-AJ 535/p42b.

22. CADN-AJ 527/1892/#3. For another example of clemency, in which a Frenchman showed that he has a profession but particular circumstances made it impossible for him to exercise it, see CADN-AJ 531/1900/#30.

23. CADN-AJ 535/p104b.

24. CADN-AJ 534/p137.

25. National Archives of the United States, College Park, Maryland (USNA) 84/350/17/23/4.

26. CADN-AJ 530/1899/#29.

27. Julia A. Clancy-Smith, *Mediterraneans: North Africa and Europe in an Age of Migration, C. 1800–1900* (Berkeley: University of California Press, 2011); Ilham Khuri-Makdisi, *The Eastern Mediterranean and the Making of Global Radicalism, 1860–1914* (Berkeley: University of California Press, 2010); Leila Tarazi Fawaz and C. A. Bayly, eds., *Modernity and Culture: From the Mediterranean to the Indian Ocean* (New York: Columbia University

Press, 2002); Adam Mestyan, "Power and Music in Cairo: Azbakiyya," *Urban History* 40, no. 4 (2013): 681–704.

28. CADN-AJ 535/p16, 535/p27.

29. This accords with the findings of Ann Laura Stoler, "Rethinking Colonial Categories: European Communities and the Boundaries of Rule," *Comparative Studies in Society and History* 31, no. 1 (1989): 134–161.

30. FO 847/43/64.

31. "*fa-yara anna wafatahuma nashiʾatan ʿan idkhalihima ashkhasa bi-tarfihima bi-halat il-khafiya wa muʿamilatihima iyahum bi-halat al-tasatir.*" The tortured translation produced by the consular dragoman: "it appears that the cause of the murder was that they should have introduced clandestinely some persons into their premises and dealt with them in a secret manner." (FO 847/2/68).

32. CADN-AJ 529/1896/#19.

33. CADN-AJ 530/1898/#15, 530/1899/#13, 531/1900/#33, 532/p95, and the two cases cited below.

34. French laws to control recidivism were at the root of the push to identify individual subjects in the late nineteenth century. See Martine Kaluszynksi, "Republican Identity: Bertillonage as Government Technique," in *Documenting Individual Identity*, ed. Jane Caplan and John C. Torpey (Princeton, N.J.: Princeton University Press, 2001), 123–138.

35. CADN-AJ 533/p13b.

36. CADN-AJ 533/p122.

37. CADN-AJ 533/p24, 533/p77, 534/p136, 536/p196, 538/p164.

38. CADN-AJ 530/1899/#3, 530/1899/#17, 530/1899/#21, 531/1899/#56.

39. CADN-AJ 532/#21, 533/p26b, 533/p28. On the last charge, the tribunal elected not to send him to France for trial, but it sentenced him to seven months nevertheless. CADN-AJ 534/p72, 534/p78.

40. CADN-AJ 533/p66, 533/p110.

41. Nathan Brown, "Brigands and State Building: The Invention of Banditry in Modern Egypt," *Comparative Studies in Society and History* 32, no. 2 (1990): 258–281; Rebecca Bryant, "Bandits and 'Bad Characters': Law as Anthropological Practice in Cyprus, c. 1900," *Law and History Review* 21, no. 2 (2003): 243–270; Anne Marie Clément, "Fallahin on Trial in Colonial Egypt: Apprehending the Peasantry Through Orality, Writing, and Performance (1884–1914)" (Ph.D. dissertation, University of Toronto, 2012); Kasaba, *A Moveable Empire*; Eugene L. Rogan, *Frontiers of the State in the Late Ottoman Empire: Transjordan, 1850–1921* (New York: Cambridge University Press, 1999); Karen Barkey, *Bandits and Bureaucrats: The Ottoman Route to State Centralization* (Ithaca, N.Y.: Cornell University Press, 1994).

42. For an 1883 example of state prosecution of *qatʿ al-tariq*, see Dar al-Wathaʾiq al-Qawmiya, Cairo, Dabtiya Iskandariya (DWQ-DI) 738/358.

43. Brown, "Brigands and State Building."

44. For the Egyptian government's definition of vagrancy, see Harold Tollefson, *Policing Islam: The British Occupation of Egypt and the Anglo-Egyptian Struggle over Control of the Police, 1882–1914* (Westport, Conn.: Greenwood, 2000), 76.

45. Ann Laura Stoler, *Carnal Knowledge and Imperial Power: Race and the Intimate in Colonial Rule* (Berkeley: University of California Press, 2002).

46. Caitlin Anderson makes the link between transfer of the poor between parishes within Britain and repatriation as a means of dealing with distressed British subjects abroad. "Britons Abroad and Aliens at Home: Nationality Law and Policy in Britain 1815–70" (Ph.D. dissertation, Cambridge, 2004).

47. CADN, Fonds Alexandrie: Recensement—Tunisiens (RT) 71/206–10.

48. CADN-AJ 536/p84.

49. DWQ. I have not seen these cards myself, but I have images of three of them.

50. FO 847/43/64. The initial consular reply was quite guarded, reserving the right to deport and saying that the consulate had no record of previous searches or convictions.

51. Governor of Alexandria to British consul #59/30 of March 14, 1890, in FO 847/18/16.

52. FO 847/20/24.

53. No dossier is preserved for this case.

54. FO 847/21/3.

55. See explanation in FO 78/4459/25 (Cookson to FO, November 25, 1892).

56. See narrative in Tollefson, *Policing Islam*, chap. 3–4.

57. FO 847/52/48.

58. For a detailed critique, see Will Hanley, "Grieving Cosmopolitanism in Middle East Studies," *History Compass* 6, no. 5 (2008): 1346–1367.

59. See, for instance, Mine Ener, *Managing Egypt's Poor and the Politics of Benevolence, 1800–1952* (Princeton, N.J.: Princeton University Press, 2003); Michael David Bonner, Mine Ener, and Amy Singer, eds., *Poverty and Charity in Middle Eastern Contexts* (Albany: SUNY Press, 2003); Julia A. Clancy-Smith, "Europe and Its Social Marginals in Nineteenth-Century Mediterranean North Africa," in *Outside In*, ed. Eugene L. Rogan (London: I. B. Tauris, 2002), 149–182.

60. Ussama Makdisi, *The Culture of Sectarianism: Community, History, and Violence in Nineteenth-Century Ottoman Lebanon* (Berkeley: University of California Press, 2000); Hannah Arendt, *The Origins of Totalitarianism*, new ed. (New York: Harcourt Brace Jovanovich, 1973).

61. This project is suggested, in different ways, by Prasenjit Duara, *Rescuing History from the Nation: Questioning Narratives of Modern China* (Chicago: University of Chicago Press, 1995); Dipesh Chakrabarty, *Provincializing Europe: Postcolonial Thought and Historical Difference* (Princeton, N.J.: Princeton University Press, 2000).

62. This is the import of Rebecca Saunders, ed., *The Concept of the Foreign* (Lanham, Md.: Lexington, 2003).

11. Ottomans

1. Archivio Storico del Ministero degli Affari Esteri, Rome (ASMAE) Cairo 64/2/d. The case was not pursued.

2. Başbakanlık Osmanlı Arşivi, Istanbul (BOA) A.MTZ (05) 14-A.

3. The chief works in this vein include Ariel Salzmann, "An Ancien Regime Revisited: 'Privatization' and Political Economy in the Eighteenth-Century Ottoman Empire," *Politics and Society* 21, no. 4 (1993): 393–423; Dina Rizk Khoury, *State and Provincial Society in the Ottoman Empire: Mosul, 1540-1834* (Cambridge: Cambridge University Press, 1997); Eugene L. Rogan, *Frontiers of the State in the Late Ottoman Empire: Transjordan, 1850-1921* (New York: Cambridge University Press, 1999); Ussama Makdisi, *The Culture of Sectarianism: Community, History, and Violence in Nineteenth-Century Ottoman Lebanon* (Berkeley: University of California Press, 2000); Jens Hanssen, Thomas Philipp, and Stefan Weber, eds., *The Empire in the City: Arab Provincial Capitals in the Late Ottoman Empire* (Würzburg: Ergon in Kommission, 2002); Selim Deringil, " 'They Live in a State of Nomadism and Savagery': The Late Ottoman Empire and the Post-Colonial Debate," *Comparative Studies in Society and History* 45, no. 2 (2003): 311–342; Marc Aymes, "Provincialiser l'empire: Chypre et la Méditerranée ottomane au XIXe siècle," *Annales* 62, no. 6 (2007): 1313–1344. For a convenient summary (though emphasizing the eighteenth century), see Dina Rizk Khoury, "The Ottoman Centre vs. Provincial Power Holders," in *The Cambridge History of Turkey*, ed. Suraiya Faroqhi, vol. 3: *The Later Ottoman Empire, 1603-1839* (Cambridge: Cambridge University Press, 2006), 135–156.
4. This consensus is so widespread that Egypt's independence is assumed rather than argued. For a sense of the position, consult I. Gershoni and James P. Jankowski, *Egypt, Islam, and the Arabs: The Search for Egyptian Nationhood, 1900-1930* (New York: Oxford University Press, 1987); James P. Jankowski and Israel Gershoni, eds., *Rethinking Nationalism in the Arab Middle East* (New York: Columbia University Press, 1997); M. W. Daly, ed., *The Cambridge History of Egypt*, vol. 2: *Modern Egypt, from 1517 to the End of the Twentieth Century* (Cambridge: Cambridge University Press, 1998). But see Aimee M. Genell, "Empire by Law: Ottoman Sovereignty and the British Occupation of Egypt, 1882–1923" (Ph.D. diss., Columbia University, 2013).
5. 42 L. J. Ad. 17; *L. R. 4 A. & E. 59.*
6. For powerful summary interpretations of this broad literature, see Frederick Cooper, *Colonialism in Question: Theory, Knowledge, History* (Berkeley: University of California Press, 2005); Jane Burbank and Frederick Cooper, *Empires in World History: Power and the Politics of Difference* (Princeton, N.J.: Princeton University Press, 2010).
7. Much of this work has been decidedly Western in focus: Daniel Gorman, *Imperial Citizenship: Empire and the Question of Belonging* (Manchester: Manchester University Press, 2006). More interesting for my purposes is the fledgling literature on the citizenship of imperial subjects. The literature on French empire is notable here: Alice L. Conklin, *A Mission to Civilize: The Republican Idea of Empire in France and West Africa, 1895-1930* (Stanford, Calif.: Stanford University Press, 1997); Elizabeth Thompson, *Colonial Citizens: Republican Rights, Paternal Privilege, and Gender in French Syria and Lebanon* (New York: Columbia University Press, 2000); Gary Wilder, *The French Imperial Nation-State: Negritude and Colonial Humanism Between the Two World Wars* (Chicago: University of Chicago Press, 2005); Mary Dewhurst Lewis, *The Boundaries of the Republic: Migrant Rights and the Limits of Universalism in France, 1918-1940* (Stanford, Calif.: Stanford University Press, 2007).

8. Two promising preliminary interventions in this vein are Ariel Salzmann, "Citizens in Search of a State: The Limits of Political Participation in the Late Ottoman Empire," in *Extending Citizenship, Reconfiguring States*, ed. Michael P. Hanagan and Charles Tilly (Lanham, Md.: Rowman & Littlefield, 1999), 37–66; Engin Fahri Isin, "Citizenship After Orientalism: Ottoman Citizenship," in *Citizenship in a Global World: European Questions and Turkish Experiences*, ed. Fuat Keyman and Ahmet Icduygu (London: Routledge, 2005), 31–51. See also my "When Did Egyptians Stop Being Ottomans? An Imperial Citizenship Case Study," in *Multilevel Citizenship*, ed. Willem Maas (Philadelphia: University of Pennsylvania Press, 2013), 89–109.

9. All three terms are used, for example, in a case file from 1881 (National Archives of the UK: Foreign Office [FO] 847/3/17). See also Yoav Di-Capua, *Gatekeepers of the Arab Past: Historians and History Writing in Twentieth-Century Egypt* (Berkeley: University of California Press, 2009), 49–50.

10. Gershoni and Jankowski, *Egypt, Islam, and the Arabs*.

11. Classics of this literature includes C. Ernest Dawn, *From Ottomanism to Arabism: Essays on the Origins of Arab Nationalism* (Urbana: University of Illinois Press, 1973); Hasan Kayalı, *Arabs and Young Turks: Ottomanism, Arabism, and Islamism in the Ottoman Empire, 1908-1918* (Berkeley: University of California Press, 1997); Butrus Abu Manneh, "The Christians Between Ottomanism and Syrian Nationalism: The Ideas of Butrus al-Bustani," *International Journal of Middle East Studies* 2 (1980): 287–304; William L. Cleveland, *The Making of an Arab Nationalist: Ottomanism and Arabism in the Life and Thought of Satiʿ al-Husri* (Princeton, N.J.: Princeton University Press, 1971). More recently, see Hanssen, Philipp, and Weber, *The Empire in the City*; Abigail Jacobson, "Negotiating Ottomanism in Times of War: Jerusalem During World War I Through the Eyes of a Local Muslim Resident," *International Journal of Middle East Studies* 40, no. 1 (2008): 69–88; Michelle Campos, *Ottoman Brothers: Muslims, Christians, and Jews in Early Twentieth-Century Palestine* (Stanford, Calif.: Stanford University Press, 2010).

12. Ami Ayalon, *Language and Change in the Arab Middle East: The Evolution of Modern Political Discourse* (New York: Oxford University Press, 1987), 43–53.

13. Di-Capua, *Gatekeepers of the Arab Past*, 63 (quotation), 75, and *passim*.

14. Daniel Panzac, "The Population of Egypt in the Nineteenth Century," *Asian and African Studies* 21 (1987): 11–15.

15. Ibid., 26–27. Much of the jump in foreign numbers in 1917, for example, is attributable to the reclassification of more than 11,000 Ottoman foreigners who were previously considered local subjects.

16. Maurus Reinkowski, "Uncommunicative Communication: Competing Egyptian, Ottoman, and British Imperial Ventures in Nineteenth-Century Egypt," *Die Welt Des Islams* 54, no. 3–4 (2014): 399–422; Oded Peri, "Ottoman Symbolism in British-Occupied Egypt, 1882–1909," *Middle Eastern Studies* 41, no. 1 (2005): 103–120; Feroz Ahmad, "Mukhtār Pasha," in *Encyclopaedia of Islam* (Leiden: Brill, 1993); M. Cavid Baysun, "Muhtar Paşa," in *Diyanet İslâm Ansiklopedisi* (Istanbul: Türkiye Diyanet Vakfı, 1979).

17. Genell, "Empire by Law."

18. Details listed in Stefano G. Poffandi, ed., *1897 Indicateur Égyptien Administratif et Commercial*, 11th ed. (Alexandria, 1896), 51. BOA Y.PRK.MK 20/80 discusses the finances of the High Commission.

19. A certain Isma'il Sabri sent an Arabic-language letter under the title of *mutasarrif* of Alexandria to the Ottoman foreign ministry in 1899 (BOA Y.A.HUS 339/17). The Port Said agent Autiglise is mentioned in a letter of complaint from the Ottoman consul in Bombay concerning shoddy work in issuing passports (BOA A.MTZ [05] 29-B/270).

20. For example, BOA HR.HMŞ.İŞO 186/83, DH.MKT 2210/139, DH.MKT 796/62.

21. BOA HR.HMŞ.İŞO 140/15.

22. FO 847/2/47.

23. BOA DH.MKT 2667/93.

24. BOA DH.SN.THR 57/63.

25. BOA DH.MKT 1680/143, DH.MKT 182/15.

26. BOA DH.MKT 604/40.

27. Jurji Zaydan, *Yawmiyat rihla bahriya* (Damascus: Fajr al-Nahdah, 2010), 19–26. Thanks to Beth Holt for drawing my attention to this book.

28. Ibid., 20.

29. The phrase "*la hawla wa la quwwa illa bi-llah*" appears frequently in the text.

30. A reissued Ottoman novel on this episode is Bekir Fahri, *Jönler* (Istanbul: İletişim Yayınları, 1985). See also Wajda Sendesni, "Les Jeunes-Turcs en Égypte (1895–1908), histoire politique et intellectuelle" (Thèse de doctorat, École des hautes études en sciences sociales, 2009).

31. BOA HR.SYS 2781/1.

32. As an example, he cited the case of Atanik Eknayan.

33. See also BOA DH.TMIK.M 123/38, from May 1902, in which an Armenian notable travels to Alexandria and then to France, seeking foreign protection.

34. The archetypal model is adopted in Rogers Brubaker, *Citizenship and Nationhood in France and Germany* (Cambridge, Mass.: Harvard University Press, 1992); Patrick Weil, *How to Be French: Nationality in the Making Since 1789* (Durham, N.C.: Duke University Press, 2008).

35. T. H. Marshall, *Citizenship and Social Class, and Other Essays* (Cambridge: Cambridge University Press, 1950).

36. For the edict announcing Egyptian nationality, see *al-Waqa'i al-Misriya* (WM) 70, no. 74, July 4, 1900.

37. Gianluca Paolo Parolin, *Citizenship in the Arab World: Kin, Religion, and Nation-State* (Amsterdam: Amsterdam University Press, 2009).

38. Ibid., 74.

39. Ibid., 80.

40. Ibid., 74.

41. Ibid., 79.

42. Ibid., 75.

43. Ibid., 80.

44. The best elaboration of the provincial results of Tanzimat "emancipation" is Makdisi, *Culture of Sectarianism.*

45. BOA HR.HMŞ.İŞO 174/7. Thanks to Matt Ellis for giving me a copy of this dossier.

46. Dror Ze'evi, *Producing Desire: Changing Sexual Discourse in the Ottoman Middle East, 1500-1900* (Berkeley: University of California Press, 2006), 66.

47. Maurits H. van den Boogert, *The Capitulations and the Ottoman Legal System: Qadis, Consuls, and Beratlis in the Eighteenth Century* (Leiden: Brill, 2005), 33, citing Colin Imber.

48. BOA Ş.D 322/28.

49. BOA HR.HMŞ.İŞO 165/71. Also National Archives of the United States, College Park, Maryland (USNA) 84/350/17/23/4/2/6.

50. BOA HR.HMŞ.İŞO 169/7.

51. Arret of June 6, 1889, *Bulletin de législation et du jurisprudence égyptiennes* (BLJE) I: 145.

52. Arret of January 20, 1890, BLJE II: 107; Arret of 1890, BLJE I: 156, Arret of April 2, 1890, BLJE II: 398; Arret of June 11, 1909, BLJE II: 185. This jurisprudence goes back to the court's establishment in 1876, when it was ruled that consular certificates prove nationality for the purposes of the Mixed Tribunals and that it is not the court's business to probe the validity of the certificates (Arret of December 7, 1876, *Jurisprudence des tribunaux de la réforme en Égypte: recueil officiel* II: 38–41).

53. Arret of the Alexandria Court of Appeal, May 8, 1890, cited in Octave Borelli and Paul Ruelens, eds., *La législation Égyptienne annotée* (Bruxelles, 1892), 211.

54. See the discussion in chapter 12 of two Tunisian lawyers who became local subjects. CADN, Fonds Alexandrie (FA) 442 ("*Au sujet du changement de nationalité des tunisiens qui désirent acquérir la nationalité égyptienne, 1913-26*").

55. FO 847/6/25.

56. CADN, Fonds Alexandrie: Jugements (AJ) 516/36.

57. FO 847/27/5.

58. FO 847/39/35.

59. A similar inaccuracy characterizes the description of Ahmed Mohamed Bahadur, tried in the Native Courts for the murder of a British subject, as an "Ottoman subject" (FO 847/49/3).

60. FO 369/138.

61. FO 847/36/1, 847/43/54.

62. FO 847/43/54.

63. See, for instance, the list of naturalized subjects in the consular census of 1888–1889 (FO 881/5968).

64. FO 847/36/13. See also Nazan Maksudyan, "The Fight Over Nobody's Children: Religion, Nationality, and Citizenship of Foundlings in the Late Ottoman Empire," *New Perspectives on Turkey*, no. 41 (2009): 151–180.

65. CADN-AJ 537/p8. This proved advantageous for the widow Anissa, however: Ottoman nationality was not transferred to foreign wives, so when her husband died she reverted to her original status (inherited from her father), which was that of an Algerian French protégé.

66. CADN, Fonds Alexandrie: Recensement Algériens (RA) 46/1061 (1880), 51/1306, 51/1307, 51/1310 (1892) 53/1497 (1903), 58/1972 (1914). CADN, Fonds Alexandrie, Recensement Tunisiens (RT) 72/305 (1883).

67. BOA HR.HMŞ.İŞO 221/11.

68. BOA HR.HMŞ.İŞO 48/14.

69. Anhoury was a litigious individual. See *Bulletin de législation et du jurisprudence égyptiennes* (BLJE) 13 (1901), 21 and 14 (1902).

70. BOA DH.SN.THR 25/25; İ.HR 427/19.

71. BOA HR.SYS 2127/4.

72. FO 369/694/73092.

73. Key references include Dipesh Chakrabarty, *Provincializing Europe: Postcolonial Thought and Historical Difference* (Princeton, N.J.: Princeton University Press, 2000); Prasenjit Duara, *Rescuing History from the Nation: Questioning Narratives of Modern China* (Chicago: University of Chicago Press, 1995); Cooper, *Colonialism in Question*.

74. For a call to expand the European-dominated paradigm, based on Asian evidence of transnationalism, see Elaine Lynn-Ee Ho, "Citizenship, Migration, and Transnationalism: A Review and Critical Interventions," *Geography Compass* 2, no. 5 (2008): 1294–1296. She also argues that the literature on migration and citizenship suffers from an analytical bias toward receiving states (1292).

75. Signal examples of this work include Mahmood Mamdani, *Citizen and Subject: Contemporary Africa and the Legacy of Late Colonialism* (Princeton, N.J.: Princeton University Press, 1996).

76. For a discussion of the misuse of Middle Eastern history in liberal political imaginings, see my "Grieving Cosmopolitanism in Middle East Studies," *History Compass* 6, no. 5 (2008): 1346–1367.

12. Locals

1. The court's judgment was printed as "al-Hukm fi qadiyat al-ʿuthmaniyin," *Al-Ahram* (Cairo), June 16, 1898.

2. Despite gender, property, age, and literacy requirements, Cairo (for example) had more than sixty thousand registered voters for its single seat on the Legislative Council. Elections were held in 1883, 1889, 1895, 1901, 1907, and 1913. Quotation from Cromer, *Reports by His Majesty's Agent and Consul-General on the Finances, Administration, and Condition of Egypt and the Soudan* (1904), 10.

3. The appellants timed their appeal so as to miss the annual sitting of the voters' commission, preferring to have their case heard by the Native Court of Appeal.

4. The text of this law in Filib Jallad, *Qamus al-idarah wa-al-qadaʾ*, 3rd ed. (Cairo: Matbaʿat Dar al-Kutub wa-al-Wathaʾiq al-Qawmiya, 2003), 1312–1316.

5. I take *raʿiya* here to mean the collective "flock" rather than the singular "subject."

6. Ehud R. Toledano, *State and Society in Mid-Nineteenth-Century Egypt* (Cambridge: Cambridge University Press, 1990), 155.

7. Ibid., circa 177.

8. Harold Tollefson, *Policing Islam: The British Occupation of Egypt and the Anglo-Egyptian Struggle Over Control of the Police, 1882-1914* (Westport, Conn.: Greenwood, 2000), 36.

9. Alexander Kitroeff, *The Greeks in Egypt, 1919-1937: Ethnicity and Class* (London: Ithaca, 1989).

10. Nancy Y. Reynolds, *A City Consumed: Urban Commerce, the Cairo Fire, and the Politics of Decolonization in Egypt* (Stanford, Calif.: Stanford University Press, 2012).

11. For Egypt, Samera Esmeir, *Juridical Humanity: A Colonial History* (Stanford, Calif.: Stanford University Press, 2012). For the Pacific context, Adam McKeown, *Melancholy Order: Asian Migration and the Globalization of Borders* (New York: Columbia University Press, 2008).

12. The National Archives of the UK: Foreign Office (FO) 847/2/63. This case is discussed in chapter 5.

13. Sawsan Messiri, *Ibn al-Balad: A Concept of Egyptian Identity* (Leiden: Brill, 1978), 1–5, 19. Compare nineteenth-century Tunisia, where *baldi* was used for "notable" and *twansa* for "the allegedly 'authentic' inhabitants." Julia A. Clancy-Smith, *Mediterraneans: North Africa and Europe in an Age of Migration, C. 1800-1900* (Berkeley: University of California Press, 2011), 38.

14. Messiri, *Ibn al-Balad*, 14.

15. Kenneth M. Cuno and Michael J. Reimer, "The Census Registers of Nineteenth-Century Egypt: A New Source for Social Historians," *British Journal of Middle Eastern Studies* 24, no. 2 (1997): 204–205.

16. Toledano, *State and Society*, 151.

17. Messiri, *Ibn al-Balad*, 26.

18. Toledano traces the paths followed by *fallahin* (peasants) as they became *abna' al-balad* (city dwellers). *State and Society*, chap. 9. He provides clear evidence of the ways that migrants sought to integrate themselves into the existing urban fabric but does not show how that fabric changed by their advent. He endorses the centrality of city dwellers, when in fact Alexandria's nineteenth-century growth had an important rural aspect.

19. Michael Ezekiel Gasper, *The Power of Representation: Publics, Peasants, and Islam in Egypt* (Stanford, Calif.: Stanford University Press, 2009).

20. This was perhaps the meaning of the category "seminomads" that appears in the 1882 census.

21. See, for instance, FO 847/18/16, in which one accomplice of the Maltese bad subject was identified as an *ibn ʿarab*.

22. On the administration of bedouins to the west of the Nile delta, see Matthew Ellis, "Between Empire and Nation: The Emergence of Egypt's Libyan Borderland, 1841–1911" (Ph.D. diss., Princeton University, 2012).

23. "Imtiyazat al-ʿurban bi-masr: asluha wa masiruha," *Al-Hilal* 14 (1904): 212–214.

24. The comparison with the separate nationality of Native Americans bears comparison. In her seminal article on American citizenship, for example, Linda Kerber consistently writes about individuals and the way that they affiliate legally with states.

In her discussion of Indians, however, she writes mostly of nations rather than nationals, of rights of a collectivity rather than rights of individuals. Linda K. Kerber, "The Stateless as the Citizen's Other: A View from the United States," *American Historical Review* 112, no. 1 (2007): 17–18.

25. On this term, see Eve Troutt Powell, *A Different Shade of Colonialism: Egypt, Great Britain, and the Mastery of the Sudan* (Berkeley: University of California Press, 2003), 17, 70.

26. A police register from 1882, for example, identifies one local subject as a "Jewish subject of the [local] government" (*israʾiliya min raʿaya al-hukuma*). Dar al-Wathaʾiq al-Qawmiya, Cairo, Dabtiya Iskandariya (DWQ-DI) 734/58. This construction parallels designation of a foreigner as (for example) a "Maltese subject of the English state" (*malti min atbaʿ dawlat al-inkliz*).

27. See chapter 7, and Jean-Luc Arnaud, "Des Khawaga au Caire à la fin du XIXe siècle: éléments pour une définition," *Egypt/Monde Arabe* 11 (1992): 39–46. While every *khawaga* was in a certain sense foreign, and there were *khawaga*s of foreign nationality, in the main the term designates cultural rather than legal distinction.

28. *Barbari* and *raʿiya* become categories of nationality, *ibn ʿarab* a category of settlement, and the distinction between *fallahi* and *ibn al-balad* is communicated through mapping of place.

29. Cuno and Reimer, "Census Registers," 204–205.

30. FO 847/14/39.

31. Diane Singerman and Paul Amar, eds., *Cairo Cosmopolitan: Politics, Culture, and Urban Space in the New Globalized Middle East* (Cairo: AUC Press, 2006), 253. Quotation from Arjun Appadurai, *Modernity at Large: Cultural Dimensions of Globalization* (Minneapolis: University of Minnesota Press, 1996), 179.

32. FO 847/27/8.

33. For an extended discussion of the use of *ahli* in Lebanon in the first half of the nineteenth century, see Ussama Makdisi, *The Culture of Sectarianism: Community, History, and Violence in Nineteenth-Century Ottoman Lebanon* (Berkeley: University of California Press, 2000).

34. FO 847/2/68. Enseng Ho describes members of the Hadrami diaspora who become "natives" wherever they settled throughout the Indian Ocean. "Empire Through Diasporic Eyes: A View from the Other Boat," *Comparative Studies in Society and History* 46, no. 2 (2004): 210–246.

35. FO 847/2/63.

36. Esmeir, *Juridical Humanity*; Timothy Mitchell, *Rule of Experts: Egypt, Techno-Politics, Modernity* (Berkeley: University of California Press, 2002), chap. 2.

37. Gasper, *The Power of Representation*.

38. Lila Abu-Lughod, *Veiled Sentiments: Honor and Poetry in a Bedouin Society* (Berkeley: University of California Press, 1986).

39. Rebecca Saunders, ed., *The Concept of the Foreign* (Lanham, Md.: Lexington, 2003), esp. 1–67.

40. Ariel Salzmann, "Citizens in Search of a State: The Limits of Political Participation in the Late Ottoman Empire," in *Extending Citizenship, Reconfiguring States,*

ed. Michael P. Hanagan and Charles Tilly (Lanham, Md.: Rowman & Littlefield, 1999), 45.

41. Ministère des Affaires Étrangères, Centre des Archives Diplomatiques de Nantes (CADN), Fonds Alexandrie: Recensement – Algériens (RA) 47/1145.

42. CADN-RA 47/1121. He was readmitted in 1887, however.

43. CADN-RA 46/1055.

44. These pseudoforeign movements are described in Joel Beinin and Zachary Lockman, *Workers on the Nile: Nationalism, Communism, Islam, and the Egyptian Working Class, 1882–1954* (Princeton, N.J.: Princeton University Press, 1987); Ilham Khuri-Makdisi, *The Eastern Mediterranean and the Making of Global Radicalism, 1860–1914* (Berkeley: University of California Press, 2010).

45. Mustafa Kamil, *Égyptiens et Anglais* (Paris: Perrin, 1906), 88. On the general tenor of his advocacy during this period, see Ziad Fahmy, "Francophone Egyptian Nationalists, Anti-British Discourse, and European Public Opinion, 1885–1910: The Case of Mustafa Kamil and Yaʿqub Sannuʿ," *Comparative Studies of South Asia, Africa and the Middle East* 28, no. 1 (2008): 170–183.

46. Kamil, *Égyptiens et Anglais*, 93–94.

47. The Syrian "interlopers" were a common target for nationalist critique in the 1890s. For other examples, see I. Gershoni and James P. Jankowski, *Egypt, Islam, and the Arabs: The Search for Egyptian Nationhood, 1900–1930* (New York: Oxford University Press, 1987), 16.

48. See coverage in *Al-Ahram* (Cairo), March 5, 1896.

49. Kamil, *Égyptiens et Anglais*, 163–164. Speech of June 7, 1897.

50. Ibid., 164.

51. The sources of law that the court cited were imperial *fermans* based on unspecified "international agreements" (*muʿahadat duwaliya*).

52. The court did not specify the origin of this latter group, which would have contained Syrians but especially Turkish-speaking Ottomans.

53. "The absence of a nationality law does not preclude the existence of a nationality, because nationality does not depend on a law for its existence. It depends only on the existence of an independent government for the nation (*umma*) possessing the nationality (*jinsiya*) . . . because nationality laws are not set down to establish nationality, but rather to announce the conditions and procedures that must be fulfilled and followed for its acquisition and loss."

54. The court referenced the Conscription Law of 1880 (Jallad, *Qamus*, 391–398) and the Employment Law of 1895 or 1897, which states: "Sont considérés comme égyptiens les sujets ottomans nés en Egypte et ayant leur résidence habituelle, ainsi que les sujets ottomans qui y résident habituellement depuis au moins quinze ans." Employment Law of 1901, quoted in Philippe Gélat, *Répertoire général annoté de la législation et de l'administration egyptiennes* (Alexandrie: J. C. Lagoudakis, 1906), 2:566.

55. This decision was taken by the Council of Ministers on 17 Shawwal 1307 (June 5, 1890). Gélat, *Répertoire*, 1:555.

56. Ibid., 5:291.

57. Ibid., 2:407, 5:652.

58. Muhammad al-Muwaylihi, *Hadith ʿIsa ibn Hisham, aw fatrah min al-zaman* (Cairo: Kalimat, 2013), 31; Muhammad Muwaylihi, *What ʿIsa ibn Hisham Told Us; Or, A Period of Time*, trans. Roger Allen (New York: New York University Press, 2015), 1:70.

59. Gélat, *Répertoire*, 3:566. Recall that article 13 of the Islahat Fermanı of 1856 had established that public servants were named "without distinction of nationality" (*cinsiyet*).

60. For the edict announcing Egyptian nationality, see *Al-Waqaʾi al-Misriya* (WM) 70, no. 74 (July 4, 1900).

61. Gélat, *Répertoire*, 3:586.

62. Mahkamat al-istiʾnaf ruling of February 27, 1900, in *Al-Majmuʿa al-Rasmiya lil-Mahakim al-Ahliya* (MRMA) (1900), 43–47.

63. Mahkamat al-Muski al-Juzʾiya ruling of December 23, 1900, in MRMA (1900), 306–310, Mahkamat al-Giza al-Juzʾiya ruling of August 25, 1900, in MRMA (1900), 311–312, Mahkamat al-Naqd wa-al-Ibram ruling of October 29, 1901, in MRMA (1900), 120–122, Mahkamat al-Istiʾnaf ruling of December 19, 1901, in MRMA (1901), 127–132.

64. Gélat, *Répertoire*, 3:585.

65. FO 847/36/13.

66. Thomas W. Gallant, *Experiencing Dominion: Culture, Identity, and Power in the British Mediterranean* (Notre Dame, Ind.: University of Notre Dame Press, 2002), on British imperial rule in the Ionian Islands, touching on some of the issues treated here.

67. Summary statistics in FO 97/410 (Police Registers, 1845–1848) and FO 78/1337 (Police Registers, 1851–1857) show that twenty-three of 167 convictions were given to Ionian defendants.

68. Certain Ionians reemerge as Greek Egyptians in the 1917 census, which is discussed below.

69. FO 847/40/76.

70. CADN, Fonds Alexandrie (FA) 442 ("Au sujet du changement de nationalité des tunisiens qui désirent acquérir la nationalité égyptienne, 1913–26"). This folder contains thirty-odd letters concerning this question.

71. In subsequent years, the policy was tempered. By 1926, the consul agreed to remove the names of Tunisians who requested it, simply informing them that they would be considered French subjects when in Tunisia.

72. The wish to change nationality, to become local, was nothing new. One of the men requesting a nationality change reported that his brother had done the same thing two decades earlier, in 1890. In 1889, a Docteur Basile Apostolidis wrote, asking that his name be removed from the rolls (CADN-RA 46/1099).

73. In ʿAbduh's case, ʿalim can be translated as "cleric," as it was with the clerical functions of the position that he was most concerned.

74. CADN, Fonds Alexandrie: Jugements (AJ) 527/1893/#28, 30.

75. CADN-AJ 528/#12, 528/#45, 529/#40, 530/#34, 531/#45–46, 536/p179b, 537/p101b. In the two cases in 1895 (a year in which there seems to have been a crackdown on unlicensed agents), Shaykh Ahmad was tried with a slate of codefendants.

76. These procedures were set out in the "Ordinance of the Sharia Courts" of 9 Rajab 1297/June 17, 1880, found in Jallad, *Qamus*, 4:145–156. Cited by Kenneth M. Cuno, "Disobedient Wives and Neglectful Husbands: Marital Relations and the First Phase of Family Law Reform in Egypt," in *Family, Gender, and Law in a Globalizing Middle East and South Asia*, ed. Kenneth Cuno and Manisha Desai (Syracuse, N.Y.: Syracuse University Press, 2009), 9. See also Enid Hill, *Mahkama!: Studies in the Egyptian Legal System: Courts and Crimes, Law and Society* (London: Ithaca, 1979), 56.

77. Cour d'Appel d'Aix archives, Archives Départementales des Bouches-du-Rhône, Centre d'Aix-en-Provence (CAA) 2U2 115 (1899), shows that ʿAbduh relied on an interpreter in French court.

78. In so doing, they could draw on long Algerian experience.

79. Had he been a British subject or a local, it is unlikely that ʿAbduh would have faced such substantial prison sentences for the same offenses.

80. CAA 2U2 115. ʿAbduh traveled to France seeking a reduction of the one-year sentence he received in 1899.

81. Ho, "Empire Through Diasporic Eyes."

82. "Man huwa al-misri al-haqiqi?" *Al-Ahram* (Cairo), September 9, 1911. Thanks to Hussein Omar, who alerted me to this article.

83. See, for instance, Gasper, *The Power of Representation*; Wilson Chacko Jacob, *Working Out Egypt: Effendi Masculinity and Subject Formation in Colonial Modernity, 1870–1940* (Durham, N.C.: Duke University Press, 2011); Esmeir, *Juridical Humanity*.

84. The most notable articulations of this view are contained in Frederick Cooper and Ann Laura Stoler, eds., *Tensions of Empire: Colonial Cultures in a Bourgeois World* (Berkeley: University of California Press, 1997).

85. Will Hanley, "Grieving Cosmopolitanism in Middle East Studies," *History Compass* 6, no. 5 (2008): 1346–1367.

Epilogue: Egyptians in a World of Universal Nationality

1. See the important qualification of this document in *Critical Inquiry* 40, no. 4 (2014), notably Samuel Moyn, "The Universal Declaration of Human Rights of 1948 in the History of Cosmopolitanism," *Critical Inquiry* 40, no. 4 (2014): 365–384; Lydia He Liu, "Shadows of Universalism: The Untold Story of Human Rights around 1948," *Critical Inquiry* 40, no. 4 (2014): 385–417.

2. Richard W. Flournoy and Manley O. Hudson, eds., *A Collection of Nationality Laws of Various Countries, as Contained in Constitutions, Statutes, and Treaties* (New York: Oxford University Press, 1929).

3. United Nations, *Laws Concerning Nationality* (New York: United Nations, 1954). The United Nations also published a supplement in 1959, as part of book 8 of its Legislative Series.

4. Gerry J. Simpson, *Great Powers and Outlaw States: Unequal Sovereigns in the International Legal Order* (Cambridge: Cambridge University Press, 2004); Linda Bosniak, *The*

Citizen and the Alien: Dilemmas of Contemporary Membership (Princeton, N.J.: Princeton University Press, 2006); Ayelet Shachar, *The Birthright Lottery: Citizenship and Global Inequality* (Cambridge, Mass.: Harvard University Press, 2009).

5. See the striking reading of Kamal Sadiq, *Paper Citizens: How Illegal Immigrants Acquire Citizenship in Developing Countries* (New York: Oxford University Press, 2009).

6. Hannah Arendt, *The Origins of Totalitarianism*, new ed. (New York: Harcourt Brace Jovanovich, 1973).

7. Goswami's persuasive development of Benedict Anderson's concept of modularity, for instance, does not recognize this factor. Manu Goswami, "Rethinking the Modular Nation Form: Towards a Sociohistorical Conception of Nationalism," *Comparative Studies in Society and History* 44, no. 4 (2002): 770–799.

8. Matthew Connelly argues: "The debate over the merits of state- versus society-centred approaches to explaining social change . . . privileges comparative analyses of different countries, presupposing that countries are the relevant units of analysis." "Seeing Beyond the State: The Population Control Movement and the Problem of Sovereignty," *Past and Present* 193 (2006): 201. On nongovernmental organizations, see ibid. On anticolonial movements, see Cemil Aydin, *The Politics of Anti-Westernism in Asia: Visions of World Order in Pan-Islamic and Pan-Asian Thought* (New York: Columbia University Press, 2007); Manu Goswami, "Imaginary Futures and Colonial Internationalisms," *American Historical Review* 117, no. 5 (2012): 1461–1485. On transnational communities, see Prasenjit Duara, "Transnationalism and the Predicament of Sovereignty: China, 1900–1945," *American Historical Review* 102, no. 4 (1997): 1030–1051; Engseng Ho, "Empire Through Diasporic Eyes: A View from the Other Boat," *Comparative Studies in Society and History* 46, no. 2 (2004): 210–246.

9. Most prominently, Jane Burbank and Frederick Cooper, *Empires in World History: Power and the Politics of Difference* (Princeton, N.J.: Princeton University Press, 2010). See also Ann Laura Stoler, Carole McGranahan, and Peter C. Perdue, eds., *Imperial Formations* (Santa Fe, N.M.: School for Advanced Research Press, 2007); Craig J. Calhoun, Frederick Cooper, and Kevin W. Moore, eds., *Lessons of Empire: Imperial Histories and American Power* (New York: New Press, 2006); and the journal *Ab Imperio*.

10. Archives d'outre mer, Aix-en-Provence (AOM) Fond Ministeriels 1AFFPOL/1294, 3.

11. Samuel Moyn, *The Last Utopia: Human Rights in History* (Cambridge, Mass.: Belknap Press of Harvard University Press, 2010), 30, *passim*.

12. Linda K. Kerber, "The Stateless as the Citizen's Other: A View from the United States," *American Historical Review* 112, no. 1 (2007): 15–20.

13. James C. Scott, *The Art of Not Being Governed: An Anarchist History of Upland Southeast Asia* (New Haven, Conn.: Yale University Press, 2009).

14. Duara, "Transnationalism and the Predicament of Sovereignty," 1030–1033.

15. The most important were the *Journal du Droit International*, founded in 1874 (it still bears the name of its founder, Clunet, but changed its name to *Journal du Droit International Privé*) and the *Revue de Droit International Privé et de Droit Pénal International*, founded in 1905 (Darras).

16. Turan Kayaoğlu, *Legal Imperialism: Sovereignty and Extraterritoriality in Japan, the Ottoman Empire, and China* (Cambridge: Cambridge University Press, 2010); Eileen P. Scully, *Bargaining with the State from Afar: American Citizenship in Treaty Port China, 1844-1942* (New York: Columbia University Press, 2001); Pär Kristoffer Cassel, *Grounds of Judgment: Extraterritoriality and Imperial Power in Nineteenth-Century China and Japan* (Oxford: Oxford University Press, 2012).

17. Étienne Balibar, "Citizen Subject," in *Who Comes After the Subject?*, ed. Eduardo Cadava, Peter Connor, and Jean-Luc Nancy (New York: Routledge, 1991), 38–39.

18. Frederick Cooper, *Citizenship Between Empire and Nation: Remaking France and French Africa, 1945-1960* (Princeton, N.J.: Princeton University Press, 2014).

19. Moyn, "The Universal Declaration of Human Rights of 1948 in the History of Cosmopolitanism," 371.

20. Note quoted in *Foreign Relations of the United States 1914*, 1090, quoted in Feroz Ahmad, "Ottoman Perceptions of the Capitulations, 1800–1914," *Journal of Islamic Studies* 11, no. 1 (2000): 17. Italics mine.

21. The classic references are Afaf Lutfi Sayyid-Marsot, *Egypt's Liberal Experiment, 1922-1936* (Berkeley: University of California Press, 1977); I. Gershoni and James P. Jankowski, *Egypt, Islam, and the Arabs: The Search for Egyptian Nationhood, 1900-1930* (New York: Oxford University Press, 1987); I. Gershoni and James P. Jankowski, *Redefining the Egyptian Nation, 1930-1945* (New York: Cambridge University Press, 1995).

22. Selma Botman, *Engendering Citizenship in Egypt* (New York: Columbia University Press, 1999); Wilson Chacko Jacob, *Working Out Egypt: Effendi Masculinity and Subject Formation in Colonial Modernity, 1870-1940* (Durham, N.C.: Duke University Press, 2011); Hanan Kholoussy, *For Better, for Worse: The Marriage Crisis That Made Modern Egypt* (Stanford, Calif.: Stanford University Press, 2010); Marilyn Booth, *May Her Likes Be Multiplied: Biography and Gender Politics in Egypt* (Berkeley: University of California Press, 2001); Eric Davis, *Challenging Colonialism: Bank Misr and Egyptian Industrialization, 1920-1941* (Princeton, N.J.: Princeton University Press, 1983); Robert L. Tignor, *State, Private Enterprise, and Economic Change in Egypt, 1918-1952* (Princeton, N.J.: Princeton University Press, 1984); Arthur Goldschmidt, Amy Johnson, and Barak Salmoni, eds., *Re-Envisioning Egypt 1919-1952* (Cairo: AUC Press, 2005); Abdeslam Maghraoui, *Liberalism Without Democracy: Nationhood and Citizenship in Egypt, 1922-1936* (Durham, N.C.: Duke University Press, 2006).

23. Joel Beinin and Zachary Lockman, *Workers on the Nile: Nationalism, Communism, Islam, and the Egyptian Working Class, 1882-1954* (Princeton, N.J.: Princeton University Press, 1987); Wilson Chacko Jacob, "Eventful Transformations: al-Futuwwa Between History and the Everyday," *Comparative Studies in Society and History* 49, no. 3 (2007): 689–712; Hanan Hammad, "Between Egyptian 'National Purity' and 'Local Flexibility': Prostitution in al-Mahalla al-Kubra in the First Half of the 20th Century," *Journal of Social History* 44, no. 3 (2011): 751–783.

24. Such an approach is conceivable in other Middle Eastern contexts, for instance in Cyrus Schayegh, "The Many Worlds of ʿAbud Yasin; Or, What Narcotics Trafficking

in the Interwar Middle East Can Tell Us About Territorialization," *American Histori-cal Review* 116, no. 2 (2011): 273–306.

25. Ramzi Sayf Rizq Allah, *Tanazuʿ al-Ikhtisas bain al-Mahakim al-Ahliya wa al-Mahakim al-Mukhtalita* (Cairo: Matbaʿat Fath Allah Ilyas Nuri wa Awladihi, 1938), 97.

26. ʿAbd al-Hamid Abu Haif, *al-Qanun al-Duwali al-Khass fi Awruba wa Masr* (Cairo: Matbaʿat al-Iʿtimad, 1924), 141–148.

27. Duara, "Transnationalism and the Predicament of Sovereignty," 1043–1045.

28. F. Robert Hunter, *Egypt Under the Khedives, 1805–1879: From Household Government to Modern Bureaucracy* (Cairo: AUC Press, 1999).

29. Partha Chatterjee, *The Nation and Its Fragments: Colonial and Postcolonial Histories* (Princeton, N.J.: Princeton University Press, 1993).

30. Elizabeth Thompson, *Colonial Citizens: Republican Rights, Paternal Privilege, and Gender in French Syria and Lebanon* (New York: Columbia University Press, 2000), 2.

31. Ibid., 72. Thompson does a good job, however, of showing how a sense of civil and social entitlements grew alongside demands for political citizenship.

32. Ibid., 5.

33. Ibid., part II, esp. 72.

34. Ibid., 102–103.

35. John T. Chalcraft, *The Striking Cabbies of Cairo and Other Stories: Crafts and Guilds in Egypt, 1873-1914* (Albany: SUNY Press, 2004), 175.

36. This argument is articulated in Ann Laura Stoler, "Rethinking Colonial Categories: European Communities and the Boundaries of Rule," *Comparative Studies in Society and History* 31, no. 1 (1989): 134–161; Frederick Cooper and Ann Laura Stoler, eds., *Tensions of Empire: Colonial Cultures in a Bourgeois World* (Berkeley: University of California Press, 1997); Anne McClintock, *Imperial Leather: Race, Gender, and Sexuality in the Colonial Conquest* (New York: Routledge, 1995); Dipesh Chakrabarty, *Provincializing Europe: Postcolonial Thought and Historical Difference* (Princeton, N.J.: Princeton University Press, 2000); and a host of other scholarship.

37. Ministère des Affaires Étrangères, Centre des Archives Diplomatiques de Nantes (CADN), Fonds Alexandrie: Recensement – Algériens (RA) 58/1949.

38. It appears that this regulation was derived from article 1 of the Islahat Fermanı of 1856, which required that the grand rabbi of each locality be an Ottoman subject.

39. This resembles the situation of the Tunisian lawyers mentioned in chapter 12, who were fired from their jobs when government employment and nationality were in conflict.

40. See Umut Özsu, *Formalizing Displacement: International Law and Population Transfers* (Oxford: Oxford University Press, 2014).

41. See the discussion of hospitality for strangers in Austin Sarat, Lawrence Douglas, and Martha Merrill Umphrey, eds., *Law and the Stranger* (Stanford, Calif.: Stanford University Press, 2010), 5, *passim*.

42. Ministère des Affaires Étrangèrs, Étude du 30 November 1939 (Afrique-Levant) au sujet de l'assainissement du statu de la protection et de l'immatriculation en Egypte. Copy in AOM Fond Ministeriels 1AFFPOL/1294.

43. AOM Fond Ministeriels 1AFFPOL/1294 (Extraits d'une note de la Legation de France au Caire en date du 8 juillet 1939), 7.

44. Egyptian Décret-loi no. 89 of 1937, concerning legislation applicable by the Mixed Courts, published in *Al-Waqaʾi al-Misriya* (WM) 92, October 13, 1937.

45. Immanuel Wallerstein, "Citizens All? Citizens Some! The Making of the Citizen," *Comparative Studies in Society and History* 45, no. 4 (2003): 652, treating the postrevolutionary French context.

46. Joel Beinin, *The Dispersion of Egyptian Jewry: Culture, Politics, and the Formation of a Modern Diaspora* (Cairo: AUC Press, 2005).

47. Khaled Fahmy, "The Anatomy of Justice: Forensic Medicine and Criminal Law in Nineteenth-Century Egypt," *Islamic Law and Society* 6, no. 2 (1999): 252.

48. This idea should not to be confused with a similar political science formulation, which aims to "revitalize the particularist values of 'nationality' without reviving 'nationalist' demons." See Erica Benner, "Nationality Without Nationalism," *Journal of Political Ideologies* 2, no. 2 (1997): 189–206.

49. Frances Bartkowski, *Travelers, Immigrants, Inmates: Essays in Estrangement* (Minneapolis: University of Minnesota Press, 1995), xvi.

Bibliography

Abu Haif, ʿAbd al-Hamid. *Al-Qanun al-Duwali al-Khass fi Awruba wa Masr*. Cairo: Matbaʿat al-Iʿtimad, 1924.

Abu-Lughod, Lila. *Veiled Sentiments: Honor and Poetry in a Bedouin Society*. Berkeley: University of California Press, 1986.

Abu Manneh, Butrus. "The Christians Between Ottomanism and Syrian Nationalism: The Ideas of Butrus al-Bustani." *International Journal of Middle East Studies* 2 (1980): 287–304.

Agamben, Giorgio. *State of Exception*. Chicago: University of Chicago Press, 2005.

Agmon, Iris. *Family and Court: Legal Culture and Modernity in Late Ottoman Palestine*. Syracuse, N.Y.: Syracuse University Press, 2006.

——. "Recording Procedures and Legal Culture in the Late Ottoman Shariʿa Court of Jaffa, 1865–1890." *Islamic Law and Society* 11, no. 3 (2004): 333–377.

Ahmad, Feroz. "Mukhtār Pasha." In *Encyclopaedia of Islam*. Leiden: Brill, 1993.

——. "Ottoman Perceptions of the Capitulations, 1800–1914." *Journal of Islamic Studies* 11, no. 1 (2000): 1–20.

Allen, Roger. *A Period of Time: A Study and Translation of Hadith ʿIsa Ibn Hisham by Muhammad al-Muwaylihi*. Reading: Ithaca, 1992.

Anastassiadou, Meropi. *Salonique, 1830–1912: une ville ottomane à l'âge des Réformes*. Leiden: Brill, 1997.

Anderson, Benedict. *Imagined Communities: Reflections on the Origin and Spread of Nationalism*. Rev. and extended ed. London: Verso, 1991.

Anderson, Caitlin. "Britons Abroad and Aliens at Home: Nationality Law and Policy in Britain 1815–70." Ph.D. diss., Cambridge University, 2004.

Anghie, Antony. *Imperialism, Sovereignty, and the Making of International Law*. Cambridge: Cambridge University Press, 2005.

Appadurai, Arjun. *Modernity at Large: Cultural Dimensions of Globalization.* Minneapolis: University of Minnesota Press, 1996.

Archibugi, Daniele, ed. *Debating Cosmopolitics.* London: Verso, 2003.

Arendt, Hannah. *The Origins of Totalitarianism.* New ed. New York: Harcourt Brace Jovanovich, 1973.

Arminjon, Pierre. *Étrangers et protégés dans l'Empire ottoman.* A. Chevalier-Maresq & cie, 1903.

Arnaud, Jean-Luc. "Des Khawaga au Caire à la fin du XIXe siècle: éléments pour une définition." *Egypt/Monde Arabe* 11 (1992): 39–46.

Arnold, David. "European Orphans and Vagrants in India in the Nineteenth Century." *Journal of Imperial and Commonwealth History* 7, no. 2 (1979): 104–127.

Asad, Talal. *Formations of the Secular: Christianity, Islam, Modernity.* Stanford, Calif.: Stanford University Press, 2003.

Asad, Talal, Judith Butler, Saba Mahmood, and Wendy Brown. *Is Critique Secular? Blasphemy, Injury, and Free Speech.* Berkeley: Townsend Center for the Humanities, University of California, 2009.

Aslanian, Sebouh David. *From the Indian Ocean to the Mediterranean: The Global Trade Networks of Armenian Merchants from New Julfa.* Berkeley: University of California Press, 2011.

Ayalon, Ami. *Language and Change in the Arab Middle East: The Evolution of Modern Political Discourse.* New York: Oxford University Press, 1987.

Aydin, Cemil. *The Politics of Anti-Westernism in Asia: Visions of World Order in Pan-Islamic and Pan-Asian Thought.* New York: Columbia University Press, 2007.

Aymes, Marc. "Provincialiser l'empire: Chypre et la Méditerranée ottomane au XIXe siècle." *Annales* 62, no. 6 (2007): 1313–1344.

Bailyn, Bernard. *The Peopling of British North America: An Introduction.* New York: Knopf, 1986.

Baldwin, James E. "Islamic Law in an Ottoman Context: Resolving Disputes in Late Seventeenth/Early Eighteenth-Century Cairo." Ph.D. diss., New York University, 2010.

Balibar, Étienne. "Citizen Subject." In *Who Comes After the Subject?*, ed. Eduardo Cadava, Peter Connor, and Jean-Luc Nancy, 33–57. New York: Routledge, 1991.

Barkey, Karen. *Bandits and Bureaucrats: The Ottoman Route to State Centralization.* Ithaca, N.Y.: Cornell University Press, 1994.

Bartkowski, Frances. *Travelers, Immigrants, Inmates: Essays in Estrangement.* Minneapolis: University of Minnesota Press, 1995.

Bar, Ludwig von. *The Theory and Practice of Private International Law.* Translated by G. R. Gillespie. 2nd ed. Edinburgh, 1892.

Baysun, M. Cavid. "Muhtar Paşa." In *Diyanet İslâm Ansiklopedisi.* Istanbul: Türkiye Diyanet Vakfı, 1979.

Beckles, Hilary. " 'Black Men in White Skins': The Formation of a White Proletariat in West Indian Slave Society." *Journal of Imperial and Commonwealth History* 15, no. 1 (1986): 7.

Behar, Cem. *A Neighborhood in Ottoman Istanbul: Fruit Vendors and Civil Servants in the Kasap İlyas Mahalle.* Albany: SUNY Press, 2003.

——. "Qui compte? Recencesements et statistiques démographiques dans l'Empire ottoman du XVIe au XX siecle." *Histoire and Mesure* 13 (1998): 135–146.

——. "Sources pour la Démographie Historique de l'Empire Ottoman. Les tahrirs (dénombrements) de 1885 et 1907." *Population* 1–2 (1998): 161–178.

Beier, A. L., and Paul Ocobock, eds. *Cast Out: Vagrancy and Homelessness in Global and Historical Perspective*. Athens: Ohio University Press, 2009.

Beinin, Joel. *The Dispersion of Egyptian Jewry: Culture, Politics, and the Formation of a Modern
Diaspora*. Cairo: AUC Press, 2005.

Beinin, Joel, and Zachary Lockman. *Workers on the Nile: Nationalism, Communism, Islam, and
the Egyptian Working Class, 1882-1954*. Princeton, N.J.: Princeton University Press, 1987.

Benner, Erica. "Nationality Without Nationalism." *Journal of Political Ideologies* 2, no. 2
(1997): 189–206.

Benton, Lauren A. *A Search for Sovereignty: Law and Geography in European Empires, 1400-1900*.
Cambridge: Cambridge University Press, 2010.

——. *Law and Colonial Cultures: Legal Regimes in World History, 1400-1900*. Cambridge: Cambridge University Press, 2002.

Berque, Jacques. *L'Égypte, impérialisme et révolution*. Paris: Gallimard, 1967.

Bhabha, Homi K., ed. *Nation and Narration*. London: Routledge, 1990.

Boll, Alfred. *Multiple Nationality and International Law*. Leiden: M. Nijhoff, 2007.

Bonner, Michael David, Mine Ener, and Amy Singer, eds. *Poverty and Charity in Middle Eastern Contexts*. Albany: SUNY Press, 2003.

Booth, Marilyn. *Bayram al-Tunisi's Egypt: Social Criticism and Narrative Strategies*. Oxford:
Ithaca, 1990.

——. *May Her Likes Be Multiplied: Biography and Gender Politics in Egypt*. Berkeley: University
of California Press, 2001.

Borelli, Octave, and Paul Ruelens, eds. *La législation Égyptienne annotée*. Bruxelles, 1892.

Borg, Alexander. "Language." In *Malta: Culture and Identity*, 27–50. Malta: Ministry of Youth
and the Arts, 1994.

——. "On Some Mediterranean Influences on the Lexicon of Maltese." In *Romania Arabica*,
ed. J. Ludtke, 129–150. Tubingen: Gunter Narr, 1996.

Bosniak, Linda. *The Citizen and the Alien: Dilemmas of Contemporary Membership*. Princeton,
N.J.: Princeton University Press, 2006.

Botman, Selma. *Engendering Citizenship in Egypt*. New York: Columbia University Press,
1999.

Braude, Benjamin. "Foundation Myths of the Millet System." In *Christians and Jews in the
Ottoman Empire: The Functioning of a Plural Society*, 2 vols., ed. Benjamin Braude and Bernard Lewis, 1:69–87. New York: Holmes & Meier, 1982.

Bredbenner, Candice Lewis. *A Nationality of Her Own: Women, Marriage, and the Law of Citizenship*. Berkeley: University of California Press, 1998.

Brinton, Jasper Yeates. *The Mixed Courts of Egypt*. 2nd ed. New Haven, Conn.: Yale University Press, 1968.

Briscoe, W. R. B. "Marriage with Foreigners." *Law Magazine and Review: A Quarterly Review of
Jurisprudence* 37 (1912): 129.

Brock, Gillian, and Harry Brighouse, eds. *The Political Philosophy of Cosmopolitanism*. Cambridge: Cambridge University Press, 2005.

Brown, Nathan. "Brigands and State Building: The Invention of Banditry in Modern Egypt." *Comparative Studies in Society and History* 32, no. 2 (1990): 258–281.

Brown, Philip Marshall. *Foreigners in Turkey: Their Juridical Status*. Princeton, N.J.: Princeton University Press, 1914.

Brubaker, Rogers. *Citizenship and Nationhood in France and Germany*. Cambridge, Mass.: Harvard University Press, 1992.

Bryant, Rebecca. "Bandits and 'Bad Characters': Law as Anthropological Practice in Cyprus, C. 1900." *Law and History Review* 21, no. 2 (2003): 243–270.

Burbank, Jane. *Russian Peasants Go to Court: Legal Culture in the Countryside, 1905-1917*. Bloomington: Indiana University Press, 2004.

Burbank, Jane, and Frederick Cooper. *Empires in World History: Power and the Politics of Difference*. Princeton, N.J.: Princeton University Press, 2010.

Burns, Kathryn. *Into the Archive: Writing and Power in Colonial Peru*. Durham, N.C.: Duke University Press, 2010.

Burton, Antoinette M., ed. *After the Imperial Turn: Thinking with and Through the Nation*. Durham, N.C.: Duke University Press, 2003.

——. *At the Heart of the Empire: Indians and the Colonial Encounter in Late Victorian Britain*. Berkeley: University of California Press, 1998.

Cachia, Anna, and Pierre Cachia. *Landlocked Islands: Two Alien Lives in Egypt*. Cairo: AUC Press, 2000.

Calhoun, Craig J., Frederick Cooper, and Kevin W. Moore, eds. *Lessons of Empire: Imperial Histories and American Power*. New York: New Press, 2006.

Cameron, D. A. *An Arabic-English Vocabulary for the Use of English Students of Modern Egyptian Arabic*. London, 1892.

Campos, Michelle. *Ottoman Brothers: Muslims, Christians, and Jews in Early Twentieth-Century Palestine*. Stanford, Calif.: Stanford University Press, 2010.

Cannon, Byron. *Politics of Law and the Courts in Nineteenth-Century Egypt*. Salt Lake City: University of Utah Press, 1988.

Caplan, Jane. " 'This or That Particular Person': Protocols of Identification in Nineteenth-Century Europe." In *Documenting Individual Identity*, ed. Jane Caplan and John C. Torpey, 49–66. Princeton, N.J.: Princeton University Press, 2001.

Caplan, Jane, and John C. Torpey, eds. *Documenting Individual Identity: The Development of State Practices in the Modern World*. Princeton, N.J.: Princeton University Press, 2001.

Cassel, Pär Kristoffer. *Grounds of Judgment: Extraterritoriality and Imperial Power in Nineteenth-Century China and Japan*. Oxford: Oxford University Press, 2012.

Çelik, Zeynep. *The Remaking of Istanbul: Portrait of an Ottoman City in the Nineteenth Century*. Berkeley: University of California Press, 1993.

Chakrabarty, Dipesh. *Provincializing Europe: Postcolonial Thought and Historical Difference*. Princeton, N.J.: Princeton University Press, 2000.

Chalcraft, John T. *The Striking Cabbies of Cairo and Other Stories: Crafts and Guilds in Egypt, 1873-1914*. Albany: SUNY Press, 2004.

Chang, Richard T. *The Justice of the Western Consular Courts in Nineteenth-Century Japan.* Westport, Conn.: Greenwood, 1984.

Chatterjee, Partha. "The Nationalist Resolution of the Women's Question." In *Recasting Women*, ed. Kumkum Sangari and Sudesh Vaid, 233–253. New Brunswick, N.J.: Rutgers University Press, 1990.

——. *The Nation and Its Fragments: Colonial and Postcolonial Histories.* Princeton, N.J.: Princeton University Press, 1993.

Cheah, Pheng, and Bruce Robbins, eds. *Cosmopolitics: Thinking and Feeling Beyond the Nation.* Minneapolis: University of Minnesota Press, 1998.

Cheta, Omar. "Rule of Merchants: The Practice of Commerce and Law in Late Ottoman Egypt, 1841–1876." Ph.D. diss., New York University, 2013.

Chevalier, Louis. *Laboring Classes and Dangerous Classes in Paris During the First Half of the Nineteenth Century.* Princeton, N.J.: Princeton University Press, 1981.

Clancy-Smith, Julia A. "Europe and Its Social Marginals in Nineteenth-Century Mediterranean North Africa." In *Outside In*, ed. Eugene L. Rogan, 149–182. London: I. B. Tauris, 2002.

——. *Mediterraneans: North Africa and Europe in an Age of Migration, C. 1800–1900.* Berkeley: University of California Press, 2011.

——. *Rebel and Saint: Muslim Notables, Populist Protest, Colonial Encounters (Algeria and Tunisia, 1800–1904).* Berkeley: University of California Press, 1994.

Cleland, Wendell. *The Population Problem in Egypt: A Study of Population Trends and Conditions in Modern Egypt.* Lancaster, Penn.: Science Press, 1936.

Clément, Anne Marie. "Fallahin on Trial in Colonial Egypt: Apprehending the Peasantry Through Orality, Writing, and Performance (1884–1914)." Ph.D. diss., University of Toronto, 2012.

Clercq, Alexandre J. H. de, and Charles de Vallat. *Guide pratique des consulats.* 2 vols. Paris, 1880.

Cleveland, William L. *The Making of an Arab Nationalist: Ottomanism and Arabism in the Life and Thought of Satiᶜ al-Husri.* Princeton, N.J.: Princeton University Press, 1971.

Cogordan, George. *Droit des gens: la nationalité au point de vue des rapports internationaux.* 2nd ed. Paris, 1890.

Cole, Juan Ricardo. *Colonialism and Revolution in the Middle East: Social and Cultural Origins of Egypt's ʿUrabi Movement.* Princeton, N.J.: Princeton University Press, 1992.

Colley, Linda. *Captives: Britain, Empire, and the World, 1600–1850.* London: Jonathan Cape, 2002.

——. *The Ordeal of Elizabeth Marsh: A Woman in World History.* New York: Pantheon, 2007.

Conklin, Alice L. *A Mission to Civilize: The Republican Idea of Empire in France and West Africa, 1895–1930.* Stanford, Calif.: Stanford University Press, 1997.

Connelly, Matthew. "Seeing Beyond the State: The Population Control Movement and the Problem of Sovereignty." *Past and Present* 193 (2006): 197–233.

Cooper, Frederick. *Citizenship Between Empire and Nation: Remaking France and French Africa, 1945–1960.* Princeton, N.J.: Princeton University Press, 2014.

——. *Colonialism in Question: Theory, Knowledge, History.* Berkeley: University of California Press, 2005.

Cooper, Frederick, and Ann Laura Stoler, eds. *Tensions of Empire: Colonial Cultures in a Bourgeois World.* Berkeley: University of California Press, 1997.

Cuno, Kenneth M. "Disobedient Wives and Neglectful Husbands: Marital Relations and the First Phase of Family Law Reform in Egypt." In *Family, Gender, and Law in a Globalizing Middle East and South Asia*, ed. Kenneth Cuno and Manisha Desai, 3–18. Syracuse, N.Y.: Syracuse University Press, 2009.

——. *Modernizing Marriage: Family, Ideology, and Law in Nineteenth- and Early Twentieth-Century Egypt*. Syracuse, N.Y.: Syracuse University Press, 2015.

Cuno, Kenneth M., and Michael J. Reimer. "The Census Registers of Nineteenth-Century Egypt: A New Source for Social Historians." *British Journal of Middle Eastern Studies* 24, no. 2 (1997): 193–216.

Dalrymple, William. *White Mughals: Love and Betrayal in Eighteenth-Century India*. New York: Penguin, 2004.

Daly, M. W., ed. *The Cambridge History of Egypt*. Vol. 2: *Modern Egypt, from 1517 to the End of the Twentieth Century*. Cambridge: Cambridge University Press, 1998.

Davis, Eric. *Challenging Colonialism: Bank Misr and Egyptian Industrialization, 1920–1941*. Princeton, N.J.: Princeton University Press, 1983.

Dawn, C. Ernest. *From Ottomanism to Arabism: Essays on the Origins of Arab Nationalism*. Urbana: University of Illinois Press, 1973.

Deringil, Selim. *Conversion and Apostasy in the Late Ottoman Empire*. Cambridge: Cambridge University Press, 2012.

——. *The Well-Protected Domains: Ideology and the Legitimation of Power in the Ottoman Empire, 1876–1909*. London: I. B. Tauris, 1998.

——. "'They Live in a State of Nomadism and Savagery': The Late Ottoman Empire and the Post-Colonial Debate." *Comparative Studies in Society and History* 45, no. 2 (2003): 311–342.

Di-Capua, Yoav. *Gatekeepers of the Arab Past: Historians and History Writing in Twentieth-Century Egypt*. Berkeley: University of California Press, 2009.

Dicey, Albert Venn, and Arthur Berriedale Keith. *A Digest of the Law of England with Reference to the Conflict of Laws*. London: Stevens, 1922.

Duara, Prasenjit. *Rescuing History from the Nation: Questioning Narratives of Modern China*. Chicago: University of Chicago Press, 1995.

——. "Transnationalism and the Predicament of Sovereignty: China, 1900–1945." *American Historical Review* 102, no. 4 (1997): 1030–1051.

Dubois, Laurent. *A Colony of Citizens: Revolution and Slave Emancipation in the French Caribbean, 1787–1804*. Chapel Hill: University of North Carolina Press, 2004.

Egypt, Direction du Recensement. *Recensement général de l'Égypte, 15 Gamad Akher 1299 / 3 mai 1882*. Cairo, 1884.

El Shakry, Omnia S. *The Great Social Laboratory: Subjects of Knowledge in Colonial and Postcolonial Egypt*. Stanford, Calif.: Stanford University Press, 2007.

Eldem, Edhem, Daniel Goffman, and Bruce Alan Masters. *The Ottoman City Between East and West: Aleppo, Izmir, and Istanbul*. Cambridge: Cambridge University Press, 1999.

Eley, Geoff, and Ronald Grigor Suny, eds. *Becoming National: A Reader*. New York: Oxford University Press, 1996.

Ellis, Matthew. "Between Empire and Nation: The Emergence of Egypt's Libyan Borderland, 1841–1911." Ph.D. diss., Princeton University, 2012.

Elshakry, Marwa. *Reading Darwin in Arabic, 1860-1950.* Chicago: University of Chicago Press, 2013.

Encyclopedia of the Languages of Europe. Oxford: Blackwell, 1998.

Ener, Mine. *Managing Egypt's Poor and the Politics of Benevolence, 1800-1952.* Princeton, N.J.: Princeton University Press, 2003.

Ergene, Boğaç A. *Local Court, Provincial Society, and Justice in the Ottoman Empire: Legal Practice and Dispute Resolution in Çankırı and Kastamonu (1652-1744).* Leiden: Brill, 2003.

Esmeir, Samera. *Juridical Humanity: A Colonial History.* Stanford, Calif.: Stanford University Press, 2012.

Fahmy, Khaled. *All the Pasha's Men: Mehmed Ali, His Army, and the Making of Modern Egypt.* Cambridge: Cambridge University Press, 1997.

——. "The Anatomy of Justice: Forensic Medicine and Criminal Law in Nineteenth-Century Egypt." *Islamic Law and Society* 6, no. 2 (1999): 224-271.

——. "For Cavafy, with Love and Squalor: Some Critical Notes on the History and Historiography of Modern Alexandria." In *Alexandria, Real and Imagined*, ed. Anthony Hirst and Michael Silk, 263-280. Aldershot: Ashgate, 2004.

——. "Justice, Law, and Pain in Khedival Egypt." In *Standing Trial*, ed. Baudouin Dupret, 85-115. London: I. B. Tauris, 2004.

——. "Towards a Social History of Modern Alexandria." In *Alexandria, Real and Imagined*, ed. Anthony Hirst and Michael Silk, 281-306. Aldershot: Ashgate, 2004.

Fahmy, Khaled, and Rudolph Peters. "The Legal History of Ottoman Egypt." *Islamic Law and Society* 6, no. 2 (1999): 129-135.

Fahmy, Ziad. "Francophone Egyptian Nationalists, Anti-British Discourse, and European Public Opinion, 1885-1910: The Case of Mustafa Kamil and Yaʿqub Sannuʿ." *Comparative Studies of South Asia, Africa, and the Middle East* 28, no. 1 (2008): 170-183.

——. "Jurisdictional Borderlands: Extraterritoriality and 'Legal Chameleons' in Precolonial Alexandria, 1840-1870." *Comparative Studies in Society and History* 55, no. 2 (2013): 305-329.

——. *Ordinary Egyptians: Creating the Modern Nation Through Popular Culture.* Stanford, Calif.: Stanford University Press, 2011.

Fahri, Bekir. *Jönler.* Istanbul: İletişim Yayınları, 1985.

Fahrmeir, Andreas. *Citizenship: The Rise and Fall of a Modern Concept.* New Haven, Conn.: Yale University Press, 2007.

——. "Governments and Forgers: Passports in Nineteenth-Century Europe." In *Documenting Individual Identity*, ed. Jane Caplan and John C. Torpey, 218-234. Princeton, N.J.: Princeton University Press, 2001.

Fawaz, Leila Tarazi. *Merchants and Migrants in Nineteenth-Century Beirut.* Cambridge, Mass.: Harvard University Press, 1983.

Fawaz, Leila Tarazi, and C. A. Bayly, eds. *Modernity and Culture: From the Mediterranean to the Indian Ocean.* New York: Columbia University Press, 2002.

Féraud-Giraud, M. *Traité de la juridiction française dans les échelles de Levant et de Barbarie.* 2nd ed. Paris, 1886.

Flournoy, Richard W., and Manley O. Hudson, eds. *A Collection of Nationality Laws of Various Countries, as Contained in Constitutions, Statutes and Treaties.* New York: Oxford University Press, 1929.

Foucault, Michel. *Discipline and Punish: The Birth of the Prison*. New York: Vintage, 1995.

——. Power/Knowledge: Selected Interviews and Other Writings, 1972–1977. Pantheon, 1980.

Freitag, Ulrike. "The City and the Stranger: Jeddah in the Nineteenth Century." In *The City in the Ottoman Empire: Migration and the Making of Urban Modernity*, ed. Ulrike Freitag. Abingdon: Routledge, 2011.

Frendo, Henry. "National Identity." In *Malta: Culture and Identity*, ed. Henry Frendo and Oliver Friggieri, 1–25. Malta: Ministry of Youth and the Arts, 1994.

Frey, Linda, and Marsha Frey. *The History of Diplomatic Immunity*. Columbus: Ohio State University Press, 1999.

Gallant, Thomas W. *Experiencing Dominion: Culture, Identity, and Power in the British Mediterranean*. Notre Dame: University of Notre Dame Press, 2002.

Ganachari, Aravind. " 'White Man's Embarrassment': European Vagrancy in Nineteenth-Century Bombay." *Economic and Political Weekly* 37, no. 25 (June 22, 2002): 2477–2486.

Gasper, Michael Ezekiel. *The Power of Representation: Publics, Peasants, and Islam in Egypt*. Stanford, Calif.: Stanford University Press, 2009.

Gélat, Philippe. *Répertoire général annoté de la législation et de l'administration égyptiennes*. 5 vols. Alexandrie: J. C. Lagoudakis, 1906.

Gellner, Ernest. *Nations and Nationalism*. Ithaca, N.Y.: Cornell University Press, 1983.

Genell, Aimee M. "Empire by Law: Ottoman Sovereignty and the British Occupation of Egypt, 1882–1923." Ph.D. diss., Columbia University, 2013.

Georgelin, Hervé. *La fin de Smyrne: du cosmopolitisme aux nationalismes*. Paris: CNRS, 2005.

Gershoni, I., and James P. Jankowski. *Egypt, Islam, and the Arabs: The Search for Egyptian Nationhood, 1900–1930*. New York: Oxford University Press, 1987.

——. *Redefining the Egyptian Nation, 1930–1945*. New York: Cambridge University Press, 1995.

Gibb, H. A. R., and Harold Bowen. *Islamic Society and the West: A Study of the Impact of Western Civilization on Moslem Culture in the Near East*. London: Oxford University Press, 1967.

Go, Julian. *American Empire and the Politics of Meaning: Elite Political Cultures in the Philippines and Puerto Rico During U.S. Colonialism*. Durham, N.C.: Duke University Press, 2008.

Goldschmidt, Arthur, Amy Johnson, and Barak Salmoni, eds. *Re-Envisioning Egypt, 1919–1952*. Cairo: AUC Press, 2005.

Gordon, Robert W. "Critical Legal Histories." *Stanford Law Review* 36 (1984): 57–125.

——. " 'Critical Legal Histories Revisited': A Response." *Law and Social Inquiry* 37, no. 1 (2012): 200–215.

Gorman, Daniel. *Imperial Citizenship: Empire and the Question of Belonging*. Manchester: Manchester University Press, 2006.

Goswami, Manu. "Imaginary Futures and Colonial Internationalisms." *American Historical Review* 117, no. 5 (2012): 1461–1485.

——. "Rethinking the Modular Nation Form: Towards a Sociohistorical Conception of Nationalism." *Comparative Studies in Society and History* 44, no. 4 (2002): 770–799.

Green, Abigail. "The British Empire and the Jews: An Imperialism of Human Rights?" *Past and Present* 199, no. 1 (2008): 175–205.

Guha, Sumit. "The Politics of Identity and Enumeration in India C. 1600–1990." *Comparative Studies in Society and History* 45, no. 1 (2003): 148–167.

Haag, Michael. *Alexandria: City of Memory*. New Haven, Conn.: Yale University Press, 2004.

Hacking, Ian. "Making Up People." In *Reconstructing Individualism*, ed. Thomas C. Heller and Christine Brooke-Rose. Stanford, Calif.: Stanford University Press, 1986.

Hall, Catherine. *Civilising Subjects: Colony and Metropole in the English Imagination, 1830–1867*. Chicago: University of Chicago Press, 2002.

Hammad, Hanan. "Between Egyptian 'National Purity' and 'Local Flexibility': Prostitution in al-Mahalla al-Kubra in the First Half of the 20th Century." *Journal of Social History* 44, no. 3 (2011): 751–783.

Hanley, Will. "Foreignness and Localness in Alexandria, 1880–1914." Ph.D. diss., Princeton University, History, 2007.

——. "Grieving Cosmopolitanism in Middle East Studies." *History Compass* 6, no. 5 (2008): 1346–1367.

——. "Papers for Going, Papers for Staying: Identification and Documentation in the East Mediterranean." In *A Global Middle East: Mobility, Materiality, and Culture in the Modern Age, 1880–1940*, ed. Liat Kozma, Avner Wishnitzer, and Cyrus Schayegh. London: I. B. Tauris, 2014.

——. "Statelessness: An Invisible Theme in the History of International Law." *European Journal of International Law* 25, no. 1 (2014): 321–327.

——. "The 1876–83 Reform and Its Implementation: Many Institutions or One?" In *New Approaches to Modern Egyptian Legal History*, ed. Khaled Fahmy and Amr Shalakany. Cairo: AUC Press, forthcoming.

——. "When Did Egyptians Stop Being Ottomans? An Imperial Citizenship Case Study." In *Multilevel Citizenship*, ed. Willem Maas, 89–109. Philadelphia: University of Pennsylvania Press, 2013.

Hansen, Randall. "The Politics of Citizenship in 1940s Britain: The British Nationality Act." *Twentieth-Century British History* 10, no. 1 (1999): 67–95.

Hanssen, Jens, Thomas Philipp, and Stefan Weber, eds. *The Empire in the City: Arab Provincial Capitals in the Late Ottoman Empire*. Würzburg: Ergon in Kommission, 2002.

Hartog, Hendrik. "Pigs and Positivism." *Wisconsin Law Review* 4 (July/August 1985): 899–935.

Harvey, David. *The Condition of Postmodernity: An Enquiry Into the Origins of Cultural Change*. Oxford: Blackwell, 1989.

Heater, Derek Benjamin. *A Brief History of Citizenship*. Edinburgh: Edinburgh University Press, 2004.

Hewitson, Mark, and Timothy Baycroft, eds. *What Is a Nation?: Europe, 1789–1914*. New York: Oxford University Press, 2006.

Hill, Enid. *Mahkama!: Studies in the Egyptian Legal System: Courts & Crimes, Law & Society*. London: Ithaca, 1979.

Hirsch, Francine. *Empire of Nations: Ethnographic Knowledge and the Making of the Soviet Union*. Ithaca, N.Y.: Cornell University Press, 2005.

Hobsbawm, E. J. *Nations and Nationalism Since 1780: Programme, Myth, Reality*. 2nd ed. Cambridge: Cambridge University Press, 1992.

Hobsbawm, E. J., and T. O. Ranger, eds. *The Invention of Tradition*. Cambridge: Cambridge University Press, 1983.

Ho, Elaine Lynn-Ee. "Citizenship, Migration and Transnationalism: A Review and Critical Interventions." *Geography Compass* 2, no. 5 (2008): 1286–1300.

Ho, Engseng. "Empire Through Diasporic Eyes: A View from the Other Boat." *Comparative Studies in Society and History* 46, no. 2 (2004): 210–246.

——. *The Graves of Tarim: Genealogy and Mobility Across the Indian Ocean.* Berkeley: University of California Press, 2006.

Horowitz, Richard S. "International Law and State Transformation in China, Siam, and the Ottoman Empire During the Nineteenth Century." *Journal of World History* 15, no. 4 (2004): 445–486.

Huber, Valeska. *Channelling Mobilities: Migration and Globalisation in the Suez Canal Region and Beyond, 1869-1914.* Cambridge: Cambridge University Press, 2013.

Hunt, Alan. *Explorations in Law and Society: Towards a Constitutive Theory of Law.* New York: Routledge, 1993.

Hunter, F. Robert. *Egypt Under the Khedives, 1805-1879: From Household Government to Modern Bureaucracy.* Cairo: AUC Press, 1999.

Ilbert, Robert. *Alexandrie, 1830-1930: histoire d'une communauté citadine.* 2 vols. Cairo: IFAO, 1996.

Inalcik, Halil, and Donald Quataert, eds. *An Economic and Social History of the Ottoman Empire, 1300-1914.* New York: Cambridge University Press, 1994.

Isin, Engin Fahri. *Being Political: Genealogies of Citizenship.* Minneapolis: University of Minnesota Press, 2002.

——. "Citizenship After Orientalism: Ottoman Citizenship." In *Citizenship in a Global World: European Questions and Turkish Experiences*, ed. Fuat Keyman and Ahmet Icduygu, 31–51. London: Routledge, 2005.

Issawi, Charles Philip. *The Economic History of the Middle East, 1800-1914: A Book of Readings.* Chicago: University of Chicago Press, 1975.

Jacobson, Abigail. "Negotiating Ottomanism in Times of War: Jerusalem During World War I Through the Eyes of a Local Muslim Resident." *International Journal of Middle East Studies* 40, no. 1 (2008): 69–88.

Jacob, Wilson Chacko. "Eventful Transformations: al-Futuwwa Between History and the Everyday." *Comparative Studies in Society and History* 49, no. 3 (2007): 689–712.

——. *Working Out Egypt: Effendi Masculinity and Subject Formation in Colonial Modernity, 1870-1940.* Durham, N.C.: Duke University Press, 2011.

Jallad, Filib. *Qamus al-idarah wa-al-qadaʾ.* 3rd ed. 3 vols. Cairo: Matbaʿat Dar al-Kutub wa-al-Wathaʾiq al-Qawmiya, 2003.

Jankowski, James P., and Israel Gershoni, eds. *Rethinking Nationalism in the Arab Middle East.* New York: Columbia University Press, 1997.

Jasanoff, Maya. "Cosmopolitan: A Tale of Identity from Ottoman Alexandria." *Common Knowledge* 11, no. 3 (2005): 393–409.

Jondet, Gaston. *Atlas historique de la ville et des ports d'Alexandrie.* Cairo: IFAO, 1921.

Kaluszynksi, Martine. "Republican Identity: Bertillonage as Government Technique." In *Documenting Individual Identity*, ed. Jane Caplan and John C. Torpey, 123–138. Princeton, N.J.: Princeton University Press, 2001.

Kamil, Mustafa. *Égyptiens et Anglais.* Paris: Perrin, 1906.

Karpat, Kemal H. "Millets and Nationality: The Roots of the Incongruity of Nation and State in the Post-Ottoman Era." In *Christians and Jews in the Ottoman Empire*, 2 vols., ed. Benjamin Braude and Bernard Lewis, 1:141–169. New York: Holmes & Meier, 1982.

Kasaba, Resat. *A Moveable Empire: Ottoman Nomads, Migrants, and Refugees.* Seattle: University of Washington Press, 2009.

Kayalı, Hasan. *Arabs and Young Turks: Ottomanism, Arabism, and Islamism in the Ottoman Empire, 1908-1918.* Berkeley: University of California Press, 1997.

Kayaoğlu, Turan. *Legal Imperialism: Sovereignty and Extraterritoriality in Japan, the Ottoman Empire, and China.* Cambridge: Cambridge University Press, 2010.

Kennedy, David. "International Law and the Nineteenth Century: History of an Illusion." *Nordic Journal of International Law* 65 (1996): 385–420.

Kerber, Linda K. "The Stateless as the Citizen's Other: A View from the United States." *American Historical Review* 112, no. 1 (2007): 1–34.

Kern, Karen M. *Imperial Citizen: Marriage and Citizenship in the Ottoman Frontier Provinces of Iraq.* Syracuse, N.Y.: Syracuse University Press, 2011.

Khalid, ʿAlaʾ. "Al-shariʿ al-kabir" [The great street]. *Amkenah*, no. 7 (2006): 7–52.

Khater, Akram Fouad. *Inventing Home: Emigration, Gender, and the Middle Class in Lebanon, 1870-1920.* Berkeley: University of California Press, 2001.

Kholoussy, Hanan. *For Better, for Worse: The Marriage Crisis That Made Modern Egypt.* Stanford, Calif. Stanford University Press, 2010.

Khoury, Dina Rizk. *State and Provincial Society in the Ottoman Empire: Mosul, 1540-1834.* Cambridge: Cambridge University Press, 1997.

——. "The Ottoman Centre Versus Provincial Power Holders." In *The Cambridge History of Turkey.* Vol. 3: *The Later Ottoman Empire: 1603-1839*, ed. Suraiya Faroqhi, 135–156. Cambridge: Cambridge University Press, 2006.

Khuri-Makdisi, Ilham. *The Eastern Mediterranean and the Making of Global Radicalism, 1860-1914.* Berkeley: University of California Press, 2010.

Kitroeff, Alexander. *The Greeks in Egypt, 1919-1937: Ethnicity and Class.* London: Ithaca, 1989.

Knop, Karen. "Citizenship, Public and Private." *Law and Contemporary Problems* 71 (2008): 309–341.

Koessler, Maximilian. " 'Subject,' 'Citizen,' 'National,' and 'Permanent Allegiance.' " *Yale Law Journal* 56, no. 1 (1946): 58–76.

Koskenniemi, Martti. *The Gentle Civilizer of Nations: The Rise and Fall of International Law, 1870-1960.* Cambridge: Cambridge University Press, 2002.

Kuran, Timur. *The Long Divergence: How Islamic Law Held Back the Middle East.* Princeton, N.J.: Princeton University Press, 2011.

Kymlicka, Will. "Territorial Boundaries: A Liberal Egalitarian Perspective." In *Boundaries and Justice*, ed. David Miller and Sohail H. Hashmi, 249–275. Princeton, N.J.: Princeton University Press, 2001.

Lewis, Mary Dewhurst. *The Boundaries of the Republic: Migrant Rights and the Limits of Universalism in France, 1918-1940.* Stanford, Calif.: Stanford University Press, 2007.

——. *Divided Rule: Sovereignty and Empire in French Tunisia, 1881-1938.* Berkeley: University of California Press, 2013.

——. "Geographies of Power: The Tunisian Civic Order, Jurisdictional Politics, and Imperial Rivalry in the Mediterranean, 1881–1935." *Journal of Modern History* 80, no. 4 (2008): 791–830.

Library of Congress News Releases. "Analysis Reveals Changes in Declaration of Independence," July 2, 2010. http://www.loc.gov/today/pr/2010/10-161.html.

Liu, Lydia He. "Shadows of Universalism: The Untold Story of Human Rights Around 1948." *Critical Inquiry* 40, no. 4 (2014): 385–417.

Lloyd, Martin. *The Passport: The History of Man's Most Travelled Document.* Stroud: Sutton, 2003.

Lloyd, Tom. "Thuggee, Marginality, and the State Effect in Colonial India, c. 1770–1840." *Indian Economic and Social History Review* 45, no. 2 (2008): 201–237.

Lohr, Eric. *Russian Citizenship: From Empire to Soviet Union.* Cambridge, Mass.: Harvard University Press, 2012.

Lopez, Shaun T. "The Dangers of Dancing: The Media and Morality in 1930s Egypt." *Comparative Studies of South Asia, Africa, and the Middle East* 24, no. 1 (2004): 97–105.

Lorca, Arnulf Becker. "Universal International Law: Nineteenth-Century Histories of Imposition and Appropriation." *Harvard International Law Journal* 51 (2010): 475–552.

Lucassen, Leo. "A Many-Headed Monster: The Evolution of the Passport System in the Netherlands and Germany in the Long Nineteenth Century." In *Documenting Individual Identity*, ed. Jane Caplan and John C. Torpey, 235–255. Princeton, N.J.: Princeton University Press, 2001.

Mabro, Robert. "Alexandria 1860–1960: The Cosmopolitan Identity." In *Alexandria, Real and Imagined*, ed. Anthony Hirst and Michael Silk, 247–262. Aldershot: Ashgate, 2004.

Maghraoui, Abdeslam. *Liberalism Without Democracy: Nationhood and Citizenship in Egypt, 1922-1936.* Durham, N.C.: Duke University Press, 2006.

Mahmood, Saba. "Religious Freedom, the Minority Question, and Geopolitics in the Middle East." *Comparative Studies in Society and History* 54, no. 2 (2012): 418–446.

Major, Andrew J. "State and Criminal Tribes in Colonial Punjab: Surveillance, Control, and Reclamation of the 'Dangerous Classes.'" *Modern Asian Studies* 33, no. 3 (1999): 657–688.

Makdisi, Ussama. *Artillery of Heaven: American Missionaries and the Failed Conversion of the Middle East.* Ithaca, N.Y.: Cornell University Press, 2008.

——. *The Culture of Sectarianism: Community, History, and Violence in Nineteenth-Century Ottoman Lebanon.* Berkeley: University of California Press, 2000.

Maksudyan, Nazan. "The Fight Over Nobody's Children: Religion, Nationality and Citizenship of Foundlings in the Late Ottoman Empire." *New Perspectives on Turkey* 41 (2009): 151–180.

Mamdani, Mahmood. "Beyond Settler and Native as Political Identities: Overcoming the Political Legacy of Colonialism." *Comparative Studies in Society and History* 43, no. 4 (2001): 651–664.

——. *Citizen and Subject: Contemporary Africa and the Legacy of Late Colonialism.* Princeton, N.J.: Princeton University Press, 1996.

Mancini, Pasquale Stanislao. *Della nazionalità come fondamento del dritto delle genti, prelezione al corso di dritto internazionale e maritime.* Torino, 1851.

Mansel, Philip. Levant: *Splendor and Catastrophe on the Mediterranean*. New Haven, Conn.: Yale University Press, 2011.

Marshall, T. H. *Citizenship and Social Class, and Other Essays*. Cambridge: Cambridge University Press, 1950.

Mawani, Renisa. "Specters of Indigeneity in British-Indian Migration, 1914." *Law and Society Review* 46, no. 2 (2012): 369–403.

Mazower, Mark. *Salonica, City of Ghosts: Christians, Muslims, and Jews, 1430-1950*. New York: Vintage, 2006.

McCarthy, Justin. "Nineteenth-Century Egyptian Population." *Middle Eastern Studies* 12, no. 3 (1976): 1–39.

——. *Population History of the Middle East and the Balkans*. Istanbul: Isis, 2002.

McClintock, Anne. *Imperial Leather: Race, Gender, and Sexuality in the Colonial Conquest*. New York: Routledge, 1995.

McKeown, Adam. *Melancholy Order: Asian Migration and the Globalization of Borders*. New York: Columbia University Press, 2008.

Messick, Brinkley Morris. *The Calligraphic State: Textual Domination and History in a Muslim Society*. Berkeley: University of California Press, 1993.

Messiri, Sawsan. *Ibn al-Balad: A Concept of Egyptian Identity*. Leiden: Brill, 1978.

Mestyan, Adam. "Power and Music in Cairo: Azbakiyya." *Urban History* 40, no. 4 (2013): 681–704.

Mikhail, Alan. *Nature and Empire in Ottoman Egypt: An Environmental History*. Cambridge: Cambridge University Press, 2011.

Mitchell, Timothy. *Colonising Egypt*. Cambridge: Cambridge University Press, 1988.

——. *Rule of Experts: Egypt, Techno-Politics, Modernity*. Berkeley: University of California Press, 2002.

Moatti, Claude, and Wolfgang Kaiser, eds. *Gens de passage en Méditerranée de l'antiquité à l'époque moderne: procédures de contrôle et d'identification*. Paris: Maisonneuve & Larose, 2007.

Mongia, Radhika Viyas. "Race, Nationality, Mobility: A History of the Passport." *Public Culture* 11, no. 3 (1999): 527–555.

Monkkonen, Eric H. *Police in Urban America, 1860-1920*. Cambridge: Cambridge University Press, 1981.

Morgan, Diane, and Gary Banham, eds. *Cosmopolitics and the Emergence of a Future*. Basingstoke: Palgrave Macmillan, 2007.

Moustapha Bey, Abd El Hamid. "De la forme du mariage des étrangers en Egypte." *L'Egypte Contemporaine* (1918): 311–329.

Moyn, Samuel. *The Last Utopia: Human Rights in History*. Cambridge, Mass.: Belknap Press of Harvard University Press, 2010.

——. "The Universal Declaration of Human Rights of 1948 in the History of Cosmopolitanism." *Critical Inquiry* 40, no. 4 (2014): 365–384.

Muller, Hannah Weiss. "An Empire of Subjects: Unities and Disunities in the British Empire, 1760–1790." Ph.D. diss., Princeton University, 2010.

Municipalité d'Alexandrie. *Lois, décrets, arrêtés et règlements intéressant la municipalité d'Alexandrie, 1890-1920*. Alexandria: Société de Publications Égyptiennes, 1920.

Muwaylihi, Muhammad al-. *Hadith ʿIsa ibn Hisham, aw fatrah min al-zaman.* Cairo: Kalimat, 2013.
——. *WhatʿIsa ibn Hisham Told Us, or, A Period of Time.* Trans. Roger Allen. 2 vols. New York: New York University Press, 2015.
Nakash, Yitzhak. "Fiscal and Monetary Systems in the Mahdist Sudan, 1881–1898." *International Journal of Middle East Studies* 20, no. 3 (1988): 365–385.
Noiriel, Gérard. *The French Melting Pot: Immigration, Citizenship, and National Identity.* Minneapolis: University of Minnesota Press, 1996.
——. "The Identification of the Citizen: The Birth of Republican Civil Status in France." In *Documenting Individual Identity,* ed. Jane Caplan and John C. Torpey, 28–48. Princeton, N.J.: Princeton University Press, 2001.
Nord, Philip G. *The Republican Moment: Struggles for Democracy in Nineteenth-Century France.* Cambridge, Mass.: Harvard University Press, 1995.
Novak, William J. "The Legal Transformation of Citizenship in Nineteenth-Century America." In *The Democratic Experiment: New Directions in American Political History,* ed. Meg Jacobs, Julian E. Zelizer, and William J. Novak, 85–119. Princeton, N.J.: Princeton University Press, 2003.
Oppenheim, Lassa. *International Law: A Treatise.* 2nd ed. 2 vols. London: Longmans, 1912.
Owen, Roger. *The Middle East in the World Economy, 1800–1914.* London: I. B. Tauris, 1993.
——. "The Population Census of 1917 and Its Relationship to Egypt's Three Nineteenth-Century Statistical Regimes." *Journal of Historical Sociology* 9, no. 4 (1996): 457–472.
Özsu, Umut. *Formalizing Displacement: International Law and Population Transfers.* Oxford: Oxford University Press, 2014.
Panzac, Daniel. "Alexandrie: évolution d'une ville cosmopolite au XIXe siècle." *Annales Islamologiques* 14 (1978): 195–215.
——. "The Population of Egypt in the Nineteenth Century." *Asian and African Studies* 21 (1987): 11–32.
Parker, Kunal M. *Making Foreigners: Immigration and Citizenship Law in America, 1600–2000.* Cambridge: Cambridge University Press, 2015.
Parolin, Gianluca Paolo. *Citizenship in the Arab World: Kin, Religion, and Nation-State.* Amsterdam: Amsterdam University Press, 2009.
Pedersen, Susan. "Getting Out of Iraq—in 1932: The League of Nations and the Road to Normative Statehood." *American Historical Review* 115, no. 4 (2010): 975–1000.
Peirce, Leslie. *Morality Tales: Law and Gender in the Ottoman Court of Aintab.* Berkeley: University of California Press, 2003.
Pélissié du Rausas, Gérard. *Le régime des capitulations dans l'Empire ottoman.* 2nd ed. 2 vols. Paris: A. Rousseau, 1910.
Peri, Oded. "Ottoman Symbolism in British-Occupied Egypt, 1882–1909." *Middle Eastern Studies* 41, no. 1 (2005): 103–120.
Peters, Rudolph. "State, Law, and Society in Nineteenth-Century Egypt." *Die Welt des Islams* 39, no. 3 (1999): 267–272.
Platt, D. C. M. *The Cinderella Service: British Consuls Since 1825.* London: Longman, 1971.
Pocock, J. G. A. "The Ideal of Citizenship Since Classical Times." *Queen's Quarterly* 99, no. 1 (Spring 1992): 35–55.

Poffandi, Stefano G., ed. *1897 Indicateur Égyptien administratif et commercial*. 11th ed. Alexandria, 1896.

Pomeranz, Kenneth. *The Making of a Hinterland: State, Society, and Economy in Inland North China, 1853–1937*. Berkeley: University of California Press, 1993.

Powell, Eve Troutt. *A Different Shade of Colonialism: Egypt, Great Britain, and the Mastery of the Sudan*. Berkeley: University of California Press, 2003.

Price, Charles Archibald. *Malta and the Maltese: A Study in Nineteenth-Century Migration*. Melbourne: Georgian House, 1954.

Rafeq, Abdul-Karim. "Ownership of Real Property by Foreigners in Syria, 1869 to 1873." In *New Perspectives on Property and Land in the Middle East*, ed. Roger Owen, 175–240. Cambridge, Mass.: Harvard University Press, 2001.

Ramzi Sayf Rizq Allah. *Tanazuᶜ al-Ikhtisas bain al-Mahakim al-Ahliya wa al-Mahakim al-Mukhtalita*. Cairo: Matbaᶜat Fath Allah Ilyas Nuri wa Awladihi, 1938.

Reimer, Michael J. *Colonial Bridgehead: Government and Society in Alexandria, 1807–1882*. Cairo: AUC Press, 1997.

Reinkowski, Maurus. "Uncommunicative Communication: Competing Egyptian, Ottoman and British Imperial Ventures in 19th-Century Egypt." *Die Welt des Islams* 54, no. 3–4 (2014): 399–422.

Rey, Francis. *De la protection diplomatique et consulaire dans les échelles du Levant et de Barbarie*. Paris, 1899.

Reynolds, Nancy Y. *A City Consumed: Urban Commerce, the Cairo Fire, and the Politics of Decolonization in Egypt*. Stanford, Calif.: Stanford University Press, 2012.

Rizk, Yunan Labib. "The Women Killers." *Al-Ahram Weekly* 434 (June 17, 1999).

Robinson, Jennifer. *Ordinary Cities: Between Modernity and Development*. London: Routledge, 2006.

Robinson-Dunn, Diane Liga. *The Harem, Slavery, and British Imperial Culture: Anglo-Muslim Relations in the Late Nineteenth Century*. Manchester: Manchester University Press, 2006.

Rodgers, Daniel T. *Age of Fracture*. Cambridge, Mass.: Harvard University Press, 2011.

Rogan, Eugene L. *Frontiers of the State in the Late Ottoman Empire: Transjordan, 1850–1921*. New York: Cambridge University Press, 1999.

——, ed. *Outside In: On the Margins of the Modern Middle East*. London: I. B. Tauris, 2002.

Rose, Lionel. *Rogues and Vagabonds: Vagrant Underworld in Britain, 1815–1985*. London: Routledge, 1988.

Rosenberg, Clifford D. *Policing Paris: The Origins of Modern Immigration Control Between the Wars*. Ithaca, N.Y.: Cornell University Press, 2006.

Rothman, E. Natalie. *Brokering Empire: Trans-Imperial Subjects Between Venice and Istanbul*. Ithaca, N.Y.: Cornell University Press, 2012.

Rothschild, Emma. *The Inner Life of Empires: An Eighteenth-Century History*. Princeton, N.J.: Princeton University Press, 2011.

Rubin, Avi. "Ottoman Judicial Change in the Age of Modernity: A Reappraisal." *History Compass* 7, no. 1 (2009): 119–140.

——. *Ottoman Nizamiye Courts: Law and Modernity*. New York: Palgrave Macmillan, 2011.

Ruiz, Mario M. "Intimate Disputes, Illicit Violence: Gender, Law, and the State in Colonial Egypt, 1849–1923." Ph.D. diss., University of Michigan, 2004.

Sadiq, Kamal. *Paper Citizens: How Illegal Immigrants Acquire Citizenship in Developing Countries*. New York: Oxford University Press, 2009.

Sahlins, Peter. *Unnaturally French: Foreign Citizens in the Old Regime and After*. Ithaca, N.Y.: Cornell University Press, 2004.

Said, Edward W. *Culture and Imperialism*. New York: Knopf, 1993.

Salem, Mahmoud-Zaky. *La doctrine de Mancini sur la nationalité et son application au droit égyptien*. Dijon: Bernigaud et Privat, 1923.

Salzmann, Ariel. "An *Ancien Regime* Revisited: 'Privatization' and Political Economy in the Eighteenth-Century Ottoman Empire." *Politics and Society* 21, no. 4 (1993): 393–423.

——. "Citizens in Search of a State: The Limits of Political Participation in the Late Ottoman Empire." In *Extending Citizenship, Reconfiguring States*, ed. Michael P. Hanagan and Charles Tilly, 37–66. Lanham, Md.: Rowman & Littlefield, 1999.

Sarat, Austin, Lawrence Douglas, and Martha Merrill Umphrey, eds. *Law and the Stranger*. Stanford, Calif.: Stanford University Press, 2010.

Saunders, Rebecca, ed. *The Concept of the Foreign*. Lanham, Md.: Lexington Books, 2003.

Savigny, Friedrich Karl von, and William Guthrie. *A Treatise on the Conflict of Laws, and the Limits of Their Operation in Respect of Place and Time*. 2nd ed. Edinburgh, 1880.

Sayyid-Marsot, Afaf Lutfi. *Egypt's Liberal Experiment, 1922–1936*. Berkeley: University of California Press, 1977.

Schayegh, Cyrus. "The Many Worlds of ʿAbud Yasin; Or, What Narcotics Trafficking in the Interwar Middle East Can Tell Us About Territorialization." *American Historical Review* 116, no. 2 (2011): 273–306.

Schnapper, Dominique. *Community of Citizens: On the Modern Idea of Nationality*. New Brunswick, N.J.: Transaction, 1998.

Scott, James C. *The Art of Not Being Governed: An Anarchist History of Upland Southeast Asia*. New Haven, Conn.: Yale University Press, 2009.

——. *Seeing Like a State: How Certain Schemes to Improve the Human Condition Have Failed*. New Haven, Conn.: Yale University Press, 1998.

——. *Weapons of the Weak: Everyday Forms of Peasant Resistance*. New Haven, Conn.: Yale University Press, 1985.

Scott, James Harry. *The Law Affecting Foreigners in Egypt as the Result of the Capitulations, with an Account of Their Origin and Development*. Edinburgh: W. Green and Sons, 1908.

Scott, Joan Wallach. *Only Paradoxes to Offer: French Feminists and the Rights of Man*. Cambridge, Mass.: Harvard University Press, 1996.

Scully, Eileen P. *Bargaining with the State from Afar: American Citizenship in Treaty Port China, 1844–1942*. New York: Columbia University Press, 2001.

Sendesni, Wajda. "Les Jeunes-Turcs en Égypte (1895–1908), histoire politique et intellectuelle." Thèse de doctorat, École des hautes études en sciences sociales, 2009.

Shachar, Ayelet. *The Birthright Lottery: Citizenship and Global Inequality*. Cambridge, Mass.: Harvard University Press, 2009.

Sharkey, Heather J. "Empire and Muslim Conversion: Historical Reflections on Christian Missions in Egypt." *Islam and Christian-Muslim Relations* 16, no. 1 (2005): 43–60.

Simpson, Gerry J. *Great Powers and Outlaw States: Unequal Sovereigns in the International Legal Order*. Cambridge: Cambridge University Press, 2004.

Singerman, Diane, and Paul Amar, eds. *Cairo Cosmopolitan: Politics, Culture, and Urban Space in the New Globalized Middle East*. Cairo: AUC Press, 2006.

Slauter, Will. "Le paragraphe mobile. Circulation et transformation des informations dans le monde atlantique du XVIIIe siècle." *Annales. Histoire, Sciences Sociales* 2, no. 6 (2012): 363–389.

Slezkine, Yuri. "The USSR as a Communal Apartment, or How a Socialist State Promoted Ethnic Particularism." *Slavic Review* 53, no. 2 (Summer 1994): 414–452.

Smith, Anthony D. *Nationalism and Modernism: A Critical Survey of Recent Theories of Nations and Nationalism*. London: Routledge, 1998.

Smyrnelis, Marie-Carmen. *Une société hors de soi: identités et relations sociales à Smyrne au XVIIIe et XIXe siècles*. Dudley, Mass.: Peeters, 2005.

Somers, Margaret R. *Genealogies of Citizenship: Markets, Statelessness, and the Right to Have Rights*. Cambridge: Cambridge University Press, 2008.

Sonyel, Salahi R. "The Protégé System in the Ottoman Empire." *Journal of Islamic Studies* 2, no. 1 (1991): 56–66.

Spivak, Gayatri Chakravorty. "Can the Subaltern Speak?" In *Marxism and the Interpretation of Culture*, 271–313. Urbana: University of Illinois Press, 1988.

Stein, Sarah Abrevaya. "Protected Persons? The Baghdadi Jewish Diaspora, the British State, and the Persistence of Empire." *American Historical Review* 116, no. 1 (2011): 80–108.

Stoler, Ann Laura. *Along the Archival Grain: Epistemic Anxieties and Colonial Common Sense*. Princeton, N.J.: Princeton University Press, 2009.

——. *Carnal Knowledge and Imperial Power: Race and the Intimate in Colonial Rule*. Berkeley: University of California Press, 2002.

——. "Rethinking Colonial Categories: European Communities and the Boundaries of Rule." *Comparative Studies in Society and History* 31, no. 1 (1989): 134–161.

Stoler, Ann Laura, Carole McGranahan, and Peter C. Perdue, eds. *Imperial Formations*. Santa Fe, N.M.: School for Advanced Research Press, 2007.

Stone, Lawrence. "The Revival of Narrative." *Past and Present* 85 (1979): 3–24.

Story, Joseph, and Melville Madison Bigelow. *Commentaries on the Conflict of Laws, Foreign and Domestic: In Regard to Contracts, Rights, and Remedies, and Especially in Regard to Marriages, Divorces, Wills, Successions, and Judgments*. 8th ed. Boston, 1883.

Tagliacozzo, Eric. *Secret Trades, Porous Borders: Smuggling and States Along a Southeast Asian Frontier, 1865-1915*. New Haven, Conn.: Yale University Press, 2005.

Tahawi, Ahmad ibn Muhammad al-. *The Function of Documents in Islamic Law: The Chapters on Sales from Tahawi's Kitab al-Shurut al-Kabir*. Trans. Jeanette A. Wakin. Albany: SUNY Press, 1972.

Tan, Kok-Chor. *Justice Without Borders: Cosmopolitanism, Nationalism, and Patriotism*. Cambridge: Cambridge University Press, 2004.

Taylor, Charles, and Amy Gutmann. *Multiculturalism: Examining the Politics of Recognition.* Princeton, N.J.: Princeton University Press, 1994.

Thompson, Elizabeth. *Colonial Citizens: Republican Rights, Paternal Privilege, and Gender in French Syria and Lebanon.* New York: Columbia University Press, 2000.

Tignor, Robert L. *State, Private Enterprise, and Economic Change in Egypt, 1918–1952.* Princeton, N.J.: Princeton University Press, 1984.

Tilly, Charles. "The Emergence of Citizenship in France and Elsewhere." In *Citizenship, Identity and Social History*, 223–236. Cambridge: Cambridge University Press, 1996.

Toledano, Ehud R. *State and Society in Mid-Nineteenth-Century Egypt.* Cambridge: Cambridge University Press, 1990.

Tollefson, Harold. *Policing Islam: The British Occupation of Egypt and the Anglo-Egyptian Struggle Over Control of the Police, 1882–1914.* Westport, Conn.: Greenwood, 2000.

Torpey, John C. *The Invention of the Passport: Surveillance, Citizenship, and the State.* New York: Cambridge University Press, 2000.

Trivellato, Francesca. *The Familiarity of Strangers: The Sephardic Diaspora, Livorno, and Cross-Cultural Trade in the Early Modern Period.* New Haven, Conn.: Yale University Press, 2009.

Tucker, Judith E. *In the House of the Law: Gender and Islamic Law in Ottoman Syria and Palestine.* Berkeley: University of California Press, 1998.

United Nations. *Laws Concerning Nationality.* New York: United Nations, 1954.

van den Boogert, Maurits H. *The Capitulations and the Ottoman Legal System: Qadis, Consuls, and Beratlis in the Eighteenth Century.* Leiden: Brill, 2005.

Vertovec, Steven, and Robin Cohen, eds. *Conceiving Cosmopolitanism: Theory, Context, and Practice.* New York: Oxford University Press, 2002.

Viswanathan, Gauri. *Outside the Fold: Conversion, Modernity, and Belief.* Princeton, N.J.: Princeton University Press, 1998.

Wallerstein, Immanuel. "Citizens All? Citizens Some! The Making of the Citizen." *Comparative Studies in Society and History* 45, no. 4 (2003): 650–679.

Watenpaugh, Keith David. *Being Modern in the Middle East: Revolution, Nationalism, Colonialism, and the Arab Middle Class.* Princeton, N.J.: Princeton University Press, 2006.

Weil, Patrick. *How to Be French: Nationality in the Making Since 1789.* Durham, N.C.: Duke University Press, 2008.

Weis, Paul. *Nationality and Statelessness in International Law.* 2nd ed. Alphen aan den Rijn: Sijthoff & Noordhoff, 1979.

Weissbrodt, David S., and Clay Collins. "The Human Rights of Stateless Persons." *Human Rights Quarterly* 28, no. 1 (2006): 245–276.

Weiss, Max. *In the Shadow of Sectarianism: Law, Shi'ism, and the Making of Modern Lebanon.* Cambridge, Mass.: Harvard University Press, 2010.

Westlake, John, and Alfred Frank Topham. *A Treatise on Private International Law: With Principal Reference to Its Practice in England.* London: Sweet & Maxwell, 1905.

Wikan, Unni. "Citizenship on Trial: Nadia's Case." *Daedalus* 129, no. 4 (Fall 2000): 55–76.

Wilder, Gary. *The French Imperial Nation-State: Negritude and Colonial Humanism Between the Two World Wars.* Chicago: University of Chicago Press, 2005.

Williams, Raymond. *Keywords: A Vocabulary of Culture and Society*. New York: Oxford University Press, 1985.

Yosmaoğlu, İpek K. "Counting Bodies, Shaping Souls: The 1903 Census and National Identity in Ottoman Macedonia." *International Journal of Middle East Studies* 38, no. 1 (2006): 55–77.

Young, Robert. *Colonial Desire: Hybridity in Theory, Culture, and Race*. London: Routledge, 1995.

Zandi-Sayek, Sibel. *Ottoman Izmir: The Rise of a Cosmopolitan Port, 1840–1880*. Minneapolis: University of Minnesota Press, 2012.

Zarinebaf, Fariba. *Crime and Punishment in Istanbul, 1700–1800*. Berkeley: University of California Press, 2011.

Zaydan, Jurji. *Yawmiyat rihla bahriya*. Damascus: Fajr al-Nahdah, 2010.

Ze'evi, Dror. *Producing Desire: Changing Sexual Discourse in the Ottoman Middle East, 1500–1900*. Berkeley: University of California Press, 2006.

——. "The Use of Ottoman Sharīʿa Court Records as a Source for Middle Eastern Social History: A Reappraisal." *Islamic Law and Society* 5, no. 1 (1998): 35–56.

Zelizer, Viviana A. Rotman. *The Social Meaning of Money*. New York: Basic Books, 1994.

Index